DESTROYING THE REPUBLIC:

JABEZ CURRY

AND THE

RE-EDUCATION

OF THE OLD SOUTH

Destroying the Republic:
Jabez Curry
and the
Re-education
of the Old South

John Chodes

Algora Publishing
New York

Library of Congress Cataloging-in-Publication Data —

Chodes, John J.
Destroying the Republic: Jabez Curry and the Re-education of the Old
South / by John Chodes.
     p. cm.
Includes bibliographical references and index.
ISBN 0-87586-401-5 (trade paper : alk. paper) — ISBN 0-87586-402-3 (hard
cover : alk. paper) — ISBN 0-87586-403-1 (ebook)
     1. Curry, J. L. M. (Jabez Lamar Monroe), 1825-1903. 2. Educators—United
States—Biography. 3. Confederate States of America—Biography. 4.
Ambassadors—United States—Biography. I. Title.

LB875.C82C47 2005
370'.92—dc22

                              2005013096

60375716

Front Cover:

Portrait of Jabez L. M. Curry. Etching by John D. Felter, in *A History of the
Baptists* by Thomas Armitage, D.D., LL.D. Bryan, Taylor & Co., New York: 1890.

Printed in the United States

TABLE OF CONTENTS

INTRODUCTION

I

The career of Jabez Lafayette Monroe Curry allegorically parallels the fictional story of Colonel Nicholson in the famed Hollywood film, *The Bridge on the River Kwai*, which won six Academy Awards. In that movie Nicholson, played by Alec Guinness, was a British prisoner-of-war in Burma in World War II. He believes he is helping the demoralized English show their superiority to their Japanese captors by building a bridge better than they can. But in fact, Nicholson is "aiding and abetting" the enemy. The bridge will be used to bring Japanese reinforcements to fight the British. His own officers try to explain that reality to him but he never understands it until the last moments of the film. He is killed at that instant of realization, just as the bridge is destroyed.

Jabez Curry's story is symbolically similar. He was an aristocratic Alabamian. In the ante-bellum South he had a distinguished career in both the Alabama Assembly and the United States Congress. He tirelessly advocated the principles of state sovereignty and limited Federal governmental power. As an active promoter of education, he staunchly believed that this important function was entirely each state's responsibility and completely outside Washington's sphere.

And yet, in the years following the Civil War, Curry became the top executive of the Peabody Education Fund. This was the largest educational philanthropy of the 19th century. In a complete reversal of philosophy, Curry worked relentlessly through this agency to unite Southern private schools with the tax-

1

supported schools of the corrupt and anti-Southern carpetbag state governments.

In reality this meant fusing Southern schools to the Federal bureaucracies since the United States army of occupation controlled all the ex-Confederate states during Reconstruction. And Washington was committed to transforming the minds and souls of the defeated South's children, to eradicate the "culture of rebellion," and was intensely motivated by a form of intellectual ethnic cleansing. All the values that had led to secession would be expunged from the next generation of Southern minds.

Jabez Curry, in his position with the Peabody Fund, was tremendously successful in absorbing classic private Southern education into the alien state systems, until they achieved a virtual monopoly over the South's children.

For this, Jabez Curry is called "The Horace Mann of the South." His attainment meant that Southern culture was eliminated forever. Yet this culture was a rich one, and in many respects more intellectually advanced than the North's. It was not all about slavery and white supremacy as many Northerners, then and now, believe it was. One does not have to be a racist to believe that annihilating the Southern mind is a high crime, especially when the process turned in on itself to empty the contents of the minds of Northern children in the 20th century.

Jabez Curry was not a conscious traitor to his people. Amazingly, like Colonel Nicholson in Burma, Curry did not grasp the terrible consequences of his actions until the end of his life. And then, as with Nicholson, it was too late. Just before he died Curry sensed that he too was aiding and abetting the enemy. By that point there was no turning back. He had always believed that he was helping the South to become more productive, to compete with the North, to enter the 20th century on a level playing field. The reverse was true. Forevermore, the South would be transformed into a weak-souled colony of the United States.

This story is not about history or the Civil War or Reconstruction or about long ago events. It is about today. The decline in academic test scores over the last half century indicates how successful was the nationalizing of schools in the North, too. Washington has slowly and steadily usurped local autonomy of curriculum, standards, content and values, and not with a goal of producing better minds.

Through the story of Jabez Curry we can learn to understand the brilliant clandestine methods that were developed and implemented for Southern cultural and intellectual elimination. Similar methods are being used all over the country even now, on all of America's children, sapping the culture and intelligence of the population.

II

There have been two previous major biographies of Jabez Curry. The first, published in 1911, was co-authored by Edwin Anderson Alderman, who was then President of the University of Virginia.[1] The second, by Jessie Pearl Rice, in 1949, a professor at Columbia University.[2]

My treatment of Curry's life differs considerably from their approaches. Rice and Alderman wrote chronologically. They begin with Jabez Curry's father, then his early life, and so on in great detail. This drastically slows down the story.

I have split Curry's earlier, less meaningful years into small segments, scattering them throughout the book. This allows a wider telling of his life topically and from an entirely different perspective.

Jabez Curry was a literary stylist and his own words are more liberally used here than previously, to give the reader a sense of his wonderful prose.

Instead of beginning at the beginning, we jump right into the middle of the first powerfully significant event that would change Curry's life forever: the secession of Alabama (his home state) from the Union. This moment transports us instantly into the major conflict of the era: state sovereignty vs. centralized power.

The most serious flaw in the two previous biographies has been the lack of "consequences" of what Curry wrought; the extermination of the Southern mind and way of life. Of course this view is at odds with Rice and Alderman. They saw Jabez Curry as a man who had been transformed into a great progressive prophet. Since I disagree with that prognosis, I have taken it upon myself to straighten out the record and present a more chilling story of the Curry legacy. His through-line builds its own tale into the 20th and 21st centuries and impacts our lives negatively to this day.

Another startling failing of Alderman and Rice is their inability to explain the wonderful books that Curry wrote, that illuminate his world-view. His

---

1. Edwin Anderson Alderman and Armistead Churchill Gordon, *J.L.M. Curry: A Biography* (New York: The Macmillan Company, 1911).
2. Jessie Pearl Rice, *J.L.M. Curry: Southerner, Statesman, Educator* (New York: King's Crown Press, Columbia University, 1949).

William Ewart Gladstone (the biography of the famous British Prime Minister) and *Struggle and Triumph of Virginia Baptists* (Curry was a Baptist preacher) and *Principles, Acts and Utterances of John C. Calhoun* (this South Carolinian was a United States Vice President, Secretary of State, Secretary of War and the greatest defender of state sovereignty) and *Constitutional Government in Spain* (near the end of his life Curry was Ambassador to Spain) are completely sloughed over. It seems Alderman and Rice did not understand their significance, but all of Curry's books were parables of the Civil War and its aftermath. They speak, in a disguised form, of the continuing hateful relations between North and South that lasted for generations, even beyond Curry's death in 1903.

Curry wrote metaphorically to make sensitive topics palatable without infuriating his enemies. For instance, *Constitutional Government in Spain* was written several years (1898) after he was Minister to the Spanish Court. The United States was on the threshold of war with Spain. By showing the extreme instability, civil war, anarchy and the multitude of ineffectual constitutions that added to the political chaos, Curry was actually describing the horror that took place in the years following the American Civil War.

Alderman and Rice see the sum of his life in the same way: Jabez Curry began his career with those outdated ideals that tragically motivated so many men of the Old South. These reactionary views led to secession and war and the annihilation of the Confederacy, and its entire way of life. Out of the ashes, the modern civilization of New England was imposed on the losers, for their betterment. Curry changed and absorbed that "truth." He accepted the "more enlightened" vision that dominated 20th century America. Not only did Curry accept that new world-view but he actively and enthusiastically advocated it through the medium of state-controlled schools in the South.

It is the Peabody Fund that defined Curry as a progressive because Peabody helped end sectionalism and homogenized American society, based on that New England model, through the medium of the common school.

I take the polar opposite position. The Old South was an amazing paradox; although a slave society, it was the only part of the United States that truly understood how to achieve freedom and was home to the most brilliant intellectuals and greatest warrior freedom-fighters. And Curry's youth was spent in absorbing the classic vision of the Founding Fathers, who were mostly the same kind of brilliant Southern intellectuals and freedom-fighters. It was they who advocated a limited central government which would be kept in place by powerful, independent states.

But, the horrors of war and the further horrors of Reconstruction took their toll on Jabez's mind and he lost the thread of those classic truths. Unknowingly, he became everything he had loathed: a promoter of centralization, a believer in the despotism that had enveloped his own people. It was not until the end of his life that he grasped this.

The character and personalities and deeds of the galaxy of players that surrounded Jabez Curry seem never to have intrigued Alderman or Rice. The great political, military, religious and educational figures who had a huge impact on shaping the soul of the United States are mere shadow figures. That is a tragic mistake. Some of these men are giants whose lives also are filled with contradictions, who deserve their own biographies (which in fact, some have). Ulysses S. Grant, Rutherford B. Hayes, as presidents; John Eaton and William Torry Harris, both Commissioners of the Bureau of Education; Barnas Sears, the initial General Agent of the Peabody Fund — these are all fascinating characters. Generals Nathan Bedford Forrest, Joe Wheeler, Joe Johnston, with whom Jabez fought, and Oliver Otis Howard, the one-armed Union general, all deserve better than they have received at the hands and pens of Rice and Alderman. Fleshing them out to reveal the dynamics that made them famous or infamous was part of my intention.

Lastly, why did I write this book? Or, more exactly, why is a biography of Jabez Curry necessary now?

The story of Jabez Lafayette Monroe Curry is critically important in the current era. Without understanding his life, his times and its motivations, we cannot grasp why today's children are declining steadily, according to the test scores, and why they are ever more dispirited educationally, emotionally, intellectually. But it will all make perfect sense when we see that it was not the love of children or the love of literacy that spurred Uncle Sam to spend billions of dollars to build schools in every nook and cranny of the United States. No, it was the spirit of hatred and "bad intentions."

By this understanding, the great educational experiment has not failed; it has been a phenomenal success. It was intended to produce passive drones who would never rebel again or defy national authority. And, it has worked perfectly.

III

I would like to thank Dr. Michael Hill, President of the League of the South, for publishing *Monograph No. 6* on Jabez Curry, as part of the "Papers Series."

My thanks also to the League of the South's Institute for allowing me to teach a seminar on Curry. In preparing for that, I clarified my thoughts on how to present his story in a coherent form.

Nat Rudolph, editor of *Southern Events*, published several of my articles on various phases of Curry's life. This created an interest in his contradictory story.

Clyde Wilson, professor at the University of South Carolina, became my mentor, encouraging me to pursue and continue several difficult Civil War and Reconstruction projects including Jabez Curry, when others did not see their value or significance.

Don Livingston, professor at Emory University, acted as my "sounding board" and advisor and saw the value of the Jabez Curry story as a seminar.

An unknown librarian at the gigantic and renowned New York Public Library at 42nd Street in New York City taught me how to find specific types of government documents in the vast, confusing mass of data available.

My appreciation also goes to Algora Publishing, whose courage in defying "politically correct" trends inspired the house to publish this book.

CHAPTER 1. ADVOCATE FOR STATE SOVEREIGNTY

On January 21, 1861, Jabez Curry and the other representatives from Alabama sent this message to the United States Congress:

> Sir: Having received information that the State of Alabama, through a convention representing her sovereignty, has adopted and ratified an ordinance, by which she "withdraws from the Union of the United States of America," and resumes the powers heretofore delegated to the Federal Government, it is proper that we should communicate the same to you, and through you to the House of Representatives, over which you preside, and announce our withdrawal from further deliberations of your body.
>
> The causes which, in the judgment of our State, rendered such action necessary, we need not relate. It is sufficient to say, that duty requires our obedience to her sovereign will, and that we shall return to our home, sustain her action, and share the fortunes of her people.[1]

Alabama had seceded from the Union. Other Southern states soon followed. The Confederacy was in the process of being formed. The Civil War was rapidly approaching.[2]

---

1. *Congressional Globe*, 36th Congress, 2nd Session (Washington DC: Reprint Edition by United States Historical Documents Institute, Inc., 1970), p. 497.
2. The term "Civil War" is inappropriate for this conflict. From this point onward this war shall be referred to as "The War for Southern Independence." It was not a civil war because the South was not attempting to take over the capital at Washington and install itself as the government of the United States. It was not a "War Between the States"; it was a war between two separate countries, the United States of America and the Confederate States of America. It was not the "War of the Rebellion," because Southerners and most Northerners believed that secession was perfectly legal and was a right that was granted at the ratification of the Constitution.

Since 1857, Jabez Curry had been in the United States Congress as a member of the House of Representatives. There he had been a fiery advocate for all the classic values that the Old South had stood for: state sovereignty, a strict interpretation of the Constitution, the right to own property in human form (slavery), and secession.

Curry viewed secession as the principle that when a state's independence was threatened or violated, it had the absolute constitutional right to break its ties with the United States, since that country was a union based on a voluntary association of equals. As such, it could not be held together by force.

The South Feels Hated by the North

Alabama and the other seceding states felt that they had been threatened, violated, intimidated and forced into an inferior position by the hatred of the mass of Northerners as individuals and by the Northern states and Federal government.

When Jabez Curry was a United States Congressman, he made a speech about this hatred:

"Between the extremes of opinion that have long distracted and now threaten to convulse the country, I find no middle ground of practical usefulness on which a friend of moderate counsels can stand." He then quoted a Massachusetts Republican who described the state of things: "A handful of talented but misguided men in Massachusetts, animated by a monomania of fanatical devotion to a single idea [the abolition of slavery], poisoned the conscience and corrupted the judgment of too many of our fellow-citizens in the Commonwealth. I showed the nature and influence of their most malign teachings; how party action in the North and South was running in the channel of a desperate and deplorable sectionalism, and more than all, in Massachusetts; that all political influence in this State was founded in hate, treacherous, furious, fiendish hate, of our fellow-citizens in the Southern States."[1]

When a friend of Curry's, Jonathan Haralson, wrote Jabez on the eve of Alabama's secession, asking for advice "to guide the whirlwind and direct the storm," Curry responded with this letter. His defense of slavery is presented in these pages not to justify it but so that the modern reader may understand how pre-war Southerners experienced it.

---

1. Jabez Curry speech in the United States House of Representatives, December 10, 1859. He quoted Caleb Cushing, former Attorney-General, who was from Massachusetts.

8

"Inapplicable and misused, as the term has been, in previous periods of our history, the present is truly the crisis of our destiny and must terminate in the vindication and security of our peculiar type of civilization, or the subjugation of the South to an abolition dynasty. The election of Lincoln reverses the past policy of our General Government. It inaugurates a new and different system of policy. The federative character of our Union [power divided between states and central government] presupposes common sympathy and equality among the parts. Hereafter these are not to be exhibited in its practical workings towards the South. A geographical majority will impress tone and character upon its future operations. Lincoln and his party can no more liberate themselves from the thralldom of the associations and ideas which give them power, than a beast of prey can be transformed into a timid and inoffensive lamb. They must conform to the law of their being; to the inexorable necessities of their existence. The cohesive power, which holds the Black Republicans in the party and gives it coherency and personality, is hatred of the institution of the South and a fixed purpose to destroy them. They have the will, they have the numerical majority, to reduce us, as members of the same government, to inferiority, and if the means are wanting to accomplish that object, they will soon make them.... With Republicans administering the Government, and a sectional, hostile public opinion giving color to and directing their legislative measures, the Government becomes foreign to us.... The North complains of her assumed responsibility for the sin of African slavery, reproaches, slanders and stigmatizes our men and women at home and abroad, denounces us as 'barbarians,' incites murder and arson and treason, violates the plainest provisions of the Constitution, without which the Government would never have been formed; elects the chief of a rebel section to preside over us, and then — when we propose to withdraw and relieve their tender consciences of all connection with the 'scene of villanies' — sneeringly and defiantly threaten us with coercion, with subjugation, with the sword and halter! If the South has nature in her, she will not bear it."[1]

Punitive Policies Benefit North

Near the end of his long letter to Haralson, Curry presented the economic side of secession:

---

1. Letter to Jonathan Haralson, of Selma, Alabama, November 21, 1860, from the J.L.M. Curry Papers, Library of Congress, Washington, D.C.

"We have fought wars to protect the men and property of the North and indemnify her losses. We have paid bounties and stipends to pensions and give employment to her citizens. We have endured burdensome taxation to encourage her manufacturers and give advantages over European competitors. But of 1,100 millions of dollars collected from customs in the last seventy years, the South has paid two-thirds of the sum, while nearly four-fifths have been disbursed at the North.... The fiscal operations of the government have concentrated capital in Northern cities, and made them the centers of commerce, the starting points of ocean steam lines, and in conjunction with the navigation and coast trade, laws have destroyed and prevented direct trade between Europe and our Southern ports. The North, by political connection with us, drains the South annually of millions of dollars."[1]

Slavery; One Reason for Northern Hatred

In a poetic and beautifully crafted speech in Congress, Jabez Curry presented one of the reasons for the schism that had split the United States into two antagonistic camps:

"There are occasions when a whole people, like an individual, hold their breath in suspense, anxiously awaiting the issue of events. There are critical periods, which, like night, intervene between successive days, and mark the destiny and the history of a people. The excitement prevailing in the public mind throughout this country, the manifestation of interest both here and elsewhere, admonish, as that this, perhaps is such an occasion. Nor does this excitement and this profound agitation of the public mind arise from...the publication and circulation of an incendiary pamphlet; nor sir ... from that murderous incursion which was recently made into the Commonwealth of Virginia [John Brown's raid]. These are but scenes in the act of a general drama, incidents of a principle, the revelations, more or less shadowy, of a purpose. The real cause of the agitation in the public mind, the radix of the excitement, is the anti-slavery sentiment of the North; the conviction that property in man is a sin and a crime."[2]

Jabez Curry owned many slaves and his views on that institution reflect the aristocratic ante-bellum South, and as a reality; it was a culture that had been molded for centuries by the slave labor system. He admitted that the South

---

1. Ibid.
2. Jabez Curry speech in United States House of Representatives, December 10, 1859.

could not disentangle itself from property in man "save by the fatal operation called Caesarian."[1]

But — Slavery Drives Northern Economy

"African slavery is now a great fact; a political, social, industrial, humanitarian fact. Its chief product is king [cotton] and freights northern vessels, drives northern machinery, feeds northern laborers, and clothes the entire population. Northern, no less than southern capital and labor are dependent in great degree upon it, and these results were wholly unanticipated by the good men who are so industriously paraded as clouds of witnesses against the institution."[2]

Few Southerners Owned Slaves

Northerners generally hated the entire South, as if the entire population were slaveholders; but only a tiny minority owned property in human form. In 1860, there were 5.3 million whites in the South. Of that number, approximately 300,000 or six percent were slave-holders.[3]

The number of slave-holders who could be considered as aristocrats was only 150,000, or three percent. The rest owned five or fewer slaves and worked beside them in order to make a living.[4]

Test Oaths Would Divide South

The Republicans planned to give test oaths to all officeholders to affirm their loyalty to abolitionist principles; this was of course perceived in the South as another demonstration of their hatred for all things Southern. Curry explained the consequences:

"The famous English test act, by which a man was excluded from civil office unless he partook of the sacrament after the manner of the Church of England, is to be re-enacted, and applied to the Southern States. All who cannot pronounce the shibboleths of Republicanism are to be proscribed and banished from all influence in our Government and Union. Non-slave-owners and Republicans are to hold all the office.... Such an expedient would incapacitate Southern men. The conscientious and Constitution-loving would be excluded; the unprin-

---

1. Alderman and Gordon, p. 121.
2. Jabez Curry speech in the United States House of Representatives, March 14, 1860.
3. J. Steven Wilkens, *America: The First 350 Years* (Monroe, La., Covenant Publications, 1988), p. 153.
4. James Ronald Kennedy and Walter Donald Kennedy, *The South Was Right* (Gretna: Pelican Publishing Co.), p. 83.

cipled and the traitor would be appointed. It would be as effectual as the penal code against the Papists of Ireland.... The object is to divide the South into two distinct bodies without interest, sympathy, or connection, and another Ireland is to be made on this side of the ocean, with new parties of Orangemen and Brunswickmen."[1]

Republican Philosophies Mean War

Curry continued,

"The ideas, the principles, the politics of the Republican Party are necessarily and inherently and essentially hostile to the Constitution and to the rights and interests of the South. The arguments used assume an antagonism between the sections, an irrepressible conflict between opposing and enduring forces; and if slavery be what you allege it to be in your school rooms, your pulpits, through your public lectures, your political addresses, your legislative resolves, your congressional speeches, he is the most criminal who stops short in his career and hesitates at the exercise of the necessary means for its extinguishment. If slavery be a crime against God and against humanity, if it be a curse to society, if it contains the fruitful seeds of immedicable woes, it is as idle to talk of moderation and the Constitution and non-interference with the rights of the South, as it would be to propel a skiff up the surging cataract of Niagara."[2]

1860 Republican Party Platform: No Secession

Secession was legitimized through the ratification process of the Constitution. Virtually every state had agreed to accept that document only with the proviso that they could withdraw from the Union if the Federal government overstepped its mandated authority. But the 1860 Republican platform defied that provision, provoking further hate and confrontation.

Section 3 of their platform read:

> "That to the union of the States this nation owes its unprecedented increase in population, its surprising development of material resources, its rapid augmentation of wealth, its happiness at home and its honor abroad. And we hold in abhorrence all schemes for disunion, come from whatever source they may; and we congratulate the country that no Republican member of Congress has uttered or countenanced the threats of disunion so often made by Democratic members."[3]

---

1. Jabez Curry speech in the United States House of Representatives, December 10, 1859.
2. Ibid.
3. General Benjamin LaFevre, *Campaign of '84* (Chicago: Baird and Dillon, 1884), p. 41.

1860 Republican Party Platform: No Slavery

Slavery cannot be defended in the 21st century any more than in the 19th. But then it was a legal institution in one-third of the United States and sanctioned by the Constitution. And, slavery focused a paradox that even now is difficult to reconcile. State sovereignty embraces the principle that it is the citizens of a state or territory who have the exclusive privilege of creating their own social institutions, with no veto power from outside forces, like Congress, no matter how abhorrent those institutions may be to outsiders. By that reasoning, the attempt by the Republicans to prevent unpopular or detestable ways of life is not enlightened but dictatorial.

Section 8 of the Republican Party platform for 1860 reads:

> "That the normal condition of all the territory of the United States is that of freedom; that as our republican fathers, when they abolished slavery in all our national territory [did they?] ordained that "no person shall be deprived of life, liberty, or property [but slaves were legally defined as property] without due process of law," it becomes our duty, by legislation, whenever such legislation is necessary, to maintain the provision of the Constitution against all attempts to violate it; and we deny the authority of Congress, of a territorial legislature, or any individual, to give legal existence to slavery in any territory of the United States."[1]

This clause was highly offensive and provocative, not only to the South, but also to the Democrats, the dominant political entity in the country, who were firm advocates of state sovereignty.

Horatio Seymour, New York's Governor, Defends Slavery

The Democratic Governor of New York, Horatio Seymour, articulated the right to local self-government without external interference, when he said:

"The people of the North are uniformly opposed to slavery, not from hostility to the South, but because it is repugnant to our sentiments. In conformity with our views we have abolished slavery here, and having exercised our rights in our own way, we should be willing to let other communities have the same rights and privileges we have enjoyed. We are bound to act upon our faith in the principles of self-government. The Republican organization proposes an assault upon the Southern states by a system of agitation and excitement, directly at war with the purposes of the Constitution. They constantly discuss questions belonging to other states, to the entire neglect of their own local affairs. They

---

1. Ibid., p. 41.

organize their party on the ground that all and every difference of opinion about their own concerns are to be overlooked, provided they agree in their views about an institution [slavery] which does not exist in their own states, and does not exist in states where they admit they have no constitutional right to interfere."[1]

1856 Democratic Party Platform Defends Sovereignty/Slavery

The Democratic Party was a national party with considerable support both North and South. Resolution No. 1 of the 1856 party platform proclaimed:

> "Resolved, that we reiterate with renewed energy of purpose and well considered declarations of former conventions upon the sectional issue of domestic slavery, and concerning the reserved rights of the States — 1. That Congress has no power under the Constitution to interfere with or control the domestic institutions of the several States, and that all such States are the sole and proper judges of everything appertaining to their own affairs not prohibited by the Constitution; that all efforts of the Abolitionists or others, made to induce Congress to interfere with questions of slavery, are calculated to lead us to the most alarming and dangerous consequences, and that all such efforts have an inevitable tendency to diminish the happiness of the people and endanger the stability and permanency of the Union, and ought not to be countenanced by any friend of our political institutions."[2]

Constitution Protects Slavery

Despite the Republican platform's claim that "our republican Fathers, when they abolished slavery in all our national territory … ," Jabez Curry demonstrated that, in fact, the Fathers had protected "the peculiar institution." He stated it this way:

"The treaty of peace between Great Britain and the United States, signed in Paris, on the 3rd of September, 1783, on the United States side, by three Northern men; Adams, Franklin, and Jay, and which treaty was subsequently, by the Constitution, made the supreme law of the land, recognized "property in negroes." The Constitution of the United States discriminates specially in favor of slave property; provides for its increase, for its permanence, for its security, and for its representation in this body [Congress]. It recognizes property in slaves; and the Supreme Court has affirmed our right to emigrate to, and occupy with slaves, the common territory; and from this recognition and guarantee, protection is an inevitable sequitor."[3]

1. David Croly, *Seymour and Blair, Their Lives and Services* (New York: Richardson and Co., 1868), p. 63.
2. LaFevre, p. 36.

North-South Hatred Escalates Into War

Full-scale sectional warfare came to the United States in stages. The first crack in the Union appeared in 1820, via the Missouri Compromise. It prohibited slavery north of the 36° 30' line. This limited the expansion of the South. Thomas Jefferson, in despair, called this legislation "the [death] knell of the Union."

Then, in 1846, David Wilmot, a Democratic member of Congress from Pennsylvania, introduced his famous "Proviso." This was an amendment to a pending bill for the appropriating of two million dollars for the purchase of part of Mexico. It provided that slavery could not exist in this territory. It passed the House but failed in the Senate, but its impact was enormous. It split the country like a wedge. It caused great bitterness in the South and provoked the initial impulse for secession and war.

The year 1854 produced the Kansas-Nebraska Act. This took the issue of slavery out of the hands of Congress and left it entirely with the citizens of the territory. Curry said: "Prior to its adoption, Congress had arrogated a despotic, because unlimited, power over the Territories, fixing their normal condition, regulating their institutions, prescribing their civilization, and controlling their destiny."[1]

Instead of resolving the issue, it created a wave of terror and violence that was the opening phase of the War for Southern Independence.

Edwin Anderson Alderman dramatically introduced the horror of "Bleeding Kansas" this way: It "is as full of bitterness and woe as a Greek tragedy. The very name reeks with the evil memories of intolerance, and the ferocity of human hate, growing out of quasi-moral and political questions."[2]

A Northern Abolitionist organization, the Emigrant Aid Company, promoted anti-slavery settlers into Kansas. Pro-slavery groups in Missouri and throughout the South countered with their emigrants. Towns were established by both factions; Lawrence and Topeka by the "Free-Staters" and Leavenworth and Atchinson by the pro-slavery settlers. The first statehood elections in 1854 and 1855 went to the Southerners. Armed Missourians intimidated voters and election officials stuffed ballot boxes. The first territorial legislature, in 1855, ousted all the free-state members and moved the capital to Lecompton. In retaliation, the Abolitionists set up a rival government at Topeka, but the constitution

---

3. Jabez Curry speech in the United States House of Representatives, March 14, 1860.
1. Jabez Curry speech in the United States House of Representatives, February 23, 1858.
2. Alderman and Gordon, p. 118.

15

they set up was irregular and was rejected by Congress. Violence followed. In May 1856, Southern men raided Lawrence. A few days later, a band led by John Brown murdered five Southerners. That produced guerrilla war by both sides, abetted by desperadoes and opportunists, which terrorized Kansas.

The territorial governor, Robert Walker, called a convention at Lecompton to draft a state constitution. The free-state "Jayhawkers" refused to attend and the constitution that ensued was pro-South. There were Northern charges of fraud but President Buchanan recommended that Congress accept it. Instead, Congress returned it for a territorial vote. It was rejected.

Curry had this to say about the charges of fraud:

"The action of Kansas has been sober, methodical, and blameless; and but for its action on slavery and that she has cast her lot with the South, scarce a word of other than simulated dissent would have been heard from any quarter.... Desiring admission into the great sisterhood of Sovereign States, she is met with cold rebuffs and refusals, and to sustain the project of remanding her back to territorial pupilage, the most singular pretexts are alleged, the most monstrous doctrines are avowed, the most glaring injustice is proposed to be done, the most reckless inconsistency is practiced.... If the convention had the right to form and ordain a constitution, then the action of the Territorial Legislature was not irregular, inoperative, and void, and Congress has no right to prescribe a different mode of adopting the constitution, or send it back to find out the opinion of a majority of the voters of the State. This would be concentrating alarming power in Congress, giving it ample authority over the constitutions of the States, and allowing it to make decisions as to the extent of the elective franchise; for, if it can look behind a republican constitution, regularly framed and presented, to find out whether a majority voted for it, it can decide who shall constitute that majority and who should vote in the election. The States, inchoate and complete, will become provincial dependencies upon a central satrap, and this Confederacy be converted into a national dictatorship."[1]

In a later speech Curry further denied the fraud charges: "I cannot close without repelling an accusation which has been made on this floor, that the President and the Democratic party, in favoring the admission of Kansas, with the Lecompton constitution, were endeavoring to fasten a 'fraud' upon the country, and 'force a constitution upon the people of Kansas against their will.' ... Violence and wrong were committed on both sides, and there is much connected

---

1. Jabez Curry, speech in the United States House of Representatives, February 23, 1858.

with the question discreditable to the country. As a member of the last Congress, I repel with scorn all imputation, whether it comes from a Republican or a disorganizing and recusant Democrat, of a purpose to 'consummate a fraud,' or 'force' an unwilling State into the Union. It is demonstrable that the Lecompton constitution was legally and validly made and ordained as the organic law of the people of Kansas, so far as they had the power to institute a government.... The country will not forget that there was no allegation of the slightest fraud, not a single vote at any of the elections."[1]

Then, Lawrence became the de facto capital until the Wyandotte Convention of 1859 completely denied slavery. It was this constitution that Congress finally accepted.

Curry immediately grasped the true significance of what was happening in Kansas: "The rejection of Kansas, with the Lecompton constitution, speaks of the dissolution of, or sectionalizes, the Democratic party, which is the strongest ligament that binds the Union together. It will be the unmistakable annunciation that no more slave states are to be admitted to this Union; that the South is to be degraded and reduced to inferiority; that there is to be no extension of her limits, no enlargement of her boundaries; that slavery shall be restricted with constantly narrowing confines; that for her, within this Union, there is to be no future but bleak, gloomy, hopeless despair."[2]

Kansas became a state in 1861, with the capital at Topeka. During the War for Southern Independence, Kansas suffered the highest mortality rate of any state in the Union.

John Brown's Raid

John Brown shifted the killing, hate and terror from Kansas to the doorstep of the nation's capital, a Federal armory on the borderline of free and slave states. It brought sectional guerrilla war to the main stage, lighting the spark for the next step: full-scale war.

Jabez Curry made this comment about John Brown's raid: "The recent incursion that has been made into the State of Virginia ... is in my judgment, the necessary, logical, and inevitable sequence of [Republican] principles and doctrines."[3]

---

1. Jabez Curry speech in the United States House of Representatives, March 14, 1860.
2. Alderman and Gordon, p. 119.
3. Jabez Curry speech in United States House of Representatives, December 10, 1859.

John Brown was an ardent Abolitionist. He kept a station in the Underground Railroad in Richmond, Pennsylvania. In 1855, Brown settled with five of his sons in Kansas to help win the state for the Northern cause. He became a "captain" of the colony on the Osawatomie. The success of the Southern forces, particularly their sack of Lawrence, aroused Brown. To "cause a restraining fear" he, with four of his sons and two others, murdered five Southerners on the banks of the Pottawatamie River. He later said he was an instrument in the hand of God. His exploits received wide publicity in Abolitionist journals, and as "Old Brown of Osawatomie," he became nationally known.

Late in 1857, he began to enlist men for a project to liberate slaves through armed intervention by establishing a stronghold in the Southern mountains to which the slaves could flee and where a servile insurrection could be stirred up. Early in 1859, Brown rented a farm near Harpers Ferry, Virginia (now West Virginia) and collected followers and arms.

On the night of October 16, 1859, with twenty-one men, he crossed the Potomac and without much resistance captured the United States arsenal at Harpers Ferry, made the inhabitants prisoners, and took possession of the town. Strangely enough, he then merely settled down while the aroused local militia blocked his escape. That night a company of Marines commanded by Colonel Robert E. Lee arrived, and in the morning assaulted the engine house of the armory into which Brown's force had retreated. Ten of Brown's men were killed in the resulting battle, and Brown himself was wounded. News of the raid aroused wild fears in the South and it came as a great shock to the North. On December 2, 1859, Brown was hanged at Charles Town.

Interlude: Curry's Personality and Physiology

Let us pause and momentarily change the level of intensity, as we present a short humorous physical description of Jabez Curry.

"He is in build rather below the usual size, compactly built, dark skinned, and has an intellectual head surmounted by a covering of hair, albeit not lengthy in its dimensions, presenting very much the appearance of the picture one sees of the unkempt condition of a Shetland pony. This we say with all due respect to the learned doctor. Yet the impossibility of discovering whether his hair was parted at all, suggested the illustration of an unrefined nature, and we cannot forbear giving the public the benefit of it. Dr. Curry is possessed of a nervous manner, that renders him almost irresistible as a speaker. He is quick, sharp, and incisive as a Damascus blade; woe betide the opponent who comes within reach of his invective."[1]

Now, for his personality:

"He had the social instincts of an aristocrat, and exemplified in the best fashion the grand air of an age now gone, which greatly exalted manners and bred a quality of behavior that seems archaic and overwrought in our more direct era, but which was, in reality, very beautiful and distinguished, and by its passing has somehow robbed life of something that made for the lessening of vulgarity. His demeanor, like that of so many of his contemporaries, was a wonderful mingling of dignity and condescension, of gaiety and reserve, of intense self-consciousness without a suggestion of selfishness. Life and living were for him serious, beautiful, reverential things. He esteemed himself highly and he rigidly lived up to the standard he demanded of himself. The age of chivalry had not gone for him in his attitude towards women, for he had been singularly blessed in his relations with womanhood; nor the age of romance in his feeling for childhood and youth. He loved good talk and pleasant people, a good table and the good things the flesh of man craves, including a good story. With a varied human experience enriched by wide travel there were few themes upon which he could not discourse interestingly. He could listen charmingly enough, but bore with ill-concealed impatience any lack of attention to his own speech, and distinctly did not belong to the class of talkers who make of the noble art of conversation a series of sallies and silences. Macaulay and Dr. Johnson were more after his heart than the polished epigrams of the great French talkers. He loved the approval of his fellows and was almost naïve in his desire for applause and in the exhilaration and increase of power the applause gave him. Though bold and courageous in his opinions, he was unhappy if he was out of sympathy with his environments, and the master craving of his heart was for adaptability to his time. He could be a little overpowering at times in his suggestion of self-confidence and easy strength, and in a certain distaste for opposition, but never to the point of offense; and behind his high bearing, and sometimes imperious ways, lurked quick tears of sympathy and swift impulses of gentleness and helpfulness to every living thing."[2]

---

1. *Religious Herald* newspaper, 1875; exact date unknown.
2. Alderman and Gordon, p. 437.

Secession

Now, let us once again return to the subject at hand. The next logical step for the South, after years of hate, violence, political and economic encirclement, was secession. But — did Alabama and the other Southern states have the legal right to secede or was their action a rebellion?

Jefferson Davis, the President of the Confederacy, defined secession as "the assertion of the inalienable right of a people to change their government, whenever it ceased to fulfill the purpose for which it was ordained and established. Under our form of government, and the cardinal principles upon which it was founded, it should have been a peaceful remedy. The withdrawal of a State from a league has no revolutionary or insurrectionary characteristics. The government of the State remains unchanged as to all internal affairs. It is only its external or confederate relations that are altered. To term this action of a sovereign a 'rebellion,' is a gross abuse of language. So is the flippant phrase which speaks of it as an appeal to the 'arbitrament of the sword.' In the late contest [the War for Southern Independence] in particular, there was no appeal by the seceding States to the arbitrament of arms. There was on their part no invitation nor provocation to war. They stood in an attitude of self-defense, and were attacked for merely exercising a right guaranteed by the original terms of the compact. They neither tendered or accepted any challenge to the wager of battle. The man who defends his house against attack cannot with any propriety be said to have submitted the question of his right to it to the arbitrament of arms."[1]

Davis also described how the ratification of the Constitution was directly linked to each state's right to secede if necessary:

> The debates in the Virginia convention were long and animated.... Among the members were Madison, Mason, and Randolph, who had been members of the [Constitutional] Convention at Philadelphia. Mr. Madison was one of the most earnest advocates of the new Constitution, while Mr. Mason was as warmly opposed to its adoption; so also was Patrick Henry, the celebrated orator. It was assailed with great vehemence at every vulnerable or doubtful point, and was finally ratified ... [with a demand for] certain amendments as a more explicit guarantee against consolidation.... That the powers granted under the Constitution, being derived from the people of the United States, may be resumed by them, whenever the same shall be perverted to their injury or oppression, and that every power not granted thereby remains with them and at their will.

---

1. Jefferson Davis, *The Rise and Fall of the Confederate Government* (New York: D. Appleton and Company, 1881), p. vol. 1, p. 184.

New York, the eleventh State to signify her assent, did so, after an arduous and protracted discussion, and then by a majority of but three votes — 30 to 27....

Accompanying it was a declaration of the principles in which the assent of New York was conceded.... "That the powers of government may be reassumed by the people, whensoever it shall become necessary to their happiness."[1]

Jefferson Davis also pointed out the contradictory view that existed within the Republican party. Abraham Lincoln went to war to prevent secession. Yet Horace Greeley, one of the highest ranking Republicans, editor of the New York *Tribune* — the leading organ of the party which triumphed in the election of 1860 — had said, soon after the result of the election was ascertained, with reference to secession:

We hold, with Jefferson, to the inalienable right of communities to alter or abolish forms of government that have become oppressive or injurious; and if the cotton States shall decide that they can do better out of the Union than in it, we insist on letting them go in peace. The right to secede may be a revolutionary right but it exists nonetheless.... We hope never to live in a republic whereof one section is pinned to the other by bayonets.[2]

Finally, Jefferson Davis concluded his exploration of this topic with a chapter entitled *Coercion, the Alternative to Secession*. He wrote:

If no such right as that of secession exists — if it is forbidden or precluded by the Constitution — then it is a wrong; and, by the well settled principle of public law, for every wrong there must be a remedy, which in this case must be the application of force to the State attempting to withdraw from the Union.

Early in the session of the convention that formed the Constitution, it was proposed to confer upon Congress the power "to call forth the force of the Union against any member of the Union failing to fulfill its duty under the articles thereof." When this proposition came to be considered, Mr. Madison observed that "a union of the States containing such an ingredient seemed to provide for its own destruction. The use of force against a State would look more like a declaration of war than an infliction of punishment, and it probably would be considered by the party attacked as a dissolution of all previous compacts by which it might be bound." ... Mr. Hamilton, in the convention in New York, said: "To coerce the States is one of the maddest projects that was ever devised.... What picture does this idea present to our view? A complying State at war with a non-complying State; Congress marching troops of one State into the bosom of another.... Here is a nation at war with itself.... Can any reasonable man be well disposed toward a government which makes war and carnage the only means of supporting itself; a government that can exist only by the sword?

---

1. Davis, vol. 1, pp. 109-110.
2. Editorial in New York *Tribune*, November 6, 1860, quoted by Davis, vol. 1, p. 252.

... But can we believe that one State will ever suffer itself to be used as an instrument of coercion? The thing is a dream, it is impossible."[1]

Lincoln's Victory by Conflicts Over State Sovereignty

In the Presidential election of 1860, the Republicans received 1.8 million votes.

The Democrats, being deeply divided into Northern and Southern factions, fielded two different candidates as if they were different parties. This brought on their defeat. For Stephen Douglas, representing the North, 1.3 million votes were cast. John Breckenridge, spokesman for the South, received three-quarters of a million.

The Republicans, although a minority, gained control of the national government.

The philosophical differences between Douglas and Breckenridge revolved around the meaning of state sovereignty. Douglas, from Illinois, had been both a member of the House of Representatives and a Senator. As Chairman of the Committee on Territories, he was a key person in Washington due to the escalating conflict over slavery in the territories.

He was a classical state sovereignty proponent. Douglas said that only the citizens of each territory could determine for or against slavery. He called his doctrine "popular sovereignty." His opponents, with contempt, said it was "squatter sovereignty." His position meant that the Federal government could not intervene with slavery in any way.

John Breckenridge also believed that slavery or no slavery should be left to a territory's voters, but where he differed with Douglas exposed a contradiction in the Southern Democrat's position. On one hand he wanted Washington not to interfere with slavery yet simultaneously Breckenridge and the South demanded that the Federal government should protect slave-owners through the Fugitive Slave Law. This provided for the return, between states, of escaped slaves. But intervention and non-intervention were inconsistent viewpoints.

Last Days of the Union

In November 1860, following Lincoln's victory, Curry addressed his fellow Alabama citizens in the Methodist Church in Talladega on "The Perils and Duty of the South." He advised secession for the state as the only logical remedy for the existing evils.

---

1. Davis, vol. 1, pp. 177, 178.

In one of his last Congressional speeches, Curry prepared Washington for the inevitable break:

"Every community must be able to protect itself. Power must be met with power. If the majority can control this government; interpreting the Consti tution at its will, then this Government is a despotism. Whether it is wise or unwise or whether merciful or cruel, it is a despotism still. This power of self-protection, according to my judgment and my theory of politics, resides in each State. Each has the right of secession, the right of interposition for the arrest of evils within its limits. The means of resistance to oppression are ample; and it is a sad misfortune, sir, that these effective remedies have not been applied oftener. A more frequent application of the remedy would make the will commensurate with the means, inspire moral greatness, embolden courage, make resistance a duty, and equality a necessity. If our Democratic friends, with the aid of American [Party] friends, or of Republicans, who may come to the rescue, as I trust many of them will, may not be able to interpose for the security of the South, and for the preservation of the Constitution, I for one, shall counsel immediate and effective resistance, and I shall urge the people of Alabama, to which I owe my first and undivided allegiance, to fling themselves upon their ultimate defense, their reserved rights and inalienable sovereignty."[1]

In late November 1860, Curry was in Washington to be present at the new session of Congress. He remembered this momentous juncture: "Little else was thought or talked about than the threatened secession of the slave-holding States. The debates in Congress were excited and inflammatory; menacing, not pacific; partisan, not statesmanlike. Few realized the criticalness of the situation, or seemed to forecast the consequences. Few at the North credited the intense earnestness of the South. When the telegram was received that South Carolina had seceded, it was met with derisive laughter from the Republican side. Oxenstiern's advice to his son, to travel and see with how little wisdom the world is governed, had a painful verification."[2]

Then, as presented at the beginning of this chapter, Curry defiantly informed Congress that Alabama was cutting its ties to the United States. Six other states joined her: South Carolina, Mississippi, Florida, Georgia, Louisiana and Texas.

---

1. Alderman and Gordon, p. 135.
2. Ibid., p. 145.

Curry went back to Montgomery, where the excitement over secession was intense and vented itself in the roaring of cannon and the ringing of bells. At the Convention Hall, the doors were flung open at the announcement and it was thronged with an enthusiastic and cheering multitude. At night the city was brilliantly illuminated and the streets were crowded with men, women and children. A mass-meeting was held in front of Montgomery Hall and Curry addressed that mob. "Recognizing to its fullest extent the right of secession, and owing to her [Alabama] my allegiance and fealty, when she calls I will respond, where she goes I will go; her people shall be my people, and her destiny my destiny."[1]

---

1. Ibid., p. 148.

CHAPTER 2. CURRY AND THE CONFEDERACY

Thirty-six years after the War for Southern Independence, Jabez Curry wrote these tragic, bitter words about that era.

"It is almost impossible for any at the present time to realize, to enter into the spirit of, or to share the feelings and convictions of the people of the South in 1860.... A revolution, the bloodiest and most eventful war of modern times, produced ... the overthrow of secession as a right of a sovereign state. Such a complete and radical transformation has occurred in our Constitution, in laws, in social institutions, in organized labor, in party shibboleths, in schools, in public opinion, in literature, that one might as well strive to transport himself to the antediluvian period as to assume the thoughts and sympathies and manners of the period of 1860.... No justice can be done to the people of the South in the acts of 1861-1865, if they are to be interpreted by the standards of 1900."[1]

Curry finished his thoughts with this: "The Southern people have shared the fate of all conquered peoples. The conquerors write their history.... As they have been the objects of persistent misrepresentation, and authentic records have been perverted to their prejudice, their descendents are liable to receive and hold opinions hostile and derogatory to their fathers.... If the act of secession cannot be justified, the Southern people will be stigmatized as a brave and rash people deluded by bad men, who attempted in an illegal and wicked manner, to overthrow the Union. It is charged that there was a wanton and precipitate sev-

---

1. J.L.M. Curry, *Civil History of the Government of the Confederate States, With Some Personal Reminiscences* (Richmond: B.F. Johnson Publishing Co., 1911), p. 24.

ering of the relations to the Union and that the masses were hurried along against their better judgment by ambitious and unscrupulous leaders. Dr. Palmer, in his address before the recent Confederate re-union [May 30–June 3, 1900] forcibly says: 'It is simply folly to suppose that such a spontaneous uprising as that of our people in 1860 and 1861 could be effected through the machinations of politicians alone. A movement so sudden and vast, instantly swallowing up all minor contentions, would only spring forth from great faith planted in the human heart, and for which men were willing to die ... State sovereignty as against national supremacy. As there was no compromise between the two, the only resort was an appeal to the law of force.'"[1]

The Impending War

Alexander Stephens, one of the leading Southern Unionists and later Vice President of the Confederacy, was aware that Abraham Lincoln did not have unanimous support in the North. The United States Congress was controlled by the Democrats. They would neutralize him, surely. Secession would not be necessary.

The opposing perspective came from South Carolina, the first state to secede. Through the "South Carolina Plan" the Confederacy would be formed no later than Lincoln's inauguration; James Buchanan, the outgoing President, was a state sovereignty proponent. He would never block secession, but the Republicans would be more aggressive. Prudence required an operating government be in place by January 20.

South Carolina seceded on December 20, 1860. "The union subsisting between South Carolina and the other States under the name of the United States of America, is hereby dissolved. South Carolina proclaims itself an independent commonwealth."

South Carolina acted alone, without waiting for cooperative action, but expressed a desire for the formation of a Southern Confederacy. Commissioners were appointed to the other Southern states and deputies were elected to meet those from states who might secede. Their purpose was to form a provisional government, propose a constitution, and plan for a permanent nation.

Mississippi followed, then Florida, then Alabama, Georgia and Louisiana. On February 13, 1861, Virginia called for a secession convention in Richmond. The majority opposed. She remained within the Union.

---

1. Ibid., pp. 185, 186, 143.

On March 4, Abraham Lincoln was inaugurated as President. His address argued against the right to secede and asserted his intention to "hold, occupy, and possess the property and places belonging to the Government, and collect the duties and imposts," but "beyond what may be necessary for these objects, there will be no invasion, no use of force against or among the people any-where."[1]

William Seward, Lincoln's Secretary of State, in official papers and private talks repudiated the right or even the wish to use any armed force in subjecting the Southern states against the will of the majority of the people and declared that the President "willingly" accepted as true the cardinal dogma that the Federal government could not reduce them to obedience by conquest. He may have been led to this opinion by the belief that the seceding states would soon find their position untenable and would be forced back into the Union. His was a temporizing policy; he was playing a subtle game for delay; and he was misled as to the transient nature, the "passing mania" of the secession bent of the South.

Dr. Russell of the London *Times* wrote, after visiting the Confederacy: "Assuredly, Mr. Seward cannot know anything of the South or he would not be so confident that all would blow over."[2]

Ft. Sumter and War

Seward refused to receive diplomats from the Confederacy. If he received them, it would have signified that the United States recognized the Confederacy as a legitimate separate country. Only through clandestine, semi-official means, through Judge Campbell of the Supreme Court, were secret negotiations carried on. Through Campbell, Seward said that the United States intended to evacuate Ft. Sumter. This would avoid conflict. Lincoln's Cabinet voted 5 to 4 for its abandonment. But Lincoln was stalling. Seward deceived Judge Campbell as to Washington's real intentions, which were to reinforce and hold the fort.

The merchant vessel *Star of the West*, bringing reinforcements to Sumter, was driven back by Charleston's shore batteries and thereafter, on April 14, after a thirty-four hour bombardment, Major Robert Anderson surrendered the fort.

The next day Lincoln called for 75,000 volunteers to subdue the "combinations," meaning the "insurrection." He asked Virginia for her quota of 8,000. Gov-

---

1. Davis, p. 256.
2. Jabez Curry, *Civil History of the Government of the Confederate States, etc.*, p. 98.

ernor Letcher, although both an anti-slavery and anti-secession man, refused to invade sister states. "You have chosen to inaugurate civil war," he said.

The other border states took the same stand. North Carolina, Arkansas, Missouri and Tennessee had all voted against secession, "but Tennessee will not furnish a single man for coercion," Governor Isham said, "but 50,000 if necessary for the defense of her rights or those of our Southern brothers."

Claiborne Jackson, the governor of Missouri, called Lincoln's demand "inhuman and diabolical ... illegal, unconstitutional and revolutionary in its object."

Officers of the United States military stationed all over the world who were Southerners by birth or residence, and not a few who were neither but who believed that the cause of the South was just, hastened to the service of the Confederacy. They did not come to perpetuate slavery but were animated by the sentiment of constitutional freedom and the sovereignty of the states.

A New Nation

In the meantime, Jabez Curry, as a deputy from Alabama, was present when the Convention of the Seceding States met at Montgomery on February 4, 1861. They assembled in the Senate chamber of the capital. Howell Cobb was elected president of the convention. He had been a Congressman and the governor of Georgia, and United States Treasury Secretary under President Buchanan.

A sample of the other distinguished men who participated includes Alexander Stephens, who had served six terms in the Georgia legislature and would be Jefferson Davis' Vice President. The future Secretary of State of the Confederacy, Robert Toombs, a vocal opponent of Jefferson Davis, was there as well as the German-born Christopher Memminger, who would be the new nation's Treasury Secretary. Robert Walker, the governor of the Kansas Territory during the "Bloody Kansas" era, who convened the Lecompton constitutional convention, was also in attendance.

The immediate business of the convention was to prepare a constitution, and organize a provisional government. The convention was in session until May.

Curry wrote: "When the Constitution was adopted Jefferson Davis was elected President. Mr. Davis reached Montgomery on the 17th of February and was inaugurated the following day. He stood on the steps of the capital, looking West, as he read his inaugural.... A platform had been erected on the East side of General Washington's statue and there Mr. Davis took the oath of office. The day was very disagreeable, It rained and snowed and some said it augured unfavorably as to our cause from the unpleasantness of the day."[1]

Davis concluded his inaugural speech with these lofty sentiments: "It is joyous, in the midst of perilous times, to look around upon a people united in heart; where one purpose of high resolve animates and actuates the whole, where the sacrifices to be made are not weighed in the balance against honor, and right and liberty and equality. Obstacles may retard, they cannot prevent the progress of a movement sanctioned by its justice, and sustained by a virtuous people."[2]

Curry continued: "When the oath of office was administered, with great solemnity, and reverence, he bowed and kissed a large open bible which lay before him. Then sounded the cannon. The first gun was fired by the granddaughter of President Tyler. She was a pretty little girl about twelve years old."[3]

Some Cabinet Members and Vice President

They were all distinct individuals. Curry had known the Confederacy's Vice President, Alexander Stephens, since his college days: "His life, amid difficulties and dangers, appears a miracle. Tall, spare, not weighing over one hundred pounds, nearly bloodless, with a feminine voice and appearance, he seemed incapable of physical labor or fatigue. He was spoken of as a 'refugee from a graveyard.' Of parentage of moderate means, he was educated up to graduation from the University of Georgia by some generous and sympathetic woman who discovered in him personal virtues and mental precocity. At the bar Stephens attained exceptional success. His legal knowledge, diligently acquired, his disciplined faculties, his marvelous eloquence, were the elements of his professional distinctions. He was a representative, Vice President and governor. As a stump speaker he had few equals. His remarkable physique, penetrating voice, ingenious frankness, humor, satire, repartee, eloquence, made him a great favorite."[4]

Stephen Mallory was Secretary of the Navy; a Floridian, who originally had been against secession. A Unionist and Chairman of the United States Naval Committee. He was the most imaginative of all the Cabinet members, and invented or developed new devices of war: mines, torpedoes, submarines, iron-

---

1. Jabez Curry, hand-written autobiographical notes, April 1876, Curry Papers, Library of Congress.
2. Alderman and Gordon, p. 156.
3. Jabez Curry, hand-written autobiographical notes, April 1876.
4. J.L.M. Curry, *Civil History of the Government of the Confederate States, etc.*, p. 56.

clads. He was one of the few high-level Confederate officials who conceptualized methods to win the war.

Judah Benjamin was the Attorney-General. From Louisiana, he was born of Jewish parents in the West Indies, a nationally prominent lawyer and a state-machine Senator. While in the Senate, he challenged Jefferson Davis to a duel over a slight. Davis apologized.

LeRoy Pope Walker was from Curry's home state of Alabama. He was Secretary of War. Since Jefferson Davis literally tried to be a total commander-in-chief of the military, he reduced Walker's role to a clerical paper-shuffler. Although disorganized, he was effective in developing arms and ammunition production where there had been almost nothing.

Robert Toombs is called, by one author, "The Danton of the Rebellion," but Curry idolized him. Toombs was Secretary of State. Curry described him this way: "Perhaps no one was more active, bold and able in asserting the rights of the Southern States and their purpose not to submit to inequality and injustice than Senator Toombs. He was one of the most remarkable men of the century; lawyer, farmer, statesman. An orator swaying multitudes as the storm swept the forest, holding grave senators breathless under the exposition of damages and remedies.... I recall an incident in a secret session of the Provisional Congress, held in the House of Deputies in the capital at Richmond, when the success of the Confederacy was under consideration and foreign succor, financial schemes and other expedients were under discussion. After a warm debate, Toombs took the floor, and in less than an hour, in a style dazzling, free, incisive, delivered a powerful speech on our available means of safety. Every deputy sat with rapt and concentrated attention, amazed at the extraordinary ability of the man and surprised and delighted at the seemingly wise and adequate scheme which he presented. When he closed there was almost a painful silence for a considerable time, and then Robert Smith of Mobile, arose and said: 'Mr. President, if the gentleman from Georgia does not bring in bills to carry out what he has suggested, he is a worse traitor than Benedict Arnold.'"[1]

Toombs, aged 50, was the first Cabinet member to turn against Jefferson Davis. A successful lawyer at 30, a member of Congress at 34, a senator at 40, he originally believed in the Union, then turned violently against it and advocated rebellion. Toombs expected to be the President of the Confederacy. He loved literature, and studied French with his daughters.

---

1. Ibid., p. 18.

The more Toombs criticized Davis, the more he was isolated from him. Jefferson Davis was a West Point graduate (1828) and an officer in the Black Hawk War. He married the daughter of former President Zachary Taylor. She died within three months. In 1845 he married a great beauty, Varina Howell. In the same year, he was elected to Mississippi House of Representatives. He commanded a regiment in the Mexican War. He was a senator, then ran for governor in 1851; he was beaten by only one thousand votes. He served as United States Secretary of War in 1855 under Franklin Pierce.

As President of the Confederacy, Jefferson Davis made many enemies because of his arrogant style. He did not pretend to listen to opposing views. He kept Congress in the dark on important matters. When the war turned against the South, the anger of Congressmen and Cabinet-members came out into the open but Davis was invulnerable to criticism. He felt he was more qualified to be military commander in the field than President. Davis was one of the few who recognized that the war would be long and bloody.[1]

The Capital Moves to Richmond

The original capital of the Confederacy was at Montgomery, Alabama; the impulse to move it to Richmond, Virginia, was based on military necessity. Davis, as commander in-chief, saw the need to be near the scene of the major fighting for rapid decision-making. Montgomery was far away and communications were slow.

When the Montgomery government voted to make Richmond the capital, Virginians ratified the secession ordinance. The next day their state was invaded.

Montgomery was a small town with only two hotels and it was very hot in the summer. Virginia was the South's producer of war materiel and food. Its geographical position made it easier to win over the border states.

Curry Observes Battle of Bull Run

On July 20, 1861 the Confederate Congress met for the first time in Richmond. Jabez Curry was a member. He had been elected from the 4th District of Alabama, which consisted of Randolph, Calhoun, Talladega and Shelby counties.

---

1. Biographical sketches based on *Profiles in Rebellion*, Clifford Dowdey (Garden City: Doubleday & Co., 1946), pp. 14-15.

On July 20, Curry left his home in Talladega for the new capital. He arrived in Richmond the following morning and learned of the impending collision of the two armies.

"Hearing that a battle was imminent at Manassas, I took the train ... to hasten to the scene of the conflict. The cars were so crowded that the whole day hardly sufficed to enable us to reach Manassas. The battle had been fought, the victory won; and the Federal soldiers in complete rout, had fled to Washington. I rode over the battlefield and along the line of retreat, and to me the carnage seemed dreadful. It was my first sight of men killed in battle. One thing impressed me powerfully; the utter disorganization and want of discipline in our army. Victory had demoralized our troops as much as defeat had the enemy. To my inexperienced eye it seemed as if a well-appointed brigade could have captured our whole army. Everything was in confusion, and men and officers seemed to be straggling at will."[1]

The Confederate Constitution

Jabez Curry was a deputy from Alabama to the Convention of the Seceded States which met in Montgomery on February 4, 1861. One of its main functions was to create a constitution. Its work was completed just after the inauguration of Jefferson Davis, on February 18th.

Davis said: "The Constitution formed by our Fathers is that of the Confederate States, in their exposition of it; and in the judicious construction it has received we have a light which reveals its true meaning."[2]

Curry participated in the creation of this fundamental document. He said that the original Constitution was an object of veneration. Attachment to it was akin to idolatry. Curry noted, with great pride, that the United States Constitution was the work of Southern statesmen, adding that "the Federal government, the creature of the Constitution, had been shaped and administered, for many years, by Southern men."[3]

In the deliberations to create a permanent Confederate Constitution, the convention looked to the history of the United States to find the weakness and failings of the original. Alexander Stephens said of the men who put this new instrument together: "They were men of substance, of solid character, of moral

---

1. Jabez Curry, hand-written autobiographical notes, April 1876.
2. J.L.M. Curry, *Civil History of the Government of the Confederate States, etc.*, p. 51.
3. Ibid., pp. 145-6.

worth, versed in the principles and practice of government, and some of them were amongst the first men of the continent."[1]

Curry emphatically claimed that the Confederacy was not dissatisfied with the United States Constitution, only with its administration; and its avowed purpose was to restore its integrity and secure its faithful observance with the goal of taking away from the majority in Congress unlimited power. He described how this was achieved: "Every possible infringement upon popular liberty, or upon State rights, every oppressive or sectional use of the taxing power, was carefully guarded against, and civil service reform was made easy and practicable. Stubborn and corrupting controversies about tariffs, post offices, improvements of rivers and harbors, subsidies, extra pay, were avoided. The taxing power was placed under salutary restrictions. Responsibility was more clearly fixed. Money in the treasury was protected against purchasable majorities and wicked combinations. Adequate powers for a frugal and just administration were granted to the General Government. The States maintained their autonomy, and were not reduced to petty corporations, or counties, or dependencies.

"The study of the Confederate Constitution would be useful at present, as there never was a time when the need of restrictions and guarantees against irresponsible power was more urgent. The public mind has been schooled against any assertion of State rights or of constitutional limitations, and taught to look with aversion and ridicule upon any serious attempt to set up the ancient landmarks."[2]

The Provisional Constitution was no mere interim makeshift document. It represented a serious effort to incorporate Southern state rights principles into organic law. The preamble omitted the "general welfare" clause, which had been used to add imperial powers to the United States Constitution, and referred pointedly to the "sovereign and independent States." As such, each state was permitted to have peace-time armies and navies, but they could not wage war with foreign powers unless invaded.

The President

Radical changes were made to the President's office. First, his tenure was for six years, not four, as in the United States. He was ineligible for a second

---

1. Ibid., p. 62.
2. Alderman and Gordon, p. 165.

term. Curry noted: "Under the [United States] system, the President is practically an appointee of irresponsible bodies of men and the triumph of the party is of more consequence than the public welfare. The patronage of the President rewards partisans and silences free thought. When the President is a candidate for a second term he is tempted to use this immense patronage to secure renomination."[1]

This appointing power, Curry observed in 1900, meant the control of 170,000 Federal positions. This generated great corruption. Curry bitterly denounced this arrangement because "continuance in public office is no longer dependent on fidelity to duty. Men are put into official positions as a reward for partisan service, or for favors."[2]

Another change was that the Confederate President was responsible for appropriations. Congress could not make them except by a two-thirds vote of both Houses. And, the President had "line-item" veto power.

To a degree, the Confederate President's powers were based on the British model. While there was a wide difference between a Presidential and a Cabinet government, like the one in Britain, there was in the Confederacy a modified form of the unwritten British constitution which allowed the President to be heard on the floor of the two Houses through his advisors. This gave the President more responsibility and accountability for economy in appropriations.

In Britain, the Executive was required to select his Cabinet from Parliament. The Confederate Constitution followed that ideal but did not make it mandatory.

Curry's Contributions to the Constitution

The *Journal of the Congress of the Confederate States of America* was the equivalent of the *Congressional Record* in the United States. It depicts the debates and law-making process. It shows several of Jabez Curry's contributions to the Constitution. This May 9, 1861 entry relates to the responsibilities of the President and Vice President:

> Secret Session. Mr. Curry offered the following resolutions, viz:
>
> Resolved, that the Committee on the Constitution be requested to inquire into the expediency of an amendment to the Constitution authorizing the Vice President to act as, and discharge the duties of, the President, when that officer

---

1. J.L.M. Curry, *Civil History of the Government of the Confederate States, etc.*, p. 74.
2. Ibid., p. 74.

shall consider the public defense requires his absence from the seat of govern-ment.

Resolved, that it is the judgment of this Congress that the President, as soon as the public convenience will justify it, should take command in person of the Army of the Confederate States.[1]

Congress

As for economy, the Confederate Constitution forbade Congress to appro-priate any money other than for its own expenses, except at the specific request of the President. Curry made the following revision:

Tuesday, March 5, 1861. The Ninth clause of the Confederate Constitution: Congress shall appropriate no money from the Treasury unless it be asked and estimated for by some one of the heads of Department, and submitted to Con-gress by the President, except for the purpose of paying its own expenses and contingencies, or for the payment of claims against the Confederate States, the justice of which has been judicially declared by a tribunal for the investigation of claims against the government, which it is hereby made the duty of Congress to establish.

Mr. Curry then offered the following as a substitute for the clause, to wit:

9. Congress shall appropriate no money from the Treasury except by a vote of two-thirds of both Houses, taken by yeas and nays, unless it be asked or esti-mated for by some one of the heads of Department; or except for the purpose of paying its own expenses and contingencies; or for the payment of claims against the Confederate States, the justice of which has been judicially declared by a tribunal for the investigation of claims against the government, which is hereby the duty of Congress to establish.

It was agreed to.[2]

The Confederate Congress was thwarted from financing state projects by denying it power to appropriate money "for internal improvements intended to facilitate commerce" except in certain navigational aid circumstances. This pre-vented the absorption of the states into the central government by subsidizing their own affairs.

Confederate Congressmen could serve in the army, since the United States ban on plural office-holding was omitted.

To prevent unrelated amendments from being tacked onto legislation, every law had to relate to only one subject, which must be expressed in the title.

---

1. *Journal of the Congress of the Confederate States of America, 1861-1865*, Document No. 234, 58th United States Congress, 2nd Session, February 1904, Washington D.C. Government Printing Office, May 9, 1861, p. 200.
2. Ibid., p. 872.

Philosophical Conflicts over Constitution

The radical state rights men were determined to complete the break with the United States Constitution, while the conservatives tried to combat experiments and innovations that would move them away from the original document. The Constitution Committee was almost evenly divided between the two points of view. Rivalry was keen and arguments interminable.

Alexander Stephens wrote his brother Linton (who was Curry's roommate in college) that he was "in agony" lest "some serious mischief" be done to the old Constitution and he told of "some very bad passions and purposes" at work.

Georgia and Alabama and to some extent Mississippi, states with strong "cooperationist" or Union elements, most often supported conservative doctrines. Florida and South Carolina voted most consistently for radical departures from the previous balance between the states and central government.

The completed Constitution was a mixture of rigid adherence to tradition, a desire to write a truly Southern Constitution and the recognition of practical flaws in the previous one.

Abolished was the theory that the central government possessed inherent powers; it was now only an agent of the states.

The preamble designated the Confederacy as a "permanent federal government," with each state "acting in its sovereign and independent character." The powers of the central government were "delegated," not "granted."[1]

Slavery

In the United States Constitution, the issue of slavery was thrust as far as possible out of sight and a euphemistic paraphrase avoided the frank naming of what portended future trouble. This timidity was one of the causes that brought forth the terrible war.

No proposition was made by the Confederate Congress to re-open the slave trade and the Provisional Constitution reads: "The importation of African negroes from any foreign country other than the slave-holding States of the United States is hereby forbidden." The permanent document also affirms that same prohibition.[2]

The Fugitive Slave paragraph of the United States Constitution was actually weakened by the Confederacy, by shifting to the governor of the state to

---

1. From Wilfred Buck Yearns, *The Confederate Congress* (Athens: University of Georgia Press, 1960), p. 26.
2. J.L.M. Curry, *Civil History of the Confederate States, etc.*, p. 90.

which the slave fled the responsibility of either returning him or compensating the owner for his loss.

The Supreme Court

The failure of the Confederate Congress to establish a Supreme Court is an interesting chapter in the history of the state rights controversy. The Provisional Constitution set up a Supreme Court "constituted of all the District Judges" who should sit "at such times and places as the Congress shall appoint." It was soon evident that Western judges would have difficulty making the long trek to Richmond for its session; moreover, the judges realized that they might be charged for bargaining with each other for the support of their district court decisions. On July 31, 1861 Congress suspended the Supreme Court until it could be organized under the Permanent Constitution.

Jefferson Davis, believing in the cohesive force of a strong judiciary, in February 1862 asked Congress for the Court, "in accordance with the mandate of the Constitution." Within weeks Senate and House bills providing for a Supreme Court with a Chief and three Associate Justices were proposed. After a long postponement, both Houses dropped the matter without bringing it to a vote. Georgia Senator Benjamin Hill's warning that a government without a Supreme Court would be a "lame and limping affair" fell on deaf ears.

By 1863, more senators agreed and on January 19 Hill introduced a bill much like the one from the year before. Discussion this time was vigorous and thorough Tempers flared, inkwells were hurled, personal spite and partisan politics broke out into the open. The climax came when Mr. Clay proposed to strike from the Judiciary Act of March 1861 two sections that conferred upon the Supreme Court appellate jurisdiction over the highest state courts.

The Senate nationalists attacked Clay's amendment on the grounds that appellate jurisdiction would stabilize the nation by guaranteeing that the laws of Congress would be enforced: that in the Confederacy there could be no such misrepresentation of the Constitution that permitted "usurpation typifying the history of the United States' Court." But the majority rejected this "poisonous" doctrine so reminiscent of John Marshall, the famed Supreme Court Chief Justice who had advocated Federal centralization over state sovereignty. Clay contended that the disputed sections placed the state courts so much within the "power of the courts of the Confederate States [the national government] that the Constitution would become only an instrument to favor the consolidation of the government."

Mr. Yancey warned that this very principle "more than any other thing" had disrupted the United States and was intended to "chain" the states to "the ear of the government."

These fireworks reveal the principal reasons why the Confederacy had no Supreme Court. That absence, plus the fact that the district courts had no appellate jurisdiction over the state courts, either, finished the Federal court system. The Confederate government usually prosecuted its cases in state courts in the knowledge that their decisions would be more respected than those of the district courts.[1]

"By March" 1861 Curry wrote, "a permanent Constitution was adopted, and submitted to the separate States for their ratification.... The New York *Herald*, in April, published the full text of our Constitution, and advised the North to adopt it as a settlement of difficulties."[2]

Curry and the Flag Committee

Jabez Curry was assigned to four committees in the Provisional Congress. Three were of minor significance; one was highly important. The Postal Committee, the Commercial Affairs Committee and the Rules Committee did not produce earth-shaking legislative proposals. The fourth, the Flag and Seal Committee, did. From Curry and its other members came the immortal and universally recognizable "Stars and Bars" flag.

On Thursday, February 28, 1861, "Mr. Curry presented a design for the flag." On March 4 came the following report:

> The number of [designs) has been immense, but they may be divided into two great classes. First, those which copy and preserve the principle features of the United States flag, with slight and unimportant modifications.
>
> Second: Those which are very elaborate, complicated or fantastical. The objection to the first class is, that none of them at any considerable distance could readily be distinguished from the one which they imitate. Whatever attachment may be felt from association, for the "Stars and Stripes," an attachment which your committee may be permitted to say they do not share, it is manifest that in inaugurating a new government we cannot with any propriety, or without encountering very obvious practical difficulties, retain the flag of the Government from which we have withdrawn. There is no propriety in retaining the ensign of a government which, in the opinion of the States composing the Confederacy, had become so oppressive and injurious to their interests as to require their separation from it.... It is superfluous to dwell upon the

---

1. Yearns, pp. 37-39.
2. Alderman and Gordon, p. 156.

practical difficulties which would flow from the fact of two distinct and probably hostile governments, both employing the same or very similar flags. It
would be a political and military solecism. It would produce endless confusion
and mistakes. It would lead to perpetual disputes.... It must be conceded however, that something was conceded by the committee to what seemed so strong
and earnest a desire to retain at least a suggestion of the old "Stars and
Stripes".... A flag should be simple, readily made, and above all, capable of being
made up in bunting. It should be different from the flag of any other country,
place or people. It should be significant. It should be readily distinguishable at
a distance. The colors should be contrasted and durable, and lastly, and not the
least important point, it should be effective and handsome.

The committee humbly thinks that the flag they submit combines these
requisites. It is easy to make. It is entirely different from any national flag. The
three colors of which it is composed — red, white and blue — are the true
republican colors. In heraldry they are emblematic of the three great virtues of
valor, purity and truth.... If adopted, long may it wave over a brave, a free, and a
virtuous people.[1]

Curry's Observations of Fellow Congressmen

Curry: "The legislation amounted to very little. Mr. Davis gave Congress
very little information beyond what was published in the newspapers. He was
apparently expected to put into statutes what he deemed best for the interests of
the Confederacy. Possibly, probably, it was best not to communicate publicly
secrets to Congress, for very little occurred in either House that did not
promptly find its way into the newspapers.

"We had some excellent men in the House. Mr Rives was a scholar, an
experienced statesman, a high-toned gentleman. Garnett of Georgia was a man
of abundant possibilities. He died and I made one of the addresses on the
occasion. Staples and Preston were eloquent men. Henry Foote of Tennessee was
sui generis [in a class by himself]. Whether partially demented or more disaffected
with the South, it was difficult to decide. His insane hatred of the President, led
him into the most violent and vituperative harangues. With a prolific mind, a
fluent tongue, varied but inaccurate information, indominatable industry and a
genius for hating, he came into the House every day with pockets full of resolutions and bills, which he disgorged upon an unwilling and impatient body. With
personal courage joined to audacity and unscrupulousness, he sometimes
uttered terrific philippics. But generally, he was so hasty in his conclusions and
so bitter in his attacks, that his influence was zero."[2]

---

1. *Journal of the Congress of the Confederate States of America, 1861-1865*, p. 101.
2. Alderman and Gordon, p. 164.

Curry Opposes Kentucky and Missouri into Confederacy

Bills were introduced into Congress providing for the admission of Missouri and Kentucky into the Confederacy. Toombs, Wigfall and other prominent Congressmen favored their admission and the measure was enacted into law. But Curry said: "I opposed them ineffectively, and almost alone, on the grounds that their admission would be in utter contravention of all the principles underlying our secession and the formation of the Confederacy; that a majority of the people in Kentucky and Missouri were not in sympathy with us, and that the representatives would have no constituents. My predictions were too faithfully verified. The States were soon in the complete control of the Federal army; and those who sat as representatives of these States owed their pretense of an election to the votes cast by soldiers in our army from those States. With some honorable exceptions, the representatives were worse than useless."[1]

Efforts to Gain European Recognition

Curry: "A Liverpool [England] journal declared cotton to be the greatest question of the civilized world. Many of the leading men of the South trusted in the commercial and industrial supremacy of cotton, a power as great as armies and navies, and relied on it as a political factor to 'force the hand' of Great Britain and secure the recognition of the Confederate States as an independent power.

"[English] looms, which had consumed 40,000 bales in a week, could not hope for 4,000. Disturbances were serious and operatives were thrown on parishes for relief."[2]

England and France immediately recognized the Confederacy's right as a belligerent because Lincoln blockaded Southern ports. This meant the United States acknowledged the Confederacy as a sovereign entity, for the blockade stopped European ships.

And by 1862, despite many Confederate defeats, England was moving closer toward official recognition, especially when Union General, Benjamin "Beast" Butler committed atrocities in occupied New Orleans.

Curry, Guardian of State Sovereignty

As a member of the United States Congress, Jabez Curry had always attempted to curb Federal spending as a way to keep the national government

---

1. J.L.M. Curry, *Civil History of the Government of the Confederate States, etc.*, p. 112.
2. Ibid., p. 112.

within its mandated sphere. Whenever he observed legislation that tended toward centralization, he reacted. Here, we see that same logic in the Confederate Congress:

> The undersigned [which included Toombs and several other notables] protest against the passage of the "Act to provide for connecting the Richmond and Danville and the North Carolina Railroads, for military purposes." This act, in effect, places one million dollars of the bonds of the Confederate States at the disposal of the President, to be used and applied at such times and in such sums as he may deem proper.... It must also follow as a "necessity" that, by thus conferring upon the President the power to invade public, corporate and individual rights in order to build the road.... [He will be] exercising dictatorial powers over the lives, liberties and properties of the people under the color of giving improved facilities to the Quartermaster's and Commissary Departments ... under the same pretension that they now witness the Constitution of the United States subverted, martial law declared, and the writ of habeas corpus suspended. The old Government never exercised this power. This was one of the prospective evils against which the people of the South were warned, and was one of the special grounds urged in favor of separation from it.[1]

Curry Observes Retreat from Corinth

Curry: "About the last of May [1862] I visited my brother's family in Perry County, then extended my journey to Tupelo, Mississippi. The trains were crowded with soldiers, new or lately furloughed, limping to the army stationed at Corinth and Tupelo. I stopped with a connection by marriage, Mr. Freeman, and soon came in young General Pegman who had been sent forward by General Beauregard to select a suitable camp for our troops, falling back from Corinth. [Corinth is in extreme Northeast Mississippi, near the Tennessee line; a strategic railroad center.]... In the afternoon, General Beauregard arrived and at once General Pegman, with intelligence, communicated the results of his observations and presented a hastily drawn map or diagram. General Beauregard listened attentively, examined the map and with his rare engineering skill, soon suggested several changes, so as to increase offensive and defensive advantages. I spent two weeks with the army.... The enemy did not pursue and I had ample opportunities for visiting the troops."[2]

These notes do not express how disturbed Curry was over the military situation in Mississippi and Alabama. On June 20, 1862, he wrote Jefferson Davis a six-page letter describing conditions as he saw them. "The retrograde movement from Corinth to Tupelo was more like a rout than a retreat," and he blamed the

---

1. *Journal of the Congress of the Confederate States of America, 1861-1865*, p. 781.
2. Jabez Curry, hand-written autobiographical notes, April 1876.

commanders for the confusion and disorder. He stated that the "loss of property and destruction of the Rail Road rolling stock were in keeping with what has been the practice since fallings-back have become masterly military movements." He condemned the Quartermaster and Commissary departments for inefficiency. He described the sickness in the Army as terrible, amounting to "60 percent of the whole force." Curry stated that there was great dissatisfaction among the troops he saw because the men were tired of inactivity and retreats, and because General Bragg, instead of electing and promoting officers by seniority, arbitrarily appointed them and thrust them upon regiments and companies "in the teeth of the law and the unanimous wishes of the men." He named an Alabama regiment to which three field officers from other states, "two of whom are said to be brothers-in-law of Secretary Mallory," had been appointed to the exclusion of officers who had won distinction at Shiloh. Curry reported that there was no despondency among the men as to the final outcome, and that Price and Stonewall Jackson were universally favored because they fought and advanced. He wrote of his fear that failure to advance into Tennessee and protect Memphis would result in another falling back, which would cause the Confederacy to be divided into three portions that could not communicate with each other.[1]

Curry on Battle of Richmond and Jefferson Davis

Curry continued, "In August the great but indecisive battle around Richmond had occurred, freeing Richmond from the probability of an early attack. I said 'indecisive' because the results were not proportionate to the fighting, but McClellan's repulse was decisive. Many thought his army should have been captured."

Curry says the battle was indecisive but, in fact, it was one of the great victories of the war for the Confederacy. General McClellan had pushed the Union Army into the suburbs of Richmond. Then Robert E. Lee replaced the wounded and defense-minded Joseph E. Johnston, who had constantly fallen back. Lee brilliantly went on the offensive and came close to trapping and annihilating McClellan's forces, who had to evacuate the Peninsula, leaving behind thousands of dead and huge amounts of war materiel.

Yet Curry may have been taking an indirect swipe at Jefferson Davis for being an autocratic leader who would not listen to any other advice except his own.

---

1. Jabez Curry to Jefferson Davis letter, June 20, 1862, Duke University Library.

Jessie Pearl Rice, Curry's biographer, mentions that there is no indication that he was an admirer of Davis. His silence proves that he was not. Curry was an aristocrat and adhered to a code of discretion. As a confirmation of this, during the war, Curry was on the command staff of Joseph E. Johnston. He respected, even idolized, Johnston and his diary and autobiographical notes reflect this. They are filled with laudatory comments about him.

Later in the war Curry fought with General Joseph "Fighting Joe" Wheeler, who shocked Curry with his atrocities against Southern civilians. Instead of relating Wheeler's barbarism, Curry merely avoided writing about him at all.

Jessie Pearl Rice says that Curry "believed in team play. Disapproving of Jefferson Davis' treatment of Congress, as he seemingly did, it is possible, even probable, that he refrained from the personal invective to which others at times gave play. His memoirs, all written after the fall of the Confederacy and after Curry himself was past forty, seldom border on any personal criticism. His philosophy called for remembering the good things about people."[1]

War Defeats Become Political Defeat

Curry: "Frequently I presided in the House, and when the Speaker, Mr. Babcock, was absent, I was elected Speaker Pro Tem. If I had been a member of the next Congress, I should probably have been chosen to preside, as very many of the members had very decidedly expressed their preference in that direction."[2]

But that was not to be. In May 1863, Jabez Curry announced that he was a candidate for re-election to the Confederate Congress. His district comprised Calhoun, Randolph, Talladega and Shelby counties. At first he had no opposition. Then a candidate appeared: Marcus Cruikshanks. Curry said he was a "very worthy man." Curry wanted both of them to debate together. Cruikshanks refused. He conducted his political agenda with tactics that proved to be invincible. "Silence is the true eloquence of power," said a great French statesman, "because it admits of no reply." Curry had no way to respond to Cruikshanks' insidious attacks. And, the reality of the war undermined his positions on secession and state rights. In the August election, Curry was defeated. Cruikshanks carried three of the four counties.

---

1. Rice, p. 42.
2. Alderman and Gordon, p. 164.

These districts had opposed secession. Before the election, Vicksburg had fallen and Gettysburg was lost. These events had demoralized the voters. Secret peace organizations sprang up. Curry said: "Conscription was unpopular, impressments was odious. The currency became every day of less value. Taxes were high. Foreign markets were closed. The blockade had shut out luxuries and many conveniences. Demagogues and malcontents availed themselves of these favorable circumstances to enflame prejudices against me, as a Secessionist, in favor of a vigorous prosecution of the war. The most delusive promises of an early peace were made to the ignorant."[1]

"General Hard Times" had assumed command of the Confederacy. A Confederate paper dollar that had been worth one dollar and ten cents in August 1861 had now depreciated to the extent that it took thirteen dollars, two years later, to equal the value of a gold dollar.

Curry: "The gradual contraction of the area of the country under Confederate jurisdiction, the growing helplessness of many persons, the grief in many families at loss, or the prolonged absence of dear ones, was having an influence on public sentiment and in some counties, disaffection was rife and outspoken. This was stimulated by deserters and some civilians who had no stomach for the fight and were probably traitors to our cause." Southerners survived by improvising to get the basics. Curry described two ways: "As a substitute for sugar and molasses, a large quantity of sorghum was planted and made into rude sugar and sour molasses. We were put to great straits to get salt. The earth at the bottom, or on the floor of old smoke houses, was dug up and boiled to get the drippings which fell from the salted meat. In Alabama, salt companies were formed for digging salt wells in some lower counties and making salt. I kept a Negro busy at the business of salt-making, about two years."[2]

Curry had no time for self-pity after being defeated for re-election. Immediately, he made the decision to join the army. As a first step, on September 22, 1863, he went out with a company of Home Guards to aid in the impending great battle at Chickamauga but the annihilation of the Federal army had occurred before he got there.

Curry: "I went over the battlefield, before the Federal dead were buried, and then visited the army occupying Missionary Ridge, Lookout Mountain, and the valley between. From Lookout Mountain, one of the grandest views in the

---

1. Jabez Curry, hand-written autobiographical notes, April 1876.
2. Ibid.

world is presented. The two armies; the Federals were in Chattanooga, lay at the beholder's feet."[1]

Mrs. Curry, Last Days in Congress, War

This is a good place for another short interlude and a few insights into Curry's personal life with his wife, Ann Alexander Bowie. They had been married in March 1847. This was the same year that Curry had initially been elected to the Alabama legislature. They had two children, Susan and Manly.

While Curry's post-war diaries have several gushing comments about his love for Mary Wortham Thomas, "the second Mrs. Curry," he has very little to say, positive or negative, about Ann. The one perspective we have is Jabez's comment that she was "feeble." That is not flattering. Here, we see that while he was away in Richmond, in 1863, Ann "remained at home while I was in Congress. She was at the head of a sewing circle ... for making clothes for soldiers. Although a feeble woman, she had indomitable perseverance and energy and great prudence and tact in encouraging others. By her liberality and energy, she had accomplished a large amount of work and won great praise in the county for her patriotic labors."[2]

February 1864 would be the end of Curry's term as a Congressman. He was active to the end. During his last month in Richmond, he was placed on a joint committee to prepare an address to the people of the Confederacy. It was a review of what Congress had accomplished and a statement of the duties of the citizens. It outlined the necessity for secession, the conviction in the South that secession was the only recourse, and the peaceful intent inherent in that action. It laid the war guilt on the United States, enumerated the South's disadvantage in military materiel, and praised the heroic response of Southern men and women to the Confederacy's need. It pointed out how the discontented had generated hostility toward the government because of three years of war and how the North refused to negotiate with the South on any terms. It absolved the mass of Northern people from guilty knowledge of the Republican leaders' intentions and prophesied the fall of the Republicans. It also charged the North with ignoring the international rules of warfare by attacking the entire population of the South, pillaging, burning, ransacking, looting, mistreating the wounded, and committing atrocities. It charged the enemy with attempting to impose the fate

---

1. Alderman and Gordon, p. 171.
2. Jabez Curry, hand-written autobiographical notes, April 1876.

of Ireland or Poland on the Southern states, to make the Confederacy a colony, with its people in bondage.[1]

Then, Curry wrote: "Congress adjourning and my term of service expiring on the 18th of February, I left for Alabama and reached home on the 24th. As all persons were subject to conscription, the Secretary of War had given me a furlough of sixty days to make my arrangements for entering the army." Then, "I purchased cavalry equipment, intending to join the 53rd Alabama Cavalry Regiment, in which my brother, Thomas, was a Captain. General J.E.B. Stuart had previously written a letter to President Davis, asking my appointment as a Judge of a Military Court for his corps. General Longstreet also tendered me a position on his staff." Yet, instead, "Very soon I received, unsolicited, an appointment from President Davis, as Commissioner under the Habeas Corpus Act, to serve with General Joseph E. Johnston's army, but not under him. My duties were judicial, to investigate charges of disloyalty, conspiracy, unlawful trading and treason, preferred against civilians."[2]

Here, Curry explains the significance of the Habeas Corpus Act: "On February 27, 1862, Congress enacted a law authorizing President Davis to suspend the privilege of the Writ of Habeas Corpus, and declare martial law in such districts as he thought in danger of attack by the enemy. It was limited to thirty days after the meeting of the next Congress. [In October 1862 and in the winter of 1863, the writ was again suspended.] As the condition of the Confederacy grew more desperate ... the feeling of the suspension was very bitter and led by Vice President Stephens who denounced suspending the writ and its consequences; martial law, as absolutely unknown under the Confederate Constitution. Stephens said that only Congress might suspend the writ, but always subject to strict safeguards, like the right to a trial in a civil court."[3]

Jabez Curry joined Johnston in April 1864, just as the general was about to commence his famous slow withdrawal toward Atlanta.

---

1. *Address of Congress to the People of the Confederate States* (published in pamphlet form, copy in Curry Papers), p. 8.
2. Jabez Curry, hand-written autobiographical notes, April 1876.
3. Ibid.

Chapter 3. Curry's Early Georgia Years

Lincoln County: The Dark Corner

Jabez Lafayette Monroe Curry was born Sunday, June 25, 1825, in Lincoln County, Georgia. Jabez Curry is a wonderfully descriptive writer, so it would be best if he informs us about the intriguing, dangerous, beautiful world he lived in: "Lincoln County, Georgia takes its name from General Lincoln of Revolutionary War history. It occupies the angle of land situated between the Little and Savanna rivers. Judge Longstreet, in *Georgia Scenes*, has perpetuated the name of The Dark Corner of Lincoln, where I had the honor to be born. In somber phrases he perpetuated the moral darkness which once reigned over that portion of the country. This portion of Georgia and the adjacent parts of South Carolina, were the scenes in the Revolutionary War of many border forays and bloody personal contests. The Tories infested both sides of the Savannah River, and very often between families a vendetta strife was waged with fury and unforgiveness. The Tory party in England, sustaining George III and Lord North in their policy toward the American colonists, gave name to the Loyalists or those who affiliated in opinion and action with the mother country. Tory became a term of contempt, reproach, hatred, and no more stinging insult could be offered than to call one a Tory, or the son of a Tory. Boyle O'Reilly sings:

> Whatever the race, the law, the land,
> Whatever time or throne
> The Tory is always a traitor to every class
> But his own."[1]

47

Indian Wars in Georgia

Curry: "In 1835 the Indian troubles spread consternation and the hostile Indians were regarded with horror. The horrible massacre of Major Dade's command, incapable of being exaggerated, sent a thrill of apprehension throughout Georgia and Alabama. In 1836 the Creek Indians, with fire and tomahawk, were committing depredations along the Chattahoochie River, and many families abandoned plantations and fled for safety. Governor Schley made a requisition for troops and forty-four companies promptly assembled at Columbus. Robert Toombs, then a lawyer, raised a company, composed of volunteers from Wilkes and Lincoln Counties, and went off 'to the wars.' It is not easy now to realize the fears that existed and how much the people were excited by the uprisings of 'the savages.'"[1]

Maternal Ancestors

"My maternal ancestors were of the families of Winn and Lamar. The Winns were Welsh. General Winn, after whom Winnsboro, in South Carolina, was called, was an officer of much local distinction in the Revolutionary Army. So great was his popularity that he was elected representative in the United States Congress for many years. As a member, he was a colleague of Mr. Calhoun and voted for the War of 1812.

"The Lamars were Huguenots who from fled from France because of religious persecution. Some of the family settled in South Carolina and from there spread into Georgia and other states. The Lamars have been quite distinguished. One of them was President of Texas, prior to annexation: Mirabeau B. Lamar. Two of them, Henry G. and John B. were members of Congress from Georgia. Another was a judge and the father of Lucius L. Lamar, of Mississippi, just elected senator from that State. Others have been prominent as bankers, lawyers, and farmers. Mr. Howell Cobb is a Lamar. Peter Lamar, my uncle, was for many years a prominent member of the Georgia legislature.

"I can hardly call myself an Anglo-Saxon, as in my veins flow English blood, Scotch, Welsh and French.

"William Curry of the Curry and Walker families; Scotch and English, was my father.[2]

---

1. Jabez Curry, hand-written autobiographical notes, April 1876.
1. Jabez Curry, *Reminiscences of Youth*, hand-written notes, no date, Curry Papers.
2. William Curry was a farmer, owned a country store and served several sessions in the state legislature.

"Susan Winn, of the Winn and Lamar families, Welsh and French, was my mother. They were married in 1823. One child was born before me, Jackson C. Curry. He died in Demopolis, Alabama, in 1863, a Captain in the Confederate States army. He was a man of sterling sense and as honest a man as ever lived. He was a Deacon in the Baptist Church. He left two sons and three daughters."[1]

My Name

"My parents gave me the too long name of Jabez Lafayette Monroe Curry. The 'Jabez' is an honored Bible name and was borne by Jabez Marshall, a popular Baptist preacher in Georgia, and by Jabez Curry, who died in Perry City, Alabama, in 1873; a favorite nephew of my father. [General] Lafayette was the nation's guest when I was born, and my father, in token of his gratitude to the friend of Washington, saddled me with the name but I threw it aside and substituted Lamar.[2] Monroe was President at that time. I know of no good from my long name, but not a little inconvenience."[3]

My Mother and Step-Mother

"My mother and an infant brother died in 1827. Of course I do not remember ever to have seen my mother. Very many persons have told me she was exceedingly beautiful. It has been a source of sincerest regret that I was not trained in my youngest years by a loving mother. Delicate and susceptible, my life might have been different, but God knows best. I have a thousand times wished for her likeness, but in her day there were no photographs and few persons had portraits painted.

"One of my earliest recollections is a faint remembrance of my father's second marriage. His wife was Mrs. Mary Remsen. They married on 4 September 1829. Her maiden name was Murray and she was the daughter of a Revolutionary War soldier.... My step-mother was a real mother to me and loved me as she did her own children. I gladly and gratefully bear this testimony to her faithfulness, kindness and love."[4]

---

1. Jabez Curry, hand-written autobiographical notes, April 1876.
2. Jabez Curry, hand-written autobiographical notes, April 1876.
3. Marquis de Marie Joseph Paul Yves Roch Gilbert du Motier Lafayette (!) was born into an aristocratic family, joined George Washington's army despite official French opposition. Congress appointed Lafayette a Major-General. He became close friends with Washington. Wounded at Brandywine, he shared the hardships at Valley Forge and received a divisional command. He was responsible for French aid to the American cause.

Early School Days

"When about four years old I was sent to an 'old-field' school where Reading, Writing and Arithmetic were taught by Joel Fleming. The school house was in the forest. In a grove of oak, and hickory, hard by a spring of clear, cool water, was a log house, about twenty feet square, the openings stopped with billets of wood and daubed with clay. There was a chimney with a large, open fireplace. On one side of the cabin was a rude door, swung on wooden hinges. There was no window but opposite the fireplace one of the logs had been sawed out. There was no shutter to this opening as it gave light to the general writing desk of the school, which was an unplanned plank extended horizontally the whole width of the room. At a given signal every writing scholar put himself at the desk and set about the serious work of learning to write. During the exercise the faces of the pupils were turned away from the teacher and an awkward stroke of the pen, or a blot on the paper, was punished by a crack on the knuckles. There were no gold or steel pens in those days and goose quills were used. Ink was kept in small vials, and enough cotton was put in the vials to absorb the ink. There were no globes, nor blackboards, nor desks, nor wall maps, nor chairs. The benches were made of slabs of timber, with legs or pins inserted in auger holes, and were so high that the feet of a young girl in a proper sitting position could not possibly reach the floor. In the absence of support, relief was sought for the spinal column or overtaxed bones by leaning against the wall, or by frequent changes of position. In mild weather the larger boys were permitted to retire from the schoolhouse and seek mutual aid in the solitude of the grove. The scholars were permitted to study aloud and the chattering of magpies could not have exceeded the noise of the miniature Babel. At noon we had recess or play-time, continued to the humor of the teacher and suspended by loud and repeated crying on his part of "Books, books, books."[1]

The "Turn-Out"

"We had no long vacations. When a holiday was needed for any special purpose, it was given by the teacher. Sometimes a gentle compulsion was used on the part of the pupils to force it. This was a process called, in those days, a 'turn-out.' I remember such an event well. It was agreed to 'turn-out' the teacher. The girls and little boys knew the secret and kept it. On the appointed morning,

---

4. Jabez Curry, hand-written autobiographical notes, April 1876.
1. Jabez Curry, *Reminiscences of Youth*, hand-written notes.

some boys reached the school house earlier than Mr. Fleming, and went in and fastened the door securely. When he arrived and demanded admission, it was refused unless he would consent to the holiday. He withdrew to the foot of the large oak tree and sat down to await events. Other boys, who remained outside and unseen, approached stealthfully from behind the tree and suddenly seized the teacher and held him fast. Long strips of mulberry bark, brought for the purpose, were used in tying the hands and feet of the prisoner. All the school now came forward and from behind some neighboring trees might be seen some patrons of the school, watching and enjoying the scene. Mr. Fleming was tenderly lifted, for he was much loved, and carried to the neighboring stream of water and dunked. I waded in and with both hands threw water on the immersed man. He asked that his tobacco might not be permitted to get wet. In a few minutes he agreed to the holiday. The bands were cut and teacher, boys and watchers had a jolly time. Such was the custom then, and the 'turn-out' did not interfere with the discipline of the school, nor diminish pedagogic dignity."[1]

The Great Meteor Shower

"In the year 1834, as I remember, was the great meteoric shower. My uncle very thoughtfully awoke me and took me to a window that I might see the wonderful display. It seemed as if every star had been loosed from its place and was careening from the heavens. The brightness was so great that I think I could have read ordinary print. Too young to appreciate or be alarmed, I soon went to sleep, and the next day and for weeks afterwards, the extraordinary phenomenon was the subject of ignorant speculation. It was generally believed that many 'stars' fell to the ground and the negroes and their companions in superstition regarded the display as a premonition of the day of judgment. As an example, a neighbor was playing cards with his fellows when his body-servant, a faithful but timid Negro, rushed into the room and frantically besought his master to throw down his cards, for the world was coming to an end. The servant was ordered out of the room but soon returned more terrified than ever and mingled prayers and admonitions with his entreaties to cease wickedness in such an awful time. The master said. 'Jack, do you know the North Star?' 'Of course I do, master.' 'Well Jack, go out into the yard and fix your eye on the North Star and when it gives way, come and tell me and I'll quit playing.'"[2]

---

1. Jabez Curry, hand-written autobiographical notes, April, 1876.
2. Ibid.

Georgia Courts and Lawyers

"While living at the Court-House [as he attended the famous Waddell's school, in 1834-35] I had an opportunity of seeing the Superior Court in session.... Lawyers were not so numerous as they are now and I looked upon one of the profession as a sort of demi-god.... Robert Toombs was the first person I remember distinctly as a lawyer and when, years afterwards, as a representative from Alabama, I met him in Washington City, he was helpfully kind to me because of his friendship with my father. At that Lincoln [county] bar at that time, such lawyers attended as Joseph Henry Lumpkin, afterwards the first Chief Justice of the Supreme Court of Georgia; George W. Crawford, afterwards governor and a member of [President] Fillmore's Cabinet; Andrew J. Miller, many years president of the Senate; Charles J. Jenkins, afterwards governor, and Alexander Stephens. Such a combination of legal ability and forensic eloquence would do credit to any court in England or the United States.

"At that time Georgia jurisprudence was peculiar. There was no Court of Appeals and the judge of each circuit expounded the law as he understood it. The jury, being practically the last tribunal, the lawyers put forth for their persuasion their utmost powers and Georgia lawyers became renowned for all the elements that enter into effective, extemporaneous debate.... With eager ears did I listen to the arguments in the courtroom, wondering why such vehement exhibitions did not result in personal encounters, and my astonishment had no bounds when I saw these heated contestants, on the adjournment of the court, walking arm-in-arm to the tavern and telling anecdotes in a manner that the most famous raconteur cannot surpass."[1]

Georgia Doctors

"The transition from lawyers to doctors is easy. The medical profession did not thrive in a sparsely settled country. Medical colleges were not numerous and young men with diplomas, seeking fields for work, were not abundant. It was often necessary to send twenty or thirty miles for medical assistance. The doctors traveled on horseback, or in sulkies, and always carried medicines in their little saddlebags, constructed with partitions so as to be available for liquids, powders, etc. The dental, surgical and medical branches were all combined. Pulling teeth was unadulterated barbarism and the instrument of torture was 'tooth-drawers,' which sometimes lifted the sufferer from his seat and

---

1. Ibid.

brought away together the tooth and a piece of the jawbone. Blood-letting was practiced on a scale that would have pleased Sangrado, and while there were no barbers practicing venesection in conjunction with the tonsorial art, phlebotomy was by no means, as an art, confined to the doctors. Jalep, ipecacuanha, calomel, paregoric and laudanum were the favorite curative expedients.

'He pukes, he purges and he sweats 'em,
And if they die, why then, he lets 'em.'

"Calomel, like some patent medicines, was a specific for all diseases, for adults and infants, and was administered in doses which often ruined the constitutions of the patients.... I recall that when my stepmother and my father's purse had suffered much from many doctors, Dr. Dent was brought in by carriage from Augusta. He won my profound admiration by helping me in my lesson in Virgil, which he translated with facility."[1]

The Waddell School

"My step-mother, when she married my father, had a son, David H. Remson, who grew up as one of us. My father sent him and my brother, Jackson, to Willington, in Abbeville County, South Carolina, to school. This had been a famous school, taught by Dr. Moses Waddell, where McDuffie [George McDuffie, 'The Orator of Nullification'], Petigru [James Lewis Petigru, defender of the Union in the days of South Carolina's nullification battle with the Federal government], Longstreet [Judge Longstreet, of *Georgia Scenes* fame], John C. Calhoun [the defender of state sovereignty], Bowie [James Bowie, the soldier and adventurer who invented the deadly knife named after him, who died at the Alamo], and other distinguished men had been prepared for college. *The Debating Society*, an amusing incident recorded in *Georgia Issues*, occurred here.... I was too young to be sent so far away from home. So I was sent to Lincolnton, the Courthouse, to board with my grandmother and attend a school taught by a Mr. McCleary, a Presbyterian preacher....

"The next year [1834] I was sent to Willington [to the Wadell School] and boarded with Mr. Harris. He gave us biscuits every Sunday morning and corn bread the rest of the time. There must have been one hundred scholars from Georgia and South Carolina....

"At sunrise Dr. Waddell was wont to wind his horn, which was immediately answered by horns in all directions. At an early hour the pupils made their

---

1. Ibid.

appearance at the log cabin schoolhouse. The Doctor, entering the cabin and depositing his hat, would reappear at the door with his school horn in his hand. He then would call out loud, 'What boy feels most flatulent this morning?' ...

"The pupils, each with a chair bearing his name sculpted in the back of it, retired to the woods for study, the classes being divided into squads according to individual preference. In the spring and summer months these squads scattered through the oak and hickory woods in quest of shade; but in the cold weather the first thing done by them was to kindle log-heap fires. Whosoever imagines that the boys did not study as well as they would have done under the immediate eye of the teacher is mistaken. I have been to many schools conducted according to various systems of education, but nowhere have I seen such assiduity in study, nowhere have I ever witnessed such emulation to excel. It was a classical school. The multiplicity of studies now advertised at fashionable academies was unknown in those early times. The debating club on Friday afternoons was an important institution, and regarded by the teacher as a very necessary part of his scholastic system, for to converse and speak in public were esteemed necessary accomplishments to Southern youths."[1]

"The next year and two years afterwards my brothers and myself were kept at home and sent to school at 'Double Branches,' to Daniel Flynn. Mr. Flynn was an Irishman, a graduate of the University of Dublin and had been educated for a Romish priest. He was an excellent scholar, especially in the ancient languages, and a very popular and successful teacher. I studied under Mr. Flynn Latin and Greek and Algebra and Geometry and was usually an apt scholar, and fond of books."[2]

Fighting

"My father was a farmer and a country merchant. His store drew customers from a wide circle. Musters and elections were held at or near the store. 'Drinking' was common in those days and as a consequence there were many fisticuff fights. A ring was formed and friends and neighbors stood around to see a 'fair fight.' Coats and vests were removed and a regular set-to occurred, not however according to the Queensbury rules. Hitting below the belt, biting, kicking, I believe, are now forbidden. Then, anything was allowable, justifiable, as far as nature furnished means of attack or defense. Blows fell thick and fast,

---

1. Alderman and Gordon, p. 23.
2. Jabez Curry, hand-written autobiographical notes, April 1876.

followed by clinching and wrestling. When the combatants fell, scratching, biting, pulling hair, and gouging were resorted to, and I have seen men horribly disfigured and maimed by having thumbs or fingers thrust into sockets of the eyes. No one interfered and sometimes cries of encouragement were given by the friends. When either of the men engaged cried 'enough,' the victor ceased the conflict or was forcibly removed. Sudden quarrels or combats sometimes grew out of politics, or trading, or more frequently from liquor. No weapons were used, and carrying concealed weapons was not common."[1]

Georgia Politics

"Politics caused much excitement and ill-feeling. The parties were then called the 'Troup party,' and 'The Clarke party' or the 'Union Men' or 'Nullifiers.' ... Georgia politics, in the first half of this century, took hue and shape very largely from local questions and personal favoritism or hostility. The Yazoo frauds [after the Revolutionary War, Georgia sold vast tracts of her Western lands, but this territory was claimed by the Indians, Spain and the United States. In 1795 the Georgia legislature was bribed into passing the Yazoo Act, named after the river, which sanctioned the sale of even larger tracts to unscrupulous speculator groups. A later legislature repudiated this corruption. The confusion over payments became a national scandal], the controversy in reference to the Cherokee Indians, the claims of Crawford to the Presidency [William Harris Crawford, allied to Troup as leaders of the Georgia tidewater region. In a duel, Crawford killed a partisan of John Clarke, his rival. Clarke, in another duel, wounded Crawford. He was a United States Senator and a minister to France; Secretary of War and the Treasury under Madison and Monroe. In 1824, he ran for President and finished third. Since no candidate received a majority of the electoral votes, the result was decided by the House. John Quincy Adams was chosen]; the secession of Walter T. Colquitt, Mark A. Cooper and Edward J. Black from the Whig party in 1840, and their refusal to support William Henry Harrison, are illustrations of the local and personal character of the contests.

"In my large collection of pamphlets I find *Some of the Objections to Mr. Crawford as a Candidate for President of the United States*, twenty-eight pages; *A Vindication of the Recent and Prevailing Policy of the State of Georgia*, ninety pages, attributed to Judge A.S. Clayton, and bristling with arguments, satire and abuse; *Proceedings of a Public Meeting* in Athens, in 1832, in which Crawford and others participate; a

---

1. Jabez Curry, *Reminiscences of Youth*, hand-written notes.

circular of W.T. Colquitt in 1840, *To the People of Georgia, and Especially to the State's Rights Party*.

"Without a knowledge of these discussions no one can properly write the history of the old State."[1]

Horse Racing

"In the afternoon of elections there were nearly always races. Riding or plow-horses, which had some 'bottom' or speed were used and were ridden by the owners or their friends. In 1836 or 1837 there occurred in Augusta a famous race between Argyle, belonging to Hampton, of South Carolina, and John Bascom, belonging to Crowell, of Georgia. It was a kind of interstate contest, resulting in victory for Georgia. Thousands of people went to Augusta to witness the race and thousands of dollars exchanged hands. Bascom was subsequently taken to Long Island, where he successfully ran against Post-Boy.

"In 1883, lying one night on the platform at the station in Hearne, Texas, suffering from fever and awaiting the train to take me to Austin, I engaged in a conversation with an old Negro man who many years previously had emigrated from Augusta. As I recalled names of prominent citizens whom he knew in his youth and mentioned the famous race, the old man said he had witnessed the contest and with much animation he recounted the particulars and lived over the excitement of his early days."[2]

Georgia Militia

"Militia musters for companies and for regiments were held several times a year and were laughable farces. The officers were ignorant of the manual of arms and of evolutions in the field. Rifles, shotguns, walking sticks and corn-stalks were the medley representatives of the required fire-arms. The uniform of a Georgia colonel has often been satirized as consisting of a paper collar and a pair of spurs, but despite the ridicule as to title and dress, the office was much coveted. I remember seeing once a militia general, and his coming to the county created as much excitement as the coming of a circus. My eyes are yet dazzled by the flashy trappings of the caparisoned horse, the cocked hat, the buckskin gauntlets, the gilt spurs and epaulettes, the shining sword-scabbard, the brass buttons, the braid and bands and the red silken sash. The pride, the pomp and

---

1. Ibid.
2. Ibid.

circumstance in those piping times of peace surpassed anything I saw when the terrible reality of war came upon us."[1]

Courting

"At weddings and 'infares' [the latter were entertainments given the day after the marriage by the husband or his parents] and guests amused themselves with innocent plays or the country dance. 'Quiltings' were a favorite mode of bringing the young people together. A patch-work of pieces of cloth or silk being sewed together and framed invited young ladies to spend the day in quilting. About sunset the young men came, and until the 'wee small hours' of the next morning the young people had a merry time in games and dancing. The fiddler was often a Negro man, who was proud of his accomplishments and of the brief authority he exercised."[2]

White and Black Preachers

"Episcopalians and Roman Catholics were unknown. As preachers were scarce, protracted meetings and camp meetings furnished additional means of religious instruction and awakening. My father's house was always open for the preachers, although we were not at that time a member of any church, and nearly every Sunday the family could attend a 'meeting' somewhere. Carriages were very scarce. Gigs were common. Generally church-goers rode on horseback or walked. I have seen men and women stop before reaching the church house and put on their shoes and stockings.... A Negro minister by the name of Henry Adams was an able minister, well educated, very popular, modest and well-behaved. Some foolish jealousy existed toward him and I can remember the withdrawal at the instigation of a partisan of a white preacher, of a part of the congregation once he preached, but the greater part gladly remained.... Seats in the rear of the churches were set apart for the Negroes and hundreds of them were church members."[3]

Hunting and Fishing

"Opossum and raccoon hunting was very common. Very often have I, with other boys and some of my father's Negroes, hunted for half the night. It was a boyish ambition to be out all night. The skill of the Negroes in finding their way

---

1. Ibid.
2. Ibid.
3. *Alabama Baptist* newspaper fragment, no date, from J.L.M. Curry Papers.

in the woods by star-light, used to excite my boyish admiration. Another amusement was bird-hunting. When a field was cleared and 'new ground,' as it was called, was made, the brush and tops of trees were piled into heaps to remain until dry enough for burning. In the cold nights, birds would find shelter in the heaps. Taking torches of pinewood in one hand and brushes of dogwood in the other, we would surround a 'brush heap,' give it a shake and as the birds would fly out, would strike them down. It was cruel but exciting sport. Hare or rabbit hunting was very common. Boys engaged in it, also men. My father used to, nearly every year, invite his neighbors to come to a rabbit hunting. They would divide into two parties and hunt in competition and then enjoy a 'big dinner.'

"Fishing with hook and line and with a seine were common. I remember well the first fish, a little minnow, I ever caught, and Napoleon was not prouder of one of his great victories, than I was of my piscatory success. In the spring time the shad, a migratory fish, would come from the sea up the fresh water rivers and large numbers were taken in seines and finger traps. I used to rejoice when on Saturdays I could go to the Savannah River and see the neighbors and go with them in little boats to the traps."[1]

Slaves

"As compared with the aggregate white population, the number of slave-owners was small, and the number of slaves on a plantation varied from one to a thousand. On the plantations in Lincoln County, to which these reminiscences are confined, the life was patriarchal. Log or frame houses were built near the owner's house, the whole making a little village, and custom was to supply, every year, each adult slave with a blanket, two pairs of shoes, and three suits of clothes. The food consisted of meat, generally pork, meal, vegetables and milk. Where slaves were few they ate what the white people ate as did the cook and house servants. While the Negroes, as slaves, were, of course, required to render obedience and service, the relation between master and slave and servant was one of much familiarity and often real affection. Disobedience and theft were punished but severe punishment was not common. Self-interest, humanity and the law forbade it. I. Bosworth Smith, in the nineteenth century, brackets as equal the horrors of the middle passage and of the cotton plantation. Testimony is of little value to those whose theories require certain facts, but I never saw a

---

1. Jabez Curry, hand-written biographical notes, April 1876.

Negro cruelly whipped, nor a blood-hound. There were cruel masters and over-seers, it would be absurd to deny, and of the 'peculiar institution,' I am no advocate. No one rejoices more than I over the disappearance of Negro slavery, but my recollections of slaves are of the tender kind. My nurse and my plantation playmates were Negroes. Hundreds of times have I gone, day and night, into the cabins and shared their homely meals and listened to the stories which have since been embodied in that popular book, *Uncle Remus*. Many nights have I, accompanied by the Negroes, hunted 'coons' and 'possums' and returning hungry and tired, have eaten roasted potatoes and drank persimmon beer."[1]

The Move to Alabama

"In 1837 my father visited Alabama, and bought land in Talladega County, a place called Kelly's Springs, from the number of large limestone springs upon it, and paid about thirty-nine dollars an acre. In December of that year, or January of the next, he sent his Negroes, with an overseer, to Alabama to prepare for and plant a crop. He owned a large body of land in Lincoln County and a number of lots in other counties of Georgia. He sold his home-place, where he was born and where his parents and my mother and two brothers are buried. Strangers now own the place, and the graveyard, I suspect, is much neglected."[2]

1. Ibid.
2. Ibid.

Chapter 4. Curry Goes to War

In April 1864, after being defeated for a second term in the Confederate Congress, Jefferson Davis appointed Jabez Curry as a Commissioner under the Habeas Corpus Act to serve with General Joseph E. Johnston.

"I went to Dalton, Georgia in April and having little to do in connection with my office [as Commissioner] I spent much of my time in visiting the various camps and familiarizing myself with military movements. Many brigades were addressed by me and my services in this line were sought after. General Johnston had a grand review to infuse fresh confidence into his men. The display of banners and music and mimic warfare was very magnificent.

"A great religious revival pervaded the army, while in camps, meetings were held every night. Chaplains and other preachers held religious services. I heard General M.P. Lowry, a Baptist minister, in command of a Mississippi brigade, an officer much trusted by General Johnston, quite often. Hundreds of soldiers would gather in the open air to hear the simple gospel and the converts were very numerous.

"When General Johnston, in May, began his retreat towards Atlanta, when confronted by Sherman's superior forces, as my regular official duties were perforce, suspended, I was attached to General Johnston's staff as a special aide, at his request, and so served until his removal. General Johnston conducted this campaign with unsurpassed skill and strategy, thwarting the enemy's plans and designs, inflicting heavy losses upon him, losing not over 5,000 of his own men, whose enthusiastic confidence he preserved to the end.... On the 14th of May, there was a severe engagement at Resaca. While occupying a sugar-loaf hill, nearly denuded of trees, we saw the enemy coming down a valley on our left most beautifully repulsed by Colonel Conolly of Alabama.

"The enemy's artillery shelled the hill fearfully and as we were sheltered on the opposite side, just under the brow, a little bird, perched on a high branch, sang most sweetly and defiantly, intensified by the showers of shot and shell.

"On the 25th, 26th and 27th of May, severe fighting occurred near New Hope Church in the resistance of a heavy flank movement by General Sherman. The lines of the contestants were so near that it was dangerous to get behind the protection of the breastworks. The noise of the 'Minnie balls' was like the buzzing of bees. During these fierce and continuous engagements, there occurred one of the most compelling sorties of the campaign. Some of the Union forc84es made a desperate and bold effort to break through our ranks. They were met by as gallant a defense as soldiers ever made. The Confederates under Cleburne, Cockrell, Granberry, Kelly, Wheeler, Lowry and others equally worthy of mention, displayed heroic courage, and when the attacking party was repulsed, the ground was so covered with dead and disabled, that one could have traversed the ground by walking on the bodies. I never saw on a battlefield such havoc and destruction of human life.

"Frequently I rode with General Johnston at night and he would, when in a talkative mood, tell me of Marlborough's and Wellington's and Napoleon's campaigns which seemed as familiar to him as the alphabet. When he had traveled as far as he intended, he would dismount, wrap himself in a blanket and be asleep in five minutes. He was singularly reticent in reference to his plans. He kept his own counsel, but had marvelous facility in finding out the movements and the plans of the enemy. The cavalry was utilized and made to subserve its legitimate office of acting as eyes and ears for infantry and artillery.

"I once saw the general in a towering rage, and only once. It was near Cartersville, Georgia. He always sent the engineers ahead, as he fell back before Sherman's army, to make topographical reconnaissance of the country his troops would occupy as they retreated. He was looking for a place to halt and offer an effective resistance to Sherman's advance. Finally a position was selected, and he halted his army and issued a battle order. It was joyfully received by the men, who were eager for a fight and confident in their power to resist the Federal advance. I have never seen anything like the enthusiasm this battle order of Johnston's elicited from the army. He knew that Sherman's army would be divided into two columns at this point, one going by Rome and the other farther east. General Johnston planned the attack on the west wing, and hoped to put it to rout before the other column could reinforce it. He divided his forces into three divisions, with Hood in command at the right, Polk at the center and Hardee on the left. When all was ready, General Johnston ordered the attack to begin. Everybody waited with every nerve strained, but the attack did not begin. Hood was to lead the onslaught, but his command did not advance on the enemy. Johnston paced up and down impatiently, not knowing why General Hood had not advanced as ordered. He had sent aides to find out what was the trouble, but none of them returned. At length he sent his adjutant general, Mackall, to see what was the matter. I can see him now as he waited impatiently, pacing to and fro, erect, soldierly, a model general. Still he said nothing. Finally General Mackall returned and reported that Hood sent word he had been flanked on his right by the enemy and could not advance. He was not sure he could even hold his position.

"Johnston said this could not be so. He had reports from his cavalry under General Wheeler that showed this to be impossible. It turned out, I believe, that Hood was deceived, for a braver soldier than General Hood never lived. At any rate, this delay arrested the engagement, and night fell. General Johnston, however, determined to resist the enemy's advance, and gave orders to that effect. Earthworks were hastily thrown up, and all the arrangements made for a determined resistance. After everything was ready I rode with General Johnston and the staff the whole length of the line, from one end to the other.

"Major Harvie and Wade Hampton's son were with us. We did not go back to our sleeping place; we had no tents, till after dark, and then a military conference was held. The artillery firing, which had begun during the day, ceased at nightfall. At the conference, General Hood said he was afraid he would not be able to hold his position. General Polk made a similar report, saying his position was such that the enemy's side fire would be disastrous to his men. General Hardee was the only one of the three generals who said he thought he would be able to hold his position. General Johnston told me afterward that Hardee's position was the weakest of the three.

"After these discouraging reports, General Johnston decided to order a retreat without attacking the enemy, and, sending for Wheeler, he told him to take a position between the Confederate forces and the Federals, and protect the retreat..., Johnston was firm, abrupt in his manner of speaking and thoroughly self-reliant; yet he was kind-hearted, a true friend and very sympathetic."[1]

Joseph Eggleston Johnston, the Soldier

Joe Johnston was the son of a Revolutionary War soldier. He married the daughter of his father's war-time comrade. His father, Peter Johnston, fought with "Light-Horse Harry" Lee, Robert E. Lee's father, then became a lawyer, a circuit judge in Virginia, then Speaker of the Virginia House of Delegates.

Peter married a niece of Patrick Henry; Joseph Eggleston was the result, on February 3, 1807. The original Joseph Eggleston had been a Revolutionary War Captain and Peter's friend. With such a tradition, Joseph had to become a soldier.

In 1829, Joseph graduated from West Point, with Robert E. Lee. In the 1830s he fought against the Seminoles in Florida with Lt. Jefferson Davis.

But Joseph found that army promotions and pay were discouraging. So, he did the logical thing. He married the grand-daughter of an officer who had fought with George Washington; Louisa McLane. Louisa's father had been Secretary of State and Minister to England in the Jackson Administration. Now he was president of the Baltimore and Ohio railroad. Joseph E. hoped to work for him. In 1838, he resigned from the army and became a civil engineer but things did not work out as he had planned, so he grudgingly crept back into the military in 1839.

Once again, he fought the Seminoles in Florida. He was shot in the head. The bullet went around his skull, under the skin, but it was not a serious wound.

For the next eight years he worked on army engineering projects, then became a combatant in the war with Mexico. Twice he was badly wounded, then promoted to Lt. Colonel in 1847.

Just before the War for Southern Independence, Joseph E. was promoted to Quartermaster General. His background had prepared him to master the art of logistics; the managing of armies.

Johnston was a loyal Virginian. When the state seceded, he resigned from the United States army and joined his home state's military. Robert E. Lee commanded Virginia's forces. He assigned Joseph E. to organize the volunteers and commissioned him a Brigadier General.

Then the Confederate Congress passed an act, offering a General's rank in the national army to five officers who had been in the United States army. Johnston was one of the five. As a Brigadier-General in Virginia, he was the

---

1. Jabez Curry article in the *Washington Post*, March 24, 1891, on the occasion of Joseph E. Johnston's death.

highest ranked. But Jefferson Davis, when issuing the commissions, placed Johnston fourth. He was greatly offended: "It seeks to tarnish my fair fame as a soldier and a man, earned by more than thirty years of laborious and perilous service. I had but this, the scars of many wounds all honestly taken in my front, and in the front of battle."[1]

Davis downgraded Johnston because they had radically different views of how the war should be fought. Davis was convinced that defending cities, forts, lines and posts was imperative.

Johnston believed as strongly that this strategy gave the battle initiative to the North, since at the outset the Union had a six-to-one numerical advantage. This ratio would increase with time. He felt that mobility and speed balanced out the South's disadvantage in men.

So, from the beginning, mutual confidence was lacking. Neither Jefferson Davis nor Johnston yielded his views but Joseph E. had to obey. Distrust became open anger when Johnston did not take Washington after the opening battle, the rout at Bull Run. Davis blamed him for the great missed opportunity to end the war then and there.

Both Davis and Johnston were basically the same; high tempered, impetuous, jealous of honor and they hated rivals. Both needed absolute devotion without question.

In late 1861, the Department of Northern Virginia was created. Johnston commanded it. He had 41,000 men; the Federals, 150,000. He wanted to attack Washington but Davis prevented it.

The Peninsula Campaign

In April 1862, General George McClellan attempted to capture Richmond by way of the peninsula between the York and James rivers. He prepared to besiege Yorktown; Johnston evacuated the town. After bitter fighting at Williamsburg, Johnston's men withdrew again. At Norfolk, another retreat. Union gunboats on the James River were now nine miles from Richmond. The Northern armies had advanced over seventy miles.

When the spring rains caused flooding which isolated parts of McClellan's forces along the swollen Chickahominy River, Johnston attacked at Seven Pines. The Union men held. Here Johnston was severely wounded because, as always,

1. Bradley T. Johnson, editor, *A Memoir of the Life and Public Service of Joseph E. Johnston* (Baltimore: R.H. Woodward and Co., 1891), p. 1.

he was at the front. Robert E. Lee took over. In the famous "Seven Days" battles at Mechanicsville, Cold Harbor, Savage's Station, Frayser's Farm and Malvern Hill, the Union forces were steadily pushed back toward their starting point. Lee almost annihilated McClellan's army and he abandoned the peninsula altogether.

Johnston never commanded in Virginia again. He was reassigned to the Department of the West where Braxton Bragg, Kirby Smith and John Pemberton opposed Grant and Rosecans.

Johnston asked Jefferson Davis if he could concentrate the three Confederate armies to crush Grant. Davis refused. Once again the conflict was one of holding territory vs. mobility and attacking the Federals piecemeal. Johnston asked to be relieved of his command. Davis refused his request.

In early 1863, for the defense of Vicksburg, Davis relieved Bragg and put Johnston in charge, but he became seriously ill and Bragg resumed as leader.

When Vicksburg fell, Johnston took charge of the Army of the Tennessee. His plan, again, was to smash Grant through mobility, flexibility, and abandoning specific locations. Again Davis would not allow that. Yet Grant's success in this campaign was due to using Johnston's ideas — movement, not protecting places.

When Braxton Bragg was defeated at Missionary Ridge, outside of Chattanooga, Johnston rushed to defend Dalton, which was between Chattanooga and the strategically important city of Atlanta. With its many rail lines, it supplied Lee's army of Northern Virginia. Taking this city would also cut off most of the Confederate states. This is where Jabez Curry joined Johnston's staff.

Ulysses S. Grant had twice as many men. The Confederates had little food, clothing or weapons. At this point Grant was promoted. He now commanded all Union forces. William Tecumseh Sherman faced Johnston.

Johnston was promised troops which never arrived. Davis ordered him to attack Sherman. This was suicidal. Sherman advanced with three separate spearheads. Johnston fought a slow, defensive deliberate strategic withdrawal, inflicting heavy casualties. He was criticized by Davis for this. Yet Lee, who played the same retreating game, was idolized.

Suddenly Johnston was removed and replaced by Hood. Lee, who was usually subordinate and respectful said: "If General Johnston was not a soldier, America has not produced one. If he is not competent to command that army, the Confederacy has no one who was competent."[1]

Hood attacked, as Johnston had not, and his army was slaughtered. Atlanta fell. Lee ordered Johnston to "assume command of the Army of the Tennessee and all troops in South Carolina and drive back Sherman."[1]

Johnston saw that it was too late for that. Sherman was already in South Carolina, moving North to unite with Grant. Johnston could only hope to delay that link-up. His one hope was that Lee could disengage from the defense of Richmond, join him, and together with him crush Sherman. In April 1865, when Lee evacuated Richmond, just before Appomattox, Johnston believed he was trying to achieve that link-up.

April 9: Lee surrendered. Sherman moved to encircle Johnston.

April 12: Jefferson Davis and Johnston met. Davis, now out of touch with reality, wanted the war to go on. Johnston knew it was over. The Confederacy had 25,000 men left. Grant had 180,000.

April 14: At Raleigh, Johnston tried to negotiate a settlement.

April 26: Johnston surrendered at Durham Station.

Curry and Joe Wheeler's Cavalry

In July 1864, with Curry on his command staff, Johnston retreated to the fortifications at Atlanta. During the ensuing siege, Curry went on horseback to his home in Talladega for a brief furlough

In late July, while he was still away, Davis replaced Johnston. Shortly afterward, the Habeas Corpus Act expired and upon his return to duty Curry no longer had an official role.

General Joe Wheeler, who was a cavalry commander under Johnston, knew Curry well. He asked Jabez to join his staff as a special aide. Curry agreed.

If there is one specific moment that would give us a clue as to why Jabez Curry's mind changed, so that he would repudiate all that he had stood for and fought for in the first half of his life, it might begin here, with his association with Wheeler.

Wheeler was one of the great commanders of the Confederate army but he also committed almost as many atrocities against Southern civilians as did Sherman, in the desperate effort to provide food for the starving Southern troops.

Although Curry's diary is filled with flattering entries about Joe Johnston, no such comments are made about Wheeler. There are only notations about the

---

1. Bradley T. Johnson, p. 117.
1. Ibid., p. 117.

battles, not the man. This may be due to the disillusionment he experienced that such a high-ranking officer and gentleman could behave in such a barbaric way. Wheeler's cruelty probably put doubts in Curry's mind as to whether Southerners were actually morally superior to Northern men.

Wheeler had an amazing career: he was the youngest man in American history to be commissioned a Major-General, at twenty-six. He is also the only officer ever to be a corps commander in the United States Army after holding the same position in the Confederate Army.

Wheeler was just 5'5" and 120 pounds. "He was surcharged with electricity." And "He never walked, he loped ... was restless as a disembodied spirit and as active as a cat."

After the war he was a Congressman and amazingly, because of his youth in the War for Southern Independence, he still fought for the United States in the Spanish-American War. While attacking a Spanish position in Guasimas, on the road to Santiago, in Cuba, Wheeler shouted, "The Yankees are on the run!"

Before following Wheeler's accomplishments, let Curry speak of his own experiences with him. This was his first combat assignment. He was part of "an expedition to go in the rear of Sherman's army and cut his communications. We first struck the road at Dalton and captured, after a brisk little engagement, about one hundred prisoners. Our men very quickly used what commissary stores were found in the town. Moving up the railroad and tearing up rails, we encountered some colored troops, the first I had seen. We marched to Cleveland, looking to cross the Tennessee River, but the late heavy rains had swollen it as to be not fordable. We passed through Athens and some stores were 'gutted.' On this expedition, we were forbidden to encumber horses with any surplus clothing, and we ate just what we 'picked up' en route. For a portion of the time our principle food was green corn. General Wheeler was compelled to make a wide detour to cross the swollen river, which he finally accomplished, with a little resistance, east of Knoxville. While tearing up the rail road at McHillan's Depot, we had a little fight, and dispersed the enemy. As the rail road between Nashville and Chattanooga was the line of communication to be cut, the general struck across the country. He requested me to cross Clinch River at Clinton, to the right of his line of march and get what information I could. Going on with a few men, I came to a country mill, where I captured two Federal soldiers and an old woman, apparently the miller, who abused me in the most vulgar language and cursed me 'black and blue.' By the way, the population of East Tennessee was unrefined, ignorant, vicious and disloyal to the Confederacy. At the Clinch

River, opposite Clinton, the boat, being on the opposite side, a Texas soldier, heavily loaded with pistols, rode in to swim across and was drowned. The boat was ferried across and soon after I reached the village, about 100 of our men appeared and the stores soon supplied our wants. Hats, boots, shoes, blankets, were in special demand. We crossed the rail road south of Nashville but our circuitous journeying and long delay had defeated the project of breaking up communications. Tearing up the road a little, we marched toward Franklin, where we had quite a severe engagement and General Kelly, an accomplished young officer, was killed. I was within a few paces of him when he was shot. At a little town south of Franklin, we had another engagement and there I saw a woman on the street, in the middle of the fray, cheering our men. The tyranny of Federal occupation drove them nearly to despair. Traveling south, the corps forded the Tennessee River, a dangerous enterprise, below Decatur, Alabama, and General Wheeler halted to await orders and information from General Hood, who had been 'flanked' out of Atlanta and whipped."[1]

At that moment, after his brief career as a combat cavalryman, Curry was again transferred. On October 8, 1864, he started off to North Alabama to assume the role of a Judge Advocate on a military court within the jurisdiction of General George Roddey.

"Fighting Joe" Wheeler

Appointed to West Point, Joe Wheeler graduated near the bottom of his class, with the worst grades in cavalry tactics, and yet, he was characterized by Robert E. Lee as one of the two outstanding cavalrymen of the war.

In one part of the Confederacy he was hailed as a deliverer, and in another part, as a barbarian, worse than Sherman.

After graduating from West Point as a Lieutenant, at Ft. Craig in New Mexico, he was assigned to a regiment of Mountain Rifles. They were really mounted infantry. These men traveled light and had an extensive cruising range. They were scouts. Here, he learned the tactics he would use during the war.

At Ft. Craig there was much talk of secession, and the possibility of resigning from the United States military occupied the officers' time. There is no evidence that Wheeler took a pronounced stand, because he had grown up in Connecticut. But he had been born in Georgia.

---

1. Jabez Curry, hand-written autobiographical notes, April 1876.

Yet, when the actual moment of decision came, Wheeler had no hesitation. Even before Georgia seceded, he said: "Much as I love the Union, and as much as I am attached to my profession, all will be given up when the State, by its actions, shows that such a course is necessary and proper."[1]

January 1861: Georgia seceded. Wheeler was commissioned a lieutenant in the forces of Georgia. After Ft. Sumter, Wheeler was assigned to General Braxton Bragg's command to improve the defenses of Ft. Barrancas in the harbor of Pensacola, Florida. He had been trained in engineering, and he succeeded where others had failed: to re-mount the big guns that had been dislodged by Federal troops who had abandoned the fortification. For that, Wheeler was promoted to Colonel.

Wheeler's meteoric rise was due not to his brilliance but to his ability to take an order and stay on the job day and night until it was executed. He lacked the dash of Nathan Bedford Forrest, but in the matter of subordinating himself and playing the part assigned to him in a campaign, he excelled.

While he was at Pensacola, Ft. Donelson surrendered. It was on the Cumberland River at Dover, Tennessee. It commanded the river approach to Nashville. The Confederate defenses in the West began to crumble. Bragg abandoned Pensacola to keep the Mississippi and other rivers open. Wheeler went with him.

Then Ulysses S. Grant reached Pittsburg Landing, on the Tennessee River in Tennessee. His objective — Corinth, Mississippi, a key railway junction. This set up the battle of Shiloh Church. On April 6, 1862, Wheeler's 19th Alabama Cavalry Regiment was to drive the Federal's left flank into Snake Creek. After bitter fighting, the flank began to turn, despite 30 percent casualties among Wheeler's men. The Federals were trapped but their reinforcements arrived and the Confederates, bled white, were pushed back in a panic-filled rout.

Wheeler, with the remnants of his force, slowed the Union advance with a brilliant rear-guard defense. Confederate General Withers said: "Colonel Wheeler ... throughout the fight had proved himself worthy of all trust and confidence, a gallant commander and an accomplished soldier."[2]

Wheeler was twenty-five. Before this he had never led more than a platoon in warfare but now he observed, first-hand, what a broken and retreating army

---

1. John W. DuBose, *General Joseph Wheeler and the Army of Tennessee* (New York: The Neale Publishing Co., 1912), p. 52.
2. DuBose, p. 75.

looked like from the rear. This would be of incalculable value in the three years that lay ahead.

He covered the retreat to Corinth and Bragg's withdrawal from Kentucky and Tennessee, to Chattanooga, and also Joe Johnston's withdrawal to Atlanta. Always, he sacrificed his men to stall the enemy.

Often his fast, destructive movements behind Union lines gave the impression of a larger force, which made the Union commanders postpone offenses to reinforce areas where Wheeler operated.

Wheeler only had one rival: Nathan Bedford Forrest. He was 41 years old, and a Brigadier-General of cavalry. Forrest joined Braxton Bragg at Sparta, Georgia, expecting to be the commander of Wheeler's troops. That did not happen. They had separate commands. Forrest was furious, and jealous when Bragg gave Wheeler most of his cavalry (since Bragg constantly quarreled with Nathan Bedford).

Perryville, in Kentucky, was another Shiloh. A Confederate victory in the daytime, they were slaughtered during the night. Wheeler covered their agonizing retreat.

Bragg abandoned Kentucky and in a frightening pull-back to Cumberland Gap, it was Wheeler who again saved the Southerners from annihilation. The roads were clogged with wagons filled with wounded and dying, demoralized, divided troops and refugees. All this chaos slowed movement.

Wheeler and his cavalry fought rear-guard battles in the day and blocked the roads with trees at night. It was here that Wheeler innovated mounted infantry warfare on a large scale. Soon Bragg was demoted and placed under Johnston's command at Chattanooga.

Wheeler's men were some of the most mentally deranged in the entire Confederacy. They raided friend and foe for supplies, and with equal cruelty. Atrocities were committed indiscriminately to get what they needed.

When Union General Rosecrans replaced Buell after Perryville, Wheeler went on the offensive: "The turnpike, as far as the eye could reach, was filled with burning wagons." He took thousands of prisoners. As a result, Bragg nominated Wheeler for Major-General.

January 1863: Once again Wheeler joined Forrest, now in the attempt to re-capture Ft. Donelson, to open up the Cumberland River. Forrest protested the plan. He felt it was suicidal. When the mission failed, Forrest was furious and vowed never to fight with Wheeler again.

In the summer of 1863, Rosecrans attacked Chattanooga. Because Forrest, still burning with hate, never came to his aid, Wheeler's cavalry was crushed and he was almost captured. Once again the Southern armies fell back. Middle Tennessee was abandoned. Vicksburg fell. Most of the West was lost. The Union cavalry was using Wheeler's tactics and beating him at his own game.

After abandoning Chattanooga, Rosecrans made a fatal error at Chickamauga. He allowed a huge gap to open in the Union lines by mistakenly repositioning Wood's division. General Hood raced through that opening. In a panic-rout, the Federals were on the verge of extermination and were trapped in Chattanooga. Wheeler went on the offensive again, cutting communications to the besieged Union army. And again, Nathan Bedford Forrest's horsemen were shifted to Wheeler. Forrest threatened Braxton Bragg's life for that.

Inside besieged Chattanooga, Rosecrans' men were starving. A relief column of 1,000 supply wagons never reached them. Wheeler destroyed them all.

In October 1863, Ulysses S. Grant took command of the region. He sent Joe Hooker to Chattanooga. He smashed his way into Chattanooga and lifted the siege. Now the Southerners were pushed back into Georgia. Braxton Bragg was replaced by Joe E. Johnson.

May 1864: Grant became commander of all the Union armies. He ordered Sherman to take Atlanta. When Sherman attacked Tunnel Hill, it was Wheeler who delayed his advance. Sherman attempted to encircle Dalton. Wheeler drove him back.

Joe Johnston was constantly being outflanked. He felt compelled to back out of the closing trap. Dalton fell. Resaca fell. Calhoun fell. Wheeler's cavalry covered Johnston until he reached Atlanta.

Jefferson Davis then replaced Johnston with Hood. Wheeler's men dismounted and fought as infantrymen. Atlanta held. Then they re-mounted, outflanked Sherman and recaptured Dalton. But now Atlanta was encircled.

Wheeler's horsemen feinted toward Chattanooga. Sherman took the bait and withdrew men needed at Atlanta to shadow him.

August 1864: Nathan Bedford Forrest was in Alabama. Wheeler met him at Tuscumbia. They patched up their differences but "fighting Joe" was exhausted, discouraged and ready to resign. Forrest wrote that Wheeler's "whole command is demoralized to such an extent that he expressed himself as disheartened, and that, having lost influence with his troops and unable to secure the aid and cooperation of his officers, he believed it is in the interest of the service that he should be relieved from command."[1]

---

1. Nathan Bedford Forrest letter to General Richard Taylor, brother-in-law of Jefferson Davis, September 20, 1864, from *Official Records of the Confederacy*, vol. xxxix, Part II, p. 849.

General Hood refused to let Forrest and Wheeler join commands. Wheeler was ordered to defend Atlanta but before he arrived, the city was evacuated.

As Hood retreated, Wheeler's harassing tactics slowed Sherman but he also destroyed enormous amounts of private property before Sherman could gain any advantage from it.

Robert E. Lee issued this order aimed at Wheeler: "The commanding general considers that no greater disgrace could befall the army, and through it, our whole people, than the perpetuation of barbaric outrage upon the unarmed and defenseless, and the wanton destruction of private property."[1]

The Confederate government now threatened to relieve Wheeler of his command for his atrocities, but nothing was done.

By January 1865, only half of Wheeler's men had weapons or winter clothes or food. Discipline hardly existed.

By this stage of the war, Sherman advanced from Savannah to join Grant at Richmond, by marching through the Carolinas. Once again, Wheeler delayed the crossing of the Savannah River and then defeated his major Union cavalry rival, Kilpatrick, at Aiken, Georgia.

Despite his great contributions to the Southern war effort, Wheeler was finally replaced by Major-General Wade Hampton, on the grounds that although he was a "modest, zealous, gallant and indefatigable officer, he cannot properly control and direct successfully so large a corps of cavalry."[2]

When informed of the change by Hampton, Wheeler quietly said: "Certainly General, I will receive your order with pleasure."[3]

Hampton ordered Wheeler to guard the approaches to Columbia, South Carolina. It was still over-run, sacked and burned. Then Charleston was evacuated. In Virginia, the Petersburg siege tightened. Only 2,500 Southern men were left to face Sherman's huge army. Wheeler and Kilpatrick still battled. They hated each other. Atrocities and "take no prisoners" were the reality on both sides.

Lee surrendered on April 9th. Johnston, at Durham Station, North Carolina, on the 26th. Jefferson Davis would not accept the collapse of the Con-

---

1. Jabez Curry article in a fragment of an unknown newspaper, date unknown, but after 1897, Curry Papers.
2. General Beauregard to Robert E. Lee, February 12, 1865, from Brigadier General Fred C. Ainsworth and Joseph W. Kirkly, *The War of the Rebellion: A Compilation of the Official Records of the Union and Confederate Armies* (Washington: Government Printing Office, 1900), vol. xlvii, Part II, Series I, p. 1165.
3. Dubose, p. 430.

federacy. He headed to the Carolinas to continue guerrilla war, asking for Wheeler's and Hampton's cavalry to protect him. At that moment Wheeler said that while Davis "saw the necessity of further retreat, he did not realize the completeness of our undoing. He still hoped the tide of calamity might be turned. Around him was preserved the semblance of power and the routine of government, and on the day of my arrival, I remember that a young cadet underwent a regular form of examination for promotion to the office of lieutenant."[1]

Wheeler asked for men who would follow Davis, even to death. All of his six hundred men volunteered. Davis went on, ahead. On May 10 he was captured near Irwinsville, Georgia. Wheeler was seized as he slept one night, while en route to reach Davis. He was imprisoned at notorious Ft. Delaware. Hundreds died there. After months of solitary confinement, Wheeler was paroled.

Curry Commands 5th Alabama Cavalry

On October 5, 1864, while Jabez Curry was with Joe Wheeler, he received a new assignment — to go to North Alabama to assume the role of Judge Advocate with a military court, within the jurisdiction of General Philip Roddey. Curry recalled: "We reached Courtland, General Roddey's headquarters on the 17th." Roddey "greatly desired my presence and assistance, on account of the disturbed state of affairs in Alabama, [so] I was appointed his aide pro tempore. There was much disloyalty in that portion of the State, and the facility of intercourse with the Federal army made cautious dealing very necessary."[2]

Roddey had been a tailor, a sheriff and a steamboat owner before the war, and by the end commanded a Confederate cavalry division. He served as Braxton Bragg's escort at Shiloh, then in middle Tennessee and Northern Alabama with Wheeler and Nathan Bedford Forrest. Operating independently now, he was responsible for the defense of Northern Alabama.

On October 30, generals Hood and Beauregard and their troops reached Courtland, en route to Nashville. On November 2, Roddey and his men arrived at Tuscumbia, where Hood was encamped and readying for his proposed invasion of Tennessee. Beauregard had already departed.

Curry, still disturbed that Hood had replaced his hero, Joe Johnston, had some caustic comments to make about him: "The difference between his

---

1. John P. Dyer, *Fighting Joe Wheeler* (University, Louisiana: Louisiana State University Press, 1941), p. 228.
2. Jabez Curry, hand-written autobiographical notes, April 1876.

[Hood's] and General Johnston's handling of troops was most manifest. General Hood seemed at a loss of what to do; and his equipment and appointments, for which no blame attaches to him, were most inadequate."[1]

Roddey, with his cavalry brigade, conducted scouting observations to see if the Union armies were moving from Memphis.

Hood's men crossed the Tennessee River by pontoon bridge to Florence, then pressed northward toward Tennessee. Roddey and Curry remained near Corinth.

Then, one of Roddey's officers, Josiah Patterson, who commanded the Fifth Alabama Cavalry Regiment, was temporarily reassigned. Curry was voted to lead the Fifth by its officers. He was promoted to Lieutenant-Colonel. This was his first combat leadership role.

Curry took over the Fifth on November 21. There was a dress parade marking the transition. He made a stirring speech. With his usual zeal and adaptability, Curry set to work to learn the art of leading warriors. He said: "I soon mastered Wheeler's tactics, and drilled the regiment every day, Sunday excepted, when not engaged in active service. The regiment was undisciplined and badly armed, and not homogeneous. While my relations with the regiment were pleasant, and I had the entire confidence of officers and men, it was a sore trial to put and keep in 'fighting trim' men who were generally not well officered, and who were partially demoralized by serving in the immediate vicinity of their homes and families. It is simple justice, however, to say that I never saw more gallantry and courage than were frequently displayed by some of the officers and men. In this connection, I can do no better than stop and pay tribute to General Roddey. He has been much misrepresented, and since the war his conduct has not been free from censure. I never witnessed in him any other than a jealous and watchful purpose to serve his country to the best of his ability. He had a difficult command, requiring much tact and patience to manage, and a wide extent of territory to guard; and of his personal courage there can be no question."[2]

Curry's Fifth Alabama rode into Sherman's rear, cut railroad lines and communications, scouted Union strength, and acted as a rear-guard, like Wheeler, to cover Confederate withdrawals.

1. Ibid.
2. Ibid.

Curry's diary has terse comments about his first month as a battlefield commander: "On 29 November assumed command of the 5th Alabama regulars, of General Roddey's brigade. Left Corinth on the 10th of December. Crossed Tennessee River at Ganier's Ferry on the 14th. Left Ganier's on the 23rd. Recon of Florence. Reached Rogersville on the 24th. Ordered back by General Hood and camped near Florence on the 25th. His army, retreating in disorder and confusion." Hood's armies had just been decimated at Franklin and Nashville. On Christmas Day Curry fell back to Florence. It was a cold, wet day with no food for men or horses. "I have no pleasant associations of that Christmas." Then, "On the 26th two gun boats came to Florence and smashed up a small battery, supported by my regiment and Stewart's battalion, both commanded by Colonel Patterson. Same night, crossed river, near Bainbridge on pontoon bridge. 28th, marched to Pond Spring. 29th, fought Yanks at Mallaid's Creek and was driven to Courtland and camped at Yocon Creek. Fought the Yanks, repulsed, narrowly escaped capture, and encamped three miles south of Tuscumbia."[1]

Elsewhere, he commented: "Infantry and cavalry were completely demoralized, regarding our defeat as accomplished and resistance as hopeless. With such men as I could organize I had several skirmishes with Yankees, very nearly not escaping capture, as the enemy charged within a few paces and fired in very uncomfortable proximity. I should have surrendered, but that I dreaded the imprisonment and the separation from my family."[2]

For the first half of January 1865, Curry's 5th Alabama and the Union cavalry played hide-and-seek through Franklin, Lawrence and Morgan counties of Northern Alabama. Then Colonel Patterson rejoined the 5th Alabama, temporarily regaining command again, near Sim's Mill in Morgan County. This allowed Curry to take a short furlough and rush home. His wife, Ann, was desperately ill. The privations brought on by the war were partially responsible for her condition. Curry stayed a week with her, but the harsh compulsion of military orders forced him back to the front. He never saw her again. She died on April 9, believing that Jabez had been killed.

In March 1865, Curry's responsibilities were expanded. The 5th Alabama was his again as well as Stewart's battalion. Events were moving quickly as the Federal armies pushed for their final offensive to end the war. The Union general, Wilson, gathered his forces for a major strike through Alabama.

---

1. J.L.M. Curry, diary for 1864, J.L.M. Curry Papers, Library of Congress.
2. Jabez Curry, hand-written autobiographical notes, April 1876.

When Patterson, for the third time, took over the 5th Alabama from Curry, Jabez found himself reporting to the legendary cavalryman Nathan Bedford Forrest. Curry's assignment was to watch Wilson's movements as Forrest, although vastly outnumbered, courageously moved up to confront the Federal offensive.

Curry watched half of Wilson's division, but was cut off and delayed for two days as he detoured around the Federals to rejoin Forrest. Now Curry, à la Wheeler, was to protect the rear of the Confederate column.

Curry wrote in his diary: "Deploying what men I had, I skirmished with the enemy through Plantersville, slowly falling back to give the wagons time to get out of the way. While resisting the attack, a ball, with a heavy thump, struck and entered my haversack, perforating my coat, breaking a hair brush, and making sixty holes in a New York *Tribune*, which I had been carrying for two weeks without an opportunity to open and read it. This paper, now in the Confederate Museum in Richmond, undoubtedly saved my life. When [Horace] Greeley [the editor of the *Tribune*] was a candidate for the Presidency, [in 1872] I sent him, by a friend, a jocular message, that if elected he could not take the oath of office, as he certainly had given 'aid and comfort' to his country's enemy."[1]

Curry and Forrest

Nathan Bedford Forrest was the most significant commander that Jabez Curry fought with. The following overview is from a biography of Forrest:

"The history of this country presents no parallel to the career of Nathan Bedford Forrest, who won a place among the foremost soldiers of a war distinguished for generals of ability and high professional training.

The exploits of Forrest are among the chief glories of the Confederacy. In Virginia the Confederate army was led by some of the greatest generals the world has known, and it went from victory to victory. In the West, on the other hand, the Southern army suffered from poor leadership, and its history is of heroic valor and endurance in the face of heavy odds and in spite of every disaster.

A single ray of victory gilded the darkness of Confederate defeat in the West; the career of Forrest. Until his last battle at Selma, where he was overwhelmed by sheer weight of numbers, the great cavalryman seldom fought without conspicuous success. In the midst of armies defeated and breaking up,

---

1. Alderman and Gordon, p. 186.

his skill and courage shone with a brilliant light. With the passing of time and a proper understanding of what Forrest accomplished with the smallest of means, his fame has so grown that there are not wanting those who hold him to be the greatest military genius that the American continent has produced."[1]

Nathan Bedford Forrest was born July 13, 1821, in, of course, Bedford County, Tennessee. His father was a blacksmith who married an Amazon, by 19th century standards. Miriam Beck was almost six feet tall and 186 pounds.

While Nathan was still a child, Miriam was attacked by a panther and badly injured. Nathan treed the animal, shot it and gave the scalp and ears to his mother.

Later, Nathan was a farmer in Mississippi. In 1841, at 20, he joined a militia company to fight in Texas. They reached New Orleans but from there Texas was unreachable. Most of the company went home. Nathan made his way, alone, to Houston, only to learn that Texas did not need any more soldiers. He was too broke to return and was forced to work as a farm-hand to earn enough to go back.

In 1845, Nathan shot a man to death and wounded another. He was defending his uncle, who was caught up in a feud. Nathan was wounded, his uncle killed. He was acquitted: self-defense.

Nathan raised cotton, sold real estate, traded in slaves and became very wealthy. In Memphis, he broke up a lynching with just a knife, and as a result was elected Alderman.

Nathan Bedford Forrest believed in state sovereignty and secession. In July 1861, despite his wealth (which could have bought him an officer's rank), he enlisted as a private in Josiah White's Mounted Rifles. But, soon he used his money to raise eight companies of cavalry and their weapons and equipment. He was commissioned a Lt. Colonel.

His first battle was at Sacramento, Kentucky. He outmaneuvered and routed a large Union cavalry unit. Nathan's commander, General Clark, wrote this report: "It was one of the most brilliant and successful cavalry engagements that the present war has seen."[2]

February, 1862, Ft. Donelson: When Ulysses S. Grant attacked, the fort's commander, General Floyd, tried to fight his way out to Nashville. Forrest's cavalry led the break-out but confusion led Floyd to surrender. Only Forrest and his men escaped in heavy snow.

---

1. Hamilton James Eckenrode, *Life of Nathan B. Forrest* (Atlanta: B.F. Johnson Publishing Co., 1918), preface.
2. Ibid., p. 31.

April 1862: Shiloh: Forrest now commanded a full regiment. His scouts saw General Buell marching to reinforce Grant. The plan was to attack before they joined. Forrest led the way, blocking the Union reinforcements. Success: 3,000 surrendered. But just when the Federals seemed on the edge of annihilation, other reinforcements arrived and drove back the Southerners. Forrest covered that disastrous retreat, slowing Grant, but this required hand-to-hand fighting and Nathan was shot in the back. He continued battling but would spend weeks in the hospital.

June 1862: Forrest became famous when he brazenly charged directly into the town of Murfreesboro in Tennessee, and the Union defenders surrendered. He took 1,200 prisoners and 500 horses. This showed Forrest's over-all genius for strategy. As a result, he was promoted again, this time to Brigadier-General.

Union General Buell tried to trap Forrest with two cavalry pincers. Forrest escaped by traveling through the woods instead of using the roads.

Buell telegraphed General Nelson: "Destroy Forrest if you can." Nelson replied: "It is hopeless, with infantry, to chase Forrest's command mounted on race horses."[1]

Nathan Bedford received his weapons, clothes and food from the Union supply wagons he captured.

Several times he seemed hopelessly trapped against wide, unbridgeable rivers but he, his men, and their horses would swim across to safety.

Forrest's raids were so successful that Ulysses S. Grant postponed major offenses because of the massive amount of supplies destroyed and prisoners taken.

December 1862: Joe Wheeler and Forrest combined for the first time to retake Fort Donelson, with cavalry. Nathan Bedford objected to the plan. They had too few men. But Wheeler was the superior officer. The attack went on.

After three assaults failed, they retreated. Forrest, enraged, said: "General Wheeler, I advised against this attack and said all that a subordinate officer should have against it. Nothing you can say or do will bring back my brave men, lying dead or wounded or freezing around that fort tonight. I mean no disrespect to you, you can have my sword if you wish it, but there is one thing I want you to put in that report to General Bragg. Tell him I will be in my coffin before I will fight again under your command."[2]

---

1. Ibid., p. 49.
2. Ibid., p. 62.

Forrest never again served under Wheeler. Thereafter, they fought on opposite flanks of the Southern armies.

Spring 1863: Forrest's next success made headlines all over the South. Union General Rosecrans hoped to force Braxton Bragg out of south Tennessee, into Georgia. Colonel Abel Streight led the assault with 2,000 men on mules, because of the mountainous terrain.

Forrest chased Streight for 24 hours in heavy rain, as Streight circled behind Bragg. They clashed at Sand Mountain. Forrest's first two assaults were repelled with heavy losses and yet it was Streight who withdrew. At Hog Mountain, there was hand-to-hand fighting at night. Forrest had three horses shot out from under him. Streight was routed. At Black Warrior River, he was beaten again and retreated to Lawrence. Streight's men were so exhausted, they slept while being attacked. He surrendered.

The Confederate Congress declared its "thanks are due to General N.B. Forrest ... especially for the daring, skill and perseverance shown in the pursuit and capture of the largely superior forces of the enemy."[1]

May 1863: A Confederate officer who felt that he had been unjustly treated attempted to assassinate Forrest, shooting him with a pistol. Forrest was badly wounded but he still killed his assailant. Before dying, the officer asked for forgiveness.

September 1863: Forrest covered Braxton Bragg's retreat from Chattanooga toward Dalton. Outside Chattanooga, at Chickamauga Creek, possibly the fiercest battle in American history was fought. Wheeler was on Bragg's right flank, Forrest on the left.

Forrest outflanked the Federals under General Thomas. To support Thomas, Rosecrans withdrew men from other sections of the line. This created a gap. Longstreet poured through. The Federal front collapsed, the troops were routed and nearly obliterated.

Forrest attacked almost into Chattanooga, trapping the Union army within the city. But Bragg was too fearful to pounce on the disorganized Federals and wipe out the remainder. Once again this infuriated Forrest. To placate him, Jefferson Davis promoted him, this time to Major-General. From this point on, he raided independently.

---

1. Ibid., p. 79.

February 1864: Forrest smashed the forces of General Smith at Okolona. It was so decisive that Sherman had to abandon his plan to take Selma, Alabama, with its war workshops and arsenal.

March 1864: With larger forces, Forrest attacked Fort Pillow. It was on a sand bar, north of Memphis. In a bitter struggle over trench lines, walls and obstacles, Forrest's men slaughtered the defenders because they would not surrender. Negro Union soldiers were also butchered. The United States Congress tried to prove the massacre was racially motivated. This was proved false. The Negroes also had refused to surrender.

Spring 1864: Joe Johnston replaced Bragg and slowly withdrew into Georgia. Sherman was afraid of Forrest's success in demolishing his rail lines while operating on Johnston's flanks. Sherman sent General Sam Sturgis and 8,000 infantry and cavalry to block Forrest.

At Brice's Cross-Roads he collided with Nathan Bedford's 4,800 men. This turned out to be one of the bloodiest engagements of the war. In hand-to-hand combat the Union cavalry was crushed. Then, Forrest turned on the slow-moving infantry. He attacked them from the front and rear, causing panic at a blocked bridge where 3,000 Federals were slaughtered.

Sherman wrote Secretary of War Stanton about this disaster: "I cannot but believe that Sturgis had troops enough. I know I would have been willing to try the same task with that force; but Forrest is a devil, and I think he has got some of our troops under cover. I have two officers at Memphis who will fight all the time. I will order them to make up a force and follow Forrest to the death, if it costs ten thousand lives and breaks the Treasury. There never will be peace in Tennessee until Forrest is dead."[1]

This is how Nathan Bedford Forrest's mind worked as he prepared for action. General Taylor planned for him to harass Sherman's lines of supply to slow his advance. Taylor met Forrest at Meridian, Mississippi to discuss the plan. Taylor described the moment: "To my surprise, Forrest asked many questions; how was he to get over the Tennessee [River]; how was he to get back if he was pressed by the enemy; how was he to be supplied; and what should be his line of retreat; what was he to do with prisoners. I began to think he had no stomach for the work, but at last, having separated the chances of success from the causes of failure with the care of a chemist in a laboratory, he asked for Fleming, the manager of the railway. Fleming appeared, a little man on crutches

---

1. Ibid., p. 114.

but with the energy of a giant, and at once stated what he could do in a way of moving supplies on his line. Forrest's whole manner now changed. In a dozen sharp sentences he told his wants, said he would have an officer to bring up his supplies, asked for an engine to take him north to meet his troops, told me that he would march with the dawn and hoped to give an account of himself in Tennessee."[1]

With 4,500 men Forrest began; capturing Union strong points and forts, taking thousands of prisoners, burning bridges, destroying rail lines, cutting telegraph lines.

December 1864: General Hood put Forrest in charge of all his cavalry but Hood kept falling back into Tennessee. In a suicidal attack Hood lost one-third of his army at Franklin, and yet the Federals withdrew.

After Franklin, Forrest pursued the retreating Union forces toward Nashville. He planned to engage them along the route, at Murfreesboro, and seemed to be at the point of capturing a strong contingent but his own infantry panicked. Forrest rode among them, calling out, "Rally men, for God's sake, rally!" But the soldiers continued to run. Forrest, riding up to the fleeing color-bearer, told him to halt. When he did not, Forrest shot him dead, dismounted, seized the flag, rallied his men, and they pushed the Federals back into the forts at Murfreesboro and the strong points in Nashville. Hood recklessly attacked again and was crushed again. His army would have been exterminated except that Forrest's cavalry also once again acted as a rear-guard buffer.

It was snowing and freezing and many of his men had no shoes or coats, but they fought on, counter-attacked and at some points still were victorious.

Christmas Day, 1864: Hood escaped by crossing the Tennessee River. Forrest had saved his army.

January 1865: Forrest was promoted to Lt. General. The Confederate government made him Commander of Cavalry for Alabama, Mississippi and East Louisiana. Starting as a private, Nathan Bedford had now risen to the second highest rank in the Confederate army. No other man had made that kind of advance.

March 1865: Union General James Wilson entered Alabama with 15,000 cavalry armed with the latest repeating rifles. His objective was Selma and its arsenal and munitions workshops. Forrest faced him with 2,000 men.

---

1. Ibid., p. 131.

Forrest soon became encircled. In hand-to-hand fighting he broke out, heading toward Selma, battling all the way. Wilson smashed through Selma's defenses and burned it to the ground.

Nathan Bedford escaped with 300 survivors to Gainesville. Here he learned that Lee and Johnston had surrendered. The war was over. Forrest told his men to go home. His cavalrymen, who had fought in one hundred battles, cut their flag into pieces. Each man took a fragment. This flag had been the gift of a young woman in Mississippi. It had been made from her bridal dress.

Forrest headed toward his home in Memphis. His friends urged him to leave the country, fearing he would be arrested and imprisoned. He said: "This is my country. I am hard at work on my plantation and keeping the terms of my parole. If the Federal government does not regard it, they will be sorry. I will not go away."[1] He was not harassed.

When the war ended, General Sherman said: "After all, I think Forrest was the most remarkable man the Civil War produced on either side. In the first place he was uneducated, while Jackson and Sheridan and other leaders were soldiers by calling. He never read a military book in his life but he was a genius for war. There was no way by which I could tell what Forrest was up to. He always seemed to know what I intended to do, while I am free to confess I could never tell what he was trying to do."[2]

Selma, Curry's Last Great Battle

Jabez Curry was scouting with his cavalry for Nathan Bedford Forrest when Wilson invaded Alabama with the intention of taking Selma.

Forrest, outnumbered seven-to-one, fought back with amazing courage but the strength differential was overwhelming. He was slowly pushed back into the town.

At this point Confederate general Dick Taylor saw Forrest and described the intense and frightening scene: "Forrest appeared, horse and man covered with blood, and he said that the enemy was at his heels and that I must move to escape capture. I felt anxious for him but he said he was unhurt and would cut his way through, as most of his men had done."[3]

---

1. Ibid., p. 165.
2. Ibid., p. 177.
3. Ibid., p. 159.

Forrest relied chiefly on Armstrong's brigade, numbering 1,400 men, which were placed on the left side of the battle line. Roddey's small force was on the right. The center was filled with inexperienced militia and citizens.

Curry was the last man to enter the trenches in Selma. Wilson's troops appeared. They probed the defenses with thirty minutes of intense fire. Then they charged, aiming at the weak center. The militia panicked and fled. Forrest rushed into the gap to hold it until Roddey's men could come to the rescue, but Wilson forced Roddey back. The militia was slaughtered and Forrest, Armstrong and Roddey were trapped, hemmed in by the Alabama and Cahawba rivers. They escaped death with great difficulty.

Curry described his participation in the battle: "I held my position, not violently assailed, until the enemy had gotten betwixt me and the town. Seeing everything in confusion, and our army routed, my men became uncontrollable, and sought safety. With a squad adhering to me, I crossed the fortifications, as to go into Selma was capture or death. Avoiding the road, on which were Federal troops, I soon found myself in the woods, and in a swamp. May I be spared from such another night! The Federals fired the government buildings, the foundries and naval works and magazines, which amid the awful explosions ignited and consumed the business portion of the city. The din was fearful. The rattle of musketry, the music of brass bands, the explosion of shells, the shrieks of women, made a second Tophet [a place near Jerusalem which became a name for Hell]. The burning town made an illumination which extended for several miles. Amid the hurrahing of victors, and the tramping of pursuers and pursued, I walked nearly the whole night.... The next day, with two men, I lay in the woods, until the next night, as the country was full of cavalry, we traveled; and just at daylight I paid a Negro five dollars in Confederate money, all of any kind I had, to put us across the Cahawba River in a canoe. A young horse, which a friend loaned me, swam by the boat. On the west bank of the river we were safe. My two companions soon left me, and I rode to Marion.... I found in the town General Forrest, who had effected his escape from Selma; and I promptly reported to him for duty."[1]

Curry then spent several days at Greensboro collecting what remained of his scattered and decimated command. On the 14th of April Forrest ordered Curry to the area near Montevallo and Elyton, to block the enemy from the direction of the Tennessee River. Curry was also to establish a one hundred mile

---

1. Jabez Curry, hand-written autobiographical notes, April 1876.

courier line from Greensboro to Talladega. At this stage all was confusion and chaos. No one was aware that Lee had surrendered on the 9th.

On the 17th, while trying to get his men across the flooding Cahawba River at Centreville, Curry learned from a messenger that his wife, Ann, had died on the 8th. Curry later wrote: "She was a pure, noble Christian woman, and a devoted wife. For eighteen years our lives had run peacefully and happily together. No woman sympathized more heartily with the Confederacy, or labored more self-denyingly for the soldiers and their families."[1]

Curry turned over his command to a Colonel Stewart and started home, still soldiering by patrolling and locating the proposed line of couriers but his true objective was to look after his motherless children, Susan and Manly. He reached Talladega on April 18. On the 21st, a brigade of Federal cavalry passed through Talladega. Curry was still unaware that the war had ended. "Gathering a few soldiers, I counted them [the Union cavalry] and then watched their movements, to report. While in a lane I captured a Federal soldier, and took his mule and arms. As I was protecting my prisoner from the thoughtless insults of the men who were with me, I was very near being shot. Unnoticed, another Federal soldier had approached within thirty yards of me, when I discovered him he was taking deliberate aim at me. Gathering my bridle and spurring my horse, I charged upon him, and fired my pistol. He fled and I was only too glad of an opportunity to escape, as several of his companions were in sight."[2]

A Federal garrison under General Crysler of New York occupied Talladega. From them Curry learned that the great struggle had finally ended. He surrendered and was paroled.

Meanwhile, Nathan Bedford Forrest had gathered his scattered forces at Gainesville. There, he too learned about Lee and Johnston. He told his men that the war was over: "It is the duty of every man to stand firm at his post and be true to his colors. Your past service, your gallant and heroic conduct on many fields forbids the thought that you will ever ground your arms except with honor. Duty to your country, to yourselves, and to the gallant dead who have fallen in this great struggle for liberty demand that every man shall continue to do his duty.... Keep the name you have so nobly won and leave the results to Him who in wisdom controls and governs all things."[3]

---

1. Alderman and Gordon, p. 189.
2. Jabez Curry, hand-written autobiographical notes, April 1876.
3. Eckenrode, p. 162.

CHAPTER 5. JABEZ CURRY, POLITICAL EXILE

The war was over. Jabez Curry came home to Talladega. He was forty years old and physically and mentally exhausted. His life and mind would be forever changed by his experiences in the war.

He was a widower with two small children to raise. He went to live with his late wife's family. It would be a year and-a-half before he was independent enough to rent a room for himself and Manly, now eight. Susan, thirteen, was sent to board at the Judson Female Institute.

Curry: "On the thirteenth of May, a Federal garrison, under General Crysler, occupied Talledega. I reported and was paroled. On the 30th of May, before breakfast, by order of General Canby at Mobile, I was arrested, but released on my personal parole the same day. The arrest grew out of a 'cock-and-bull' story in the New York *Tribune* that I had favored the assassination of Lincoln and the cruel treatment of Federal prisoners." Curry did not add that the charges against him also stemmed from a bill he introduced into the Confederate Congress, in which he advocated the murder of black troops and the burning of Northern cities. "General Crysler treated me uniformly with consideration and kindness but he was accused, and probably not wrongfully, of leveling 'black-mail' on citizens and taking cotton for his own use. His Quartermaster took corn and forage and meat from me without the slightest compensation and a Michigan regiment robbed me of three mules in open day-light. Of course, the rascals charged 'Uncle Sam' for these purchases.

"Corn and meat were distributed gratuitously to applicants. Thousands came to Talladega for such bounty. Such low vice was exhibited as to put the pen to blush. Where the people lived, how they graduated to such beastly crimes, was then, and still is, a mystery. The dens and purviews of the 'Five Points' [the notorious vice area of New York] could not have spawned out a fouler population. It is a sad illustration of the democratization and wrong of feeding from the public crib. When Richmond was evacuated and burned, I am told that a similar population made their hateful appearance for the first and the last time.

"The country was under martial law and the people so crushed and subjugated that a corporal could commit any depredation upon person or property with impunity. The Freedmen's Bureau was instituted and some of the fanatical or corrupt agents sought to make masters support their former slaves, or divide with them the property. Generally, the Negroes behaved well. Mine, with one exception, remained on the place as usual. I stayed at home quietly with my two children."[1]

In September 1865, a Bill of Information was filed against Curry in the Federal District Court at Montgomery, for the confiscation of his property, on the grounds that he had engaged in armed rebellion against the United States; that he had furnished money, provisions, clothing, and other materials for use by persons engaged in the "rebellion," and that he had used and circulated the paper currency and bonds of the State of Alabama, which had been issued for the purpose of waging war against the United States government.

In May, President Andrew Johnson had proclaimed an amnesty. In October, Curry went to Washington to obtain his pardon. On October 22, "I arrived at the capital city, Congress being in session. On the 23rd, unattended by any person, I saw the Attorney General and President Johnson. The latter received me courteously and kindly. To my application for pardon, he made no immediate reply; but talked freely about the conditions of the country and the state of feeling in the South.

"On my rising to leave, he expressed a wish for a further conversation, and told me to call next morning at the State Department, and the pardon would be ready for me. In Congress [before the war] I had a pleasant but not intimate acquaintance with the President, when he was a Senator from Tennessee.

"I was, of course, prompt in calling on the 24th at the State Department, then in the upper portion of the Treasury Building, and after making and signing the required oath, the pardon, with the signatures of the President and of 'W.

---

1. Jabez Curry, hand-written autobiographical notes, April 1876.

Hunter, Acting Secretary of State,' attested by the Great Seal, was handed to me."[1]

The pardon did not, by a magic stroke of a pen, make Jabez Curry a free citizen without penalties. The restrictions were severe. Its provisions made him a non-citizen and almost a non-person but it saved him from imprisonment or execution, as he was considered one of the leaders of the "rebellion."

He was barred from voting. He was banned from politics or from speaking in public about current events. It would not be until 1877 that Congress removed his disabilities. Politics had been his whole life. Now, he had no way to make a living. With his home and property confiscated, he was penniless. All this affected him deeply and this was another element which may help to explain his later mental transformation.

Curry was not only required to take the oath of allegiance, but also, among other parole conditions, to pay all costs that "may have accrued in any proceedings instituted or pending against his person or property before the day of the warrant" and to agree not to claim any property sold under the confiscation laws."[2]

Curry wrote, related to that: "This information from the District Attorney was never served on me by the Marshall, but was returned as executed; and thus I was at the mercy of as despicable and unprincipled a set of adventurers and robbers as ever, under official sanction, plundered a helpless people. I employed Judge William B. Chilton to look after my interests; and he compromised with the officials, hungry as dogs and merciless as wolves, by the payment of $250, the receipt of which lying before me, is the evidence of the robbery."[3]

Reconstruction, An Introduction

In this segment, the various aspects of Reconstruction will alternate with the personal life of Jabez Curry and with the general picture of this tragic era in Alabama and the rest of the South. It will demonstrate that life and human relations did go on despite the decade of tyranny. It is not meant to be a complete picture of Reconstruction, but simply an overview.

Since Jabez Curry was a citizen of Alabama, more emphasis will be placed on that state, but what occurred there is typical for all the Southern states.

---

1. Alderman and Gordon, p. 192.
2. Rice, p. 52.
3. Ibid., p. 51.

For the paroled Confederate soldier, the war decided both the abolition of slavery and the end of state sovereignty. Jabez expected that, but he did not expect political proscription and humiliation.

When he surrendered, certain terms had been made with him; as he thought, a contract was embodied in the parole which would secure his rights in return for laying down his arms. As long as he was law-abiding, he believed his rights were inviolate; but nearly all that occurred thereafter was in violation of the terms of surrender.

This was clearly articulated by Robert E. Lee. In August 1870, he attended a meeting of former Confederate leaders. He made this comment to Fletcher Stockdale, war-time Governor of Texas: "Governor, if I had foreseen the use these people [the Northern conquerors] had designed to make of their victory, there would have been no surrender at Appomattox Courthouse; no sir, not by me. Had I foreseen the results of subjugation, I would have preferred to die at Appomattox with my brave men, my sword in this right hand."[1]

At first Alabama lay prostrate. Her people were not interested in public questions. They were dazed about the future. There were no railroads, steamboats or basic services. The civilians were more frightened than the veterans.

Revived spirits came to the young. Social life returned. They married. This spirit did not extend to the older people. Dead sons, brothers and husbands took the meaning out of life. They died off quickly.

Lethargy passed when the Confederate leaders were arrested. Jefferson Davis, Alexander Stephens, the war governors, Admiral Semmes and many others were imprisoned and treated harshly.

Then the devastating work of the carpetbaggers, the Northern army and the crusading missionaries, brought on a renewed interest in politics, even though it was viewed as proof of "disloyalty."

The war had devastated the South. It was "similar to the property losses of the worst chapters of the two world wars."[2]

And more significantly, American democracy was transformed forever: "The Civil War and Reconstruction mark the end of the American constitutional Republic. The officially accepted history conveniently ignores the distinction between the American government after the war, as compared to the gov-

---

1. Thomas C. Johnson, *The Life and Times of Robert Lewis Dabney* (Richmond: The Presbyterian Committee of Publication, 1903), p. 499.
2. Thomas B. Keys, *The Uncivil War* (Biloxi: The Beauvoir Press, 1991), p. viii.

ernment that existed before the war. Just as the Imperialists of ancient Rome attempted to keep the trappings of Republican Rome, the Yankee myth-makers attempted to convince us that the current Federal government is a legitimate descendent and natural continuation of the American Republic."[1]

The following narrative is from South Carolina. It is included due to its power and righteous anger. It is more than a factual account. It is a cautionary tale to understand the era.

"The rule of South Carolina should not be dignified with the name of government. It is the installation of a huge system of brigandage. The men who have had it in control are the picked villains of the community. They are the highwaymen of the State.... Then they turn around and buy immunity for their acts by sharing their gains with the ignorant, pauperized, besotted crowd who have chosen them to their stations they fill."[2]

The civilization of the South "lies prostrate in the dust, ruled over by this strange conglomerate [the ex-slaves, carpetbaggers, opportunist Southerners] gathered from the ranks of its own servile population. It is a spectacle of a society turned upside-down. The wealth, the intelligence, the culture, the wisdom of the State, having broken through the crust of that social volcano on which they were contentedly reposing, and have sunk out of sight, consumed by the subterranean fires they had with such temerity braved and defied.

In the place of this old aristocratic society stands the rude form of the most ignorant democracy that mankind ever saw, invested with the functions of government. It is the dregs of the population habituated in the robes of their intellectual predecessors, and asserting over them the rule of ignorance and corruption, through the inexorable machinery of a majority of numbers. It is barbarism overwhelming civilization by physical force.

We will enter the House of Representatives. Here sit 124 members. 23 are white men, representing the remains of the old civilization. They are good looking, substantial citizens. These are men of weight and standing in the communities they represent. They are all from the hill country. The frosts of sixty or seventy winters whiten the heads of some among them. There they sit, grim and silent. They feel themselves to be but loose stones, thrown in to partially obstruct a current they are powerless to resist. They say little and do little as the days go by.... They are types of a conquered race. They staked all and lost all.

---

1. James Ronald Kennedy and Walter Donald Kennedy, p. 167.
2. James S. Pike, *The Prostrate State* (New York: Loring and Mussey, 1935), p. 58.

Their lives remain, their property and their children do not. War, emancipation, and grinding taxation have consumed them. Their struggle now is a giant complete confiscation. They endure and wait for the night."[1]

In a letter, Jabez Curry gave his own perspective of the realities of Reconstruction in Alabama: "These men, with star chamber powers, and views incurably hostile to the character of the people, began and prosecuted their work, uncovering nakedness, exposing peculiarities and weaknesses, transforming objectionable exceptions and incidents into rules of life and characteristics of a people, searching with microscopic eye every fault, heralding every intemperate expression, perverting and misconstruing every utterance. For a portrait of the South, every hasty act of violence, every instance that could bring reproach was ferreted out, multiplied, aggravated and grouped together as an illustrative whole. Everything to the contrary was ignored and concealed. No family, no community, no church could come unscathed, uncondemned, from such a merciless exposure and misconception.... The Czar of Russia or the Sultan of Turkey would not have the temerity, the cruelty to place their subjects under such a strain and burden as our States; prostrate, impoverished, helpless, were placed when reduced to provinces and put under military satraps."[2]

Jabez Curry also wrote about the enormous political changes that the war brought to the United States: "What political questions were settled by the terrible conflict of 1861-65? That is ascertainable only by reference to Amendments 13, 14 and 15. They nationalized the government and broadened citizenship beyond what the Fathers ever dreamed of. They emancipated the slaves and placed them upon equality of citizenship with the white people, compelled the seceding States to repudiate obligations growing out of conflicts with the United States, and eliminated secession as a State Right or remedy by creating national citizenship, thus transferring paramount allegiance from the State to the general government. As a legitimate consequence, the right of State interposition to arrest usurpation by the Federal government, whether by nullification or secession, has gone forever.... And the General Government has become practically the final judge of the measure and extent of the powers conferred upon it."

Curry then added: "Since the war some new theories have been promulgated as to changes in the character and authority of the Federal government.... A

---

1. Pike, pp. 12-13.
2. Fragment of typewritten letter to unknown person, no known date, from J.L.M. Curry Papers.

government [designed to be] alterable only by prescribed methods, becomes flexible and elastic, so as to be molded by circumstances, by fluctuating public opinion, or by supposed public interests. The law professor coolly sets aside the Tenth Amendment. ['The powers not delegated to the United States by the Constitution nor prohibited by it to the states, are reserved to the States respectively, or to the people.'] ... Another measures constitutional law, not by the texts, but by 'fait accompli,' and tests constitutional changes by two queries; were they in accordance with the standard of the times, have they lasted? These theories are revolutionary and efface the well-established distinction between a Constitution and an ordinary statute. Nothing can be conceived more antipodal to the true end of our Federal, constitutional, representative Republic. The Constitution becomes superfluous. Restraints and reservations are swept into desuetude, not innocuous. Oaths have no binding force. Whim, caprice, the mutable breath of the multitude, whatever fanaticism or hatred ... supersedes the fundamental law. The Constitution is wiped out.... Instead of a stable, solemn, permanent national will, we have a rope of sand, and the Constitution, as Jefferson feared, becomes 'waste paper' by construction."[1]

Based on these comments, it seems inconceivable that within a few years Curry would be so willing to promote this "rope of sand."

Anarchy in South

President Andrew Johnson instructed Union General Canby, who commanded the military district which included Alabama, to arrest any member of the Alabama legislature who attempted to hold a meeting of the General Assembly. So, from May to August 1865, there was no state government.

For six months chaos reigned except near military posts. Most of this anarchy was generated by the occupation troops. They were worse than outlaws. Much of the Federal army had been discharged at the end of the war but those who remained terrorized the people with robbery and outrages.

For years after the surrender, detachments of Union troops marched through the country, searching for cotton and booty, arresting citizens on false charges supplied by war-time Unionists.

---

1. J.L.M. Curry, *Principles, Acts and Utterances of John C. Calhoun, Promotive of the True Union of the States* (Chicago: University of Chicago Press, 1898), p. 25.

Negroes, Freedom, Destitution, Death

The fears of a Negro insurrection following emancipation proved groundless but wherever the Federal armies moved, the ex-slaves followed. Often, they returned home. All of them were restless and expectant, as was natural.

Generally, the former slaves had first learned of their freedom from their returning ex-master. He assembled them and explained their new condition with its privileges and responsibilities.

Many of the Negroes believed that freedom was paradise, and that they would never have to work again. The government would take care of them. As a result, the towns soon filled with destitute blacks. A dog and a squirrel gun were their badges of freedom.

The ex-slaves were coerced into the towns by the military where they could be more easily controlled. Only a small fraction could be fed or housed there. Thousands died from disease and starvation as they were trapped into existing in the open elements. A small-pox epidemic killed thousands more. The army did nothing and let them expire. The Negro population was reduced by one-fourth. Children died by the hundreds of thousands.

Presidential Reconstruction: Lincoln's Plan

In his inaugural address, Abraham Lincoln asserted that the Union was perpetual. Secession was null and void. The Union was unbroken.

In December 1863, Lincoln brought forth his plan of restoration. When one-tenth of the 1861 population of a Confederate state had taken an oath to support the Constitution and should establish a government on the basis of Northern ideals, it would be recognized as a legitimate Union state. Lincoln believed that recognition was an Executive prerogative.

Lincoln advocated suffrage for the best Negroes and believed that voting rights were beyond the control of the national government. His plan, both in theory and practice, was objectionable. It would recognize as a political people of a state the loyal minority. They would be an oligarchy. The principle of majority rule would be repudiated. As applied in Louisiana and Arkansas, those who claimed to be loyal were not promising material and were treated with contempt. There, the plan was severely criticized on the ground that the President was assuming absolute authority over the seceded states.

Later, Jefferson Davis said this about Lincoln's concept: "The plan of the President of the United States to restore states to the Union, did not contain a single feature to secure a republican form of government, nor a single provision authorized by the Constitution of the United States. With his usurped war power to sustain him in the work of destruction he found it easy to destroy; but he was powerless to create or restore. In the former case, he had gone imperiously forward, trampling under foot every American political principle, and breaking every constitutional limit."[1]

Presidential Reconstruction: Andrew Johnson's Plan

Andrew Johnson's political philosophies seemed to be a mass of contradictions. At first, it looked like he would be a brutal tyrant over the shattered South. He had said: "For the thousands who were driven into the infernal rebellion there should be amnesty, conciliation, and mercy. For the leaders, justice. The penalty and the forfeit should be paid. The people must understand that treason is the blackest of crimes and must be punished."[2]

Johnson hated the slave-holding aristocrats with a bitter envy. "If Johnson was a snake," said a political rival, Isham Harris, "he would lie in the grass and bite the heels of rich men's children. The very thought of an aristocrat caused him to emit venom and lash about in fury."[3]

With such a perspective, Johnson's initial plan was to humiliate and destroy the slave-holders, yet he proved to be an insightful, moderate President. His plan was "restoration": bringing the South back into the Union in the shortest time with the least amount of harsh military rule. This was not "reconstruction," which implied a long-term radical alteration of the minds, social framework and economy of the South.

Andrew Johnson was devoted to the principle of state sovereignty. He believed most political matters should be left in the hands of the Southern states. Individual traitors should be punished but the states had never legally seceded or surrendered their rights to govern their own affairs. As the first step toward normalcy, in Alabama, Johnson appointed Lewis E. Parsons as provisional governor. He was from Talladega. Originally an active participant for the Confederacy, he later bolted to the Union side.

---

1. Davis, p. 298.
2. Walter Fleming, *Civil War and Reconstruction in Alabama* (New York: Columbia University Press, 1905), p. 347.
3. C.R. Hall, *Andrew Johnson, Military Governor of Tennessee* (Princeton: Princeton University Press, 1916), p. 22.

In addition to provisional governors, Johnson had to fill thousands of patronage jobs which required picking many secession politicians and war-time Confederates. This brought "disloyal" Southerners closer to power again. Johnson accepted that reality.

Andrew Johnson believed that Southerners were reasonable men who accepted the outcome of the war and the end of slavery. To convince the American people and Congress that his views were correct, he assigned several men to travel through the South to investigate the truth of his perspective. He sent journalists Harry Watterson and Benjamin Truman and also Ulysses S. Grant.

Watterson and Truman found that conditions justified Johnson's policies; the influential whites could be trusted to maintain loyal state governments. Grant said that Southerners were more loyal than he expected.

Johnson then asked Carl Schurz to report on the South. He was a Radical Republican. His findings were very different. He said that Southern whites spent their time persecuting, beating and killing Negroes and loyalists. Schurz and the Radical newspapers reported comments made by drunks in bar rooms and idlers on street corners and magnified them into the "threatening voice of a whole people." Against these falsehoods, General Swayne, the military commander for Alabama, said there had been no trouble from Southern whites.

Destitution for Alabama Whites

In the northern counties, half the people were supported by the state. Then, for six months after peace, the state did not exist. Most of the men were war casualties. Peace-time crops were one-tenth the harvest of 1860. There were 250,000 whites officially listed as destitute. Initially, the army neglected them. As a result, most did not eat meat for months.

Then, there was a general crop failure in 1865-66. Like the blacks, thousands of whites died from starvation, exposure and disease. The rest managed, though half-starved, to survive until better times. Finally, in October 1868, soup kitchens were established in Mobile, Selma and Montgomery.

Politics, not kindness, lay behind this. These towns had less hunger than anywhere else in the state, but Ulysses S. Grant was to be elected President by the Republicans and in those locations were many Negro voters.

Congressional Reconstruction

Thaddeus Stevens was the Radical Republican leader in the House of Representatives. Charles Sumner was the Radical head in the Senate and Ben Wade, the Radical President Pro Tem of the Senate. They all loathed Andrew Johnson's moderate, conciliatory approach to healing the wounds of the war.

The Radicals had only limited success against the President and his policies until external events shifted public sentiment away from reconciliation to retribution.

Bloody riots in New Orleans and Mobile left many blacks and Unionists dead and wounded. This allowed the Radicals to bring their harsh plan for the South to the foreground. It would split the races apart forever and transform America permanently from a republic into a centralized dictatorship-in-progress.

To the Radicals the riots proved that the South still seethed with the spirit of rebellion. But the New Orleans riot had begun as a result of inflammatory speeches by Republicans to fire up the freedmen to conduct destructive acts.

Radical Republicans milked these incidents to ascend to political power. "Horrors upon horrors accumulate," wrote a Louisiana carpetbagger to General Ben Butler as he related the gory details of how "the Rebel Mayor, John C. Munro, armed his rebel police with revolvers and Bowie knives and privately ordered them to go and massacre the loyal men of New Orleans.... Andrew Johnson must and shall be made responsible for this Whole Sale massacre.... You must rouse the Northern mind against the massacre."[1]

This letter forecast the Radicals' program: revolutionary Reconstruction, a complete overturn of the South's social, political and economic existence. This meant viewing the ex-Confederacy as no longer part of the United States.

To achieve this, the Radicals pursued two brutal principles, the "State Suicide" and the "Conquered Province" theories, to prove that the South was an alien entity.

"State Suicide"

Charles Sumner formulated the "State Suicide" idea. The South, by her actions, had abdicated all constitutional rights. The Southern states had become territories under the exclusive control of Congress; there were no state govern-

---

1. William Hasseltine, *Ulysses S. Grant, Politician* (New York: Frederick Ungar Publishing Co., 1957), p. 70.

ments in the South. As territories, the South was no longer part of the United States, and Southerners were compelled to forfeit their citizenship. They were now clean slates upon which Congress would write the laws. Congress alone would establish a "republican form of government" for them. This meant universal voting for loyal blacks and whites, which would nationalize voting qualifications. "A republican form of government" also meant universal education. This would expand Federal dominance over the minds of all citizens. The Radicals also proposed the ascendancy of blacks over rebel whites to entrench the Republican Party. Since unqualified blacks would prevail in the Southern governments, a deep antagonistic wedge was driven between the races.

"Conquered Province"

Thaddeus Stevens originated the "Conquered Province" theory. It was more extreme than the Sumner plan. The "law of war" alone would rule the actions of Congress. The victors must treat the South as "conquered provinces and exterminate or drive out the present rebels as exiles from this country."[1]

Every inch of Southern soil should be confiscated for the costs of the war and for pensions to wounded Union soldiers. For Stevens, secession had been successful. The South was out of the Union. The Constitution was a "bit of worthless parchment." The South must either come back as completely new states or as conquered provinces, with perpetual ascendancy of Washington. Representative Anthony Thorton of Illinois expressed the truth of what this would mean: "If the states which attempted to secede are 'out of the Union,' either in fact or in law, then the war has failed in its avowed object. If they are 'dead and defunct' states, then the war was a fearful tragedy, resulting in the death of both the Union and the states."[2]

Jabez Curry also commented about the consequences of the "Conquered Province" policy: "The contradictory action in reference to the seceded states partook of a farce and tragedy. The states were treated sometimes as 'in,' sometimes as 'out' of the Union; sometimes as conquered territories, sometimes as states; sometimes as entitled to representation, sometimes not; sometimes as inchoate states forced to ratify amendments, and then were refused the exercise of their rights and privileges. The series of Reconstruction measures, in bald usurpation, in mad tyranny, in the essence of diabolism, in the deliberate

---

1. Fleming, p. 340.
2. *Congressional Globe, 39th Congress, First Session* (Washington, D.C.: Reprint Edition by United States Historical Documents Institute, 1970), p. 1165.

purpose to give supremacy to Negroes in some states, and to Republicans in all, has no parallel in the annals of the Borgias and the Caesars."[1]

Thaddeus Stevens' more extreme policies won out. He received from Congress the approval to divide the South into military districts under a commander with absolute power and no time-table for the end of military rule. These officers were subject only to the disapproval of the General of the Army, Ulysses S. Grant, and not the President.

This prompted Andrew Johnson to say: "Thus, over all these ten [Southern] States, this military government is now declared to have unlimited authority. It is no longer confined to the preservation of the public peace, the administration of criminal law, the registration of voters, and the superintendence of elections; but 'in all respects,' is asserted to be paramount to the existing governments. It is impossible to conceive any state of society more intolerable than this, and yet it is the condition that twelve million of American citizens are reduced by the Congress of the United States, over every foot of the immense territory occupied by these American citizens, the Constitution of the United States is theoretically in full operation. It binds all the people there, and should protect them; yet they are denied every one of its sacred guarantees. Of what avail will it be to any of these Southern people, when seized by a file of soldiers, to ask the cause of arrest, or for the production of the warrant? Of what avail to ask for the privilege of bail when in military custody, which knows no such thing as bail? Of what avail to demand a trial by jury, process for witnesses, a copy of the indictment, the privilege of counsel, or that grater privilege, the writ of habeas corpus?"[2]

The Attorney-General of the United States, in his official opinion to the President of these illegal acts by the Radical Congress, expanded the magnitude of the military usurpations: "It appears that some of the military commanders have understood this grant of power as all comprehensive, conferring on them the power to remove the Executive and judicial officers of the State, and to appoint other officers in their places."[3]

An example of this took place in Mississippi in June 1868. General McDowell was the commander of the region. He issued an order removing the civil governor, Humphreys, and replacing him with Major-General Ames. Gov-

---

1. J.L.M. Curry, *Civil History of the Government of the Confederate States, etc.*, p. 33.
2. Jefferson Davis, p. 732.
3. Ibid., p. 758.

ernor Humphreys refused to vacate his office, saying that the attempt to remove him was a "usurpation of the civil government of Mississippi, unwarranted and in violation of the Constitution of the United States." A squadron of soldiers was sent by the military commander of the post, which marched in and took possession of the office.[1]

The Radicals, 19th Century Stalinists

The fusing of lawless dictatorship with Radical revolutionary philosophy produced the 19th century's political equivalence of Stalinist collectivism. This was the moral precedent for the totalitarian horrors of the 20th century.

W.E.B. DuBois, the famed black Marxist historian, writing in the 1930s (when Stalin's redistribution programs were at their peak), saw the parallels between the conquered South and the policies of the Soviet Union. The Congressional Reconstruction laws created a "dictatorship backed by the military arm of the United States by which the government of the Southern states were to be coerced into accepting a new form of administration, in which freedmen and the poor whites were to hold the overwhelming balance of political power. As soon as the political power was successfully delivered into the hands of these elements, the Federal government was to withdraw and full democracy ensue. ["The State will wither away," as Marx proclaimed.] ... Such dictatorship must last long enough to put the mass of workers in power; that this would be, in fact, a dictatorship of the proletariat."[2]

Military in South Means Military in North

Horatio Seymour was the governor of New York before and during the War for Southern Independence. He was the Democratic Presidential opponent against Ulysses S. Grant in 1868. He said: "They [the South] are now settling down into the belief that we are their unrelenting foes: there can be no hearty Union. Unless there is a change of policy, in a little while they will accept the theory that they are a conquered people, with the rights as well as the liabilities of that condition. A military government will be forced upon us by making a military government necessary for their subjection. They will have everything to gain, and nothing to lose by revolution. We have more to fear from the South if it accepts the doctrine of subjugation than we ever had to fear from its armed rebellion; we cannot enslave them without enslaving ourselves. We cannot have

---

1. Ibid., p. 735.
2. W.E.B. DuBois, *Black Reconstruction in America* (New York: S.A. Russell Co., 1935), p. 345.

government whose Northern face shall smile devotion to the popular will, and whose Southern aspect shall frown contempt, defiance and hate to the people of eleven states

The South has comparatively little to fear from misgovernment; its lands have already been laid waste; its system of labor broken up; its homes impoverished; and its families thinned by the sword. It has seen and felt the worst.

Today the power of Great Britain is paralyzed by its harsh, unjust and contemptuous treatment of Ireland. We are taught that if a people are to be treated as outlaws, they can bide their time; they can wait for domestic strife or foreign invasion. It is not wise or safe to trample upon those who, for years, with desperate courage, held their ground against the millions we sent to the field, and the thousands of millions of treasure we spent in the contest — a contest which filled our homes with mourning, loaded us down with debt and taxation, and wrought great and lasting changes in the policy, the maxims, and structure of our government. A wise settlement of pending questions will do much to build up the prospects of the South; an unwise policy will do more to break down the wealth and prosperity of the North."[1]

Curry Marries Again

In the midst of the societal and personal agony of Reconstruction, there was still room for the human dimension of emotions and love and passion. Jabez Curry was transformed by these feelings and married a second time.

It began this way. Shortly after the war began, when Curry was a member of the Confederate Congress, he found living quarters on Grace Street in Richmond. Separated from his wife, Ann, and his two children, he was lonely.

In August 1861, Judge Chilton introduced him to the Thomas family, who lived on Second and Grace. Curry and Chilton went "into the back yard where I was introduced to Mr. and Mrs. Thomas and seven daughters who were sitting under a tree. For the first time I saw Mary. [She would become the second Mrs. Curry.] She was a sweet, beautiful, attractive, intelligent girl, seventeen years old. The family was so gentle, so cordial, that my heart was won and during my service in Congress, seldom a week passed that I did not take tea with the family.

---

1. Speech of October 30, 1866 at the Democratic National Union meeting, Cooper Institute, New York City. From Thomas M. Cook and Thomas Knox, editors, *Public Record of Horatio Seymour* (New York: I.W. England, at the offices of the New York *Sun*, 1868) p. 290.

I have never known a family where such a deference to parents, such filial love, such unreserved and respectful intercourse, such a pure atmosphere, such gentle courtesy, such sweet charities more dominated. Here began the sweetest friendship of my life. Separated from my own family, I as eagerly longed for the repetitions of my visits to this welcome home, as a school-girl even looks forward to vacation and reunion with parents. That I should have found in this family a wife, one who combined every womanly charm and excellence, who has since 1867 been to me more than I ever imagined or the heart ever craved, is one of the mysterious providences that shows a higher ruling power over our lives."[1]

Then, with the war over, and his first wife, Anne, dead, and being forced to be both mother and father to Manly and Susan, and his personal and economic life highly unsettled, Jabez was lonelier than ever. He lived in the small provincial town of Marion but he was often in Richmond.

He again called on the Thomas family, and found that Mary was now a 21-year-old woman who had lost none of her youthful and gracious qualities. They began a clandestine correspondence. Even in his own diary, Jabez did not have the courage to put her name to paper. He referred to Mary coyly as "M.W.T.," as in Mary Wortham Thomas.

On November 18, 1866, Jabez was in Richmond. That morning he preached at the Second Baptist Church. (In January, Jabez had been ordained as a Baptist minister.) In the afternoon, he assisted with the communion at the First Baptist. That night, he preached at First Baptist again. Mary Thomas accompanied him there. As he walked her home, on the corner of Fourth and Grace, he proposed. She accepted.

This would be an appropriate point to present a brief sketch of James Thomas Jr., Mary's father. He is probably responsible for bringing Curry into Richmond College as a professor, and that influenced Jabez's future decision to enter the wider field of education via the Peabody Fund. These aspects of Curry's life will be related shortly.

James Thomas Jr. was born in 1806 in Caroline County, Virginia. For half a century he was involved, with much success, in the manufacture of tobacco products. His brands were exported, and were well-known, all over the world. Despite fluctuations and depressions in trade, and the ravages of fire, he never wavered in his enthusiasm for his business, and continued to expand.

---

1. Jabez Curry, hand-written autobiographical notes, April 1876.

During the war the Confederacy was blockaded. His losses amounted to nearly a million dollars. By twenty-first century standards, that would amount to almost a billion dollars. He did not quit, and with peace once again reaped large profits.

James Thomas was a religious man, and the close contact with him as a father-in-law had a powerful influence on Jabez Curry. Mr. Thomas' obituary in 1882 made this comment: He "never enjoyed the advantages of collegiate training, and yet, in the richest sense of the word, he was an educated man. Nature endowed him with a vigorous, inquisitive and wonderfully active mind.... He was pre-eminently a lover of books. He not only feasted on their contents, but often enriched his conversations with their choicest thought. He was fond of grappling with great and difficult problems in science and religion, and was never happier than when listening to or leading in the discussion of great themes. He gave much of his time to society.

His hospitality was boundless. He spent his ample means with an almost reckless prodigality in the entertainment of his friends. The best people in Richmond, in the social sense, were accustomed to enter his home and taste his generous bounty, but we suppose that his greatest joy was in opening his door to his Christian brothers.... It would be impossible for anyone to estimate the number of those who sat at the table and partook of his charming hospitality. For half-a-century Mr. Thomas was known far and wide as an earnest and devout Christian.... He was a sincere Baptist."

Many of those who came to his home for "grappling with great and difficult problems" were the hierarchy of the Baptist community. Some were members of the Board of Directors of Richmond College, a Baptist school.

James Thomas was on that Board, too. Jabez Curry was courting Mary Wortham and was a frequent guest at the Thomas home. This allowed the Board members to observe Curry and evaluate his fitness to be a professor of that institution.

"For many years he [Thomas] was the Superintendent of the Sunday School.... As one proof of his devotion to the Sunday School, on the day his great factories were consumed by fire, he went with the school to its annual picnic, declaring that after having promised to give that day to the children, no personal interests should interfere with his word....

"Mr. Thomas stands before the public pre-eminent as a giver. We had many men who had the heart to give, but lacked the means, and some who had the means, but lacked the heart. He had both.... What a catalog it would be if it should tell of the widows he helped, the orphans he clothed, the students he educated, the business men he helped, the old preachers he relieved, the houses of worship he assisted in building, and the unfortunates that he relieved.

"His richest gifts were for Christian education.... To his magnificent and inspiring generosity, Richmond College is indebted for its present prosperity, if not, indeed, for its very existence. We are not surprised that the college had been ready to wreathe upon his brow the chaplet of honor. She had made him the President of the Board of Trustees."[1]

The Wedding

Jabez Curry and Mary Wortham Thomas were married on June 25, 1867, at the First Baptist Church in Richmond at 8:30 in the evening.

Judging by Curry's personal comments about Mary in his diary, this marriage was significantly different than his first, to Ann Bowie. He was far more enthusiastic. The sensual and spiritual union was much deeper and did not diminish with time.

As an example, on their 19th wedding anniversary, June 25, 1886, Jabez wrote the following entry in his diary. Mostly these little books are filled with terse, factual comments about meetings, appointments, speeches and travel destinations. There are few personal comments. This is an exception: "Mary and I were married in First Baptist Church in Richmond, Virginia, Dr. L.L. Burrows officiating. Nineteen years have passed and not a harsh word has passed between us. Our lives have followed on like two streams whose mingling waters are no more to be separated. Much, very much of my success is due to her. She has been an invaluable counselor, as true and loyal a wife as a man was ever blessed with. Every day reveals new beauties and excellences."[2]

Immediately after the wedding ceremony, Jabez and Mary left Richmond for New York. On June 29, they sailed for Europe. With them were a group of friends and relatives, which included Mary's half-brother William and three Baptist ministers. They spent four months in Europe, landing in Ireland and slowly working their way through England, Scotland, Belgium, Germany, Switzerland, Italy and France.

In July they were in England, touring Westminster Palace, Westminster Abbey, and the British Museum. On July 14 they heard a sermon by Spurgeon,

---

1. *Religious Herald*, newspaper, October 12, 1882, from Curry Papers.
2. J.L.M. Curry diary, Curry Papers.

the famed British minister. Later, Curry wrote an analysis of why some religious leaders, as speakers, had such a hold on the public. "The standard was different than for politicians or other public speakers, because they occupied a pulpit above the people and separated by a great gulf," so that effective elements like humor "were eliminated, tabooed, and only such bold men as Broadus and Spurgeon broke down the barrier," but "for continuity and greatness of success, for wide circulation of sermons, for marvelous capacity in reaching every one in his audience and making him feel that the sermon was especially intended for him, for extracting the marrow from apparently dry bones or neglected Scripture and feeding the people, for subduing the prejudices of class and church opponents, Spurgeon had no rival."[1]

July 24: Italy. They visited Pompeii and climbed Vesuvius. On August 1, Florence; the galleries of the Uffizi and Pitti palace; then they visited the famous American sculptor, Hiram Powers, in his studio. The group remained there until October 5. They saw the Exposition, the museums, the palaces, and all the other sites of interest.

Then back to England, sailed to New York, arrived on October 28 and went directly back to Richmond, stayed a few days, then home to Marion early in November. The honeymoon was over.

A New Career

Before being a professor at Richmond College, Jabez Curry was President of the Baptist school, Howard College.

William Curry, Jabez's father, had been an activist in the Baptist Church. Jabez himself, especially from the 1840s through the mid-1850s, when he was in the Alabama Assembly, was a well-known figure in the various Baptist associations; so, it was not entirely without precedent that in the first summer of peace he was induced to preach his first regular sermon, as a layman, at the Refuge Church in Talladega County.

In August and September he assisted his own pastor in Talladega and another minister at the Alpine Church. In Talladega, "a spectacle, novel and interesting, was that of a Confederate soldier and a Federal soldier, who walked into the water, hand-in-hand," to be baptized.[2]

---

1. Jabez Curry article in *Religious Herald*, date unknown.
2. Jabez Curry, hand-written autobiographical notes, April 1876.

In October 1865, when in Washington for his pardon, Curry preached at the 13th Street Baptist Church, and then in Richmond, at the First Baptist and the First Street Baptist churches.

Then in November, while attending the Baptist State Convention in Marion, he was elected its President. This long-standing relationship with the Baptist community led, while he was at the convention, to his being elected President of Howard College, "The Baptist College of Alabama." It was located in Marion.

Another reason for his selection was his pre-war promotion of education. As an Alabama Assemblyman he had been on the "16th Section Committee." The tax revenues of the 16th section of every township were devoted to common schools. Jabez Curry had successfully proposed legislation that created Alabama's first state-wide school system.

Howard College had been founded in 1841. It closed its doors when the Union army over-ran Marion, using the school's buildings as a hospital. It re-opened in the fall of 1865 but without the financial resources to continue endowment or scholarship commitments.

As President, Curry's role was to "travel, attend meetings of Baptist associations, and deliver addresses on behalf of Howard and general education."

This meant attracting students and money. He was "almost constantly in the field seeking funds and patronage for its maintenance."[1]

He traveled and spoke in Selma, in Montgomery, Tuskegee, Jacksonville, Talladega and elsewhere, and he still had time to teach classes in Moral and Mental Science and Political Economy.

The 14th Amendment: Nationalizing Justice Splits Races

Section One of the 14th Amendment provided that all persons born or naturalized in the United States were citizens of the United States. Formerly, they had been citizens of their own state. This destroyed the Bill of Rights restrictions on Federal power. This section has been used extensively by the Supreme Court to undermine the validity of state legislation and to draw it beneath Federal jurisdiction.

---

1. B.F. Riley, *A Memorial History of the Baptists of Alabama* (Philadelphia: Judson Press, 1923), p. 310.

Section Two gave full apportionment in Congress to Negroes. This set the stage for giving them voting rights and denying this privilege to most whites. That further split the races apart.

Section Three excluded from political office those army officers and members of Congress who aided the Confederacy; like Jabez Curry. By implication this allowed unqualified freedmen to fill these places, creating a further bitter rift between blacks and whites.

This amendment to the Constitution was based on the principles of the Congressional Reconstruction Civil Rights Act. Andrew Johnson said this about it: "It intervenes between capital and labor and attempts to settle questions of political economy through the agency of numerous officials, whose interest it will be to foment discord between the races; for as the breach widens their employment will continue, and when it is closed their occupation will end." Johnson also said that this amendment establishes "for the security of the colored race safeguards which go infinitely beyond any that the General Government has ever provided for the white race" and therefore discriminates against whites. Johnson stated that it was a step toward centralizing all legislative powers into the national government. "A perfect equality of the white and colored races is attempted to be fixed by Federal law in every State of the Union, over the vast field of State jurisdictions covered by the emancipated rights. In no one of these can any State ever exercise any power of discrimination between the different races.... Hitherto every subject embraced in the enumeration of rights contained in this bill has been considered as exclusively belonging to the states.... If acquiesced in, [it] must sap and destroy our federative system of limited powers and break down the barriers which preserve the rights of States."[1]

Alabama Rejects 14th Amendment

In the fall of 1866 the proposed 14th Amendment was submitted to the legislature of Alabama. Since there was no belief by Alabamians that further yielding to Washington would do any good toward restoring them to statehood, the people were asked to reject the amendment because the more they gave in to Washington's demands, the more was asked of them. They had ratified the 13th Amendment, which abolished slavery and which also gave Negroes security in

---

1. DuBois, p. 282.

their person and property, but Alabamians were no nearer to re-admission into the Union.

It was still believed by both Loyalists and "rebels" that Negro rights were state rights, so both sides were afraid to put their privileges into the hands of Congress through the 14th Amendment.

Alabama's governor, Patton, asked the legislature to reject it for the above reasons and because it created a penalty "after the fact"; an ex-post facto law. This was contrary to the spirit of modern civilization. It disenfranchised most whites as traitors for acts they had committed before the amendment went into effect. This form of law belonged to tyrants for the purpose of revenge. Its effect would be to vacate most governmental offices in the unrepresented states. This would produce anarchy.

Governor Patton changed his mind when he understood that rejecting the 14th Amendment would bring on far worse penalties: Alabama would be a territory permanently. The legislature still rejected it.

14th Amendment Ratified After Veto

President Johnson noted that only 25 of the 36 states were represented in Congress. He questioned the legality of the 14th Amendment. Every Southern state voted against it.

This prompted Senator James Doolittle of Wisconsin to say: "The people of the South have rejected the constitutional amendment" and we will "march on them and force them to adopt it at the point of a bayonet."[1]

When the Southern citizens and legislators fully grasped the consequences of their actions — remaining territories forever — they finally acceded, accepting the 14th. This included Alabama.

The 15th Amendment: Nationalizing Votes Splits Races

This amendment turned the classic Southern and Northern social order upside down. Voting qualifications were set in Washington, not in each state as mandated by the Constitution. In principle, it nationalized and universalized them.

The freedmen became the dominant Southern voter class as most whites were disqualified, as traitors. The freedmen, adhering to the carpetbaggers,

---

1. Dr. Michael Hill, "The 14th Amendment," in *Southern Events*, November – December 1999, p. 3.

passed laws against their former white masters, neighbors and friends. This created yet another force for a personal and political alienation of the races.

Thaddeus Stevens told Southern leaders that unless they accepted the 15th Amendment, the former Confederate states would remain territories for at least ten years, controlled by the army — and blacks would be the only voters. To terrorize them further, Stevens said: "In my county [in Pennsylvania] there are 1,500 escaped slaves. If they are specimens of the Negroes in the South, they are not qualified to vote. Twelve months hence you will have reconstruction acts with Negro suffrage."

When Southerners objected to an endless military dictatorship, Stevens responded: "Every government is a despotism. Better for the black man if he were governed by one king than twenty million."[1]

Yet even in Congress, the Radical "Committee of Fifteen," which convened to give the vote to blacks, had questions about the validity of their actions. "Doubts were entertained whether the Congress had the power, even under the amended Constitution, to prescribe the qualifications of voters in a state, or could it act directly on the subject. It is doubtful, in the opinion of your committee, whether States would consent to surrender a power they had always exercised."[2]

Jabez Curry made the following comments about this extreme transition which would lead to universal male voting rights: "A New England statesman who held a seat in the Cabinet, gravely declared that suffrage was a natural and inherent right; 'The only thing divine in human government is the equal right of men to a voice in making the laws.' Is this right unconditioned by sex, or age, or race, or mental qualifications? To justify Negro suffrage is the only excuse, pitiable and contemptible as that may be, for such an insane utterance. The experience of the wise, dictates a sharp limitation to the franchise. Suffrage of right belongs to those best able to guard and promote the public welfare. Theoretically the Mississippi Constitution is right, in requiring of the voter the ability to read and understand the Constitution."[3]

Elsewhere, Curry added: "The Athenians tried the problem of government by limiting the number of people who might, in a very narrow way, take part in the government, and only a few citizens had the leisure and time to study grave

---

1. Claude Bowers, *The Tragic Era* (Cambridge: The Riverside Press, 1929), p. 153.
2. DuBois., p. 312.
3. J.L.M. Curry, typewritten manuscript, June 12, 1900, Curry Papers, Library of Congress.

political problems. It is also to a mere handful of people that the management of the Roman State was entrusted. The government of England is committed to the governing classes, set apart by training, heredity, wealth, social position, for exerting a controlling and governing voice in shaping the political policy of the society. In the United States we have adopted a theory opposed to that of any other great organization in the world. We are trying, in the face of all political history, to govern upon the theory that every man is a political expert, entitled to have an opinion upon all economic, social and political questions."[1]

Yet, as with the 14th, Alabamians were trapped into accepting the 15th Amendment to avoid the consequences of its rejection.

Alabama Rejects Constitution; Forced Into Union

In Congress, Thaddeus Stevens authorized "Alabama and other waste territories of the United States to form constitutions so, if possible, to make them fit to associate with civilized communities."[2]

In the summer of 1867, Governor Parsons called a convention of delegates chosen by loyalists to change Alabama's constitution, as the opening step to re-admission to the Union. This convention was made up of 98 Radicals and two Conservatives. The carpetbaggers were in complete control.

In February 1868, this constitution was voted upon. Under the law, a majority of the qualified electorate had to vote for the constitution to be legally ratified. The Conservatives were thoroughly displeased with the new document and wanted Alabama to stay outside of the Union until after the Presidential election so that Ulysses S. Grant could not receive its electoral votes. Grant was still hated for his war-time atrocities and his current drift toward Radicalism.

The Conservatives devised a strategy to prevent its adoption: register all qualified whites, then have them stay away from the polls on election day.

Jabez Curry, by the terms of his pardon, was banned from political public speaking but the turmoil created by this new carpetbag constitution forced him to become an activist once again. On January 6, 1868, in Selma, he attended a meeting of the opponents of the constitution. Here, he did not speak — but he opened the proceedings with a prayer. His presence symbolized his support for the opposition.

---

1. Jabez Curry, fragment of an article in an unknown newspaper, unknown date, but after 1897, from Curry Papers.
2. Fleming, p. 548.

Then, on January 12, in Talladega, "reluctantly, after almost begging entreaties" from his friends and former constituents, he did speak, advocating its defeat. "This is the only political speech I ever made since the war."[1]

The Conservatives' tactics worked. The constitution was rejected. Although 71,000 voted for it and only 1,000 against, half the eligible voters stayed away from the polls.

Immediately the Radicals charged fraud and moved the debate into the radicalized Congress. Senator Wilson of Massachusetts said it would be unjust to leave Alabama out of the Union since she was one of the strongest states for Radical policies. Then Senator Sherman said it was absolutely necessary to admit Alabama in order to pass the 14th Amendment before the Presidential elections. Mr. Pomeroy of Kansas added that it would be a "cruel thing" to admit other states and to leave Alabama out. Congress admitted Alabama.

Andrew Johnson vetoed the bill, saying: "In the case of Alabama, it violates the plighted faith of Congress by forcing upon that State a constitution which was rejected by the people."[2]

The bill passed both Houses over his veto. It stated that Alabama and the other states had adopted, by large majorities, their constitutions, and as soon as they ratified the 14th Amendment, each would be admitted to representation in the United States Congress.

As we have seen, the same process was repeated with the 14th Amendment. Alabama rejected it; it was illegally passed, anyway, by Congress; and she became a state again in June 1868.

Jabez Curry's Diary

Again, a slight digression. Soon after the war ended, Jabez Curry began to keep a diary. Over the years his entries filled hundreds of pages of small, hardbound appointment books.

For the biographer, diaries are a major source of information and insight into the events, the soul, and thoughts of his subject. Not so with Jabez Curry.

Curry's diary is a study in frustration, aggravation and evasive dead-ends. After reading it, one wonders why he even bothered. It is clearly not designed to be a record of his life that future historians, students, scholars or biographers could use to understand him or his era.

---

1. Jabez Curry, hand-written autobiographical notes, April 1876.
2. *Congressional Globe*, June 25, 1868, pp. 3466 and 3484.

A typical entry reads: "Preached at First Baptist Church." What was the subject? The content? In hundreds of similar notations there is not a clue.

In a rare entry Jabez said: "Preached at 11 a.m. on the sale of liquor by Baptists."

Then there is: "Made a speech to the Georgia Legislature." Obviously, this is very significant. All we get is "well received." The nature, title or focus of his address are condemned to silence. We can surmise that it related to education but that is only because we know something about Curry's life from other sources — that he was there as the General Agent of the Peabody Education Fund, requesting tax money for state-controlled public schools. We would not grasp that if our only source of information was that diary.

Here is one of the few exceptions, but it also is enigmatic. There is no explanation of what Curry is pained and guilt-ridden about: "Wednesday, October 25, 1876: An invitation to lecture before the Young Men's Christian Association at Staunton. This suggests that a great mistake has marred my course. I have spent too much time piecing out other men's work. Persistent attention to one thing, having some definite object, and adhering to it, would have enabled me to accomplish something more substantial and beneficial. I must try and reform."

But, on the other hand, what little real information he does provide clearly gives the negative impression that he is a name-dropping snob. Jabez would much rather tell us of all the important people he dined with than give us a window into his inner life and thoughts.

The only sense of personal pride we can detect is when Jabez tells us about the number of talks that he gave: "During the year 1867 I preached 40 sermons, delivered 42 addresses," and when he proudly counts up the miles that he traveled to fulfill these obligations. This is from the year 1883: "30 January. Visited Chattanooga schools. 31 January. Reached home at 1:30 p.m. Traveled 2,389 miles.... 20 February. Addressed [Florida] legislature. On the 17th, visited schools in St. Augustine. 10 March. Reached Richmond, having traveled 2,272 miles."

One particular entry betrays his evasion about major events in his life. His diary entry for March 27, 1885, informs us that he was offered the biggest position in the world of education: Commissioner of the United States Bureau of Education. His only comment is: "I replied in the negative." It seems incredible. As Commissioner, Curry could control and put in place everything that he believed in. Yet he turned it down. Instead of being overjoyed at the prospect as the fulfillment of his long career, he "replied in the negative." Why? There had to be some major obstacle that he could have revealed in the privacy of his diary. Any chance to understand his reasoning was lost.

Curry Moves to Virginia

In December 1865, Jabez Curry was elected President of Howard College. In April 1868, he resigned. Radical misrule of Alabama made it impossible for him to fulfill his role. "I resigned the Presidency, as the people were too impoverished and the political outlook too discouraging to justify a continuance of efforts for endowment."[1]

Later, he softened the "resignation" to a "leave of absence," but he never returned to Howard in an official capacity.

Jessie Pearl Rice noted that Curry's "strenuous efforts to collect the notes the institution held, had met with discouraging results, and the efforts to arrest the college's downfall seemed unavailing."[2]

Although Jabez never admitted to it in his reminiscences, James Thomas, Mary's father (as suggested before) was instrumental in the transition to the next important phase of his life. Curry was elected Professor of History and English literature at Richmond College in Richmond. As Chairman of the Board of Trustees, Mr. Thomas smoothed the way for his son-in-law.

Curry moved to Virginia with very mixed emotions. "With my family I soon left for Richmond and thus ended a thirty years' residence in Alabama. No man ever had truer nor more devoted friends than honored me with their confidence and it was with reluctance I turned my face away from the State of my boyhood and manhood, which still holds my paramount affection. It seemed unwise to keep my wife and children under Radical misrule and to remain when a generation or more would be needed to recover from the disastrous consequences of the war and hostile legislation."[3]

Jabez described his new life as "Professor Curry." He wrote: "In October 1868 I entered upon my duties as professor and have since acted as Professor of Philosophy and of Constitutional and International Law. My association with the College has been pleasant and, I hope, useful. I like young men and they seem attached to me. My rule is to treat them as gentlemen and to regard me, not as a hard task-master but as a sympathetic friend."[4]

---

1. Jabez Curry, hand-written autobiographical notes, April 1876.
2. B.F. Riley, pp. 314-315.
3. Jabez Curry, *My Educational Life*, hand-written notes, Curry Papers.
4. Ibid.

But, all did not begin smoothly. The journey to Richmond almost ended in tragedy. On April 29 Curry and his family left Marion for Richmond via the Blue Ridge Mountains, Knoxville and Lynchburg. "We reached Richmond on the 3rd of May, leaving Susie and Manly at Mr. Thomas'. Mary and I started to Baltimore to attend the Southern Baptist Convention, the introductory sermon I was prepared to preach according to a previous appointment. On the 6th, between Relay House and Baltimore, some ruffian threw a stone, weighing four pounds, into the coach and struck Mary, fracturing her skull. At first I thought she had been shot with a pistol and did not learn the extent of the injury, until, on arrival at Eutaw House, Dr. M.R. Smith, the eminent surgeon, came and informed me. She did not recover her consciousness until the 9th. We had sympathy from hosts of friends. Dr. Fuller [the minister], Mr. Thomas, the doctor and myself were admitted to the room. The doctor was unremitting in his attentiveness, and to his rare skill I feel that, under Providence, were we indebted for the prolongation of her life. We left, by boat, for Richmond, on the 28th, Dr. Smith kissing his patient as he bade her goodbye. No clue to the perpetrator of the deed was ever discovered."[1]

---

1. Jabez Curry, hand-written autobiographical notes, April 1876.

CHAPTER 6. CURRY'S BACKGROUND: GOING TO ALABAMA

We will pick up the next phase of Jabez Curry's early life where we left off, at the end of *The Early Georgia Years*. "In 1837 my father visited Alabama and bought land in Talladega County, a place called Kelly's Springs, from the number of limestone springs upon it, and paid about 39 dollars per acre. In December of that year, or January of the next, he sent his Negroes, with an overseer, to Alabama to prepare for and plant a crop. He owned a large body of land in Lincoln County [Georgia] and a number of lots in other counties of Georgia. He sold his home place, where he was born and where his parents and my mother and two brothers are buried. Strangers now own the place, and the graveyard, I suspect, is much neglected.

Our starting to Alabama was delayed by the extreme illness of my mother. She was reduced to a skeleton and suffered agony. The use of colonics aggravated the disease and for months her recovery seemed hopeless. My father became so prejudiced against colonics, regarding them as a poison, that he never permitted them to be given to his family and seldom sent for a physician. In May we were able to start, my mother going in a carriage. It was a sad exodus, leaving the old homestead,

Many years later, I revisited my birthplace, but what a change! When my father emigrated he left a mansion, all needful out-houses, a grove of beautiful oaks, a fertilized vegetable garden, a yard glowing with roses and rare flowers, well-bearing orchards of selected fruit, a plantation well fenced and intersected by roads, and everything that characterized a well-to-do Southern home. Forty-six years had wrought a marvelous transformation. Nearly everything on the surface had disappeared, except the dwelling house, and that was in a dilapidated condition. The cultivated fields had been neglected and permitted to grow up in broom and sedge and sassafras and persimmon and pine. Desolation reigned supreme. I came away sick at heart, regretting that I had made the visit, for all the cherished pictures of childhood were dispelled.

"Our caravan, with carriages and wagons and servants and horses, was some time on the road, but the weather being delightful, we enjoyed the camping in tents and the 'lying out o' nights' under the canopying and star-lit heavens. The mountains, as we crossed the Georgia line into what is now Cleburne County, in Alabama, are not very high or commanding, but they were the first I had ever seen and were covered with ferns and grass. At night, the wolves, attracted by the fires, would come near our camp, and their howling excited my youthful imagination and fears.

"When we reached our new home, the Negroes at work in the fields by the road side, where the corn was waist high, abandoned everything and rushed out to meet the long expected ones, giving us a noisy and joyous welcome."[1]

Beauty of Talladega County

"The almost unparalleled beauty of the country, its fertility and healthfulness, the attractive hunting and fishing, the proximity to white settlements, began to attract adventurous emigrants as early as 1832. During the pioneer period, say, for ten years, the migration was brisk and continuous. To those who know the country only as desolated by cruel and improvident husbandry, as intersected by railroads and covered by houses and farms and manufacturing establishments, it is impossible to convey an adequate idea of the loveliness of the Eden. The numerous streams originating in, or fed from, cold springs, were so clear and pure that liquid crystal would be an imperfect simile. In spring and summer the valleys and hill-sides were covered with luxuriant grapes. Strawberries and wild fruit abounded; deer, squirrels, partridges, wild turkeys, wolves and other game were plentiful. Sometimes droves of wild pigeons, thousands and thousands in number, would pass for several days, and where they roosted would break off great branches from the trees. That such a lovely land, such an enchanted earthly paradise should have been scarred, despoiled, impoverished, converted into red, scalded hills and sterile fields by unthrifty farming and stupid, servile labor, seems a folly and a calamity."[2]

---

1. Jabez Curry article in *The Alabama Baptist*, July 1896.
2. Ibid.

Talladega County: Historical Origin

"Colonel Pickett, in his interesting history, gives an account of DeSoto's march through Alabama in 1540. He quotes contemporary authority for the statement that the province of Coosa, covering the counties of Cherokee, Benton, Talladega and Coosa, was widely known to aborigines for its fertility and beauty and that it possessed a delightful climate and abounded in meadows and beautiful rivers, and wild fruit, clambered to the top of the loftiest trees, and the lowest branches laden with delicious grapes. Between the mouths of Talladega and Tallasehatchie creeks was the town of Coosa, the capital of this rich and extensive province. The Spaniards, in their journeying, left a Negro, some hogs and cattle, a brass kettle drum and several shields. In 1798 Colonel Hawkins, then a Creek agent, visited Coosa town. Talladega is an Indian name, and means, as I have often heard, border town. What a pity the sonorous aboriginal words have been subordinated by others, which have neither the body nor significance! Alabama, Tuscalusa, Coosa, Tallapoosa, Oosacala are so much more euphonious than New York, James, Cooper, Fox and Raccoon. The battle fought and won at Talladega by General Jackson on 9 November, 1813, first brought it into prominent notice. The site of the fort was long preserved by tradition and some undestroyed debris.... [In 1832] the county was established. By act approved 3 January, 1833, commissioners were appointed to locate the county site.... The south side of Talladega creek, on the road between Talledega and Mardisville, was chosen."[1]

Frontier vs. Civilized Life

"Tennessee, Georgia and South Carolina furnished the bulk of the immigrants; North Carolina, Virginia and Kentucky contributed a smaller quota. Remoter states and Ireland had their representatives to be fused ultimately into a homogeneous and noble people. The transition from an old state, with its traditions, its fixed habits, its conservatism, its methodical procedure, to a new country, with its unsettledness, its extemporized life, its individuality, its struggle for the survival of the fittest, its strangeness and contrarieties, can hardly be realized by one who has had no such unique experience.... In this formative period were exhibited daring and resolution, tact and energy, self-reliance and executive ability. The strong, the vigorous, the bold, the astute, came to the front. This life evolves remarkable traits unknown in effete society;

---

1. Ibid.

independence, voluntariness, self-protection, mutual help, leadership, ability to meet sudden exigencies, to use most available expedients, to originate a means of livelihood and success. This frontier community was a democracy, and furnished valuable discipline. Rich and poor met on terms of equality. Ancestry counted for little. Pretensions and sham were despised. The dude was unknown. Character, worth, was the stamp which gave currency. Unbounded hospitality was a necessity and a privilege. Neighbors slept in one another's beds, ate at one another's tables. Travelers, deporting themselves well, were always welcome and frequently brought coveted intelligence from those left behind. Those who lived near together assisted in clearing ground, rolling logs, building houses, cradling wheat, shucking corn. Generous succor was constantly given, knowing it would be returned in good measure.... Volney said that America, in a few brief years, had a history correspondent with a millennium in the Old World."[1]

The First Steamboat

"In 1845 the first steamboat was built on the upper Coos, above the falls, and was launched at Greensport to ply from that point to Rome. It was an occasion of much interest; a free barbeque was prepared; thousands assembled to witness the novel spectacle, and as, with flags flying and drums beating, the fastenings were cut away, the consecrating water poured out, the boat cleaved for the first time the clear waters of the river. Those of us who were sufficiently venturesome took our places on the vessel and our shouts of exultation were taken up and re-echoed for many minutes by the thousands who, from the banks, looked with amazement upon the bold experiment.... Through the night and until the day-dawn, many of us danced country dances and Virginia reels and then left for our homes, jaded and weary."[2]

Bad Roads

"In the early days, agriculture was the chief reliance for support and for making money. Cotton, corn, wheat, oats, rye and potatoes were the principle products of the farm. Stores and mills, and carpenters' and blacksmiths' shops were necessary accompaniments. The cotton was hauled in wagons to Wetumpka, or sent down the river on flat-boats, during high water. In the winter the roads were execrable. Several times I accompanied my father's wagon to market. Six mules were needed to draw six or seven bales, and often when the

1. Ibid.
2. Ibid.

driver was belated by the mud he would travel at night to make up his lost time, and I, bearing a torch of pine, would walk before the mules that he might see how to drive. In 1850 John G. Winter constructed a plank road from Wetumpka to Winterboro. It was a great improvement over the dirt road, and it was feared, as he desired, that a rival town to Talladega might be built up. While the road continued it furnished easy communication with the head of navigations, but it was unprofitable to the builders, the bridges became dangerous and after a few years the highway, which excited such hopes and fears, fell into disuse."[1]

Flush Times: Private Currency

"In the flush times of 1837, my father visited Alabama and bought his home at Kelly's Springs. This was a time of shinplasters, of fiat money, when speculation ran high and a thousand wild schemes were eagerly seized for getting rich without work. I have before me specimens of currency issued by corporations and individuals, which without any fixity of value, in the absence of gold or silver and in the mania for making money, furnished a medium of exchange, and had an astonishing circulation. They are printed on very inferior paper and signed in ink by the persons issuing the notes. When torn or worn, they are, in some instances, pasted on a piece of paper and continued on their mission of getting something for nothing. I have one which contains the fragments of two promises to pay put together on one note. It is for fifty cents, numbered 2,080, due to the bearer when the sum of ten dollars is presented and was sent out from 'Warrington, Alabama,' a place unknown to me. One dated Wetumpka, Alabama, February 17, 1838, is signed 'W.B. McCo,' and is a promise to pay the bearer twenty-five cents when the sum of five dollars is presented. Another numbered 187, signed 'I.K.C. McCandass, Chestnut Creek,' no state is mentioned, promises to pay twelve and-a-half cents in current bank bills when the sum amounts to five dollars. Here is another. It is illustrated by a spread eagle. Another, more ambitious, is decorated with a coach and four, full of passengers.... The wider the sphere of circulation, the further these notes traveled from home, the less was the probability of their return and consequently the greater the profit for the free banker."[2]

---

1. Ibid.
2. Ibid.

Flush Times: Silkworm Madness

"We read with some incredulity of the South Sea Bubble, of Law's Mississippi scheme, in 1717-1719, when a sort of madness possessed the whole of the French nation, of the tulip craze in Holland in the 17th century, but in those days was the famous 'morus multicaulis' excitement which spread like a fatal epidemic over the country. Men are easily panic-stricken by fear, or crazed by excitement, or maddened by love of gold, and they were, in this instance, infatuated by speculation and dreamed of sudden and great wealth from the manufacture of silk. Hundreds of acres were planted in mulberry trees. Silk worms were bought, or hatched from the eggs. Rooms in dwelling houses were given up to the worms, which were well supplied with tender and succulent mulberry leaves. When the cocoons were spun, they were carefully preserved and rude attempts were made to unwind and spin the delicate fiber. Visions of riches disappeared as suddenly as they were created. The excitement collapsed. Agriculture and other pursuits were resumed, but not a few lost heavily from foolish investments. Talladega did not escape the contagion, and for several years afterwards a lot east of the Court House was known as the 'morus multicaulis' field."[1]

Franklin College

"In August 1839, my step-brother, David, my full brother, Jackson, and myself, went to the University of Georgia, then called Franklin College, located in Athens, Georgia. It would have been much better for me to have gone to the University of Alabama, but the institution had troubles and my father established an attachment for his native State. David and Jackson entered the sophomore class. I, because of insufficient age, was put in the freshman class, and very properly. Although, on my examination, I was declared capable of entering a higher class. A great mistake had been made in my previous education. Instead of studying English branches and learning grammar, arithmetic, geography, I was, at an early age, put to learning Latin and Greek to the neglect of more important elementary studies.

All three of us entered the Phi Kappa Society, because students from Alabama had generally been members of it. There was a noble rivalry between that society and the Demosthenians. They met in their respective halls on Saturday mornings and kept their proceedings entirely secret. The debates were conducted with much spirit. Through my college course I gave much attention

---

1. Ibid.

to my debating society and whatever success I have achieved as a speaker is very largely attributable to my training in this school. Linton Stephens [brother of Alexander Stephens, the Confederate Vice President], who became prominent as a lawyer and judge in Georgia, and LaFayette Lamar, my cousin of early poetic promise, who died in camp the first year of the War Between the States, entered college the same day I did and for four years we were classmates and warm friends. Alexander Stephens, who supported his brother, Linton, in College, used to come to Athens to see him and thus I became acquainted with this distinguished man. He was then a small, tallow-faced, effeminate-looking man, apparently near the grave, and yet he still lives [1876], having served his country with conspicuous and unimpeached dignity.

"The physical man was in marked contrast to the intellectual; for there was scarcely flesh enough on his bones to cover his brilliant genius ... [yet] he was capable, at the bar, on the stump, in legislative halls, of as much work as the most athletic and robust. In the years 1839-1843, I saw him several times in Athens.... Going one day into Linton's room in the 'old college' building, I was introduced to 'Brother Aleck,' who was lying on the bed, and most unprepossessing, except as his eyes shone with an unusual luster.... While he was in Federal and Confederate Congresses, Vice President of the Confederacy and Governor of Georgia, I saw him often, and because of my association and friendship with Linton, he treated me with much consideration and kindness."[1]

The Curriculum

"The curriculum was of the old-fashioned kind: Latin, Greek, and mathematics predominating, with very little science and the teaching was chiefly of the text book order. Professor C.F. McCoy, one of the best teachers I ever knew, 'kicked out of the trees' and strove with some success to make his department of mathematics and mechanical philosophy to conform to what is now universally described as a liberal education. English was ignored....

"When at college, I wrote for the newspapers, and I have kept up the habit ever since, preferring to conceal my identity, under assumed names, or under editorial anonymity. To magazines, like the *Galaxy*, *Independent*, *Forum*, *New Englander*, *Popular Science Monthly*, *Review of Reviews*, *Educational Review*, *Conservative Review*, etc., I have contributed not seldom.

---

1. Jabez Curry, hand-written autobiographical notes, April 1876.

"Looking back from present surroundings and the great progress of college education and all teaching, I am constrained to say, with undiminished loyalty for my Alma Mater, that, McCoy excepted, the president and professors, in teaching power, were not up to modern standards. Nevertheless, the instruction was of a solid character, the relation between faculty and students was most pleasant, and the four years of college were among the most pleasant and profitable of a long life."[1]

Senior Year

"In August 1842 my brother, Jackson, graduated. We had been room-mates since we entered college and now as my senior year had begun, it was necessary for me to 'study harder.' I took no room-mates as to be alone.

"Usually at commencement there were two days for original speeches. One for seniors, and the other for the Honor graduates. Eight or ten of the best seniors, those who 'stood' best in their class, were selected by the faculty as Senior Orators. I was one of the number and delivered a highly eulogistic address on Andrew Jackson."[2]

Vacation: Passing the Future Atlanta

"Our vacations were from 1 November to the 10th of January. As we had gone to Athens by private conveyance, so we returned home, with this difference. Father accompanied us in his carriage at first. Ever afterwards we came and went on horseback. An old Negro man, Ben, would ride one horse and led two others from Talladega to Athens, about 180 miles. Five days were consumed in traveling the distance, and we had our regular stopping places. Our journey lay over the very spot now occupied by Atlanta. When I first passed, there was not a house, nor the hope of a village. The Rail Road, being built to that point, a village sprang up, which was called Marthasville, after a daughter of the governor. During the war, while a soldier, I was encamped where I had several times traveled when a college boy."[3]

First Social Experience With Women

"During the three years I had been in college, I had never visited a lady. I was the least boy in the college, hardly weighing one hundred pounds and was

---

1. Jabez Curry, *My Educational Life*, hand-written notes, in Curry Papers.
2. Ibid.
3. Jabez Curry, hand-written autobiographical notes, April 1876.

exceptionally modest and timid. I was 'afraid' of female society. I had no sister, grew up unfortunately among boys and lacked the ease and freedom and self-poise of manner and ability to converse on ordinary topics, which are such a necessary part of a boy's education. My own painful embarrassment, which has never left me, taught me a lesson and now I urge young men, for many reasons, to visit the opposite sex. My cousin, LaFayette Lamar and a class-mate, Thomas W. White, now a prominent lawyer in Mississippi, begged me to accompany them in some of their visits. I resolved to go, and for days before the time arrived I thought about it, and it weighed on me like a night-mare. It seems ludicrous now to recall my feelings but I have since gone into battle with far less terror and agitation than I experienced in anticipation of a visit. The President of the college, Dr. Alonzo Church, had some beautiful and accomplished daughters, who were great favorites. I knew them very well by sight, saw them nearly every day and determined to begin with them. The appointed night came. Urging my cousin not to stay to a late hour and to help me, in the event of my failing in conversation, I 'crossed the Rubicon.' The ladies, quite skilled in drawing out young men, with a kindness which I gratefully record now, so helped me that an hour passed very agreeably and I have never been called upon to pass through such an ordeal since."[1]

Presidential Politics

"In 1840 [while at Franklin College] the Presidential election was a very excited one, between Martin Van Buren, the Democratic candidate, and William Henry Harrison, the Whig candidate. It was the campaign in which the Whigs had log-cabins, raccoon-skins, red pepper and hard cider as symbols of the rustic manners and honesty of their candidate in contrast with 'Slippery Van' and his extravagance. Immense party gatherings were held in all parts of the country and prominent orators on both sides made inflammatory stump speeches. In the town-hall in Athens, on every Saturday afternoon, there were speeches before a club, by some of the ablest men in the state. On the Democratic side were William L. Mitchell, Hopkins Holsey, Junius Hillyer, Howell Cobb and Henry R. Jackson. The two latter young men, while on the Democratic side, Judge Charles Dougherty stood alone and was more than a match for all his antagonists. Mr. Cobb was a fluent and earnest speaker and a very popular man. He afterwards was a representative in Congress, Speaker of the House, Governor of Georgia,

---

1. Ibid.

Secretary of the Treasury, President of the Provisional Congress of the Confederate States, and a general in the Confederate Army. My father, being a Democrat, I became one also and began this year to read the newspapers."[1]

The "Stump" Necessary for a Republic

"One wishes for a return of those old political campaigns, when living issues were discussed before the people, who thus were instructed as to principles and measures and had an intelligent comprehension as to the character and ends of our complex government. No such school of political science, no such method of education in civics, is to be found at the present day. I find in Horace Greeley's estimate of Lincoln, this confirmation of my opinion: 'In the absence of the stump I doubt the feasibility of maintaining institutions more than nominally republican; but the stump brings the people face to face with their rulers and aspirants to rule; compels an exhibition and scrutiny of accounts and projects, and makes almost every citizen, however heedless and selfish, an arbiter in our political controversies, enlisting his interest and arousing his patriotism. The American stump fills the place of the coup d'etat, and the Spanish American pronunciamento. It is, in an eminently practical sense, the conservator of American liberty, and the antidote to official tyranny and corruption.' "[2]

Going to Dane Law School

"When I returned to college after my winter vacation, I took lodgings in town, to live more comfortably and to have more complete command of my time. I must have averaged 12 to 14 hours a day in study. In consequence of my deficiency in mathematics, I was fearful I could not graduate. To fail after being a senior orator would have been a disgrace. I found time to visit the ladies every week, the two young men mentioned, usually going with me. As intensely as I studied, the last six months of college life were by far the most pleasant of the whole four years. When the final examination was over, my diploma was obtained quite easily. In the classics I was among the best. In Political Economy, Mental Philosophy, Geology and in studies not requiring much mathematics, I had no trouble. By intense application, my memory was so quickened that I could recite ten or fifteen pages almost verbatim. Now, from the want of practice, my memory for words is very faulty. In the distribution of honors, I was again appointed an oration. I chose my subject,

---

1. Ibid.
2. Jabez Curry, *Reminiscences of Youth*, hand-written notes.

'No more, no more, oh, never more oh rue,
The freshness of the heart shall fall like dew,'
two lines from Bryan's *Don Juan*. I do not remember a line of the speech....

"Now, at 18, I was a graduate, with an A.B.; had a diploma, and what was I to do?

"My father wanted me to go to Heidelberg, Germany, to study law. Why his wishes were not carried out I do not know. I have often regretted that they were not. He decided to send me to Harvard College in Massachusetts. In September I started out. Went by private conveyance to Athens, Georgia, and there took the rail-road for a long journey by myself. I had no experience as a traveler and in those days, traveling was not as easy and common as now. [I arrived in] Augusta, where the rail-ways in adjacent States were not permitted to connect; thence to Charleston on rails built on trestle work; thence by steamboat to Wilmington, by rail to Portsmouth, by boat to Baltimore, by rail to New York, and by boat and rail to Boston. In New York I tarried two days in 'City Hotel,' between Astor and the Battery, and that I remember because it was the first public place I had seen where ice cream was furnished to guests at dinner. From Boston to Cambridge, I was conveyed in an omnibus which was the only mode of public conveyance during my college days in Harvard....

"In a day or two I matriculated in Dane Law School. Josiah Quincy, as President of Harvard, was President of all the schools. Joseph Story, a Justice of the Supreme Court of the United States, and Simon Greenleaf, were the professors. Judge Story was a genial, cheerful, cordial man, full of humor and anecdotes, very fond of the boys and told us in his lectures charming incidents about such lawyers as Webster and Mason and William Pinkney and Sargent and Binney. Simon Greenleaf, a native of Maine, was chosen on recommendation of Judge Story. Without the affluence of learning or oratic rhetoric of Judge Story, he was a more accurate lawyer, with keener logical power....

"Judge Story was genial, courteous, affectionate to 'my boys,' as he called them and they loved him and enjoyed his talks, which abounded in anecdote, biographical incident, accounts of great cases and lawyers and in what could not fail to give the students the loftiest ideals of professional attainment and integrity. Professor Greenleaf, unlike his associate, had no poetry, no fancy, had never traveled, but he was a profound lawyer and had great capacity for luminous exposition. Besides law lectures the students had free use of the libraries, could attend the college lectures.... And sometimes Judge Story invited counsel to argue their cases before him in the Law Library, that the students might have the privilege of hearing them."

Rutherford B. Hayes

"Among my fellow students was Rutherford B. Hayes [President of the United States, 1876-1880], three or four years my senior, boarded in the same house with myself and we were quite intimate. He was a 'good fellow,' studious and upright, but not specially promising, too human in appearance; my prospects for the Presidency were equal to his. But he was vain and ambitious. I went with him in 1844 to two town meetings where he made his debut as a political speaker, and stimulated and helped him although we did not agree in politics."

Abolitionists

"The Abolitionists, at that time, were a noisy and fanatical faction, with more strength in Massachusetts than in any part of the Union, but were despised there as half-crazy and fanatical. Wendell Philips and others and some women were the leaders. I attended, at Concord, an Abolitionist meeting, hired a buggy and drove that distance to attend an anti-slavery meeting. It was held in a church and very few were present. In 1844 the Abolitionist sentiment took form and organization under the name of the 'Liberty Party' and I heard James G. Binney, the candidate of the party for the Presidency, deliver an address to not more than 200 people in Faneuil Hall. Times have changed since I was a law student."

National Politics: 1844

"1844 was a year of violent political excitement: the Democratic and Whig parties were then in existence and had their favorites. Democrats were divided in opinion. At the National Party Convention, Polk of Dallas was nominated and the party cry was 'Polk, Dallas and Texas.' The annexation of Texas was the chief party issue, although the tariff and the boundary of Oregon entered into the caucuses. Webster and Clay were the favorites among the Whigs. Henry Clay and Theodore Frelinghaysen were nominated.

"Prior to the Whig nominations, I heard S.S. Prentice of Memphis, one of the most eloquent men in America, make a speech to a packed audience in Feneuil Hall. It was one of the most thrilling specimens of platform oratory I ever listened to, and he carried his audience, at pleasure. In the same hall, I heard Vice President Richard M. Johnson, a weak but honest man, whose claim to popular support seemed to be based on a red jacket and the fact, of doubtful historical accuracy, that he killed Tecumsah [the great Indian leader]."[1]

Horace Mann

"When in Cambridge there occurred the celebrated controversy, since historic, between Horace Mann and the 'Thirty-One Boston Teachers.' Mann's earnest enthusiasm, democratic ideas, fired my young mind and heart and since I have been an enthusiastic and consistent advocate of universal education."[2]

Graduates Law School; Meets Calhoun

"Having received the degree of LLD from Harvard College, I left Cambridge in February 1845 and stopped in Washington City on my way home. Mr. Lewis was there, one of the senators from Alabama. He was the heaviest man I ever saw and when he would go from his boarding house to the Senate chamber, the little boys would follow him. He, being a friend of my father, had written for me to stop with him and I enjoyed his instructive companionship for a week. The annexation of Texas was under discussion in the Senate and I heard a number of speeches.... Mr. Lewis took me with him to see John C. Calhoun, who was then Secretary of State.... Mr. Calhoun was a brilliant talker; rapid, suggestive, profound. He received me very kindly as he was very fond of the company of young men. Mr. Calhoun was giving a sketch of Mr. Van Buren and the tariff question. This was my only interview with Mr. Calhoun and I prize the recollection of it. In all my political career I was an adherent of the Calhoun school of politics [the legitimacy of State Sovereignty, secession, nullification of despotic Federal laws]. I was very familiar with his writings and I now regard him as no whit inferior to Aristotle, Burke, Bismarck, Cavour, or any statesman or publicist that ever lived."[3]

Amusing Tale of Senator Colquitt

"In going home I traveled as far as the interior of Georgia with Walter Colquitt, a senator from that State, and two of his daughters. We traveled by rail to Covington in Georgia and then took a stage, crowded with passengers. Some 'Yankees' at night spoke about Georgia's inferiority and advocated a protective tariff. Colquitt, covered up in a corner, unable to sleep because of the talking,

---

1. The last four sections from hand-written autobiographical notes, April 1876.
2. Jabez Curry, *My Educational Life*, hand-written notes.
3. Rice, p. 15-16.

without raising up his head, began to ask questions of his Yankee companions by the Socratic method, compelling them to yield their positions. Then, until he arrived at his destination, he poured forth anecdotes to the confusion and consternation of the travelers. When he left, the Yankees were quick to inquire who their antagonist was, and when I informed them, with undisguised satisfaction, one of them said, 'No wonder he used us up so completely.' "[1]

Curry, as a Lawyer, Works for Mr. Rice

"After a short respite, I went to Talladega town and entered the law office of Samuel Rice, Esquire. Mr. Rice, a native of South Carolina, was remarkable for his intellectual acuteness and vigor and his familiarity with decisions. He was one of the best lawyers in the Court-House I ever knew. He was an editor, a member of the legislature, a Judge of the [State] Supreme Court, and an active politician. In 1845 he was nominated by the Democrats of his district for Congress but was defeated by General Felix McConnel, the incumbent, who ran as an Independent. The law office was under the printing office of the 'Democratic Watchtower,' and I wrote much for the paper. I learned to set type and correct proof. This practical knowledge of printing and proof-reading has been very much of value to me....

"Samuel Rice early identified himself with politics.... He was, however, at his best in the Court House, examining witnesses, watching his skilled antagonists, and making the worse appear the better side. He had an inexhaustible fertility of intellectual resources, and at the most unexpected time, when an adversary was sure of victory, and despair settled on the countenance of client and associate, and all seemed lost, he would spring points; ingenious, subtle, plausible, and reinstate his case before judge and jury. Quickness and versatility of intellect, acuteness of perception, fecundity of suggestion, unflagging purpose, hopefulness, invincibility, were his characteristic mental traits.... He did not make a good judge. He frankly conceded his want of judicial equipoise, and hence abandoned his place on the Supreme Court bench for a more congenial element. Deluded by his own enthusiasm and hopefulness, he was not sagacious in reading the feelings of the masses, often miscalculated and was taken by surprise by the temper of the people and the movements of public opinion. His many vicissitudes did not sour his disposition, or awaken malevolence, nor provoke revenge. Obvious faults he had, but, when a law student in his office,

---

1. Jabez Curry, hand-written autobiographical notes, April 1876.

and sitting at his table as an inmate of his home, I had unusual opportunities for studying his motives and character, and I learned to admire him for his ability and nobleness of soul, and to love him for his many and great virtues. In some respects I can truly say that Judge Rice was one of the most remarkable men I ever knew."[1]

Curry Volunteers for Mexican War

"Early in 1846, it became apparent that the adjustment of the boundary line between Texas and Mexico would lead to war. A fierce controversy arose between the Whigs and Democratic parties as to the responsibility for the war. The Act of Congress for raising troops said that war existed by acts of Mexico. The territory between the Sabine and Rio Grande rivers was in dispute and the United States, having annexed Texas, determined to push the boundary line to the extreme limit. The war was popular and volunteers were numerous and enthusiastic.

"In May 1846 a company of infantry was raised in Talladega County, Jacob Shelly, Captain. I was appointed 2nd Sergeant. Several meetings were held and I made a number of speeches. In one I warned the people against the folly of believing that Mexico could be conquered in a few months, as the Spanish were proverbially obstinate and resolute. We marched from Talladega to Wetumpka where we embarked on a boat for Mobile. At various points receptions were given and I had to make speeches. We went into camp at Mobile. After annoying delays we were, with other companies, organized into a regiment and mustered in for six months. Then the War Department refused to accept for that period of service and we were discharged. The bulk of the company re-enlisted for twelve months. It being uncertain when the troops would be ordered to the scene of the war, five of us, in a most fool-hardy spirit, resolved to go to the army, on our own charges. A small schooner, the *Duane*, a discharged revenue cutter, for unseaworthiness, was in the port of Mobile, loading with supplies to be sold; Peters, the Captain, Ingersoll, mate, and another man, were owners. There was only one sailor. We engaged passage and shipped for Point Isabel, against advice and protest from friends. To us it seemed a dashing, gallant thing. We enjoyed the anticipation, the frolic. The second day out I became sick and so continued for twelve days. Two days we were becalmed and under a hot, vertical sun we fished and read and played cards and indulged in day dreams. Then came a terrible

---

1. Jabez Curry article in *Alabama Baptist* newspaper, July, 1896.

storm, the worst I ever saw and our frail barque seemed every moment, as if it would sink. The Captain was skilled. When we reached the bar at Point Isabel, the vessel leaked rapidly and the pumps were used incessantly. By means of a pilot boat, to get into, we ran the risk of being drowned, we were, without our luggage, transported to shore. We bid a ready adieu to the *Duane*, which two days afterwards, sank in the harbor. The day after landing we made our way to the regiment of Texas Rangers. We attached ourselves to a company commanded by a Captain Acklare. We were not formally mustered into service. For the 4th of July there was a celebration. The minister from Texas to France made a speech and so did I. We remained in camp a week or more when Cunningham [one of Curry's companions from Alabama] became dangerously ill and was ordered to be sent home. An attendant being required, as I was the youngest and very feeble, I was selected and unwillingly I became the companion of the sick, hoping however to return to Mexico. By steamer, we went to Galveston and to New Orleans. The Captain, Mate and Clerk were constant in their kind attention to Cunningham, greatly relieving me, as I was feeble from sickness. From New Orleans we went by boat to Mobile, where we were transferred to a boat for Wetumpka. On the Alabama River Cunningham improved rapidly. From Wetumpka I carried him to Talladega in a spring wagon, delivering him to his friends. Having no opportunity to return I resumed the reading of the law in the office of Samuel Rice and during the year, after a long and severe examination by the Honorable George W. Stone, a Circuit Judge, I was admitted to the bar with all the privileges and duties of a lawyer."[1]

---

1. Jabez Curry, *A Soldier's Life*, hand-written autobiographical notes, Curry Papers.

CHAPTER 7. SOUTHERN PREACHING AS GUERRILLA WAR

By the terms of his Presidential pardon, Jabez Curry could not enter politics or speak about the issues related to the war. But he was still a fiery advocate for the classic ideals of the South.

Fortunately, while he was still living in Alabama, his connections with the Baptist community allowed him to become President of Howard College, a Baptist school. Before moving to Virginia and finding renewed opportunities there, Curry realized that he could make a living and have the opportunity to exhort his listeners, as he had in his political career, by studying for the ministry. He became Reverend Curry and continued the struggle in a covert way. He spoke about the issues of the South by parable, seeming to speak about religion while actually keeping the old ideas alive.

This was his plan; Jabez Curry admitted that he was not a very religious man: "In early life, my parents were not Christians, although moral, upright and regular attendants in religious worship. The only denominations in the lower part of Lincoln County were Methodists and Baptists. I remember to have heard George F. Pierce, the Bishop, when he was a young man. The first missionary sermon I ever heard was at 'Double Branches' meeting house. It was in the week, drew a large audience, and produced a profound impression. The Baptist preachers I remember were Adams, a colored man, who preached to white people, Harris and John West. The last was often at my father's. My father's house was always a welcome and hospitable home for all preachers. There were no Sunday schools near me, when I was young. In fact, I never was a member of a Sunday school until I was married. In my youth, I had no distinctive religious convictions. My sensibilities and emotions were sometimes awakened but were physical excitements and had no religious basis. All my life I was outwardly moral. I never uttered an oath and never gambled, although I learned to play cards when I was eight or nine years old. When at college, I attended church more because it was a college regulation and to see the girls, than for any other purpose.... Of the Bible, I was stupidly ignorant. During college, I had, as most boys have, at some point in their lives, skeptical notions, but I was afraid of them, and deliberately buried, without reading, Paine's *Age of Reason*, which a class-mate gave to me.

"When at law school I had no conviction of sin or desires for salvation. After my return from the Mexican War there was a protracted meeting at Kelly's Springs Lebanon Church, and my father was baptized. His baptism made a deep impression on me. During the meeting I was admitted into the church and was baptized. I have often wondered whether I committed an error. If I am a Christian, I can fix no precise date when I realized my acceptance. I have never had a rapturous experience, and to this day, with humiliation, record it, I have never had any special satisfaction in partaking of the Lord's Supper. I know the depravity of my heart, the need of regeneration, my utter inability to change my own heart and character. I believe the Bible, the atonement of Christ, its all suffi-ciency and rely simply on Christ's work and grace for salvation. I find most con-tentment in working for my Master, although I am sure that there is no certainness as procuring salvation, in any human righteousness. I have often wished and prayed for the experiences that some Christians have, but they have been denied me, or possibly, by unbelief, I have denied them to myself....

"I taught Sunday schools, made missionary and other religious addresses, conducted prayer meetings and sometimes delivered what are called exhorta-tions. I may have been called an active lay member. Once, by my church, I was chosen Deacon and declined. During the war, while in command of my regiment, I sometimes, in the absence of the chaplain, or in default of one, addressed my men on practical religion.

"In the summer of 1865, at Refuge Church in Talladega County, the pastor induced me to preach my first regular sermon. In August and September I aided L.L.D. Russroe, my pastor, in a meeting in Talladega town. All these meetings were highly successful.

"On the 27th of January 1866, I was examined by a Presbytery, with a view to ordination and on Sunday, the 28th, was solemnly set apart for the ministry. I regret that I yielded to the persuasions of others and consented to the ordination. As a layman, my preaching would have been more in accordance with my convictions and probably more effective. I had preached without being licensed or ordained and do not see that Church authorization or imposition of hands gave any additional authority or grace.... I have no inclinations or conviction that it was my duty to become exclusively a preacher. At times I have to preach and I am profoundly convinced that sacerdotal ideas connected with the ministry or preaching have been productive of untold evil."[1]

In 1866, his first year as a Baptist minister, Jabez Curry delivered 119 sermons, taught Sunday school and made speeches at religious associations and conventions. One year later he gave 150 sermons and addresses. But, was he preaching about God and salvation or "The Lost Cause" by allegory?

Fusing England's Church and State, or the South's?

Curry often wrote and spoke about the painful history of the Baptists in England and colonial America. Beginning in the 1600s the British government fused with the Anglican Church and "established" it as the Church of England, the only official body.

The situation that Curry depicted paralleled the State religion created by Washington in the former Confederacy. The carpetbaggers held the dream that Reconstruction would impregnate the South with Northern civilization. They enlisted the brute force of the Freedmen's Bureau to actualize this dream. Its commissioner, General Oliver Otis Howard, ordered the confiscation of Southern churches and the arrest of their ministers as "traitors." Northern ministers were installed as bayonets kept the parishioners and clergy at bay.

When Congress authorized half-a-million dollars to the Freedmen's Bureau for schools, including their rental and repair, this allowed General Howard to subsidize church schools and all religious endeavors, including ministers' salaries. This led to Federal policy becoming church dogma and church officials becoming Freedmen's Bureau employees. Soon they "passed beyond the common ranks of the Bureau's administrative structure to reach stations of power."[2]

This meant that many Northern clergymen "have become incurable Radicals.... They have incorporated social dogmas and political tests into their church creeds."[3]

---

1. Jabez Curry, hand-written autobiographical notes, April 1876.
2. Ralph Morrow, *Northern Methodism and Reconstruction* (East Lansing: Michigan State University Press, 1956), p. 154.
3. Fleming, p. 637.

And "every innovation of the Executive [the President] or Congress was adopted as ... a new article of religious faith."[1]

All this was unconstitutional. It defied the ban against fusing church and state. It turned churches into governmental bureaucracies.

Jabez Curry, as a Southern clergyman, desperately wanted to address these issues but the terms of his pardon prevented it. Then, ingeniously, he found a way. He wrote two books. In *Establishment and Disestablishment*, he detailed the history of the Christian religion and its entrapment with civil government, from its earliest roots in the Roman Empire.

In *Struggles and Triumphs of Virginia Baptists*, Curry focused on religious persecutions in colonial Virginia and how the Baptists severed their symbiotic relations with Britain. Curry was describing crimes of centuries before but they were the same horrors that currently afflicted the South. His examples of how colonial Virginia broke its official ties to the State provided a model of how the South could do the same.

The State As Church

In *Establishment and Disestablishment*, Curry said: "The establishment of a church means the adoption of the religion of that church as the State religion, securing the reception and upholding of its doctrines and forms, enforcing its pre-eminence and support by the power of the State. To the 'Thirty-Nine Articles' was prefixed a declaration of the King as Supreme Head and Governor of the Church, 'requiring all our loving subjects to continue in the uniform profession thereof, and prohibiting the least difference from the said articles.' The formerly universal practice of uniting Church and State in so-called Christian nations was borrowed from the practice of pagan people, whose religions were so incorporated with the civil government that not infrequently civil and religious were united in the same person. The Roman Emperor was the supreme pontiff, the gods were national, and the priests were the servants of the State. The patriarchs of biblical record were priests and rulers. In the Mosaic Dispensation there was, of course, no Christian Church; Christianity not being a prolongation or ecclesiastical succession of Judaism, but Israel was a theocracy, and judges and kings performed both civil and religious functions. From this Old Covenant fact or practice, it was not strange that under the New Covenant there

---

1. Henry C. Dean, *Crimes of the Civil War* (Baltimore: J. Wesley Smith and Brother, 1869), p. 178.

should be a tendency to imitate and adopt what had been, even though under an entirely different system, the divine sanction."

Early Church Fuses with Roman Empire

"In the earliest periods of Christianity, the power, authority, and influence were in the hands of believers, in the membership of local churches. No separation had taken place between this Christian government and the Christian people. Subsequently the original constitution of the primitive churches was lost sight of. The simplicity was corrupted by a corporation, by a hierarchy, by a long gradation of ecclesiastical dignitaries and powers, and by the alliance with civil governments. The first alliance between the government of religion, of the priesthood, of an ecclesiastical society, and the Empire was probably for their mutual benefit. 'In her weakness, the Church,' says Guizot, 'sheltered herself under the absolute power of the Roman emperors, and afterward called upon the barbarian kings to enter into the same relations with the Church which had existed between her and the Roman Empire."

Roman Empire Controls Christian Church

"It was a fundamental maxim of the Roman constitution that the care of religion was the right as well as the duty of the civil magistrate. 'After Constantine's conversion, the emperor still continued,' says Gibbon, 'to exercise supreme jurisdiction over the ecclesiastical order,' and the sixteenth book of the Theodosian code represents, under a variety of titles, the authority assumed in the government of the church.... Subsequently, the [Roman] hierarchy, in its strength, laid claim to absolute power, to the right of coercion, to the right of restraining and punishing as sins, individual reason and judgment, to the principle of the imperative transmission of its doctrines, to governing human thought, human liberty."[1]

Clergy Become Part of Government

This comment by Curry describes precisely what occurred during Reconstruction where the Northern religious leaders became carpetbag governors and part of the demagogic theocracy in the South: "The Churchmen [in Rome] became statesmen, the rulers, the administrators, the jurists, diplomats, and even

---

1. Last three sections, J.L.M. Curry, *Establishment and Disestablishment; Progress of Soul Liberty in the United States* (Philadelphia: American Baptist Publication Society, 1889), pp. 4-5, 6-7, 7-8.

the warriors of stormy days. The spiritual order, comprised largely the intelligence of the age, every possible development of the human mind; all the sciences centered in theology, and naturally enough the spiritual power was led to arrogate to itself the general government of the world."

Reformation Continues Fusion of Church and State

"When the Reformation occurred and people and rulers successfully revolted against the usurpations and corruptions of the See of Rome, the reformers unfortunately stopped short of New Testament doctrines and requirements and the countries which renounced the authority of Rome committed the fatal error of substituting something in lieu of that domination or supremacy which the Pope had exercised. The authority denied to Rome was arrogated by Protestant governments and religious organizations, and alliances were formed in several countries in Europe with Protestant churches.

The Erastian theory that Church and State are only two aspects of the same body politic prevailed for centuries. Heresy was made a crime against the State, and punishable as other crimes by the civil authorities."

The Act of Uniformity

The following parallels that which occurred in the Reconstruction South where, under military compulsion, the edicts of the Radical Congress had to be incorporated into Southern sermons. "The famous Act of Uniformity of Elizabeth I is thus described by a clergyman of the Church of England: 'On Midsummer Day in 1560, the 12,000 clergy of the Church of England should, at the sole bidding of the State and against the solemn protest of all their bishops, cease to worship God and minister the sacraments of Christ in every cathedral and parish church of England and Wales, after the manner and according to the forms by which they and their predecessors had worshipped God and administered His holy sacraments for nigh a thousand years.' ... I cannot imagine what possibly could have conceived or invented by the wit of man a more effectual means for making the Church of England, as to her corporate life, thenceforward the creature and absolute bond-slave of the State."

The Thirty-Nine Articles of the Book of Prayer

This is another parable of how the Radical Congress mandated sermons for the Southern churches, including special prayers for Ulysses S. Grant, who was hated throughout the South. "At the period when the work of the Church of England's creation was completed, parliament, in the Act of Uniformity of Elizabeth, instituted thirty-nine articles of religion, and put together a Book of Common Prayer. Precisely in the same way, as naturally and as regularly, without any innovation or breach of practice, the Parliament may, if it so chooses, make the Articles either thirty or forty, and remodel the Liturgy according to its pleasure. It may develop a new doctrine exactly as the Roman Catholic Church is in the habit of doing, and that doctrine would be as much a part of the Church of England as any doctrine now contained in its confessions of faith."[1]

1664 Seditious Conventicles

This law, to suppress sedition, inflicted on all persons, "over sixteen years of age, present at any religious meeting of five or more persons in any other manner than is allowed by the practice of the Church of England, a penalty of three months imprisonment for the first offense, of six months for the second, and seven years transportation [deportation] for the third. If the offender returned, he was doomed to death. The act was rigidly enforced, and filled the jails with ministers and laity."

This had its counterpart in the "Enforcement Acts," under President Grant, where a gathering of three or more people constituted a conspiracy, with imprisonment or death the consequence.

Loyalty Oaths: Rebellion Illegal

As in the defeated South, "the Convicle Act did not satisfy the cruel and intolerant purposes. In 1665, all persons in holy orders, who had not subscribed to the act of Uniformity, were required to take an oath that it was not lawful, under any pretense, to take arms against the king, and that they would not make any endeavor to alter the government in Church or State. Those who refused were prohibited from teaching in schools, or coming within five miles of any city, corporate town, or borough sending members to Parliament.... Of the hardships and sufferings inflicted upon Nonconformists, few in these days have the faintest conception. Malignant ingenuity could hardly go further; the persecution was wanton and enforced with merciless rigor."[2]

---

1. Last four sections, Ibid. pp. 8, 9, 13-14, 16-17.
2. Last two sections, Ibid., pp. 19, 19-20.

Virginia Wins Back Religious Freedom

This presents how the Reconstruction South could regain its freedom back through the courts: "Virginia may be considered the great battle ground for religious freedom in the last quarter of the last century. The initiative was taken in the county of Hanover in 1763, in a suit brought by Reverend Mr. Maury for damages for withholding the payment in tobacco, due, under his claim of support for the clergy of the established church. Patrick Henry pleaded the cause of the defendant. The jury gave barely nominal damages, and the victory was complete in this first resistance to the Establishment. In 1768 some Baptist preachers were imprisoned in Spottsylvania County for preaching the gospel. Patrick Henry, by his marvelous eloquence, secured their release."

Religious and Loyalty Tests are Valueless

"The Constitution, ratified by the States and accepted as the supreme law of the land, declares in Article VI. No. 3, that 'no religious test shall ever be required as a qualification to any office or public trust under the United States.' [It] ... 'excludes the establishment of any particular church or denomination as the national religion.' It antagonizes unequivocally the old despotic and intol-erant principle of excluding by religious tests, classes of persons from public trusts. Distinct and decided as was this declaration in opposition to persecution by disabilities, it did not satisfy the jealousy and fears of the friends and advo-cates of religious liberty.... In Massachusetts it was objected that the Consti-tution did not recognize the existence of God, and provided no religious tests for Federal offices. One Amos Singletary declared it to be scandalous that a Papist or an infidel should be as eligible to office as a Christian. The preachers had more liberality and better understanding of the teachings of Christ. Reverend Daniel Shute replied that no conceivable advantage could result from a religious test. Reverend Philip Payson said: 'Human tribunals for the consciences of men are impious encroachments upon the prerogatives of God.' Reverend Isaac Backus said: 'In reason and in Holy Scripture religion is ever a matter between God and the individual; the imposing of religious tests hath been the greatest single engine of tyranny in the world.' "[1]

These comments also express the futility of the loyalty oaths for Southern clergy and citizens at the end of the war, which excluded tens of thousands of men from their legitimate religious or public stations.

---

1. Last two sections, Ibid., pp. 53, 69-70.

The New Testament; Parable of State Sovereignty

Jabez Curry, in another book, *Protestantism: How Far A Failure?*, used biblical principles to show the immutable truths inherent in state sovereignty, which had been crushed out by the results of the war. "Looking exclusively to the Scriptures, it is almost impossible not to see that the primitive churches were local, not national bodies, independent of one another, especially spiritual, composed only of 'believers,' 'saints,' 'the saved,' and invested with all the powers and functions of self-controlling bodies. In the nature of things, there can be no continuous history, no succession of organization or government. A church organized yesterday on New Testament principles of membership, is as true a church of Christ as that at Antioch."[1]

New Testament as "Strict Construction" of Constitution

"The rules and doctrines, the requirements and ordinances, as embodied in the New Testament, are complete. Nothing is to be added or subtracted. The God-given and apostle-practiced example is conclusive. No subsequent supposed exigency justifies a departure. Ages have added, can add, nothing to its completeness. The principle was not germinal for future development; nor imperfect, to be supplemented by human wisdom, but all-perfect and all-wise, adapted to every generation of society. An examination of the Acts of the Apostles and Epistles, reveals the apostolic churches perfect in their offices, membership, organization, ordinances, and duties."[2]

Established Church Creates Dissolute Clergy

The following sketch of colonial Virginia also parallels the Reconstruction South, where State, Army and Church merged and where Northern clergymen became corrupted with power as carpetbag governors and this led to money-madness: "Popular displeasure was increased by the notoriously inconsistent and dissolute lives of many of the clergy, an inseparable consequence of a legal establishment. The opposition was not lessened when clergymen, greedy and exacting in the collection of tithes, resorted to the courts to compel payment from reluctant and straitened parishioners."[3]

---

1. J.L.M. Curry, *Protestantism: How Far A Failure?* (Philadelphia: American Baptist Publication Society, 1880, p. 27.
2. Ibid. p. 31.
3. J.L.M. Curry, *Struggle and Triumph of Virginia Baptists* (Philadelphia: American Baptist Publication Society, 1873), p. 39.

The English-Irish Question or the Southern Question?

Jabez Curry wrote a biography of Britain's four-time Prime Minister, William Gladstone. The reforms that Gladstone introduced to normalize the antagonistic relations between Ireland and England, coincided with the conflicts between North and South in the United States, following the war. "Ireland is a paradox. It is claimed that the rules and motives applicable to other peoples cannot be adjusted to the Irish. The North and South do not harmonize. Catholics and Protestants are like alien races.... Landlord and tenant have been irreconcilable enemies. Hates and antipathies rather than friendships and agreements have dominated. Loyalty, law and order, intelligible terms, have been misapplied. Loyalty to the sovereign, and imperial patriotism have been the exception. Secret leagues have taken the place of open political warfare. Assassination, boycotting, proscription, absenteeism, governmental distrust, oppressive discrimination, coercion, shadowing, have been varying aspects of the mobile kaleidoscope....

"Besides the intrinsic difficulties in the way of adjusting the Irish problem, the intemperance of the language of the British Premier [Parnell] shows that others more formidable have arisen from tradition, from racial or national prejudice, from a long course of governmental despotism, from the tenacity with which injustice holds onto ill-gotten gains. Abuses, the most flagrant, always find able and adroit supporters. Privileges, vested rights, oppressions embodied in statutes and proscriptions, ensconce themselves behind precedent and usage.... The Vice President of the Irish Land League, Justin McCarthy, said that Mr. Gladstone was the first English minister to deal on a liberal scale with the perplexing Irish question, and was the first who ever really periled office and popularity to serve the interests of the unhappy country."

Irish or Southern Home Rule?

"To an American, local self-government, as opposed to centralization, is so obvious and has been so thoroughly vindicated in practical action, that it is difficult to comprehend the animus or character of the opposition to it.... In 1885 [Prime Minister] Chamberlain said: 'It is little wonder that the Irish people should regard the castle [in Ireland, synonymous for the government] as the embodiment of foreign supremacy. The rulers of the castle are to them foreign in race or in sympathy, or in both.'... The people have no part in the administration, no responsibility, [so] it is natural that there should be distrust, alienation from the law, and from the administration of justice. They get the idea ... that justice could be had only by violence or physical power."[1]

Chapter 8. Reconstruction as Re-education

Jabez Curry is important to history because of his successful efforts to transform the minds and souls of the children of his own people, the Southern people, as General Agent of the Peabody Education Fund. These children would eventually fall in line with the dominant, alien Northern or New England mentality.

Here is where that process begins. And that process does not simply relate to Reconstruction or the 19th century. This tale of radical mental and social transformation relates as well to the 20th and 21st centuries. Reconstruction and its focus on re-education is the opening phase of the contemporary world.

Modern education and the pedagogical philosophies behind it are the consequence of the results of the War for Southern Independence.

Re-education through Reconstruction Constitutions

No former Confederate state could re-enter the Union until it had added a public, tax-supported education system clause to its new post-war constitution. Several Southern states refused to accept such a clause. They understood that it meant a hostile world-view would be forced upon their children. But, eventually, all the "rebel" states acquiesced. Otherwise, they would have remained territories forever.

Jabez Curry quoted the education clause of his home state to the Alabama Assembly: "'The General Assembly shall,' an imperative word, 'shall establish,

1. Last two sections, J.L.M. Curry, *William Ewart Gladstone* (Richmond: B.F. Johnson and Co., Publishers, 1891), pp. 146, 161.

organize and maintain a system of public schools throughout the State for the benefit of the children thereof.' This is not a temporary, local or subordinate duty. It is a general, continuing, paramount duty, affecting the present and the future, every family, every citizen, and every interest in the State."[1]

North Carolina's Educational Clause

Amendments to North Carolina's constitution clarified the meaning of the new public education: "Textbooks and all publications prescribed and used in the public schools should be free from sectarian and denominational and partisan bias in religion and politics." This meant free from Southern and Democratic party bias.

Also, studies pertaining to the government of the United States and that of the states, should be instructed with a view to creating a sentiment which would foster a love for the perpetual union of the states.

Conservatives were also afraid that certain subjects, which were offensive to the native whites of the state, would be required in the course of study to be prescribed in the law.[2]

In addition, there was a deep-seated aversion to taxation in the South. The people had been raised from colonial days to look with suspicion upon all improvements made at their expense for the public good. They had always believed that the less tax, the more ideal the government. Schools were not considered to be a proper part of the governmental machinery.

The Reconstruction constitution of Georgia was unconstitutional. All constitutions of the United States, both national and state, could be altered via the amendment process. But, "the constitution of Georgia shall never be amended or changed to deprive any citizen or class of citizens of the United States of the school rights and privileges secured by the constitution of said State."

Mr. Thurman, a Senator from Ohio, said this about the compulsive education clause in the Southern Reconstruction constitutions: "When did it become essential to a republican form of government that there should be public schools and that everybody should have an equal right to these schools? If that is the case, how many republican states were there when the Constitution of the United States was formed? If universal suffrage and universal education upon a

---

1. Proceedings of the Peabody Education Trust Fund, Report of the 24th meeting, 1885, p. 264, of Curry's address to the Alabama Assembly, February 6, 1885.
2. Edgar Knight, *The Influence of Education in the South* (New York: Teachers College, Columbia University, 1913), pp. 24-25.

perfectly equal footing, applicable to all, are essentially indispensable requisites of a republican form of government, how many states have you now, sir, in the United States, that are republican in form? Why sir, the very statement of the argument shows its utter fallacy."[1]

Mr. Norton, a Minnesota Senator, added: "under this clause [compulsory education], these States are under the supervision of Congress and ... Congress might legitimately take charge of the regulation of the school system of a State [if it failed to live up to the education clause].... The idea would seem to imply that if the State of Mississippi had a school system that was not agreeable to a majority of the Senators on this floor, they might correct that school system to make the State of Mississippi alter its school system to comply with the views of the Senate of the United States. Now sir, we have in Minnesota such a common school system. We think it is best adapted to our wants. I had some part in devising it. We thought it was the very best we could devise. Now, if the Congress of the United States can interfere with that, and compel us to make a system that will conform to the views of Congress, then, what becomes of the States, and why do we have States? Why have districts or counties bounded by national or imaginary lines? Why have apportionment of the representatives in the other House, and in this, according to States? Why not call us, as the Senator from Illinois says, all one people; one country and have no State governments and no local governments at all?"[2]

The Freedmen's Bureau and Education for Blacks

In 1865 Congress created a new Federal agency called the Bureau of Refugees, Freedmen and Abandoned Lands. Its name was commonly shortened to the Freedmen's Bureau. It was placed within the War Department. Supposedly, the Bureau was to help the former slaves make the difficult transition to citizenship. This noble ideal had a different reality. As part of the Army, it took on the coloration of the military's objective — to turn the former Confederacy into a colony of the victorious North. The Bureau's Commissioner, General Oliver Otis Howard, described the absolute despotic power that this agency had over the South: "Legislative, judicial and executive powers were combined in my commission."[3]

---

1. *The Congressional Globe*, 41st Congress, 2nd Session, p. 1218.
2. Ibid., p. 1218.
3. Annual Report of the Secretary of War for the Year 1869, p. 499.

The Bureau's military courts replaced all civil courts. Civilians were tried under military justice. Guilty until proven innocent, no writ of habeas corpus, no jury.

The Freedmen's Bureau illegally confiscated millions of acres of private property to re-distribute to blacks, carpetbaggers and high-ranking military officers. Then the Bureau relocated Southerners into the North to transform them away from being "rebels." Yet, the Bureau's main concern was to re-educate blacks to make them loyal Republican voters. This was the first step toward nationalizing Southern schools.

Congress authorized no funds for all this, fearing taxpayers would balk at this great new centralization of power. Therefore, the Bureau funded its schools without Congressional approval, using "off-budget" methods: "2,118 schools [are] under the care of the Bureau.... The expenses of the Bureau were met the first year with the proceeds of rents, sale of crops ... and sale of 'Confederate States' property. [This was the confiscated property.] The amount raised from all these miscellaneous sources was $1,865,645." By today's standards, that is more like 1.8 billion dollars.[1]

Jabez Curry saw Bureau education as a "continuation of hostilities against the vanquished." He characterized this education as a "scheme to subject the Southern people to Negro domination and to secure the States permanently for partisan ends."[2]

Radicals in Congress like Ben Wade in the Senate and Thaddeus Stevens in the House saw the Bureau as a tool for their own agenda. It could be used to block the Southern states from combining with Northern Democrats to oust the Republicans from power. The Bureau would control Southern patronage, and with its military backing, direct Negro labor and the black-market sale of cotton, and "educate" the ex-slaves to vote Republican.

The Bureau: Schools for Black Radical Republicans

The Freedmen's Bureau was a revolutionary engine for radical social change based on principles that were completely alien to American democratic ideals.

The Bureau was a militarized government over the South, not unlike 20th-century totalitarian regimes. The Nazis and the Communists brought their

---

1. Annual Report of the Secretary of War for the Year 1869, pp. 506 and 509.
2. Alderman and Gordon, p. 424.

Gestapo, SS and KGB men into conquered territories to either transform the minds of their captive subjects or to exterminate them.

The Freedmen's Bureau had its "Union League" division to do the same thing. The League used terror to educate the emancipated slaves to either vote Republican or face torture or death.

Among the Union League's functions was to build an army of 200,000 ex-slaves and former black Union soldiers. This huge force was divided up and used as the private troops of the carpetbag governors in every Southern state. In addition to insuring that votes received through terror kept them in power, these soldiers defended against other ambitious carpetbaggers who attempted to usurp illegal power with illegal force.

The white leadership of the Union League directed these armies to terrorize, torture and kill "reactionary" blacks who would not vote for them. The Union League was the Northern version of the Ku Klux Klan.

The League also conducted a reign of terror against Southern whites, which included widespread torture, arson and murder, to prevent them from assuming their status as citizens.[1]

The Freedmen's Bureau and its Union League controlled Negro schooling. J.P. Wickersham was a Radical Republican educator. His comments give an idea of the Bureau's intentions: "The law of Congress provided for a Freedmen's Bureau. While it authorizes the appointment of commissioners, superintendents and agents ... [it] does not appropriate money for education. Perhaps the President and the Secretary of War may find a military necessity for making such an appropriation.

In a republic, if all men vote, all men must be educated. A loaded musket in the hands of a crazy man in a crowd is not nearly as dangerous as a ballot in the hands of an ignorant man at an election. The thing of highest interest in a republic is its schools.... When our youth learn to read similar books, similar lessons, we shall become one people, possessing one organic nationality, and the Republic will be safe for all time."[2]

By 1867, the Bureau was running 1,198 day schools and 288 night schools, with 1,744 teachers. When the Negroes became voters, the teachers were strate-

---

1. See John Chodes' treatment of this section of the Freedmen's Bureau in *The Union League: Washington's Klan* (Tuscaloosa: League of the South Institute for the Study of Southern Culture and History, 1999).
2. J.P. Wickersham, *Education As An Element in the Reconstruction of the Union* (Boston: L.C. Rand and Avery, 1865), p. 9-11.

gically placed to influence them into Republicanism. A Radical politician said: "Republicans notice that where there has been the most schooling since the war, the freedmen are surest for our party."[1]

Few political organizers were more active in the South than superintendents and inspectors of Bureau schools. Negro schoolhouses became Republican party headquarters and the sites for political and military activity.

When the Reverend Duncan, the Bureau's chief school officer in Florida, refused to use his school system to distribute copies of Thaddeus Stevens' speeches proposing to pay the war debt by confiscating Southerner's property, Duncan lost his job. Many Bureau men ran for public office and were often placed in State legislatures.

White Southerners were not hostile to Negro education but to the Bureau's brand of it. Southerners wanted the curriculum to concentrate on reading, 'riting and 'rithmetic, not politics and sociology. They hoped teachers would confine their lessons to the topics usually covered by school instruction, not social equality, which often led to violence and revolutionary confrontations.

Bureau teachers viewed themselves as "political revolutionaries." The Radical *Loyal Georgian* was a newspaper of the Georgia Equal Rights Association. Its purpose was to promote the Republican Party through the schools. It received Federal aid to do this. The President, J.E. Bryant, had been a Bureau agent. He said: "If able papers are established, a Union Party may be established in every State."[2]

Jabez Curry observed Bureau education first-hand and made this caustic comment: "What sort of schools were established under the Freedmen's Bureau? ... Some fanatical 'marms' who came down here to enlighten and enflame the ignorant Negro with all sorts of ideas about his greatness and his suffrage, etc., perpetuated a crime that has never been equaled in the annals of any race. And they, with their minds filled up with all these ideas, and a little smattering of education, perhaps they would go and forage, or rob. But it was not the result of the education they had received, but the fault of those human vampires. I wish I had some words, I wish the dictionary would furnish me some other words with which I might express my detestation and contempt and hatred of their acts."[3]

---

1. George Bentley, *History of the Freedmen's Bureau* (Philadelphia: University of Pennsylvania Press, 1955), p. 95.
2. Bentley, p. 181.
3. Fragment of typewritten letter by Jabez Curry, to unknown person, unknown date, from Curry Papers.

The *Virginian* newspaper commented: "It is the grossest form of insult to have sent among us a lot of ignorant, narrow-minded, bigoted fanatics, ostensibly for the purpose of propagating the gospel among the heathen, and teaching our Negroes to read the Bible and show them the road to salvation, just as if they were Feejee Islanders and worshippers of African Fetish Gods, snakes, toads and Terrapins; but whose real object was to disorganize and demoralize still more of our peasantry and laboring population.

"...Virginians would have let these impudent assumptions pass with the contempt of silence if Bureau educators had confined themselves merely to teaching the objects of their idolatry the rudiments of English education; to read, to write, to cipher, instead of to array the colored race against their white former masters and protectors."[1]

Bureau Schools Perpetuate Racism

The Reverend John Alvord was the head of the education division of the Bureau. Although he refuted claims by Thomas Carlyle and Southern whites that Negroes were inferior and would become extinct on their own, his policies treated them as if this theory was true.

This was exposed by Henry M. Turner, the outspoken Methodist bishop, who accused the Bureau-funded Hampton Institute of perpetuating Negro inferiority. "The graduates sent out cannot be called educated by any means, for they have not the learning given by a respectable grammar school. Besides, I think colored children are taught to remember 'you are Negroes. Your place is behind.' When Turner inquired about the higher branches; mathematics, science and classical languages, a white faculty member replied, 'Oh, the colored people are not prepared for these studies yet. They are too ignorant. It will take time enough to talk about that, years from this time."[2]

The Freedmen's Bureau: Bastion of Radical Philosophy

It would not be an exaggeration to state that the 19th century Radical Republicans were the philosophical descendents of the 18th century Jacobians of the French Revolution and the precursors of the 20th century totalitarians, like Stalin. The Radicals' vision of the relation of capital to labor, of private property, of the revolutionary overturn of existing social values, paralleled the Soviet Com-

---

1. *Norfolk Virginian*, July 2, 1866.
2. Robert Morris, *Reading, 'Riting and Reconstruction* (Chicago: University of Chicago Press, 1976), p. 161.

munists'. "It has been said that the ruining of the planting class in the South through war was more complete than the destruction of the nobility and clergy in the French Revolution. The very foundation of the system was shattered."[1]

W.E.B. DuBois demonstrated that parallel when he said: "In the Freedmen's Bureau, the United States started upon a dictatorship by which the landowners and the capitalists were to be openly and deliberately curbed and which directed its efforts in the interest of a black and white labor class."[2]

Thaddeus Stevens preached the same kind of radical egalitarianism that Stalin preached, and which, in the 20th century, led to mass murder: "The whole fabric of Southern society must be changed, and it can never be done if this opportunity is lost.... How can republican institutions, free schools, free churches, free social intercourse exist in a mingled community of nabobs and serfs; of the owners of 20,000 acre manors with lordly palaces and the occupants of narrow huts inhabited by 'low white trash.' If the South is ever to be made a safe republic, let her lands be cultivated by the toil of the owners of the free labor of intelligent citizens. This must be done even if it drives her nobility into exile. If they go, all the better. It will be hard to persuade the owner of 10,000 acres of land, who drives a coach-and-four, that he is not degraded by sitting at the same table or in the same pew, with the embrowned and hard-handed farmer who has himself cultivated his own thriving homestead of 150 acres. The country would be well rid of the proud, bloated and defiant rebels."[3]

False Atrocities for Revolution

To create this Utopian totalitarian society in the South, an ongoing military state was required. For the Northern citizens and Congress to accept this continual financial and emotional strain, false horror stories had to be endlessly generated. "During the war the Union League and Loyal Leagues told stories of Southern atrocities to keep the war spirit up. Most were false. After the war Radical newspapers went to the Freedmen's Bureau for more atrocity stories." Assistant Bureau Commissioner Fullerton of Louisiana said: "This society is no more demoralized than some northern states.... By telling only the bad acts, any large community could be pictured as barbarous." Union General Tillson said:

---

1. DuBois, p. 128.
2. Ibid., p. 128.
3. Will Herberg, *The Heritage of the Civil War* (New York: Workers Age Publishing Association, 1932), pp. 11-12.

"Atrocity stories are exaggerated. Most reports are false." The stories were politically motivated and planted by Radical congressmen.[1]

The Freedmen's Bureau as Marxist Government

The Radical Republicans did achieve their paradise on earth, after a fashion. And the Bureau was at the heart of that dream, as it became the supreme government over the South.

Oliver Otis Howard explained this, showing that the Bureau was above the regular army that supposedly ruled the South: "Districts were then organized, with General Schoefield in command of Virginia; General Sickles for North and South Carolina; General George H. Thomas for Florida, Georgia and Alabama, General Ord for Mississippi and Arkansas and General Sheridan for Louisiana and Texas. All these officers, who were commanders of individual states, became ex-officio, my assistant commissioners."[2]

W.E.B. DuBois, ever the Stalinist, said: "The record of the Negro worker during Reconstruction presents an opportunity to study inductively the Marxist theory of the State. I first called this chapter [of his book, *Black Reconstruction in America*] *The Dictatorship of the Black Proletariat in South Carolina*, but it was brought to my attention that this could not be correct since universal suffrage could not lead to a real dictatorship until workers use their votes consciously to rid themselves of the domination of private capital."[3]

DuBois then added that the Congressional Reconstruction laws created a "dictatorship backed by the military arm of the United States by which the governments of the Southern states were to be coerced into accepting a new form of administration in which freedmen and the poor whites were to hold the overwhelming balance of political power. [The dictatorship of the proletariat.] As soon as the political power was successfully delivered into the hands of these elements, the Federal government was to withdraw and full democracy ensue [The State will wither away].... Such a dictatorship must last long enough to put the mass of workers in power; that this in fact would be a dictatorship of the proletariat which must endure until the proletariat or at least a leading limited group, with clear objects and effective method, had education and experience and had taken firm control of the economic organization of the South."[4]

---

1. Bentley, pp. 110, 111, 112.
2. Oliver Otis Howard, *Autobiography of Oliver Otis Howard, Major-General, United States Army* (New York: Baker and Taylor Company, 1907), p. 332.
3. Dubois, p. 381, footnote.
4. Ibid., p. 345.

Finally, DuBois said: "There is no doubt that the object of the black and white labor vote was gradually conceived as one which involved confiscating the property of the rich. This was a program that could not be openly avowed by intelligent men in 1870, but it has become one of the acknowledged functions of the State in 1933. And it is quite possible that long before the end of the 20th century, the deliberate distribution of property and income by the State on an equitable and logical basis will be looked upon as the State's prime function."[1] (This, tragically, has come to pass.)

The Freedmen's Bureau Educates Blacks

Once again, J.P. Wickersham, the Radical educator, said: "What can education do for the freedmen? Four millions of human beings have just been emancipated in the South. They are now without property, without that knowledge and those habits of self-direction and self-reliance; they are ignorant, simplehearted and superstitious.... It still depends on the North, on us, whether the freedmen are to survive the 'struggle for life' or like the native red-men, they are to perish.... American society has little patience for the weak and the thriftless. In the rough jostle of business, every man is expected to care for himself. After two centuries of bondage, can we expect the freedmen to possess the high moral and intellectual qualities which fit them to compete at once with those who are educated and who have long been accustomed to depend on themselves? For one, I do not. And the benevolence of this country must in full measure extend a helping hand to the colored man or he will perish. Let good men make haste to instruct and care for these newborn children of the nation. Let the teachers and missionaries be sent to them. Let church and State and neighborhood unite in a grand effort to save them from destruction.... We all know that the freedmen must be educated. We all know that the education that they need is not merely to read and write but ... as well to fit them for their new condition as freedmen and citizens."[2]

Jabez Curry disagreed with the notion that all blacks were illiterate: "For a long time there was no general exclusion of the slaves from the privilege of education. The first prohibitory and punitive laws were directed against unlawful assemblages of Negroes, and subsequently of free Negroes and mulattoes, as their influence in exciting discontent or insurrection was deprecated and

---

1. Ibid., p. 591.
2. Wickersham, pp. 8-9.

guarded against. Afterwards, legislation became more general in the South, pro-hibiting meetings for teaching, reading and writing. The Nat Turner insurrection in Southampton County, Virginia, in 1831, awakened the Southern States to a consciousness of the perils, which might environ or destroy them, from combina-tions of excited, enflamed, and ill-advised Negroes.... Severe and general as were these laws, they rarely applied, and were seldom, if ever, enforced against the teaching of individuals or groups on plantations, or at the home of the owners. It is often true that the mistress of a household, or her children, would teach the house servants, and on Sunday, include a larger number. There were also Sunday schools in which black children were taught to read, notably the school in which Stonewall Jackson was the leader."[1]

A 20th century book (1974), *Time on the Cross*, using 1860 Census data, dem-onstrated by implication that a substantial percent of slaves were literate; they were skilled artisans whose crafts required them to read, write and calculate. "Slaves were involved in virtually every aspect of Southern economic life, both rural and urban. They were not only tillers of the soil but were represented in most skilled crafts. In the city of Charleston, about 27 percent of the adult male slaves were skilled artisans. In several of the most important crafts of that city, including carpentry and masonry, slaves actually outnumbered the whites. Some bondsmen even ascended into such professions as architecture and engineering.

Slaves also held a large share of the skilled jobs in the countryside. On the large plantations, slaves predominated in the crafts and lower managerial ranks. To a surprising extent, slaves held top managerial posts; as overseers or general managers. When acting as overseers, slaves were responsible not only for the overall direction of the labor force but for the scheduling of field operations and purchasing supplies."[2]

Frederick Olmsted was a Northern writer and abolitionist. He is most famous as a landscape architect. Olmsted designed Central Park in New York City, Brooklyn's Prospect Park, Chicago's South Park, Montreal's Mt. Royal Park, and others. He toured the South and wrote about what he saw, which modified his views about the slave system. His statement shows that slaves were literate and capable. "In the selection of drivers [foremen] ... greater capacity of mind than the ordinary slave is often supposed to be possessed of, is certainly

1. J.L.M. Curry, *Education of the Negro Since 1860*, John Slater Fund Occasional Papers No. 3 (Baltimore: 1894), p. 8.
2. Robert W. Fogel and Stanley L. Engerman, *Time on the Cross* (New York: W.W. Norton & Company, 1974), p. 38.

needed in them. A good driver is very valuable and usually holds the office for life. His authority is not limited to the direction of labor in the field, but extends to the general deportment of the Negroes. He is made to do the duties of a policeman, and even a police magistrate."[1]

"About seven percent of all slaves were managers within the agricultural sector. 11.9 percent were blacksmiths, carpenters and coopers, etc.... The common belief that all slaves were menial laborers is false."[2]

Also, Fogel and Engerman pointed out that "slave artisans hired out on their own account, operating in the same way as their free counterparts. They advertised their services, negotiated their own contracts, received monies and paid debts themselves, obtained their own residences, and places of business. A slave artisan, unlike his free counterpart, was required to pay a fixed percentage of his income to the master. Thirty-one percent of urban slave workers were on hire during 1860."[3]

The Freedmen's Bureau Re-educates Whites

Through Freedmen's Bureau education, the blacks would be converted into revolutionary, Radical Republicans. And since they were the majority of voters during Reconstruction, the South would forever remain a Radical paradise.

But what of the whites? Their re-education was more desperately necessary. After all, they were the rebels and traitors who had dared to make war against Uncle Sam. They had to be trained to be loyal, patriotic and, above all, docile and obedient.

At a Congressional hearing, famed Union General Lorenzo Thomas presented how the army of occupation and the Republicans and many Northerners viewed Southern whites. By implication, re-education was one of the highest priorities.

Senator Robert Baldwin of Connecticut asked General Thomas a series of questions.

Baldwin: "Have you any reason to believe that the rebels still entertain hopes of another outbreak, or that any considerable portion of them do?"

---

1. Frederick Olmsted, *Journeys and Explorations in the Cotton Kingdom of America* (New York: Mason Brothers, 1862), p. 249.
2. Fogel and Engerman, pp. 39-40.
3. Ibid., p. 56.

Thomas: "I have received communications from various persons in the South that there is an understanding among the rebels to form organizations for the purpose of gaining as many advantages for themselves as possible. And I have also heard it intimated that these men were anxious to, and would do all in their power to involve the United States in a foreign war, so that if a favorable opportunity should offer itself, they might turn against the United States. I do not think they will attempt ever, an outbreak on their own account, because they all admit they had a fair trial in the late rebellion and got thoroughly worsted. There is no doubt but that there is a universal disposition among the rebels in the South to embarrass the government in its administration as they can, so as to gain as many advantages for themselves as possible."

Baldwin: "In what would their advantage consist? In breaking up the government?"

Thomas: "They wish to be recognized as citizens of the United States, with the same rights they had before the war."

Baldwin: "How can they do that by involving us in a war with England or France, in which they would take part against us?"

Thomas: "In that event their desire is to re-establish the Southern Confederacy. They have not yet given up their desire for a separate government and if they have an opportunity, to strike for it again, they will do so."

Baldwin: "Observe carefully that we meet here a demand of the conquered traitors for political power. They have been terribly defeated in the field and not being able to overthrow the government by force of arms they now haughtily insist on the right to come back and rule it. And they put forth this demand without an emotion or penitence for treason, without a sign of regret for the bloodshed and desolation they have caused; on the contrary, they are proud of what they have done."[1]

Former general and now Congressman Nathaniel Banks also insinuated that re-education was needed for Southern whites when he said that they "do not seek to govern by opinion. They do not rely on ideas for success. They govern by force. Their tradition is force.... I know that the people of the South are filled at present with the prejudice against the civilization, the institutions, the people of the North; but the moment they have felt the beneficial effects of that civilization, whenever they become acquainted with our people, as they will at no

---

1. The *Congressional Globe*, 39th Congress, 1st Session, p. 1827.

distant day, they will cordially and honestly fraternize with them. It requires a little time but the result is inevitable."[1]

Then the issue of re-education clarified itself: "What can education do for the non-slave holding whites of the South? Among this class are some intelligent men. But the great majority are deplorably ignorant. More ignorant than the slaves themselves.... At Point Lookout, only one out of twenty of the rebel prisoners could read or write. It was this ignorance that enabled the rebel leaders to create a prejudice in the minds of this class of persons against the North and to induce them to enlist in their armies....

As long as they are ignorant they will remain tools of political demagogues and therefore be incapable of self-government. They must be educated; the duty is imperative.... A republican form of government cannot exist without providing a system of free schools. A republic must make education universal among its people. Ignorant voters endanger liberty. With free schools in the South there could have been no rebellion. And free schools must now render impossible rebellion in the future. Wendell Phillips said that 'behind every one of Grant's cannon there should be placed a school house.' There should be no delay; for mark it well, a contest in which two sections of this country have been engaged is not yet ended. Instead of a war with muskets and cannon, we have a war of cunning and diplomacy. There are traitors still who use all their power to prevent the carrying out of the beneficent purpose of the government toward the common people of the South.... Educate the whole people of the South and these machinations will prove abortive, the rule of the haughty slave lord will pass away and a giant step will be taken toward making homogeneous our social as well as our political institutions throughout the nation."[2]

Jabez Curry previously refuted the idea that the slaves were illiterate. Now he retaliated against the false, politically motivated charge of white ignorance this way: "In 1860 the Northern States had a population of 19 million, had 205 colleges and universities, with 1,407 professors and 29,044 students. In the same year, the Southern States had a population of 8 million, 262 colleges and universities, with 1,488 professors and 27,055 students. These are the figures of the last Census before the war."[3]

---

1. Ibid., p. 2532.
2. J.P. Wickersham, p. 7.
3. Jabez Curry, speech at the Capon Springs Conference, June 24, 1899, from an article in a fragment of an unknown newspaper in the J.L.M. Curry Papers.

The term "illiteracy" had a secondary meaning to the Radicals. Charles Sumner informs us: "You may exclude rebels [from the government] but their children, who are not excluded, have inherited the rebel spirit. The schools and colleges of the South have been nurseries of rebellion.... In a republic, education is indispensable. A republic without education is like a creature of imagination, a human being without a soul, living and moving blindly, with no means of the present or the future. It is a monster. Such has been the rebel states. They have been for years political monsters. But such they must be no longer. It is not too much to say that had these States been more enlightened, they would never have rebelled."[1]

Senator Harris of Georgia, an ex-Confederate officer, gave both sides of the state-funded education issue when he first quoted Republican Senator Donnelly of New Jersey and then presented his own perspective.

Harris [reading Donnelly's speech]: "Is it not a shame that this nation, which rests solely upon the intelligence of the citizens and without which it could not exist for an hour, should thus far have done literally nothing either to recognize or enforce education? France, Prussia, Austria and Russia have made education an affair of the State, and have esteemed it of the highest consequence. In Prussia, the Minister of Public Instruction ranks next to the King."

Harris then presented his side: "And yet, Mr. Speaker, the governments the gentlemen has enumerated and over which he says education is so widely diffused, are the most despotic in Europe. I suspect the Minister of Public Instruction has them educated in the principles of despotism."[2]

Then the ubiquitous Mr. Wickersham added: "What can education do for the late slaveholder? The majority of those who formerly held slaves are now just what they were before and during the war and I am extremely doubtful whether there are any means by which they can be made, as a class, good and loyal citizens. If they were thus disposed, I would treat them generously; but events seem to show nearly all at heart are still opposed to free government ... free speech and free schools. If pardoned, [some] will trouble every community in which they live with ill-concealed treason. They have already been sadly mis-educated and would scornfully reject all proffers of education at our hands.... We must treat them as the Western farmers do the stumps in their clearings; work around them and let them rot out."[3]

---

1. *Congressional Globe*, 40th Congress, 1st Session, p. 166.
2. *Congressional Globe*, 39th Congress, 1st Session, p. 3174.

General Oliver Otis Howard

Major-General Oliver Otis Howard was the Commissioner of the Freedmen's Bureau. His title does not reveal his significance in American history. He was not only the supreme dictator of the South, he held a life-and-death power over five states in the North and a marginal dictatorial hold over the remainder of the Union. In many respects he was above the President.

Abraham Lincoln was killed six weeks after the Freedmen's Bureau bill was signed. Lincoln's Secretary of War, Stanton, was a Radical but pretended otherwise. He proposed a Reconstruction plan to Lincoln that seemed moderate but would advance the Radical agenda. Stanton needed a Bureau commissioner who would also seem moderate but who would be sympathetic to the Radicals. Stanton picked O.O. Howard, the commanding general of the Army of the Tennessee. When Lincoln was shot, Andrew Johnson appointed Howard.

O.O. Howard had worked his way through the ranks to Major-General, although he and his army had been defeated and routed in several key battles. Early in the war (1862), at Fair Oaks, in the Peninsula campaign, his right arm was blown off. Thereafter, he proudly pinned his empty sleeve to his chest to announce to the world his wound and his bravery.

Howard commanded one of the two great armies that had marched with relentless success to the sea: Grant and Sherman's old Army of the Tennessee. Howard was known as the "Christian General." He was irritatingly, overtly pious.

In his autobiography, Howard described how he was offered the opportunity to head the Bureau. It was early May 1865. Lee had just surrendered. Howard's army was stationed just outside Richmond. He was ordered to meet Stanton, who said: "Mr. Lincoln, before his death, expressed a decided wish that you should have the office.... Now the war is ended, the way is clear. The place will be given you if you are willing to accept it."

Howard thought, "Naturally, as the great war drew to a close, I had been pondering the subject of my future work. Should I remain in the army or not? What, as a young man of 34, had I better do?"

He accepted the offer. "The clerk in charge brought in a large, oblong bushel basket heaped with letters and documents. Mr. Stanton, with both hands holding the handles at each end, took the basket and extended it to me and with a smile said: 'Here General, here's your bureau.' "

---

3. Wickersham, p. 7.

Howard notified General Sherman of his assignment and Sherman immediately wrote back: "I hardly know whether to congratulate you or not, but of one thing you must be assured, that you possess my entire confidence.... I do believe the people of the South realize the fact that their former slaves are free, and if allowed reasonable time, and not harassed by confiscation and political complications, will very soon adapt to their condition."[1]

And yet, Howard's first circular letter to Bureau officers contradicted Sherman's advice and, as predicted, the confiscation of Southerners' land created an era of distrust and hatred.

Like others in this story, Oliver Otis Howard was a man of contradictions: a pious Christian with a moral obligation to do good for the ex-slaves, and simultaneously a brutal military dictator who did not flinch at torture and murder to achieve his Utopian goals. Howard's biographer describes how he saw himself: "The work of the Bureau [was] the fulfillment of a moral obligation. He viewed himself as the man who would lead the nation in meeting this obligation. He would make America 'a nation which cares for its children.' At last, he would be able to merge his desire to be a preacher with the fact that he was a general. He was proud to be known in the nation as the 'Christian Soldier.' "[2]

Oliver Otis Howard vs. Andrew Johnson

Andrew Johnson, moderate that he was, favored the rapid return of civil government and re-union for the South. Oliver Otis Howard, the Radical, favored a long period of subservience for the South during which a revolutionary social order would be implemented.

The President, as commander-in-chief of the armed forces, thought he was more powerful than Howard. Howard disagreed, believing that, since he was the military, he could defy the President.

Johnson called Howard a "fanatic" and wanted to replace him with a Radical Negro, knowing that most whites would not serve under a black. This would break the Bureau's power.

Johnson also said, "If I wanted authority, or if I had wished to perpetuate my own power, how easily could I have wielded that which was placed in my hands by the measure called the Freedmen's Bureau Bill."[3]

---

1. O.O. Howard, pp. 206-209.
2. William McFeeley, *Yankee Stepfather: O.O. Howard and the Freedmen* (New Haven: Yale Publications in America Studies 15, Yale University Press, 1968), pp. 85-86.
3. DuBois, p. 317.

The President also called the Bureau a proposition to transfer four million slaves from their original owners to a new set of taskmasters.

To blunt the Bureau's power, Johnson removed its key officers who obstructed his restoration policies. He did this quietly, tactfully, by transferring them from their posts in the South back to headquarters in Washington, where they were rendered harmless.

Johnson then sent General Howard on a speaking tour of the South to explain "restoration." This was done to humiliate Howard. Restoration was anathema to the Bureau. It meant returning confiscated land back to the owners. But the Bureau either sold these properties outright or sold the produce from them to generate the money to build schools, pay mercenary troops, or finance clandestine operations; all to advance its revolutionary social agenda.

It was during this tour that Howard made his first public break with Johnson and sided with the Radicals in Congress. He saw that they would overturn restoration and mandate more massive confiscations.

Interpreting the objectives of the tour to fit his own plans, Oliver Otis was quoted in the *New York Times* as saying that his role was to "investigate" (meaning to interpret) and not to just announce the President's program.

Stanton backed Howard's defiance of Johnson: "I do not understand that your orders require you to disturb the freedmen in possession [of confiscated property] at present."[1]

Howard told his Bureau officers to disregard Johnson and bar Southerners from their land, even if they signed loyalty oaths.

In April 1866, Andrew Johnson proclaimed that the war was officially and legally over. That meant that civil justice would replace military courts for civilians. But Oliver Otis Howard countered, saying, "This does not remove martial law or operate in any way upon the Freedmen's Bureau in the exercise of its legitimate jurisdiction."

Then, on April 3, 1866, the Supreme Court held, in the classic Ex-Parte Milligan Case, that martial law must be "confined to the locality of actual war." This clearly meant that civilians could not be tried by military tribunals where the regular courts were open. But the Freedmen's Bureau Bill, in opposition to and by-passing the Supreme Court, provided that in cases either involving racial discrimination or where "rebellion still existed," military justice would be provided. Of course, the Bureau would make that judgment.

---

1. McFeeley, p. 147.

The Freedmen's Bureau Spreads Into North

The Bureau was supposed to cease its existence one year after the end of war, but each year Congress extended its life. Ultimately, its educational functions still operated into the 1870s.

Being an agency created under the alleged "war powers" of Congress, its existence was marginally legal in the occupied South. Its presence in the North was positively unconstitutional and posed a definite threat of bringing military government into the loyal Union states.

And, that is exactly what happened. Oliver Otis Howard said: "Under the new Bureau law approved July 16, 1866, which extended its provisions and care to all loyal refugees and freedmen, Missouri [a Union state] and Kansas [another Union state] constituted a nominal district."[1]

This care soon extended to Maryland and Delaware, also Union states. Then, Bureau amendments allowed it to expand into any state where freedmen resided, which meant all of the United States. Now, martial law reached into all of the country.

Navy Secretary Gideon Welles called this huge expansion of the Bureau "a terrific engine" and "a governmental enormity."[2]

The Freedmen's Bureau and 1868 Presidential Election

June 1868: As a result of the Bureau's work in educating blacks to be loyal Republican voters, seven Southern states were admitted to representation in Congress. They could now participate in the upcoming Presidential election. Re-admission was their reward for enfranchising the Negroes. Senators: twelve of the fourteen were Republicans. Representatives: thirty-two of thirty-four, Republicans.

November 1868: In the Presidential election, Ulysses S. Grant carried twenty-six states. His opponent, Horatio Seymour, only twelve. Grant's popular majority was only 309,000 but he received 450,000 Negro votes. The Freedmen's Bureau had kept the Radicals in power.

End of the Bureau; Continuation of the Bureau

The Freedmen's Bureau was supposed to legally pass out of existence in 1871. But, in 1867, a small agency within the Interior Department was created. It

---

1. Oliver Otis Howard, p. 348.
2. Gideon Welles, *Diary of Gideon Welles* (Boston: Houghton Miflin Co., 1911), Vol. II, p. 432.

had only five employees: a supervisor and four clerks. It was called the Bureau of Education. Its mandate seemed innocuous: to "collect such statistics and facts as show the condition and progress of education in the various states and territories."[1]

And yet, within a few years it employed or had access to 12,000 Interior Department personnel and controlled most Southern schools and many in the North. The amazing history of the Bureau of Education and its Radical commissioner, John Eaton, will be the subject of a complete chapter later on.

A series of amendments to the original Bureau of Education bill allowed it to steadily grow in size and destructive power. One of these amendments permitted it to absorb every one of the Freedmen's Bureau's 2,118 schools, and all of its officers, who were mostly Radical career army men, so that they became part of the permanent Federal civil system: "Section 3: the Bureau of Education is hereby authorized to exercise the same powers as those hitherto exercised by the Freedmen's Bureau in its education division.... Section 7: All clerks, messengers, and employees of the Freedmen's Bureau [shall] be transferred to and retained in the Bureau of Education."[2] The effect of this was to militarize a civil agency.

Then Thomas McNeely, a representative from Illinois, spoke of the consequences of this amendment. "The bill, by its title, pretends to discontinue the Freedmen's Bureau, but it does not. On the contrary, it continues under a new name, under different officials charged with duties more expansive, clothed with authority, more unconstitutional, and without the guards thrown around it that have, with so little success, opposed the abuses heretofore practiced by that bureau.... Mr. Speaker, we have reached the time when the Freedmen's Bureau and all that belongs to it should be abolished. The people expect it. Sir, it has never had a constitutional foundation, and so apparent was this fact that those who originated it based it upon certain war powers which they claimed in a time of war was superior to and outside the Constitution."[3]

---

1. Annual Report of the Commissioner of Education, for the Year 1868, p. 2.
2. *Congressional Globe*, 41st Congress, 2nd Session, p. 2295.
3. Ibid., p. 2316.

Chapter 9. Curry's Background: Alabama Politics to Congress

Curry: "In July 1847 I became a candidate for representation [for the Alabama Assembly]. My small size and youthful appearance and the popularity of my father, gave me an advantage over my competitors. I made public speeches. I had some fluency and success as a speaker. On the first Monday in August, at the election, I received a higher number of votes than any of the candidates for the House. The first bi-annual session was held in Montgomery.... The session was distinguished by the election of a senator, William R. King and Dixon H. Lewis, leading and popular Democrats, opposed each other. King was what was called a 'Hunker,' or a Van Buren Democrat, a finished and intelligent gentleman, who had been a Senator and Minister to France. Lewis was a State's Rights or Calhoun Democrat and had been a Representative in Congress for several years and a Senator since 1845. He was superior in intellect and force to Mr. King. The Democrats had largely the ascendancy in the legislature and the excitement was very great. The two candidates had their friends most actively at work. After reaching Montgomery, I went to the 'Hall,' the leading hotel. The large reception room was crowded Mr. King was in one part, surrounded by his friends. Mr. Lewis, in another, alike surrounded. My preference for Mr. Lewis being known, I was led to him and he seated me upon his knee. I apparently was a boy, beardless and slender. Mr. Lewis was the largest man I ever saw. Mr. Yancey, afterwards so famous, was present and an ardent supporter of Mr. Lewis, who, at the election by the legislature, was elected, on the 18th ballot."

First Marriage

"On March 4, 1847 I was married to Ann Alexander Bowie.... She was the daughter of Alexander and Susan Bowie. Mr. Bowie, a graduate of South Carolina College, a member of the South Carolina legislature, and of the Nullification Convention [in response to a Federal tariff which favored Northern interests at the expense of the South, John Calhoun's principle of nullifying unconstitutional infringements of state sovereignty was advocated, including defensive force; Washington reduced the tariff], was a popular lawyer and a very eloquent speaker. He moved to Talladega County, Alabama in 1836, was a Trustee of the University and Chancellor of the Northern division. He was a fine conversationalist, a graceful writer and a scholarly, high-toned Christian gentleman.

"By the union, four children were born; Susan Lamar, born 2 September, 1850. Alexander Curry, born 11 November 1854, died 27 February 1855. Manly Bowie Curry, born 23 April 1857, and Jackson Thomas Curry, born 22 October 1859 and died 29 July 1860."

Politics, Farming, South-North Splitting

"In 1848 occurred a Presidential election. Zachary Taylor and Lewis Cass being the Whig and Democratic candidates. I made a number of speeches in favor of General Cass but the military fame of General Taylor gave him an easy success. During this and the following year I practiced law with diligence. In 1849 I represented the State as Solicitor in Talladega County and had one or two murder cases.

"In 1850 my father, having given me a plantation on Salt Creek in Talladega County, I abandoned the practice of law and began to farm. Although brought up on a farm, I knew little practically of agriculture, and, while fond of the country, my tastes did not lie in the direction of making corn and cotton. My farming, being entrusted largely to Negroes, was not profitable. I was economical and never went into debt. I preferred books to overseeing Negroes.

"My brother, Jackson, having bought a plantation, I bought his place and sold mine. I moved to the farm he owned, three miles from Talladega town and resumed again the practice of law. I lived in this place until 1865 when I removed to Marion. During these years, there was scarcely a night that there was not one or more persons at my house. Preachers, relatives and friends were always welcome.

"1850 was a year of much political excitement. Questions growing out of the acquisition of territory from Mexico deeply agitated the Southern mind. In Congress, what was called the 'Wilmot Proviso,' prohibited the introduction of African slavery into the territories, lately acquired by the expenditure of common blood and treasure, had divided political parties and had separated the North and the South. Since the close of the Mexican War, slavery, as affecting the territories, was the 'bone of contention.' A large party at the North [the Republicans] demanded that the territories should be kept free from the 'curse.' The South felt that to exclude their peculiar property from common territory was a flagrant injustice, an insulting discrimination and a violation of the Constitution. The two sections began to grow apart and feel alienation and animosity. Bills were numerous during these years, in Congress, to adjust the dispute. Calhoun and Webster were then living and they represented the two sides of the question.

"In 1849-50 certain laws were passed called 'Compromise Measures,' which included the admission of California as a 'free State,' a Fugitive Slave Law, territorial governments for New Mexico and a Texas Boundary Bill and a bill prohibiting the slave trade in the District of Columbia. The spirit and general tenor of this legislation, it was thought by many people, especially in South Carolina, Georgia, Alabama and Mississippi, was very hostile to the rights and equality of the South in the Union. In this year, 1850 and in 1851, an attempt was made to organize a party favorable to secession. I favored it but the movement was unwise, premature and unpopular In the public meetings in Talladega County I took an active part and made several speeches....

[In 1848 and 1849 Curry did not seek re-election in the Alabama Assembly. He practiced law. In 1850 he was given the farm by his father.]

"In 1853 I was elected to the legislature from Talladega County. The Speaker, Richard Walker, made me Chairman of the Committee on Internal Improvements, a member of the Committee on Education and also the Banking Committee, to examine the accounts of the Commissioner and Trustees. This session was noted for its 'State Aid' question. My committee supported bills granting endorsement of Rail Road bonds on certain well-defined conditions and the government vetoed them. In the controversy, I had to defend the bills and the principle of well-guarded aid to internal improvements. A school law was passed, beginning a system of Public Schools for the State, which had my hearty endorsement."[1]

---

1. Last three sections, from Jabez Curry hand-written autobiographical notes, April, 1876.

Pre-War Southern Schools

Here, Curry shows the flaws in his thinking, as well as an insight into the merits of state and private education. His presentation is a loaded argument in favor of tax-supported schools. His words make freedom, diversity and choice seem like chaos. He denigrates private schools because they did not fit the government-funded model. His ideas parallel those of the Radical Republicans. These comments were written in the 1890s, long after his mental transition, and explain why he sounds like a Radical.

"The conviction had not yet rooted itself in the public mind or conscience, that elementary, much less universal education was an essential factor in national progress, or the only secure basis for free representative institutions. In the schools and academies of the ante-bellum period, teaching was often superficial, inadequate and unsystematic. Each school went its own way, independent of all others. [This was not necessarily true. Sectarian religious schools, which taught a large percentage of the children, followed the same program.] Differing in organization and methods, there was no unity of a general plan, nor common curriculum, nor helpful correlation. Such schools owed their origin to private enterprise, to energy or liberality of communities, sometimes to local jealousies, and of consequence they had no official inspection, nor any examination, nor certification of teachers. [This is at least partially untrue. An inspection, certification, etc., was done within the system of church or community schools, without outside interference.]"

In 1853 "the Superintendent [of Education] had visited forty-five of the fifty-four counties, to ascertain the extent and character of the educational resources and wants of different localities and the state of public sentiment with reference to public schools. While the system and the oral and newspaper discussions it excited had imparted a powerful impulse to education, increased the attendance in most of the schools, and led to the establishment of many where none previously existed, yet the deplorable fact stared the honest patriot in the face that three-fourths of the white youth of the State had gone without instruction entirely, or had been crowded into miserable apologies for schools, without comfortable seats, without desks or blackboards, often without the necessary textbooks, and still oftener without competent teachers."[1] Here, Curry has fused non-schooling with types of education that are unacceptable to him

---

1. *Montgomery Advertiser*, newspaper, March 13, 1898.

but which probably were as excellent as any other, to give a false impression of illiteracy. This was a favorite tactic of the Radicals.

Curry's First Success In School Legislation

Curry now writes, from the distance of many years, about events in 1854: "Closely allied to, and the basis of, material prosperity, and the truest development of physical resources, is free and universal education, under State control and State support. [At that time, of course, this was anathema to the small government, low tax philosophy of the Old South.] Alexander E. Meek, then of Mobile, a brilliant speaker, of large culture, rich poetic fancy, progressiveness of aim and thought, had the patriotic purpose to develop the minds of Alabama youth. In due time, from his Committee on Education [Jabez was a member of that committee], he submitted an able report, accompanied by an elaborate bill, providing for the establishment and maintenance of a system of public schools. After an interesting debate, the bill became law."[1]

"For brevity, this is an edited version of Mr. Meek's bill. It has an element of envy and bitterness similar to that of Boston Radical Republicans during Reconstruction: 'Tuesday, January 2, 1854. Mr. Meek, from the Committee on Education, reported a bill to be entitled 'An Act to establish and maintain a system of free public schools in the State of Alabama.' "There is no subject of more momentous and vital importance to any State than that of common school education. This lies at the foundation, and enters into the elements of every enlightened and popular form of government. Without a general diffusion of knowledge among its inhabitants, no State can be prosperous, dignified and secure or exempt from those vices and crimes which are incident to barbarism.... Those States of our Confederacy [meaning the United States] which have devoted the most attention and effort to the advancement of popular instruction have, despite every disadvantage of climate and soil, been the most successful in all the arts, comforts, conveniences, securities, and other excellences, of a social and political character. This is the secret of New England's prosperity, and the wonderful magic that has made Yankee ingenuity and skill proverbial throughout the world. The common school cabins ... nurtured a race worthy to inherit the institutions of their country, and to act as the apostles of scientific advancement and republican freedom in every portion of the globe. [Wouldn't all this have sounded traitorous to Southerners in 1854?] The industrial activity

---

1. Jabez Curry, hand-written autobiographical notes, April 1876.

of the Eastern States, their manufacturing and mechanical enterprises, their maritime spirit ... are mainly owing to the fact that, so proudly asserted by one of their own sons, the gifted historian of the United States, that 'every child, as it was born into the world, was lifted from the earth by the genius of the country, and in the statutes of the land, received, as its birth-right, a pledge of public care of its morals and its mind....' [Schooling] tends to diminish crime, by removing its causes. It puts an end, partially, to the necessity for penitentiaries, jails, gibbets, pillaries, whipping posts and all the other horrid paraphernalia of a vindictive penal system. Better to purify the fountain than to attempt to scatter the muddy water after they have pervaded and poisoned the land."[1]

Death of Curry's Father

"In May 1855 my father died, calling forth from the community expressions of profound and universal grief. He was universally popular, very liberal and a faithful Christian. The directors of the Alabama and Tennessee River Rail Road Company, from which body he had been a member, passed resolutions of regard and sympathy. My father was a liberal subscriber to, and an earnest friend of this Road. In 1852 I acted as agent for the Road and traversed the counties of Talladega, Calhoun and Randolph, making speeches for and obtaining subscriptions to the capital stock of the Company. For one year I was a director but gave up the place on account of other duties."

The "Know-Nothings" and Alabama Assembly

"1855 will long be remembered in the United States for the origin, growth and defeat of the American or 'Know-Nothing' party. It was a secret organization, with degrees of orders of membership and a ritual. The party suddenly became very popular. Lodges were formed in all the cities, towns and villages and almost in every neighborhood in the United States. So strong was the organization, it became presumptuous and intolerant of opposition. The leading object was to cultivate an intense Americanism to exclude aliens from suffrage and Roman Catholics from office. Nearly all the Whigs and very many Democrats were beguiled into the party. It encountered its first most serious opposition in Virginia, when Henry A. Wise, as the Democratic candidate for governor, visited every portion of the State and made one of the most brilliant and effective canvasses ever made in the United States. His election crippled

---

1. *Journal of the 4ᵗʰ Biennial Session of the House of Representatives of the State of Alabama, Session of 1853-54*, p. 303. (Montgomery: Brittan & Blue, State Printers, 1854.)

seriously the power of the party. In many States the excitement was very high, no more so than in Alabama. I was consistently and inflexibly opposed to the Know-Nothing party and in spite of many kindly warnings as to my self-inflicted injury, I was 'pronounced' in my hostility to the Secret Party and its principles.

"The death of my father and the settlement of his large estate made it proper for me to decline candidacy for any office, but on the 3rd of July a county convention nominated me unanimously for the House of Representatives. Having apparently no option, I accepted the nomination and from that day until the election I traveled and spoke every day, Sunday excepted. The Know-Nothings were confident of success and I had to debate Lewis E. Parsons, one of the ablest lawyers in the State, afterwards governor by Presidential appointment [as a Reconstruction governor]. The crowds were large and the debates warm and excited. Several times I spoke in the face of threats of violence. Having obtained a copy of oaths and rituals, I used them unsparingly. I rode on horseback to my various appointments and enjoyed the canvas. My whole ticket was elected, I leading the poll, receiving a majority of 2,550. I was at a precinct, over thirty miles from the Court House on the day of the election and rode on horseback to the Court House that night, reaching the Square about two o'clock to be received by as glad and enthusiastic an assemblage as ever greeted me."[1]

The Internal Improvements Committee

The Alabama legislature met in December, 1855 in Montgomery. Richard Walker, the Speaker of the House, put Curry on the committee to examine and audit the accounts of the Bank Commissioner and placed him as Chairman of the Internal Improvements Committee.

There is a vast difference between the nationalized "internal improvements" that the Republicans advocated and those made by an individual state within its own boundaries. Curry, the advocate of state sovereignty, repudiated the Republican doctrine which would lead to the take-over of state functions by Washington; but each state had the legitimate right to build its own canals, roads, bridges and railroad lines. Still, there were flaws in Curry's conceptions.

Governor Collier sent the following message to the Alabama Assembly: "In my communication of December 1849 and November 1851, I expressed my views quite at length upon the propriety of encouraging the improvement of the navi-

---

1. Last two sections, from Jabez Curry's hand-written autobiographical notes, April 1876.

gation of our rivers and the construction of Rail Roads, plank roads, and other facilities of inter-communication.... During the past year a strong feeling has manifested itself to connect North and South Alabama by a more direct communication than any of the charters heretofore granted have contemplated. Many primary meetings and several conventions of delegates from quite a number of counties have been held, and numerously attended, for the purpose of enlightening and uniting public opinion and action in this most interesting project. The result of the deliberations of these conventions, I believe, is an agreement to recommend the construction of [a railroad].... In a social, commercial and political point of view, this would be a road of the first importance. It would introduce North and South Alabama to each other; sections at present detached, in which the masses of each have little intercourse with each other. Indeed, they are comparative strangers, though they live under the same government and are amenable to the same laws. That this great improvement would create a community of feeling and interest, and a sense of mutual dependence cannot be doubted, while at the same time it would furnish facilities for trade, which would be made available, to an extent greatly productive of the interest of both sections."[1]

In December 1853, Jabez Curry followed the governor's message and introduced several bills to incorporate new railroad companies This was soon followed by a notation that indicates, once again, the contradictions and blind spots in Curry's thinking on state sovereignty. He attempted to involve the Federal government in subsidizing one railroad project: "Mr. Curry, of the Internal Improvements Committee, to whom was referred joint memorials to the Congress of the United States, asking grants of land for the Wills Valley, Elyton and Beard's Bluff Rail Road companies, reported back a joint memorandum to the Congress of the United States asking similar grants for all rail road companies in this State."[2]

The governor obviously saw the contradictions. He vetoed the bill. It passed, over his veto. The attorney-general realized the dangers in this legislation. He told the governor it was unconstitutional. The state Treasurer was instructed to make no disbursements under that law.

---

1. *Journal of the 4th Biennial Session of the House of Representatives of the State of Alabama, Session of 1853-54*, p. 13.
2. Ibid., p. 334.

The State Bank Fiasco

Jabez Curry was a member of the committee to examine and audit the accounts of the Bank Commissioner. Years later, he wrote about the disastrous situation and his role in resolving it. "Perhaps no State suffered more than Alabama did in her effort to do the business of banking, and by financial hocus-pocus to save the people from the burden of a duty of contributing to the support of the government by legitimate taxation. In 1823 the State Bank was incorporated. From 1832 to 1836, branch banks were established at Mobile, and at Montgomery, Decatur and Huntsville, and bonds of the State were sold to furnish their capital. In 1836 no State taxes were collected, and the profits of banking defraying all government expenses.... Under vicious legislation, wasteful discounts, the temptation of cotton speculation and other influences leading to bad management, the banks demonstrated their inability or insecurity as government and business agencies. In 1837 the banks suspended specie payments, and up to 1842 currency had depreciated to nearly one half its face value, and in that year the State indebtedness approached fourteen million dollars. That sterling and wise patriot, Benjamin Fitzpatrick, one of the worthiest and most popular of State executives, recommended that the banks be put in liquidation and their affairs be brought to a final settlement.... That great lawyer, and afterwards, great judge of the Supreme Court of the United States, John A. Campbell, deeply interested in preserving the State's financial integrity, consented to stand for the legislature.... Campbell was the recognized leader of those who sought to save public honor and private welfare. Measures were adopted during that and succeeding sessions, looking to a gradual but final extinguishment of the state bank and branches. In 1846, under an act to settle the affairs of the banks and to apply the assets to the payment of the State bonds ... Francis Strother Lyon, Esquire, of Demopolis, the sole commissioner and trustee, had extraordinary powers vested in him. No man ever had superior proof of legislative and popular confidence, and the confidence was fully justified by his able and successful administration of the most delicate and difficult duties. His report, 25 November 1853, was referred to a joint select committee. Jamison, Jones and Dickinson of the Senate, and Bell, [Jabez] Curry and Wilkins of the House, with power and authority to examine, audit and settle the elaborate and complicated accounts.

"The committee reported that the bonded debt had been reduced to 3.6 million dollars and the circulation of outstanding bank notes, to 290,000 dollars."[1]

Curry as US Congressman

In May of 1857, Jabez Curry was nominated as the Democratic candidate for Congress for the seventh Alabama district. In accepting the nomination, he outlined his reasons for being a Democrat; weaving together the principles of Jefferson, Calhoun and Andrew Jackson. He proclaimed his support for state sovereignty and his conviction that the Federal government was a "creature of the States." He praised the Democrats for, among other issues, giving the United States a stable currency by divorcing the government from banking by crushing the United States Bank.

Curry won the election. His opponent withdrew after accompanying him for two days of debate, but Curry felt he was on a mission and went on to make speeches in every county, instructing the people on political issues and the character of the government.

In November 1857, Jabez Curry went to Washington to take his seat in Congress, with his wife Ann, his two children (Susan, seven years old, and Manly, only seven months) and a servant. He boarded at Ebbitts House, where several Congressmen and his kinsmen, Lucius Q.C. Lamar, also resided.

He was appointed to the Committee on Revolutionary War Claims. His first speech, in February 1858, was on the admission of Kansas to the Union. Revolutionary War Claims was the subject of his next speech. Curry showed his fiscal conservatism and desire to limit the size of government when he spoke against the further granting of pensions to veterans of the War of 1812. He believed in pensions for the disabled, but for them only, and sought to prove that the pensions for the Revolutionary soldiers should not be considered a precedent. Jabez described the American army during the Revolution as being in a different category than an army raised by regularly organized government agencies. Curry argued that if the bill granting these pensions was correct, then Congress also had the power to construct asylums, hospitals and homes, and to feed and shelter the veterans and their wives and educate their children. That would create a class of consumers interested in sustaining a government that would support them, a class that would advocate large expenditures and possibly infuse poisonous methods in the public mind. Curry was absolutely correct in his prediction.

---

1. Jabez Curry article, "The Session of the Alabama Legislature, 1853-54," from a fragment of an unknown Baptist newspaper, unknown date, in the Curry Papers.

Curry later said: "Some whispers of discontent were heard among my constituents but their good sense approved." Alexander Stephens sent a copy of the speech to his brother, Linton, with a letter, which said: "It is in my opinion a first rate speech. I heard it and it was delivered well, one of the best delivered speeches I have heard this session. Jabez occasionally inquires of me after you. He is the ablest man from Alabama in the House and some think of him abler than Clay of the Senate."[1]

In December, Curry spoke on "Expenditures and the Tariff." Curry was a free trade advocate. He pointed out the connection between protectionism and the constantly increasing appropriations on Congress, charging that the protectionists supported these increases to create a necessity for increased taxes.

Curry's Second Term in Congress

In 1859 Curry was returned, without opposition, for his second term in the House. He was appointed to the Committee on Naval Affairs.

The atmosphere in Congress was tense. John Brown's raid had occurred that summer and passions were running high. On December 10, Curry spoke on "The Progress of Anti-Slaveryism." Without personal invective, he made an appeal for simple justice for the Southern minority. He took as his premise that, "free governments, so far as their protecting power is concerned, are made for minorities." Once again, Curry set forth the state sovereignty position as a way to accomplish such protection under the American government. Granting the Republican Party's claim that it was not responsible for the acts of radical abolitionists, he traced the history of the anti-slavery movement for over twenty years, pointed out the manner in which it had snowballed, and called attention to the Republicans' acceptance of it. He posed rhetorical questions on anti-slavery aims and asked the Republicans to judge their honest position toward the South's desires by considering the stand they would take on them. He proclaimed that when a majority could interpret the Constitution at its will, the government was a despotism. The power of self-protection resided in each state.

With the election of Lincoln, Curry saw only one course open. On November 26, 1860, he made a speech at the Methodist Church in Talladega, *Perils and Duty of the South*, outlining again the confederation concept of government and the Southern defense of slavery. He said the "Black Republican

---

1. Jabez Curry, hand-written autobiographical notes, April 1876 and letter from Alexander Stephens to Lanton Stephens, May 9, 1858, from Stephens Papers, Manhattanville College.

party, sectional and hostile," constituted a foreign government and he advocated secession as the only remedy.

In December 1860, secession was the only topic of discussion. The debates were inflammatory. Republicans laughed derisively in the House when the telegram announcing South Carolina's secession was read.

The Confederacy began to form. Alabama governor Moore appointed Curry Commissioner to Maryland to consult with that state's government as to the best actions "to protect the rights, interests and honor of the Slaveholding States."

On January 1, 1861, Curry left Washington for the South. Back in Montgomery, the secession convention was in progress. On January 10, the ordinance of secession was passed. The action was announced, the throngs poured in. Curry listened to the bells ringing and cannon firing. That night crowds of men, women and children filled the streets. Curry was among the many who spoke to the throngs, congratulating them, confident that this day would be remembered as a great one in Alabama's history.[1]

1. Abridged from Rice, pp. 29-36.

Chapter 10. Curry's Mental Transition

The harsh reality of Reconstruction gradually wore down Jabez Curry's resolve to continue to "fight the good fight." Later, he wrote his son Manly this letter, indicating his amazing mental change: "Crushed, subjugated, impoverished as we were by the war; insulted, tyrannized over, outraged by Reconstruction Acts; but of what avail to keep alive passion, and cherish hatred? Of the abstract right of a State, in 1860, to secede, under our then form of government, I have not the shadow of a doubt. But no conquered people ever wrote the accepted history of the conquest. To go about shaking our fists and grinding our teeth at the conquerors, dragging as a heavy weight the dead corpse of the Confederacy, is stupid and daily suicidal. Let us live in the present and for the future, leaving the dead Past to take care of itself, drawing only profitable lessons from that and all history."[1]

Curry also wrote this bitter letter: "The country has been impoverished. Our political institutions have been revolutionized; our peculiar civilization destroyed; our cherished theories of government overthrown; we have a new political being; a new system of labor, new fields of industry. We are no longer the peculiar people, the conservators of constitutional liberty, the resistors of encroachment of power; the preservers of ancient forms which included justice and freedom.... We must accept these and all other legitimate facts as they are; offer loyal homage and obedient support to the only government we have."[2]

---

1. Letter from Jabez Curry to his son, Manly Curry, August 12, 1886, Curry Papers.
2. Fragment of Jabez Curry letter to unknown person, from Curry Papers.

Others of his generation refused to accept the new social order and worked to undermine it to reinstate the classic decentralized American democracy; but Curry embraced it: "A mighty revolution has been accomplished and thirty five years has not disclosed or accustomed us to the marvelous changes. The cataclysm swept away the old foundations of the republic. We shall be wise to recognize and acquiesce in the reversible changes, and adapt ourselves to environments. These changes were, in many respects, painful, and were resisted with all the resources of press and party and State. They are irrevocable. What cannot be cured must be endured, utilized and made auxiliaries to our prosperity and civilization. Perhaps nothing is such a hindrance to true progress as a determined unwillingness to learn."[1]

Yet, other notable Southern men remained true to the vision that brought on secession and war. In the summer of 1867, Robert Toombs returned from Europe where he had been hiding, and said: "I regret nothing in the past, but the dead and the failure, and I am ready today to use the best means I can command to establish the principles for which I fought."[2]

Curry wrote this in his diary about Joe E. Johnston, a warrior he greatly admired: "At night, General Joseph E. Johnston called. He is the most thoroughly posted military man I ever talked to. I think, the best commander during the war. He is quite unreconstructed, in one sense of that term. He thinks the present condition of the country justified the South in her attempt to stop that revolution which has brought about such an overthrow of true republicanism."[3]

Also, in October 1873, at the Montgomery White Sulphur Springs, Curry attended the Southern Historical Society meeting. Its unreconstructed objective was to "collect and preserve materials for an authentic history" of the South. Its members had not given up the old ideas. General Jubal Early spoke. He wore a suit of Confederate gray. Generals Beauregard, Wilcox, Fitzhugh Lee, Dabney Maury, Humes and Raphael Semmes were there, as well as Wade Hampton. A statue of Stonewall Jackson was unveiled.

Edwin Anderson Alderman, Curry's biographer, noted the amazing change in his political perspective, mirroring the Radicals: "The one-time ardent secessionist recognized secession as a thing of the past ... [and] that a wise preoccupation of the South should be in education and industry rather than in politics."[4]

---

1. Fragment of a Jabez Curry typewritten manuscript, no date, from Curry Papers.
2. Clara Mildred Thompson, *Reconstruction in Georgia: Economic, Social, Political, 1865-1872* (New York: The Columbia University Press, 1915), p. 174.
3. Jabez Curry diary, November 23, 1876.
4. Alderman and Gordon, p. 248.

Then, for the first time, Curry, the great defender of freedom and local self-government, began to doubt if freedom was for everyone. In a strange way his views once again paralleled the Radical Republicans, where the "degraded and disloyal" should have their freedoms taken away: "There is a tendency to push democracy to fatal excess and jump to the conclusion that an ideal government is equally applicable to all peoples. The enjoyment of human rights and privileges here, capacity of self-government by a people trained and disciplined, does not mean that pearls are to be cast before swine, nor that the most difficult of civil attainments can be achieved by all races, nor by ignorant and semi-pagan people. That all countries or communities should be invested with home rule is a proposition too absurd for serious argument. We may put the franchise, representation of the people, the voice of the majority, inalienable rights to choose our governors, into creeds and platforms, but we cannot shut our eyes to the fact that popular government, as it exists with us and in England, is for many years with most countries out of the question, and that many peoples would come to early grief, if they had it....

No sane man, acquainted with civil government, can seriously contend that the degraded, the indolent, the corrupt, the vicious, are entitled to the freedom which we have won after centuries of toil and trial and experience."[1]

Moving to Virginia

In 1868, Jabez Curry resigned from the Presidency of Howard College in Marion, Alabama, because he could not raise enough money to support the school. Alabama was bankrupt due to carpetbag misrule. He made the decision to move to Virginia, but there were other factors besides Alabama's devastated economy.

His wife Mary had grown up in the cosmopolitan capital of Richmond. She had been surrounded by her big, loving family and a steady stream of the significant political, religious and business leaders of the city. Her father, James Thomas, was one of the wealthier men in the city. For Mary, Marion was a boring, provincial town. And, as mentioned before, Mr. Thomas, as Chairman of the Board of Directors of Richmond College, paved the way for Jabez to receive a professorship at that school.

---

1. Jabez Curry article in a fragment of an unknown Baptist newspaper and unknown date, from Curry Papers.

Did Jabez Curry move to Virginia believing it was less tormented by Reconstruction than Alabama? That is what he said. But the reality is that "The Old Dominion" was probably more wracked by misrule. A great spirit of revenge drove the Radicals to destroy that state. Curry more likely went there to placate his wife.

The Radicals hated Virginia. Richmond was the capital and soul of the Confederacy. The most demoralizing of Union defeats occurred there: Bull Run, Manassas, the Peninsula Campaign, The Wilderness, Chancellorsville. The War, in this state, generated hundreds of thousands of Northern casualties.

As a result, Virginia was politically and militarily tortured longer than almost any other Confederate state. It was not re-admitted back into the Union until 1870.

Professor Robert Stiles, in the classic 19th century book, *Why the Solid South*, described the devastation succinctly. "Virginia suffered more than any other state during the war, because larger armies subsisted and contended upon her soil for longer periods, than upon the soil of any other state; and she suffered more from Reconstruction, because in its course her ancient domain was rent asunder, and she lost one-third of her territory [when the Union state of West Virginia was carved out of her land].[1]

Curry's Mental Transition: The Readjuster Movement

Jabez Curry was undergoing a 180-degree transformation in his thinking. State sovereignty was dissolving and nationalized power, the dream of the Radicals, was filling the empty places in his mind. This was apparent in the 1870s as he approached politics again, as his legal "disabilities" neared their end.

Virginia had always followed a policy of internal improvements consisting of canals, turnpikes and railroads and even tax-supported schools, to knit together her communities and advance prosperity, but had shunned Federal aid for these objectives. Virginia borrowed money for these projects by selling bonds.

Between 1850 and 1860, the state's debt tripled. When the war ended, all the money for public works had gone but the debt was now $38 million. The state was bankrupt; but the 1866 carpetbag legislators not only assumed full responsibility for the entire ante-bellum principle but also authorized funding of

---

1. Robert Stiles, author of Chapter VIII, "Reconstruction in Virginia," from *Why The Solid South*, Hilery Herbert, editor (New York: Negro Universities Press, 1969, reprinted from original publication date of 1890), p. 216.

the war-time interest into bonds bearing the same rate of interest as the principle. The governor believed that the pre-war policy of state/private company collaboration for internal projects should be given over entirely to private companies in order to scale back the debt.

But the Radical carpetbaggers erased "frugality" from Virginia's Bill of Rights. Their revolutionary social programs accelerated the debt.

The Democrats and Conservatives were willing to pay the "true" debts but not those additionally imposed by corruption, extravagance or social experimentation and state-run schools. But, repudiation of those elements meant the return of Federal occupation.

From this turmoil a new political party emerged — the Readjusters. Its program was the median position between the traditionalists and the Radicals. The new Jabez Curry supported the "semi-Radical" Readjuster platform, although some commentators claim he sided with the opposition, the "Debt-Payers." But, no; in reality Curry endorsed several Readjuster candidates and actively and publicly promoted their ideas, including the support of the carpetbagger controlled and developed school system.

The Readjusters believed the state's creditors should be compelled to share in the general loss occasioned by the war and Reconstruction. This gave the movement its name. It was supported by the hard-pressed communities.

When Virginia was finally re-admitted into the Union, its debt had ballooned to $45 million. The interest on this debt almost equaled the entire revenue income of the state.

In 1878, the McColloch Act would have financed the debt, through a New York bank headed by J.P. Morgan. The bill also reflected the midway position between the Radicals and Readjusters; it rejected state sovereignty while also rejecting some extreme social experiments.

In 1879, the Readjusters called a convention to block McColloch. Jabez Curry campaigned for their candidate, John Daniel, a much-decorated Confederate officer, even though Daniel advocated protective tariffs, internal improvements at national expense, and radical equality between whites and blacks. These policies had been anathema to Curry.

In the election, Readjusters took 56 House and 24 Senate seats. William Cameron, their candidate, became governor. When in power the Readjusters behaved like Radical clones; they instituted more reckless spending, they destroyed corporations through punitive taxes, they expanded the carpetbag school system and controlled commerce like a totalitarian government. The Republicans, initially fearful, now urged their support.

Now, Jabez Curry became more active in politics. In January 1874, he visited the Virginia House of Delegates. Several members proposed him for the United States Senate. Curry had to decline. He was still under the "disabilities" of his post-war pardon. In 1872, most Confederates had been granted amnesties, but it was not until 1877 that Jabez and the other "major rebels" were released from their legal restrictions.

Also in 1874, demonstrating how far Curry's views had changed, he was approached to become a candidate for State Superintendent of Public Instruction. Dr. William Ruffner, the fanatic Radical who drafted the law establishing the public schools in Virginia under the carpetbag constitution, was the current Superintendent. Curry would oppose him. It appears that Jabez had no problem joining forces with those who were intent on exterminating Southern culture and Southern minds. Only his legal disabilities stood in the way.

CHAPTER 11. JABEZ CURRY AND THE PEABODY EDUCATION FUND

On February 3, 1881, Curry wrote: "I received in Richmond a telegram from the Honorable Robert C. Winthrop, Chairman of the Peabody Education Board; 'You have been unanimously elected General Agent of the Peabody Education Fund. We greatly desire your presence here tomorrow morning or sooner.' By the first train, I went to Washington and was introduced to the Board, in session at the Riggs House. In acknowledgement of the high honor, sought by many worthy applicants, I expressed my sincere thanks, and my determination to give my best powers to carrying out the past policy, with which I was familiar. General Henry R. Jackson, a Trustee from Georgia, informed me that General Grant [also a Peabody Trustee] made the motion for my election, jocularly remarking that 'the nomination was fit to be made, notwithstanding the gentleman was not from Ohio.' [Ulysses S. Grant was from Ohio.]"[1]

The Peabody Education Fund was the largest school philanthropy of the 19th century. As a result, Jabez Curry became a nationally prominent figure.

But, the Peabody Fund, due to its previous General Agent, Barnas Sears, was extremely hostile to the South. Through Sears' policies, Peabody fulfilled the ideals of the Freedmen's Bureau. Peabody was the first step in nationalizing Southern schools. And, as was said before, controlling the Southern mind in the 19th century presaged the take-over of Northern children's minds in the 20th.

---

1. Jabez Curry, hand-written notes, *My Educational Life.*

When Jabez Curry accepted his position and continued the Peabody's prior policies, it can truly be said that "he advocated all that he hated."

It began in the summer of 1869. After an exhausting period of teaching at Richmond College and preaching, Jabez Curry went for a brief vacation to White Sulphur Springs in West Virginia. The surviving elite of the Confederacy gathered there. Robert E. Lee came for the healing waters. So did Alexander Stephens and other important men.

While there, Curry met the wealthy financier George Peabody, the creator of the fund. With him was Barnas Sears. This short encounter with the terminally ill Peabody would be the paradoxical turning point in Curry's life. He wrote: "This was the first and only time I ever met him. The interview was pleasant and I was agreeably impressed by his benevolent countenance, the dignity and care with which he received visitors and his earnest, patriotic desire that the impoverished South should be benefited by his benefaction."[1]

Sears befriended Curry, since they were both partners in the world of education and because Sears "saw something." Curry noted that, "to be among the people who were the beneficiaries of the Trust, he [Sears] took up his residence in Staunton, Virginia [Sears had lived in Massachusetts]. We had frequent conferences in reference to his work and he was often a guest at my house, where we discussed with freedom, difficult and delicate questions growing out of the administration."[2]

George Peabody established his fund in 1867 with a gift of one million dollars. In 1869, he added another million. Then, 1.1 million in State of Mississippi bonds and 348,000 dollars in Florida bonds.

George Peabody was the foremost philanthropist of his day, the first in modern America. He set an example which was to be followed by Rockefeller and Carnegie.

Peabody had no clear plan of operation for his fund. His initial idea stated his concern for "the educational needs of those portions of our beloved and common country which have suffered from the destructive ravages and the not less disastrous consequences of civil war."[3]

Before analyzing the plan of operation that Sears conceptualized, let Curry give an overview of George Peabody and his life: "He was born February 18, 1795,

1. Ibid.
2. Ibid.
3. J.L.M. Curry, *A Brief Sketch of George Peabody and a History of the Peabody Education Fund Through Thirty Years* (Cambridge: University Press, John Wilson and Son, 1898), p. 19.

in Danvers, south of Salem, Massachusetts. He attended a common village school from 1803 to 1807. At 11 Peabody was apprenticed as a shopboy in a grocery store. In 1811, he was a clerk with his brother, David, who kept a dry-goods store in Newburyport. A fire destroyed the business. At 16, George was an orphan without any money or employment. In May 1812 he sailed to Georgetown, in the District of Columbia, and with his uncle and two sons, established another dry-goods business. Then in 1814, at age 19 George became a partner with Elisha Riggs. Riggs supplied the capital and Peabody the management skill. In 1815 Riggs and Peabody moved to Baltimore as well as Philadelphia and New York."

In 1827, Peabody visited England to purchase goods. In 1829, Riggs withdrew. Peabody now headed the company. In 1837, he had a permanent residence in London as a merchant and money-broker.

In the panic of 1857, with British securities companies, banks and corporations collapsing, Peabody had amassed such a fortune that he bailed out the Bank of England.

In 1862, Peabody gave 150,000 pounds "to ameliorate the conditions of the poor and needy" in London. He added more money to build housing for the laboring poor: 5,121 dwellings for 20,000 people.

For this, the British government offered him a barony. He declined, as an American citizen. A statue of Peabody was erected in front of the London Merchant's Exchange. It was unveiled by the Prince of Wales.

Peabody had built the basis of his fortune in the South. In 1837, he made an extensive tour of the Southern states. In 1862, he said that he thought his fellow countrymen were "mad in bringing about the dreadful war that now exists." Yet, when peace returned, Peabody said, "Never during the war or since have I permitted the contest, or any passions engendered by it, to interfere with the social relations and warm friendship which I had formed for a very large number of the people of the South.... And now, after the lapse of these eventful years, I am more deeply, more earnestly, more painfully convinced than ever, of our need of mutual forbearance and conciliation, of Christian charity and forgiveness of united effort to bind up the fresh and broken wounds of the nation."[1]

Upon the public announcement of the Fund, President Andrew Johnson visited Peabody, who afterward referred to this as one of the proudest incidents of his life. In March 1867, Congress passed a resolution thanking Peabody for his

---

1. Ibid., p. 24.

gigantic gift to promote education in the South and authorizing the President to create a gold medal to be presented to Peabody.

Robert Winthrop Picks Sears as General Agent

George Peabody selected Robert Winthrop of Boston to help him plan the establishment of the fund. Winthrop was named Chairman of the notable group of men picked as trustees. In both the Massachusetts and Federal House of Representatives Winthrop was the presiding officer, as well as a Senator in the United States Congress.

As Chairman, Winthrop conducted the search for a General Agent. Dozens of the leading educators submitted plans to implement the Peabody bequest.

Barnas Sears, President of Brown University, was the winner, with this proposal: "There are two general methods to be considered; the one is of originating and carrying on a system of schools. The other is that of disbursing funds to the aid of others who shall have the schools in charge. The former method would require an extensive system of agencies. Work will not go on well without an ever-present and active superintendence and vigilance to prevent and correct abuses arising from negligence or selfishness. The latter is simpler, easier and attended with few risks.... To furnish aid where it is most needed, in strengthening and resuscitating schools.... Let good schools, springing up on the soil, growing out of the wants of the people, and meeting these wants, be sprinkled all over the South, as examples, and be made the nucleus for others, and let them be established and controlled, as far as possible, by the people themselves, and they will in time grow into state systems."[1]

Barnas Sears, Disciple of Horace Mann

Sears was born in Sandisfield, Massachusetts in 1802. He was a graduate of Brown University and later became its president; he was a student in Germany, where he trained under Alexander von Humboldt and the learned professors of Berlin and Halle and Leipsig; the pastor of a Baptist church, and afterward the head of an important theological seminary; the successor of Horace Mann as Secretary of the Board of Education of Massachusetts; the author of the *Life of Luther* and several other important volumes.

Barnas Sears was greatly influenced by the philosophies of Horace Mann and, by inference, so was Jabez Curry.

---

1. Ibid., p. 31.

Horace Mann

Horace Mann was an eloquent writer, promoter and political savant. He was known world-wide. In France, he was seen as the embodiment of the American Revolution. Born in Massachusetts in 1795, he had a harsh early farm life and was negatively influenced by Calvanistic preachings of eternal damnation which he constantly heard. This led him to construct a picture of the world where all humans would be perfected by education. He never recovered from Calvinism. Like Sears, he went to Brown University; he majored in teaching, quit, and became a lawyer in 1824. He entered the Massachusetts House of Representatives in 1827, for six years. Then, the State Senate for four years. Mann became a Unitarian, since that religion's world-view was similar to his own. He attempted to improve the condition of the insane. They had been placed in prisons. Mann created mental hospitals and proposed medical treatment for them. In 1837, he created legislation for common schools. As a result he became State Secretary of Education.

Horace Mann's annual reports embodied the idea that education was valuable, not because it promoted the salvation of the soul, as was traditionally believed, but for a higher standard of living in the present world. He collected data to show that education could be measured in economic terms, and expressed teaching theories similar to the child-centered ideas of John Dewey. Much of modern schooling research originates from his annual reports.

One of those reports was called *How Virtue Can Be Imparted By The Schools.* Mann divided morality from religion. Morality led to responsible behavior. Religion, to which he was mostly hostile, led to understanding doctrine to achieve salvation.

Mann and his disciples sounded like Radical Republicans in the 1830s when they proclaimed that "the common school is an integral part of the social order.... Common schools are nurseries of a free republic; private schools, of factions, cabals and contests of force."[1]

Because the masses of immigrants to the United States were determined to retain their own cultures, Mann made the common school the cornerstone of a policy of forced assimilation and the demonizing of parental control.

John Stuart Mill, the famed economist and philosopher, challenged Mann when he said: "A general State education is a mere contrivance for molding

---

1. Richard John Neuhaus, editor, *Democracy and the Renewal of Public Education* (Grand Rapids: William B. Eerdmans Publishing Co., 1987), p. 45.

people to be exactly like one another. And as the mold ... is efficient and successful, it establishes a despotism over the mind."[1]

It would be appropriate here to repeat what Curry said about Horace Mann, during his Dane Law School days. Mann's "earnest enthusiasm and democratic ideas fired my young mind and heart; and since that time I have been an enthusiastic and consistent advocate of universal education." And this, despite the awareness by Curry that Mann was a fanatical Abolitionist who said: "Under a full sense of my responsibility, to my country and my God, I deliberately say, better disunion, better a civil or a servile war, better anything that God in His providence shall send, than an extension of the bounds of slavery."[2]

From the beginning of the drive for government schools, Horace Mann was intent on reforming society by changing the values of children. He had little sympathy for Calvinists or Catholics and was determined to use every legal means, including State coercion in schooling, to insure that other people's children were taught the truth as he understood it.

The "Common School Revival" that began in the 1820s and received definitive form under Mann was a struggle over "education" vs. "instruction," a struggle over the role of schools in shaping the character of the American people. Local religious or ethnic diversity was seen as a problem. Schools not accountable to the political process were condemned as a threat to the best interest of society. The goal was to transform popular schooling into a powerful instrument for social unity.

"Diversity" was seen as perpetuating religious fanaticism. In Catholicism, according to Mann, "children are taught from their tenderest years to wield the sword of polemics with fatal dexterity."[3] It was hoped that the common school could, by inculcating the sublime truths of ethics and natural religion, protect the rising generation from falling into the opposite extremes of becoming "devotees on the one side or profligates on the other."[4]

Mann offered big subsides to book publishers for texts to reflect the new objectives and premises of education from a national perspective. They would be "explaining and enforcing plain and undeniable truths and avoiding prejudices and falsehoods."[5]

---

1. Ibid., p. 51.
2. Alderman and Gordon, p. 75.
3. Neuhaus, p. 28.
4. Ibid., p. 28.
5. Ibid., p. 32.

Since the "common school" expressed a political and social program, a new kind of teacher was needed. A new morality was as important as basic skills. It was the intention of the reformers to move the State into areas of public influence where religion had previously been almost unchallenged, because the Church was viewed with great suspicion. The Normal School (the teacher training school) would play an important part in the efforts of Mann to promote a form of common school religion that was said to have no sectarian character but it was, in fact, consistent with his own beliefs and profoundly subversive to those of his orthodox opponents.

Training teachers was also an effective way of avoiding the problems that a direct assault on local control of schools would cause. It made it possible for parents to believe that the common schools were under the direct oversight of local committees elected by the parents. Yet, the real control was from the teachers shaped by the State Normal Schools.

Barnas Sears' Second Plan

No ex-Confederate state could re-enter the Union unless it accepted its new constitution with the clause demanding State controlled, tax-supported schools. Southerners understood the consequences. Several states refused to approve their constitutions and tried unsuccessfully to remain outside the United States because of this clause.

But Barnas Sears seduced the South into submitting. Cleverly, he used the Peabody Fund as a matching fund. Initially, other than the Freedmen's Bureau schools, the carpetbagger systems rarely got off the ground due to the fierce resistance to them. Sears said that if a private school raised a specific amount of money, Peabody would match it, and then the State, via tax monies, would also put in the same number of dollars. Immediately, this entangled independent schools into the governmental web and made Peabody a quasi-State agency.

Sears: "State Superintendents [of education], have, at my suggestion, issued circulars containing our rules and rates of distribution.... Requests and representatives [for the Peabody money] are sent to the State Superintendent, and if, upon examination, they are found in all respects satisfactory, they are endorsed, and forwarded to the General Agent [Sears] for formal acceptance.... They will in time grow into State systems."[1]

---

1. Proceedings of the Trustees of the Peabody Education Fund. Report of the 10th meeting, 1872, p. 287.

Here, Sears gives an idea of the fund's magnitude: "Altogether the Fund assisted, in 1871, 213 towns, districts and institutions, by the disbursement of $108,900." He evades the reality that the money raised from the people is not tax dollars, but their own money, to receive a subsidy for a private school: "In connection with these contributions from the Peabody Fund, the people receiving them have expended, from their own resources, about $550,000."[1]

Sears noted the obstacles to State-run schools. His comments are accurate, as far as they go. He does not mention the most basic objection: cultural ethnic cleansing. "There was, in the beginning, quite generally, and there is now, to a considerable extent, a natural prejudice against so great an innovation upon the traditions and usages of a whole people. But the obvious necessity of educating in some way all those who enjoy the rights of suffrage and the vast superiority of public over private schools ... have already done much in the way of modifying these hereditary opinions.

The greatest obstacle now to be overcome in maintaining free schools, is the deep-seated aversion to taxation prevalent among the people. They have been educated to look with jealousy upon all improvements at their expense for the public good. The domain of individual rights has been made as wide, and that for the public interest as narrow, as possible."[2]

Barnas Sears' Third Plan

From the earliest stages of his tenure with Peabody, Barnas Sears began working with the Radical Republicans and carpetbaggers in the Southern state governments to make absolutely sure that the mandatory tax-supported schools were an integral part of the new Reconstruction constitutions.

Jabez Curry wrote that the Peabody trustees met in Virginia while the constitutional convention was in progress. The Radical leaders invited them to attend the proceedings. "Dr. Sears made an address to the convention, arguing with unanswerable logic and a wealth of illustrations, in favor of a thorough and well-sustained system of free schools. Mr. Stuart [a trustee] pronounced it one of the ablest and most effective ever delivered on that subject and said that it aided materially in giving shape and impulse to the admirable system of public schools which was soon thereafter put into the statutes of Virginia."[3]

---

1. Proceedings of the Trustees of the Peabody Education Fund, Report of the 9th meeting, 1871, p. 271.
2. Proceedings of the Trustees of the Peabody Education Fund, Report of the 12th meeting, 1874, p. 406.
3. J.L.M. Curry, *A Brief Sketch of George Peabody, etc.,* p. 42.

In a candid moment, Jabez Curry gave one more reason for Southerners to hate being taxed for public schools: "In the transition period after the war, in the chaotic condition of society, many persons holding office were incompetent, or unfaithful and corrupt. Money raised for schools was diverted to other purposes. School funds once existing were 'among the things of the past.' In one state, $420,000 of stock belonging to the Education Fund was disposed of for less than half its value, and squandered on favorites. In another state, the entire permanent school fund of the parishes disappeared, and a trust fund of $1,300,500 was diverted from its legitimate use and passed, at a heavy discount, into the hands of jobbers and brokers."[1]

Barnas Sears, after ensnaring private schools into the state systems by subsidies, moved to the next step — to expand tax-supported schools so as to be universal. Thus: "The citizens of Atlanta were unwilling to be taxed for common schools. But a $2,000 grant from Peabody was the spark that led to a $50,000 school building program."[2]

Similarly, in Petersburg: "The general system of free schools was introduced in the year 1868. A tender of $2,000 from the Peabody Fund was made to the City Council, on condition that it should raise $20,000 and establish public schools for all classes.... The offer was accepted, a Board of Education appointed, its president sent to the Northern cities for the purpose of examining their various school systems."[3]

A.D. Mayo, a Peabody executive, wrote about the consequences of the next step: "These models of well organized and well conducted schools, showed the people what a good graded school is; it did more to enlighten the communities and disarm opposition and create a sound public sentiment than all the verbal arguments. Soon the towns assumed all the expenses when the Fund was withdrawn. Between 1867 and 1898 $12 million was distributed, 8 million by taxes, 4 million by Peabody."[4]

---

1. Ibid., p. 44.
2. Proceedings of the Trustees of the Peabody Education Fund, Report of the 8th meeting, 1870, p. 204.
3 Proceedings of the Trustees of the Peabody Education Fund, Report of the 10th meeting, 1872, p. 293.
4. Annual Report of the Commissioner of the Bureau of Education, for the years, 1900- 01, *Common Schools in the South from 1861 to 1876*, by A.D. Mayo (Washington: US Government Printing Office), p. 458.

As the state systems became bigger they became bolder. The Mississippi State Superintendent of Schools said: "Our steady aim has been to make the public schools superior to the private schools, and to supplant them.... In the city of Jackson there have been several private schools, but this year nearly all of them will be abolished."[1] He does not mean they would be destroyed but rather absorbed into the state system.

Peabody and the Freedmen's Bureau

Barnas Sears joined forces with the infamous Freedmen's Bureau to expand Richmond's public schools. This is how the process of absorption into the state system took place: "Present plan of public education was inaugurated in April 1869.... An appropriation of $15,000 was made; but, as this amount was entirely inadequate for the purpose, additional aid was furnished by Northern educational societies, the Freedmen's Bureau and the Agent of the Peabody Fund, to an equal amount. With the money thus furnished, 52 schools, with 2,400 scholars, were opened and continued during the session of 1869-70. At the close of the session, the city took entire control of the schools for both white and colored children.... In April 1871, the schools of the city were made part of the State system."[2]

Sears and Normal Schools

Following the philosophies of Horace Mann, Barnas Sears put a great effort into creating state controlled teacher training Normal Schools.

Jabez Curry gave this overview: "It is a concurrent experience in all countries which have established systems of public instruction, that they are very incomplete and defective, if they do not embrace professional schools, where the science of education and the art of education are regularly taught. Dr. Sears favored State Normal Schools, on account of their superiority over Normal departments in colleges and academies, which are likely to be overshadowed by the literary and science departments. A complete theoretical and practical course, illustrated in all the branches to be taught, with their environments, was found nowhere out of the Normal Schools.

---

1. Proceedings of the Trustees of the Peabody Education Fund, Report of the 12th meeting, 1874, p. 423.
2. Proceedings of the Trustees of the Peabody Education Fund, Report of the 10th meeting, 1872, p. 292.

In the whole South there was not a single Normal school. Many annexes and departments with that name were hastily organized but these were denominational or private institutions, and rivalries and jealousies soon compelled a resort to the principle of confining aid to such schools as were under state control."[1]

Then Barnas Sears put his ideal plan into effect. "In 1868 in Tennessee, the law established a State Normal School with the understanding that the state should receive some aid from the Peabody Fund. $1,000 would be given to the support of each State Normal School."[2]

In 1878, Sears recommended to the trustees that more of the Peabody appropriations should be shifted to create and expand State Normal Schools.

In the winter of 1878, Sears went to Texas, where he proposed to the legislature, through the governor, to make a donation of $6,000 if the state would establish and maintain a first-class Normal School. The legislature agreed and founded the Sam Houston Normal School at Huntsville and the Normal School at Prairie View for Negroes.

Sears' greatest effort went into forming the Normal School at Nashville, Tennessee. This would eventually become the George Peabody College for Teachers, the centerpiece for all the Normal schools.

Sears' Death. His Unfinished Business

In March 1880, Barnas Sears became ill. In June, he was taken from his home in Staunton, Virginia, to Saratoga Springs in New York. He died on July 6. Sears was 78 years old. He left three unfinished goals which Jabez Curry would attempt to complete: the establishment of state-run Normal schools in every Southern state; the expansion of the Nashville Normal School so that it would serve the whole South; and lastly, to sponsor Congressional acceptance of national aid for Southern schools.

Sears and Curry

Ever since their first meeting in 1867 at White Sulpher Springs, Curry and Sears had maintained a strong friendship, based largely on their shared belief in education and the fact that they were both ministers. And with time, Curry transformed to believe in universal, tax-funded common schools. They had many discussions. Then, in 1877, when Sears was 74 and felt he was slipping, physi-

---

1. J.L.M. Curry, *A Brief Sketch of George Peabody, etc.*, p. 121.
2. Proceedings of the Trustees of the Peabody Education Fund, 4th meeting, 1867-68, p. 43.

cally, he invited Jabez to his home in Staunton. Curry's diary described that moment: "July 31, 1877. At 12:30 p.m. Stage for Millboro. View from mountain, magnificent. Supper at Millboro. Car for Staunton. Arrived at midnight. Found Dr. Sears' son waiting to conduct me to his father's house on the hill overlooking the town. Place much improved. The oaks encouraged; other trees and flowers along the graveled walks. Quite a variety of fruit trees. House well arranged, economizing space, and neatly furnished." August 1: "Coming from chamber to parlor, Dr. Sears gave me a cordial greeting. Until 12, in the house and under the trees, we talked of education at the South and the Peabody work."[1]

Long before this, Sears had concluded that Curry was the best qualified person to succeed him and it seems that, during their meeting at Staunton, Sears told him so.

Near the end of his life Barnas Sears wrote this strategy letter to Jabez: "We shall be more and more interested in the legislation in the several States. We come directly in contact with legislative bodies in arranging for Normal Schools. I would not be surprised if when you come to the front, as I confidently expect you will, you shall find yourself specially at ease in this congenial atmosphere. I am sure a great work is before you. I do not regret being a pioneer. I only hope the pioneer work was well done. I want no higher honor. I could have had no higher joy."[2]

Then, quietly, Sears wrote this letter to Robert Winthrop: "Speaking of our successors, I would say, have recently had Dr. Curry with me, and went over with him all my plans and dealings. I am more and more satisfied that he is our man, he is so many-sided, so clear in his view, so judicious and knows so well how to deal with all classes of men. His whole being is wrapped up in general education and he is the best lecturer or speaker on the subject in the South. He is in perfect accord with us on all points. If I can be the means of securing him, for the future General Agent, I think it will be the best thing I ever did for the Trustees."[3]

Why Did Curry Become General Agent?

Everything in Jabez Curry's background should have compelled him to reject Peabody as Sears had constructed it. Sears attached private schools to the hated carpetbagger governments and the Freedmen's Bureau. Sears planned to

---

1. J.L.M. Curry Diary, July 31, August 1, 1877.
2. Anderson and Gordon, p. 252.
3. Barnas Sears letter of September 7, 1877, to Robert Winthrop, J.L.M. Curry Papers.

nationalize Southern schools. All this should have repelled Curry, but it did not. He rationalized his new views and his decision this way: "Only a wise people can govern itself; an ignorant people must be governed.... Emancipation was a great and needed revolution, marred in its benefits by giving suffrage to men who, according to those who imposed the boon, were brutalized by slavery. Right or wrong, wise or unwise, the act is irrevocable Morally, socially, politically, its influence upon the white people, upon both races, has been deplorable, incalculably vicious. We must save ourselves. Passion, prejudice, blind obedience to the past, a Macabre spirit, will avail no good."[1]

Then his viewpoint became clearer and stronger: "We must get rid of the transmitted evils of slavery. Every consideration of justice, humanity, self-preservation, material prosperity, demands that the State, by wise and liberal provision, shall secure the proper education of the Negro. It is impossible that the two races of equal civil rights and privileges, the one educated, the other, illiterate, shall occupy the same territory without friction and peril. We are tethered to the lowest stratum of society, and if we do not lift it up, it will drag us down to the nethermost hell of poverty and degradation. In uplifting the Negro in manhood and womanhood, we are lifting ourselves."[2]

But there was a paradox, even deeper than state sovereignty versus an alien and hostile authority or a nationalized imposition of a foreign educational system. It is the Baptist conflict of soul freedom vs. an external power over the human mind. Curry never reconciled this contradiction. "Under the political systems of antiquity, the Middle Ages, and to some extent, of existing governments in Europe, the individual existed for the whole society, was at all times under its control and could be sacrificed for its benefit. In modern society and especially for us, the corporation or State control is repudiated, the spirit of individuality more prevails, and the notion predominates that governments are made for the citizens, not the citizen for the government; that there are birthrights and privileges of race, and the individual and ... the State has not right to prescribe or control opinions or forms of worship or coerce support of a system contrary to belief." Yet, that was exactly the intention of tax-supported schools.[3]

---

1. Proceedings of the Trustees of the Peabody Education Fund, 29th meeting, 1890, p. 263.
2. Fragment of Jabez Curry typewritten manuscript, no date, from Curry Papers.
3. Fragment of letter to unknown person, unknown date, Curry Papers.

Then Curry presented the antithesis of his prior thought, making a "free state" sound more like a totalitarian one with its domination over the human mind and sentiments: "A free government can be stable and secure only when intelligence and patriotism act in concert. Public opinion is a safer barrier against oppression, executive usurpation, legislative robbery, Communism, only when the public opinion is sufficiently enlightened [although, it might be "enlightened" toward Communism, as well] which is attainable by spreading as widely as possible among our people a true sense of their interests and training them in those sentiments upon which alone the fabric of a free government can ever be safely erected."[1]

And here, Curry confuses freedom with the totalitarian dream ideal of making people perfect, against their will: "Life is not worth living if we are to be surrounded by, and are incapable of rising above boorish, coarse, vulgar men and women.... It is the right of the unborn to be granted an intelligent and refined parentage."[2]

Curry on Sears

"To succeed one so competent," Curry wrote, "was an embarrassment and a stimulus, exciting fears and giving encouragement. To walk in his footsteps was an impossibility; to profit by his almost unerring wisdom and sagacity has been my daily experience. No one can study the work of Dr. Sears, as I had occasion to do, without being filled with wonder and admiration at his adaptedness to the difficult and delicate duties he had to discharge.... The best eulogy of Dr. Sears is that he met all the requirements."[3] Curry would later add: "It would be a hasty judgment to conclude that the work was finished during the period of his agency, or that free schools had been established beyond the possibility of destruction. There were many considerations which would have made it foolish to relax vigorous efforts for keeping alive and strengthening the favoring educational sentiment, and making irrepealable what had been put upon the statute books.... Some excellent men had deep-seated convictions, arising from politics, social or religious reasons, adverse to gratuitous state education. The experiment of free schools was not, in all locations, so successful as to clear away any doubts, and prejudices, and reverse those traditional habits of thought and

---

1. Proceedings of the Peabody Education Trust Fund, Report of the 35th meeting, 1896, p. 253.
2. Rena Vassar, *Social History of American Education* (Chicago: Rand McNally, 1965), pp. 97-98.
3. Anderson and Gordon, p. 261.

action which the experience of all peoples has shown it to be difficult for the mind to free itself from."[1]

Curry's Role as General Agent

Immediately after his election as General Agent, Curry resigned from Richmond College and began the first of many trips through the Southern states. The governors of Texas and Tennessee urged him to come. He did, first stopping in New Orleans with Mary and her sister. It was Mardi Gras time. They watched the famous parade, then he acquainted himself with the school officials there, and then went to Texas. He toured the Galveston and Houston schools and while there made a speech on "Education and Common Schools"; visited San Antonio and then Austin, the capital.

After calling on the governor, Curry addressed a joint session of the Texas House and Senate. This speech presented a theme that he would often repeat: "Intelligence is a necessary ingredient in the wealth of nations.... Just ahead of us in our march to freedom and the perpetuity of our institutions, and the advancement and development of the moral intelligence of the people, is a great black cloud, portentous with evil, threatening to break and to deluge us, and those to come after us, with indescribable calamities — universal suffrage! I may not comment on it, whether it be right or wrong. ... But universal suffrage necessitates universal education."[2] Wasn't that the endless theme of the Radical Republicans?

He then went on and spoke at Palestine, Texas, then to Little Rock where he lobbied for state-supported schools in the Arkansas House and Senate.

This frenetic travel pace would continue through all his years as General Agent. He was proud of his peripatetic life. This is a sample of his break-neck pace, from his diary:

> January 19, 1883. Spoke to [Georgia] legislature. House of Representatives.
>
> January 26. Visited Mobile, Alabama schools. By request, addressed both Houses of legislature.
>
> January 30. Visited Chattanooga schools.
>
> January 31. Reached home at 1:30 p.m. Traveled 2,389 miles.
>
> February 20. Addressed [Florida] legislature. On the 17th, visited schools in Tallahassee.

---

1. J.L.M. Curry, *A Brief Sketch of George Peabody, etc.*, pp. 70-80.
2. *Journal of Texas Education*, Vol. I, No. 7, Curry Papers.

March 5. Visited schools in St. Augustine.

March 19. Reached Richmond, having traveled 2,272 miles.[1]

In the first four years of Curry being Peabody's General Agent, he spoke before state assemblies twenty-three times; "more legislatures than was ever in the history of the Union conceded to any man or any cause."[2]

Curry made at least one address before every Southern state assembly; two before seven states, three before one. His speeches often began by identifying himself as a Southerner. He presented the Peabody Fund as a great unselfish helping hand that was being held out to the South in her darkest hour. With an intense sincerity born from his new viewpoint on life, he proclaimed the majesty of the new Reconstruction laws and the weight of responsibility the law-makers carried. He reminded the legislators of their oath to support the new constitutions of their state and quoted to them the mandate for education that the constitution now imposed. He pictured the public schools as the colleges of the people and their maintenance as the test of political intelligence and statesmanship. He described education as one of the major influences that results in the growth of man. He saw education and religion as factors which differentiated men from animals. Education was the natural right of man and the denial of that right to white or black, rich or poor, with the inherent denial of the right of fullest moral and intellectual development of those made in God's image, was equivalent to blasphemy.

Then Curry would turn to its importance to good government and to civilization, contrasting the cost of a child's education with the cost of caring for criminals, and threw figures out to establish the relationship between ignorance and crime. Horace Mann had made the same kind of presentation to the Massachusetts legislature.

Curry marshaled facts to prove that poverty was the inevitable result of ignorance and that universal and free schools were essential to the preservation of property, asserting that property in a barbarous community was not worth the risks inherent to possession. He added that the recognition of property rights required advanced intelligence, that property was secure only when it acknowledged its duties and paid for its privileges through taxes.[3]

---

1. J.L.M. Curry diary for 1883.
2. Curry letter to Robert Winthrop, September 23, 1885, from Curry Papers.
3. From Rice, pp. 106-107.

The tragedy of Curry's thinking, which other Americans, both North and South, Conservative and even Radical, saw, was that schooling with a political motivation could train children for barbarism instead of civility, for criminality instead of good behavior, for slavery instead of freedom. Later, we shall follow one prominent Radical Republican's mental journey toward that shattering insight.

Was Curry effective in his appeals? Yes. Here are two random samples to demonstrate that. Immediately after he spoke to the Georgia legislature, in December 1888, the House, "with ringing vote, approaching unanimity," increased the appropriations for 1889 and 1890. And when he presented his story about the importance of establishing a state Normal school in North Carolina, in January 1890, that Senate passed a bill for one of the following day and the State Superintendent of Education wrote that the bill would go through the House enthusiastically.

Edwin Alderman Sees Curry Speak

Jabez Curry's biographer, Edwin Anderson Alderman, recorded his personal reaction to seeing him make a public speech: "I saw him for the first time in 1883. A thriving North Carolina town was proposing to tax itself for adequate school facilities. This was not then an every day occurrence in North Carolina. Curry stood before them and pleaded with passion and power for the children of the community. I remember how he seized a little child impulsively, and with dramatic instinct placed his hand upon his curly head, and pictured to the touched and silent throng the meaning of a little child to human society. It was the first time I had ever heard a man of such power spend himself so passionately in such a cause. I had seen and heard men speak that way about personal religion and Heaven and Hell, and struggles and wrongs long past, but never before about childhood. It seemed to me, and to all young men who heard him, that here was a vital thing to work for, here indeed a cause to which a man might nobly attach himself, feeling sure that though he himself might fall, the cause would go marching grandly on. There dwelt in him a leonine quality of combat and struggle, a delight of contest, a rising of all his powers to opposition that had only one master in his soul, and that master was the Christian instinct for service. I once heard him declare to an audience that it was the proudest duty of the South to accomplish the education of every child in its borders; high or low, bond or free, black or white. The only response to his appeal was silence. He shouted, 'I will make you applaud that sentiment.' With strident voice and shaking of the head, after the manner of the oratory of the olden time, he pleaded for human freedom. He pictured to his audience the ruin that may be wrought by hate, and the beauty of justice and sympathy until he awakened within them the god of justice and gentleness that lies sleeping in the human heart, and the applause rolled up to him in a storm."[1]

Curry Deceives about Pre-War Southern Schools

Then, Curry spoke about Southern illiteracy and ignorance as the Radicals had. As they misrepresented the ante-bellum South, so did he: "In order to have a right understanding of the aim and the work of the [Peabody] fund, it needs to be iterated and kept constantly in view that when Mr. Peabody made his gift there was not, and there never had been any state system of compulsory and tax-sustained public schools."[2]

Had Curry forgotten his own role in bringing tax-sustained public schools to Alabama?

Barnas Sears was more realistic. He said that,

[In] South Carolina: public education existed for the poor from 1811.

In Georgia, free public schools from 1845.

In Louisiana: not long after its admission to the Union, it gave support to parish schools.

Texas: This state, from the beginning, made liberal provisions for education.

Tennessee: Prior to the secession of this State, there was an efficient school law for the education of white children.[3]

Then Curry, the Baptist minister, showed an astonishing bias against religious schools, saying: "Churches never did and never ought [educate all children], even if they could. Sectarianism in schools is abhorrent and under the narrowness of sectarianism, schools can never be progressive." Curry was saying that soul and mental freedom and diversity are reactionary and that the undeviating State view is a positive.[4]

---

1. Edwin Anderson Alderman, *J.L.M. Curry: An Address* (Brooklyn: Eagle Press, 1903), pp. 18-19. This address was delivered in Richmond, Virginia, April 26, 1903, under the auspices of the Conference for Education in the South, two months after Curry's death.

2. J.L.M. Curry, *A Brief Sketch of George Peabody, etc.*, p. 38.

3. Proceedings of the Trustees of the Peabody Education Fund, Report of the 15th meeting, 1877. pp. 103, 105, 111, 112, 117.

4. Article about Jabez Curry speech on education, in the *Jacksonville-Times-Union and Citizen*, no date.

Ulysses Grant, Peabody Trustee

Ex-President Ulysses S. Grant, as a Peabody trustee, had nominated Jabez Curry for his General Agent's role.

Because of Grant's presence, the Curry of old would never have accepted this position. To Southerners, and many Northerners, he was known as "The Butcher," for his indifference to Union army casualties and his "total war" cruelty. After the war, he was still hated by winner and loser alike for his extreme radicalism and autocratic military rule as president. Grant's policies continued to leave the South a virtual colony of the United States.

It would be appropriate now to give a short overview of Grant's post-war career, to demonstrate how implausible it was that Jabez Curry would be willing to associate with him on any level.

And it is also interesting to note that Grant, like Curry, underwent an amazing negative mental transformation in peace-time, from being a moderate to a "Red Republican."

The Congressional Reconstruction laws mandated by the Radicals put Grant on an equal basis with President Johnson. "In July [1867] Congress gave more powers to the District Commanders, giving them the right to suspend or remove any civil functionary. But more than all, the Supplementary Statutes made the acts of the District Commanders subject to the approval of the General of the Army [Grant], while the same original power of removal or suspension was conferred on him. This actually charged Grant with the supreme duty of supervising the reconstruction of the Union.

The authority now entrusted to Grant as General-in-Chief, made him in many respects, independent of the President. He accepted the prerogative, believing it necessary for the preservation of those results which the war had been fought to secure."[1]

Grant Begins as a Moderate

Initially, after the war, Andrew Johnson had testified that he acted frequently on Grant's advice and that the general was "the strongest man in support of my policy."

The intense vindictive feeling toward the South directly after the war was moderated by Grant, "and only Grant's interposition preserved the good faith of the government, or rescued many, civilians as well as soldiers, from impris-

---

1. Adam Badeau, *Grant in Peace* (Hartford: S.S. Scranton and Co., 1887), p. 14.

onment or pecuniary ruin; for he urged the restoration of their property as well as remission of their personal penalties. In consequence there grew up a remarkable feeling at the South.... In November 1865 Grant made a tour through Virginia, North and South Carolina, Georgia and Tennessee [at the request of the President], to investigate and report upon the condition and feelings of the population. Everywhere he was received with the greatest respect by those who regarded him the year before as the chief of their adversaries.

At the conclusion of his tour, Grant reported to Johnson that 'the mass of thinking men of the South accepted the situation in good faith.' And while he recommended that a strong military force should still be retained in the Southern states, he declared his belief that the citizens of that region are anxious to return to self-government within the Union as soon as possible."[1]

Grant's Mental Transition

Andrew Johnson's idea of how to bring the South back into the Union was completely at odds with the Radical dominated Congress. The conflict deepened and threatened to tear the Federal government apart.

Johnson went on a national tour, called "going around the circle," to explain his more moderate policy to the American public. He took Grant with him to give silent support and to deter the Radicals from acts of violence and assassination attempts.

The tour stopped in Cincinnati, where Grant's father lived. Immediately afterward, there was a change in Grant's attitude. For the first time, he did not believe that the people approved of Johnson. Grant held the erroneous belief that the supreme law of the land was the will of the people and not the Constitution. Believing the election would go against Johnson, Grant supported the Radical Congress.

For Jabez Curry, Ulysses S. Grant's lack of insight into the American system of government should have been a basic reason to be cautious about associating with him through the Peabody Fund. Curry had spent his life defending the Constitution.

Grant, seeing the battle going on between Andrew Johnson and Congress, slowly became convinced that the President was planning a coup against that legislative body. Grant wrote General Sheridan that "Johnson becomes more violent with the opposition he meets with, until now but a few people who were

---

1. Ibid., p. 72.

loyal during the Rebellion seem to have any influence with him. None have, unless they join in a crusade against Congress, and declare the body itself illegal, unconstitutional, revolutionary. Commanders in the Southern states will have to take care to see, if a crisis does come, that no armed headway can be made against the Union."[1] Grant ordered all arms in the South to be removed to Northern arsenals.

Mutiny and Threatened Coups

When Andrew Johnson declared that the Reconstruction Acts were unconstitutional and that he did not have to obey them, Grant disagreed; but Johnson ordered him to give the Presidential opinion to all district commanders. Instead, Grant informed the commanders they should make their own interpretations of their duties. Johnson observed this disobedience but was powerless to punish the officers or Grant, since the general alone controlled the army and was now independent and outside civil control. The situation approached mutiny.

Then, there were violent upheavals in Maryland, which was a Union state. Maryland was hostile to the United States ever since Lincoln sent troops into Baltimore in 1861 to arrest the state legislators to prevent their possible vote for secession.

The post-war clash was between State and Baltimore City authorities. The governor appealed to Andrew Johnson for armed assistance. Johnson tried to induce Grant to order troops into Maryland. Grant refused. It seemed this conflict would result in Grant and the Radicals using the army for a coup against the President. But Grant met with the opposing parties in Maryland and convinced them to settle their dispute in the courts.

Johnson decided to send Grant out of the country to forestall a military take-over, and to put General Sherman in his place. He ordered Grant to Mexico to prevent an armed conflict with that country, which had placed troops along its borders during the war.

Grant refused, saying that Johnson had given him a civil order, not a military command which he had to obey. Sherman went, instead.

Grant, the Tenure of Office Act; Impeachment

The Congressional Reconstruction acts provided that the Southern state governments should be subjected, in all respects, to their military commanders. These military governors were only responsible to Ulysses S. Grant. These laws,

---

1. Ibid., p. 51.

created by Edwin Stanton, were designed to isolate and humiliate Andrew Johnson. But Johnson counter-attacked and removed Stanton from office, which then provoked a Congressional counter-offensive through the "Tenure of Office Act" and impeachment proceedings.

This act became law in March 1867 over Johnson's veto. It forbade the President from removing any Federal office-holder "appointed by and with the advice and consent of the Senate" without the approval of the Senate. It also provided that members of the President's Cabinet should be held in office for the full term of the President who appointed them, and one month thereafter, subject to removal only by the Senate. With this measure the Radical Republicans could keep Stanton, their favorite Radical, in power, to prevent interference with their plans.

To bring about a Supreme Court test of the Tenure of Office Act, Johnson dismissed Stanton but the High Court, intimidated by the Radicals, refused to judge the case.

Then Johnson appointed Grant "Secretary of War Ad Interim," but immediately upon taking that office, Grant showed his radicalism. At his first cabinet meeting, he defended the constitutionality of the Reconstruction acts and said he would stand behind the military governors.

Then a Senate resolution stated that the causes for Johnson to remove Stanton were inadequate. Grant would have to resign his interim position. Andrew Johnson pleaded with him to stay, to test the law. Grant refused, fearing jail.

Johnson appointed General Lorenzo Thomas as Secretary of War, but Stanton, barricading himself in the department, refused to yield.

Johnson's alleged violation of the Tenure of Office Act was the principle charge in the impeachment proceedings against him. When the impeachment failed, in May 1868, Stanton finally gave up his office.

Grant and the Impeachment

Grant was originally against impeachment but after his own conflicts with Andrew Johnson, he favored it. He did not visit the Senate during the trial, except when he was a witness. When the Senate debated Grant's correspondence with the President, he was summoned to give testimony as to his conversations. On the stand, Grant shrewdly refrained from any display of personal animosity. But to the press, Grant said: "The acquittal of Mr. Johnson would threaten the country, and especially the South, with revolution and bloodshed."[1] Grant quietly urged senators to vote for impeachment.

Radical Ben Wade, as the Presiding Officer in the Senate, would become president if Johnson was convicted. So Wade tried to make deals with Grant over appointments. Grant listened but made no comment.

At first, Grant was disappointed at Andrew Johnson's acquittal. Later, he changed his mind, fearing Ben Wade's bitterness and lack of restraint. Similar fears had influenced some Republican senators to vote for acquittal.

Grant, O.O. Howard, and the Freedmen's Bureau

Oliver Otis Howard and his Freedmen's Bureau churned out false outrage stories about the South's extreme instability, violence and murder to prove the need for a continued military presence.

Ulysses S. Grant fell into Howard's propaganda trap. He came to believe that Unionists in the South would not be safe without Northern armed protection and that blacks were being massacred. Grant wrote to Howard: "Dear General: will you be kind enough to send me a list of authenticated cases of murder and other violence upon freedmen, Northern or other Union men, refugees in the Southern States for the last six months or a year. My object is to make a report showing that the courts in the States excluded from Congress afford no security, and to recommend that martial law be declared over such districts as do not afford the proper protection."[2]

Ulysses S. Grant, Presidential Candidate

As a career soldier, Grant had a limited understanding of the Constitution and the nature of this form of government. He said: "This is a Republic, where the will of the people is the law of the land." Andrew Johnson tried to enlighten him when he wrote Grant that "while ours is a government of the people it is also one based upon a written Constitution."[3]

Navy Secretary Gideon Welles wrote in his diary; "Grant is an insincere man.... Very ambitious, has a low cunning, and is unreliable, perhaps untruthful." With no knowledge of the Constitution, or "the elementary principles of civil government," the general was likely to become "an instrument of evil."[4]

---

1. *The New York Times*, April 4, 1868.
2. Ibid., p. 59.
3. House Executive Documents, 40th Congress, 2nd Session, No. 57, pp. 4, 5.
4. Welles, Diary, Vol. III, pp. 184-5.

Argus Editorial: "Grant on Unconstitutional Laws"

The *Argus*, an Albany, New York newspaper, pointed out another example of Ulysses S. Grant's lack of understanding of the Constitution. "In the late semi-weekly *Tribune* will be found the following editorial: 'I stated that the law was binding on me, constitutional or not, until set aside by the proper tribunal.'

So wrote General Grant to President Johnson in the correspondence about Stanton's restoration in the War Office.... We cannot speak too plainly in condemnation of this doctrine. Nothing can make manifest the utter incompetency and unfitness of a man for the Chief Magistry than such an expression of want of judgment and good sense as above made by General Grant and endorsed by the *Tribune*. It is but saying to a despotic Congress, 'pass just such laws as you please, against or outside of the Constitution, if you make me President I will consider them constitutional and binding and see that they are carried out until set aside by a proper tribunal.' Now, let any law, however oppressive or unconstitutional, be passed and Congress take from the Supreme Court jurisdiction of review, as they have done in the cases of the Reconstruction laws, and the despotism over our land is complete. 'Do as you please,' says Grant, 'and I will serve you.' With what propriety can he say we have a constitutional government if the Constitution may thus be ignored by the Legislative and Executive departments?"[1]

Ulysses S. Grant: Radical President

Grant was elected President in 1868. Democrats, both North and South, were fully aware of his policy to continue to keep the former Confederacy under permanent military occupation to guarantee the "Succession of 1872," his own re-election.

In one example of this, Governor Holden of North Carolina was speaking with a Reverend Smith. Holden bragged to Smith that he had a private black mercenary army of 80,000 "that I control by my word." [These were Union League troops, which kept him in illegal power against other carpetbaggers and Southern Democrats.] Smith replied, "That is a dangerous power. Very dangerous power in the hands of one man." Reverend Smith then said Holden replied: "General Grant would hold the government of the United States no matter what the election was in 1872; that he [Grant] desired him [Holden] to be emperor and his son to succeed him as emperor."[2]

---

1. Albany *Argus* newspaper, April 23, 1868.
2. Stanley Horn, *The Invisible Empire: The Story of the Ku Klux Klan, 1866-1871* (Cos Cob, CT: John E. Edwards, 1969), p. 17.

Francis Blair, who had been the Democratic Vice Presidential candidate in 1868, said this about Grant: "I have never considered him a weak and feeble, ignorant man that some have pleased to call him, and no doubt, think him. I had a totally different opinion about him and still have. I am well aware that he cannot write newspaper articles, and for that reason is not considered a very great man by many who can write such articles. I know he never distinguished himself as a stump orator, and is greatly looked down upon by some of us who do make stump orations. But there are other qualities which he possesses which make him a most dangerous man, in my opinion, in the position which he now occupies [as President]. I do not believe he cares a straw about our frame of government. His military education and military genius necessarily make him arbitrary in his ideas of government, and he places no value at all upon any other government than which is absolutely arbitrary and military. He has surrounded himself with clerks who all wear uniforms; that is a very slight indication of the temper of his mind. But, my friends, he has other qualities in addition to that; he is a man capable of conceiving most dangerous purposes, and executing those purposes with inflexible will, and I think he has demonstrated since he has assumed the power of the Executive of this nation that he will hesitate at nothing, stop at nothing, at no deed which will not give him the supreme power in this country, and I do not expect him to halt or hesitate to do anything to give him pre-eminent power in this country, except that he shall deem it most important to attempt it.... I have tried to do my duty as a soldier but soldiering has been an episode in my life, and war is still terrible to me. Not so with Grant. It is his trade. To him, human life is cheap, and not a feather's weight in the scale of his ambition.... Mr. John Sherman, a Senator, one by no means rash in his statements, asserted upon the floor of the Senate, after the last [Presidential] election [1868], that if the vote of New York had given the election to [Horatio] Seymour [the Democratic candidate from New York], it would not have been counted."[1]

Grant Interferes in State Elections

Regularly, throughout his two terms as president, Ulysses S. Grant ordered the invasion of Southern states to terrorize voters or intimidate legislators, to guarantee that he and the Republicans remained in power. These inva-

---

1. Francis P. Blair, *Radicalism, Its Corruption and Centralization* a speech before the Missouri Legislature, Jefferson City, January 4, 1872, p. 6. Printed at the *Congressional Globe* office, Washington, D.C.

sions were usually sparked by false charges of riot or insurrection. Over time these attacks became so commonplace that they hardly generated significant press coverage. But Grant's brutal disregard for even the slightest veneer of legitimacy for such actions did not extend to Louisiana.

During Reconstruction Louisiana had the most bizarre history imaginable. It featured two competing carpetbag governments, then three. There was massive fraud and terror tactics by all sides, including civil war between the factions.

Grant appointed his brother-in-law, James Casey, Customs Collector for New Orleans. This was a graft-filled position.

Grant called in Federal troops to New Orleans to install legislators that Casey designated. Under unconstitutional laws, one of the governors could hold his office for life.

In 1874, the citizens of New Orleans armed themselves to resist these travesties. Grant issued proclamations against the uprising. His own Cabinet urged caution. One Radical Republican said: "We say frankly that we know of no case of armed resistance to an established government in modern times in which the insurgents had more plainly the right on their side."[1]

Grant ordered that under no circumstances would a government chosen by Southerners be recognized. He moved troops and warships on New Orleans. Mr. Kellogg, Grant's favorite, was made governor by force.

In the November 2 election, despite Federal troops policing the polls, the Democrats gained a majority in the State Assembly. The Radicals prepared to hold the state at all costs. They manipulated the returns to give the Assembly back to the Republicans.

Grant prepared to place Louisiana under martial law to maintain them. Again, his Cabinet urged caution. Instead, he ordered General Sheridan to New Orleans, who was hated by the citizens there for his brutal treatment of them when he commanded the city.

On November 4, Sheridan's troops arrived at the State House. They marched through the corridors. An army officer produced papers denouncing the House as an illegal body. The Conservatives and Democrats were hustled out at bayonet point. Now the legislature was Republican.

---

1. Allan Nevins, *Hamilton Fish, The Inner History of the Grant Administration* (New York: Dodd, Mead & Co., 1936), p. 745.

This caused intense indignation, even in the North. Republican congressman and future president James Garfield called it: "The darkest day for the Republican Party and its hopes that I have seen since the war.[1]

Another major Republican official termed it: "The most outrageous subversion of parliamentary government by military force yet attempted in this country."[2]

Mass meetings in the North protested the action.

Sheridan then formulated a more severe plan; Congress could pass a bill declaring the opposition "banditti." Then Sheridan could arrest all the citizens he wanted to and convict them in military courts. Even Grant's Cabinet was stunned.

Carl Schurz, the extreme Radical, wisely asked: "If these things are done in Louisiana, how long before they are done in Massachusetts and Ohio?"[3]

The *Nation* asserted that to find precedents for Sheridan's acts, it would be necessary to go back to Louis XIV's marching on the Huguenots.

While public disapproval whirled into a hurricane, Secretary of War Belknap telegraphed Sheridan: "The President and all of us have full confidence and thoroughly approve of your course."[4] In reality, there was extreme dissention in the Cabinet.

Then, an impartial Congressional committee, investigating the Louisiana election, reported that Republicans had been seated in the Assembly by fraud. This also had a tremendous national impact.

Initially, Grant refused to apologize for sending the army or for Sheridan's conduct. He planned a speech rationalizing the necessity of armed intervention, but ultimately his statement was conciliatory; yet, the Republicans remained in power.

Grant and the Peabody Fund

Grant, the Radical, was committed to the re-education of the South. That is why he joined the Peabody Board of Trustees. To publicly show his commitment to re-education, several of the Peabody Trustee meetings were held in the White House. Grant attended, wearing his general's uniform.

---

1. Ibid., p. 749.
2. Ibid., p. 749.
3. Ibid., p. 751.
4. Ibid., p. 751.

In a speech to Congress he said: "I recommend a constitutional amendment … making it the duty of the several States to establish and forever maintain free public schools … [and] make education compulsory so far as to deprive all persons who cannot read and write from being voters after the year 1870."[1]

In another speech, Grant added: "The free school is the promoter of that intelligence which is to preserve us as a free nation. If we are to have another contest in the near future for our national existence, I predict that the dividing line will not be Mason and Dixon's line, but between patriotism and intelligence on one side and superstition, ambition and ignorance on the other."[2]

Once again, it is clear that the Jabez Curry of old, the advocate of state sovereignty and decentralized power, knowing all too well the dictatorial history of Ulysses S. Grant, would have declined the offer to be the Peabody Fund's General Agent. It would have been an immoral act of "sleeping with the enemy." Yet, Curry wrote in his diary: "February 4, 1881. To Riggs Hotel, met the Peabody Board of Trustees [which included Grant], who received me cordially. To Senate and House of Representatives. Dined with Peabody Trustees."

---

1. William Hasseltine, *Ulysses S. Grant, Politician* (New York: Frederick Ungar Co., 1957), p. 392.
2. Ulysses S. Grant address before the Society of the Army of the Tennessee, 1875, published in the Proceedings of the Trustees of the Peabody Education Fund, 24th meeting, 1885, p. 231.

CHAPTER 12. RUTHERFORD B. HAYES, CURRY, AND THE PEABODY FUND

When Ulysses S. Grant realized that his corrupt, unconstitutional and criminal activities were catching up with him, that he could not be nominated for a third term and that his dream of being emperor was fruitless, he stepped aside.

Rutherford B. Hayes became the Republican candidate. He won the 1876 presidential contest against the Democrat, Samuel Tilden, in the most disputed and violent election in American history, even though Tilden had a quarter million edge in popular votes.

The electoral vote numbers were close. Yet, it still seemed Tilden had won. The Republicans challenged the electoral votes in three Southern states: Florida, Louisiana, South Carolina.

Even before election day, Ulysses S. Grant, still President, had called out the military in those three states. The troops terrorized voters, smashed open ballot boxes, changed the numbers toward Hayes and shot dead poll watchers and officials who objected.

Because of this, Southerners and many Northerners hated Hayes as much as they loathed Grant. He was called "Rutherfraud" and "Your Fraudulence." His victory symbolized all that was ruthless about Reconstruction.

Here Hayes' story crossed Jabez Curry's again, when, as President, he became a Trustee of the Peabody Fund. Re-education of the South was a high priority for him.

Curry and Hayes had been classmates in Boston. Even then, Curry had a mixed attitude about Rutherford: "In 1843 to 1845 we were fellow students at

Dane Law School, in Harvard University, and enjoyed together the instructions of Judge Story and Simon Greenleaf. In 1844 we had rooms at the same house, and for several months, at the same table. This threw us into intimate relations, and I learned to respect and admire my college mate. He was several years my senior, but treated me with much kindness and confidence. As a member of the law school, and as a young man, he was of studious habits and dignified demeanor, gentlemanly in his intercourse with his fellows, frank in the utterance of his opinions, and warm in his friendships. I remembered that he argued a case in the Moot Court, by assignment of Judge Story, and his preparation was thorough, and the manner of presentation, clear and logical. He was not ranked among the most brilliant or promising students, but was sensible, thoughtful, intelligent, and always came up to the measure of what was required of him. Our remote residence, he being of Ohio and I in Alabama, and subsequently the War Between the States, prevented any personal intercourse, but his professional and military and civil success excited warm interest, notwithstanding our antipodal position in politics."[1]

The Election of 1876

The process of determining who had won the presidency dragged on for months. Election results were thrown out by special Congressional committees. Votes from one state were taken from Democrats and given to Republicans. Confusion and criminality were followed by bribery and trickery.

The clock ticked down to the final hours of Ulysses S. Grant's term. Still, there was no one to take his place. It seemed a second civil war would break out: not North vs. South, this time, but Democrat vs. Republican, which meant warfare and murder in every state in the Union. This crisis would destroy what was left of the Constitution and bring on a permanent dictatorship.

Although Tilden held a statesmanlike silence, his supporters called for war if the Republicans succeeded in stealing the election. A mass meeting in Indianapolis was told that "millions of men" would "offer their lives for the sacredness of the ballot.... Whosoever hath a sword, let him gird it on." The slogan, "Tilden or Blood!" was heard in many places. "Tilden Minute Men" clubs, dedicated to a military defense of the Democratic victory, sprang up in eleven states.

---

1. Jabez Curry article in *The Times*, Just after Hayes' death, January 24, 1893, Curry Papers.

Henry Watterson, the journalist, called for 100,000 citizens to march on Washington to seek justice for Tilden. Newspaper editor Joseph Pulitzer added that the 100,000 should "come fully armed and ready for business."

A "People's Indignation Convention" was held in Columbus, Ohio, right under Hayes' nose (he was governor of Ohio) and cheered a speaker who roared, "Resistance to tyranny is obedience to law!" The convention adopted a resolution declaring that any attempt to settle the election by the decision of the President of the Senate should be "resisted by the people to the last extremity by an appeal to arms."[1]

Hayes was prepared to meet these threats: "If a contest comes now it may lead to a conflict of arms. I can only try to do my duty to my countrymen in that case. I shall let no personal ambition turn me from the path of duty. Bloodshed and civil war must be averted. If forced to fight I have no fears of failure from lack of courage or firmness."[2]

Hayes' Background

Rutherford B. Hayes was born in 1822, in Ohio, when that state was on the western frontier. He lived in Lower Sandusky, a small, rugged community, just past the pioneer stage. Hayes was a sickly boy, but frontier life toughened him up.

He received a bachelor's degree from Kenyon College in Ohio, then a law degree from Dane Law School, with Jabez Curry. In 1845, he opened a law office in Lower Sandusky.

His first view of the South came shortly after that, when he visited a friend in Texas. He was amazed that Texans were civilized; he had expected brawling frontiersmen. Instead, they were elegant, charming aristocrats. This journey completely transformed Hayes' feeling about Southerners.

By the 1850s, Hayes began to see that his place in the world was modest. He wrote in his diary: "Two things are now ascertained ... I have neither [health] or capacity to be a first class figure in my profession; the other, that I appear to have enough of both to acquire a reasonable success enough for happiness. With this I am content."[3]

---

1. Lloyd Robinson, *The Stolen Election, Hayes vs. Tilden, 1876* (Garden City: Doubleday and Co., 1968), pp. 158-159.
2. T. Harry Williams, editor, *Diary of a President*, October 22, 1876 (New York: David McKay Company, 1964), p. 44.
3. Robinson, p. 75.

He became sober and commonplace, as Curry had observed a decade before, giving up his romantic notions of becoming a great general or statesman.

Politics became his new romantic dream. In the 1850s, he joined the emerging Republican Party, more for its financial policies than its anti-slavery stand. In 1858, Hayes was elected to the Cincinnati City Solicitor's post. He was planning to run again, when the War for Southern Independence broke out.

Being reasonable and logical, Hayes hoped that the North and South could resolve their disagreements peacefully. When the fighting began, his outlook changed. "This is a holy war, and if a fair chance opens I shall go into it; if a fair chance doesn't open, I shall perhaps take measures to open one."[1]

Resigning as City Solicitor, he joined the Ohio 23rd Regiment as a Major and went off to war. He was nearly forty. To some extent Hayes was motivated by political necessity. He realized that anyone who hoped to win public office after the war would be asked to prove that he had saved the country in battle.

Many of the politicians who became soldiers in 1861 cracked under the strain and swiftly were sent back to civilian life. Not Hayes. He thrived on it. He discovered natural abilities for leading men under fire. He went without sleep for 36 hours in a single stretch, and 19 hours of one day in the saddle. He was not a brilliant officer but a brave one and his ability to stay cool in peril brought him several promotions. By the fall of 1861, he was a Lt. Colonel and had been wounded several times.

His regiment fought in Virginia, West Virginia and Maryland. In September 1862, in a charge up a hill, Hayes was wounded in the left arm. He lay beside a wounded Confederate while the battle raged around them. "We were quite jolly and friendly. It was by no means an unpleasant experience."[2]

In October of 1864, while in the field, now a general, Hayes was nominated for Congress by his political friends. He was elected. In 1866, re-elected.

Three times he was governor of Ohio. The first time, in 1867, the votes of his former troops helped him gain that post, even though the state was Democratic. His politics became steadily more radical.

Hayes resigned after two more terms and campaigned for Ulysses S. Grant.

---

1. Ibid., p. 76.
2. Ibid., p. 78.

Curry and the Hayes Election

Curry, the Southerner, Confederate, state rights Democrat, hater of Radical Republican Reconstruction, went through another amazing mental transition related to the election of Hayes. He began by being furious, bitter and depressed over the stolen presidency but soon was a virtual "lap-dog" to Rutherford; he idolized him. This astonishing change seems to be part of his whole psychological turn-around during this period.

The process, as revealed by his diary, began this way: "Tuesday, November 7, 1876. Voted before breakfast for Tilden."

"Wednesday, November 8, 1876. News from the election of yesterday assures the success of Tilden and Hendricks. Results rather unexpected. People gathered in the streets in front of the *Dispatch* office reading and hearing telegrams from various states and shouting vociferously. We feel as if the days of Federal tyranny are numbered. Praise God from whom all blessings flow."

Curry's enthusiasm was short-lived. "Thursday, November 9, 1876. Negroes very noisy and jubilant over Hayes' election, which is not a fixed fact."

"November 20, 1876. Still much uneasiness about the Presidential election. Universal distrust of President Grant and his party. Fraud or usurpation not considered beyond their purpose or capability. I am tired of this turmoil and distrust. I want a country I can love."

Months passed. The Electoral Commission still could not settle the conflict.

"February 10, 1877. News this morning rather gloomy. Seems as if the Commission by a party vote will decide in favor of Hayes for President."

"February 24, 1877. Much dissatisfaction with the Commission. Democrats complain of having been deceived."

"March 2, 1877. Went in the afternoon and at night to the Capital. The Congress, having this morning, at 5 a.m., after a night's session, elected Hayes President.... The feeling of Democrats, quite bitter, regarding themselves as having been cheated out of the Presidency."

The next day, March 3, was very significant, for it showed how a little flattery from Hayes could transform Jabez. The day began this way: "I called at the Capital and had a pleasant interview with Senator Sherman, who had, unsought, interposed in favor of the removal of my political disabilities."[1]

---

1. Curry's pardon by Andrew Johnson at the end of the war had stripped Jabez of most of his civil rights. In 1872 a general amnesty bill was passed by Congress. But Curry and 750 of the major "traitors" were exempted. Senator Sherman cleared the way for a special bill restoring Curry to full citizenship on February 27, 1877.

Sherman asked Curry if he wished to meet the new President, but Jabez was about to leave Washington. Sherman replied, "You ought to go. He likes you very much. I have often heard him speak well of you.... I will arrange it." Curry agreed. It is astonishing that he would accept. Or, was he overwhelmed with the idea of talking to a president?

In the midst of throngs of well-wishers, Hayes had a private interview with Jabez. Hayes "expressed earnestly his desire and purpose to conduct his administration as to bring the estranged sections into harmony and fraternity. Then to my surprise and gratification he declared his willingness to put into his Cabinet some Southern men, or a Southern man, who had voted for Mr. Tilden, provided the person would give his administration an impartial support. A place in the Cabinet was tendered to me, but declined with proper and sincere expressions of thankfulness for the confidence reposed. He then said he was willing to appoint General Joseph E. Johnston, and wished my opinion as to his acceptance on the conditions mentioned.... [I said] General Johnston was so identified with the Confederacy, his promotion to a high place would awaken bitterest opposition in the North, and its strength would be such as greatly to crippled, if not defeat his policy.... He expressed a desire to make Federal appointments in the South acceptable to that section. I felt it was my duty to express strongly my conviction: 'The South will not object to have offices filled with Northern men, if they are honest and true, and go South, not to fleece the people, but to identify themselves with the country and its interests.' He responded, 'It would be better not to float the office-holders, but to select them from the residents.' I interposed, 'No, no, you cannot find in the South a sufficient number of capable and honest white Republicans to fill the offices at your disposal.' This was naturally received with some incredulity; but I reasserted what I felt to be a demonstrable truth, and I knew that putting 'Scalawags,' as they were called, in responsible places meant the defeat of his noble purpose, and the serious injury of the South."[1]

Later, Curry's diary had this comment about Hayes and that meeting: "He seems determined to unite North and South as one people." Jabez did not seem to realize that that would mean eradicating the South's culture, "uniting" the South to the North. Then he added that Hayes was "very sensible, good-mannered and patriotic."[2] How quickly Jabez had lost his righteous anger.

---

1. *My Educational Life*, hand-written notes.
2. Diary of April 28, 1877.

And, how quickly he became one of "Rutherford's boys." On October 30, 1877, Hayes came to Richmond to make a speech. Curry met him at Quantico and accompanied him. "As we came within the limits of the City of Richmond, great crowds, all the military, fire companies, etc., turned out to welcome the visitor. At a stand, near Monroe Park, the President and Cabinet spoke to many thousands. I was called for. The President introduced me as his old college mate; and I asked for three cheers, which were given and repeated."[1]

By 1880 his own words confirmed that he was, in fact, a semi-Republican, when he sent a letter to Hayes proclaiming that, because he saw himself as "occupying a sort of middle-ground between the Republican and Democratic parties, I think I can sometimes see aspects of questions to which others, differently situated, are blinded."[2]

Hayes Pretends to End Occupation of South

In order to make them accept him as president and to prevent endless legal roadblocks to his placement in the White House, and to diffuse the probability of another war, Rutherford B. Hayes promised the Democrats he would withdraw the Federal troops from the South and end Reconstruction.

But even in his nomination speech, Hayes said that the government would "protect all classes of citizens in their political rights": a veiled threat often stated by Ulysses S. Grant, Oliver Otis Howard and the Republican governors, implying that Washington would continue to generate fraudulent stories of race war to justify a continued military presence.[3]

In addition, "Hayes had promised to withdraw troops from South Carolina and Louisiana. But this would mean the collapse of Republican governors Packard and Chamberlain.... Deposing Packard and Chamberlain would split the Republican Party. Twelve Republican Congressmen announced they would vote with Northern Democrats if this was done. Then Hayes would be unable to get any legislation approved by Congress."[4]

Hayes did something that Ulysses S. Grant never dared to do. He brought Federal military power, violence and murder into the Northern states. There

---

1. Diary of October 30, 1877.
2. Jabez Curry, letter to Hayes, February 21, 1880, from Hayes Papers, Hayes Memorial Library, Fremont, Ohio.
3. Robinson, p. 110.
4. Ibid., p. 215.

were labor riots in 1877. First, the Baltimore and Ohio Railroad cut the wages of its employees by ten percent. A strike followed. A rally for the strikers became a riot. Troops fired into the crowd, killing twelve.

The strike spread to Pittsburgh. Fifty-seven strikers and soldiers died. There was millions of dollars in damage. Soldiers moved into Maryland, West Virginia, Pennsylvania, Illinois, and Missouri, to restore order. Traditionally, these internal disorders had been handled by the local militia.

Hayes, who had pledged to withdraw Federal troops from the South (and did not do so), found himself imposing military rule on the North.

He wrote in his diary on July 24, 1877: "Shall the troops of the United States be used in St. Louis [against strikers] until the governor calls?"

July 26, 1877: "Shall the United States troops be used to suppress riots in Chicago, before we issue a proclamation? [The legal precedent had been set by such actions in the South.] Riots diminishing. Discussing the propriety of allowing the US forces to be used by local authorities in states where no President's proclamation has been issued. If the troops act we will justify it. Rules are made to be broken. Ev [William Evarts, the Secretary of State] says: 'The Ten Commandments would not have been made, if they were not to be broken.' Ev says the country is ready for an exertion of its power [i.e., to step in with Federal troops instead of the militia.] But it is a difficult subject, and men are not to be court-martialed for a difference of opinion" [as was occurring in the South, simply for being Democrats].[1]

Hayes made this comment in his diary for May 11, 1879, nearly two years after he said he would pull Federal troops out of the South: The Democrats "have passed on an affirmative new measure which repeals for the day of elections many valuable laws. They call them war measures, and seem to think that as the war is over [yes, fifteen years before!], these laws should be mustered out. We are ready to muster out the soldiers but.... we don't muster in again the evils that caused the war. Besides, it is for the victors to say who shall remain, not the vanquished."[2]

Twenty years later the threat of military intervention was still a reality for the South. And Curry, possibly coming to his senses at last, described the truth: "A studied effort is being made to induce the South to believe that under McKinley as President there will be no danger of another attempt to re-enact the

---

1. T. Harry Williams, p. 90.
2. Ibid., p. 219.

Force Bill to oppress us with sectional legislation.[1] These spurious representations may gull those who wish to be deceived; but they are too 'thin' to impose on any who have recollections of the past."[2]

Hayes and Education

Like Ulysses S. Grant before him, and most Radical Republicans, Rutherford B. Hayes was a great believer that education should be controlled by Washington.

His diary entry for August 5, 1880 reads: "My hobby more and more is likely to be Common School Education, or universal education."

On December 8 of the same year, he wrote: "The New England idea is universal education. Let it not be confined to any one State or section. Let it be the National idea and be embodied in the legislation and institutions of the whole Union. Liberal education will follow free school education as surely as the light of day comes with the sun."

Then: The School Question "is one of the phases of the great question of our day. It interests in some form or other the people of all civilized nations. It convulses Italy. It stirs Germany to its base. It fills England with its debates. Here we cannot escape it."[3]

On May 15, 1878, his diary presented this idea: "Education is our greatest National concern. General education is the best preventive of the evils now most dreaded [the riots and strikes in the North]. In the civilized countries of the world the question is how to distribute most generally and equally the property of the world. As a rule where education is most general the distribution of property is most general. When we see what wealth is doing and what wealth can do, we begin to doubt the aphorism, 'knowledge is power.' As knowledge spreads, wealth spreads. To diffuse knowledge is to diffuse wealth. To give all an equal chance to acquire knowledge is the best and surest way to give all an equal chance to acquire property."[4]

---

1. The Force bills of 1870 and 1871 were Reconstruction laws, to enforce, with military power, voting rights. Congressional elections were placed under Federal control, and violators were deprived of Habeas Corpus. Fines, imprisonment and executions resulted.
2. Jabez Curry article, "Thoughts for the People," in *The Dispatch* newspaper, October 20, 1896.
3. T. Harry Williams, pp. 291 and 301.
4. Ibid., p. 142.

That seems a plea for more education; but it is also a re-statement of the carpetbagger and Radical Republican policy of confiscating the property of the wealthy Southerners to give to their cronies or freedmen.

Rutherford B. Hayes was the first president to openly advocate the nationalization of schools. He presented this anti-democratic idea in his acceptance speech at the party convention which nominated him. He said that the national prosperity depended upon the "intellectual and moral condition of the people. Therefore, liberal and permanent provision should be made for the support of free schools by the State governments, and if need be, supplemented by legitimate aid from national authority.... Supplement the local educational funds in the several states where the grave duties and responsibilities of the citizenship have been devolved on uneducated people."[1]

Hayes and the Peabody Fund

In a newspaper article appearing shortly after Hayes' death, Jabez Curry described how the President became associated with Peabody. His description of Hayes demonstrates how much his mind had turned around.

In 1877, "when Judge Watson of Tennessee, died, the Honorable A.H.H. Stuart nominated Mr. Hayes as a Trustee of the Peabody Education Fund, saying 'that the nomination of a member from the South would, under ordinary circumstances, have been proper, but there was a man of Northern birth, so eminent at that moment for patriotism and for wise statesmanship, and so honored in the South for his well-directed endeavor to restore peace and prosperity in the nation, that his name seemed naturally suggested.' From that time to the day of his death he was a faithful and punctual member of that great trust; took the deepest and most intelligent interest in Southern education, gave to our people in their struggle to establish free schools, his useful sympathy and counsel.... When I was unanimously elected General Agent of the fund in February 1881, President Hayes, as I learned, bore empathetic testimony as to my fitness, and when I presented myself and accepted the weighty responsibility he greeted me with old-time college cordiality. Ever since he has been most helpful by his wisdom and enthusiasm and his friendship."[2]

Hayes' comment in his diary for October 7, 1877, about his election to Peabody, is significant. It once again presents how Peabody had become

---

1. Gordon Canfield Lee, *The Struggle for Federal Aid, 1870-1890* (New York: Teachers College, Columbia University, 1949), pp. 73-74.
2. Jabez Curry in *The Times* newspaper, date deleted, but 1893.

enmeshed in promoting national policy in the former Confederacy. "The nomination by the Southern members of the Peabody Trustees and the unanimous election by the whole Board are agreeable things. They prove that the pacification measures are approved by the whole country."[1]

As an indication of how important Peabody was to Hayes, "the Trustees met at 12 o'clock in the library of the Executive mansion, by the invitation of President Hayes."[2]

Bringing Peabody into the heart of the national capital symbolized to Congress and the public that re-educating the South was critically important.

Curry, Hayes, and the Slater Fund

In 1882, Jabez Curry was offered the opportunity to greatly enlarge his field of educational labors by becoming the Chairman of the Education Committee of the John F. Slater Fund for the Education of Freedmen, in addition to his role as General Agent with Peabody.

The Slater Fund was another gigantic foundation, with a gift of one million dollars in 1882 from John Fox Slater, an industrialist from Norwich, Connecticut. This fund was to be used for "the uplifting of the lately emancipated population of the Southern States, and their posterity, by conferring on them the blessings of Christian education ... for the safety of our common country, in which they have been invested with equal political rights."[3]

Jabez Curry defined the difference between Peabody and Slater: "The two funds are entirely separate and distinct.... The Slater Fund was created exclusively for the Negro, and the Peabody Fund, which is older and bigger, was created for those portions of the South where the people had suffered in consequence of the war. Originally the [Peabody] fund had three million dollars but one million was lost to it by the repudiation of the bonds of certain States. It now amounts to two million dollars, and the income from this, about one-hundred thousand, is distributed every year. J. Pierpont Morgan is the treasurer and manager of the fund and invests it for the trustees.... The Peabody is never given to any but State schools, but the Slater Fund ... is given in aid to both State and denominational schools. No school receives any aid from the Slater Fund, however, which does not give industrial or manual training to its students. Two

---

1. T. Harry Williams, p. 97.
2. Proceedings of the Trustees of the Peabody Education Fund, 18th meeting, 1880, p. 257.
3. Rice, p. 159.

inscitucions receive aid from both funds; they are the schools at Hampton, Virginia and the Tuskegee Institute of Tuskegee, Alabama."[1]

Mr. Slater personally picked Rutherford B. Hayes as President of the Trustees. Hayes had discussed some of the plans for the Slater Fund with Curry during its formative period.

Atticus Heygood, a Methodist minister and President of Emory College in Georgia, was Slater's first General Agent. Since Peabody and Slater aided some of the same Negro schools, Curry and Heygood also often consulted with one another.

When Heygood became a bishop of the Methodist Episcopal Church South in 1890, he withdrew from Slater. Curry saw an opportunity to put into effect a plan he had hoped for; one General Agent for both funds. He discussed this with Hayes.

The result was that the Slater trustees substituted an "Educational Committee" for the General Agent's position. Curry was appointed as its Chairman. Curry described the process: "It was his [Hayes] suggestion that I was appointed a Trustee of the Slater Fund and Chairman of the Education Committee, with general supervision of the work. Shrinking from unnecessary publicity, he telegraphed me to meet him in Baltimore instead of Washington, where I lived, and made the proposal to me and urged my acceptance."[2]

Under Heygood, Slater aided more than fifty Negro institutions, colleges and universities in the South. The money mostly promoted industrial education: it was used to buy hand tools for shops, or farm equipment, to pay students for work on school grounds, and to pay part or all of the salaries of teachers in industrial and Normal departments.

Curry made major changes in the way that appropriations were given, reducing diffused aid to concentrate on a small number of institutions. He shifted the money from specialized trade schools to a more general manual training; student salaries were discontinued and the funds were used to pay experts in Normal work, manual training and designated special industries. Bulletins were now published showing the progress in these schools as well as special papers related to the improvement of the Negro race. From the nearly

---

1. *Times-Democrat* newspaper of New Orleans, no date, but approximately late 1880s, from Curry Papers.
2. *My Educational Life*, hand-written notes.

fifty subsidized schools, Curry gradually cut down the number so that by 1895 only twelve were funded.

As was his policy with Peabody, Curry visited all the schools receiving Slater money, and he took Hayes along with him through South Carolina, Georgia, Alabama, Mississippi, Louisiana and Tennessee.

Curry tells this story about Hayes on one of their trips together: "Riding together near Grangeburg, South Carolina, and seeing a Negro cabin in a cotton patch, he asked whether there would be any impropriety in his entering it, as he had never been inside such a home. Stopping the carriage, I conducted him to the low, dark, ill-furnished, one-room cabin, in which was a woman with a very young babe lying in a cradle. He examined the surroundings, asked in a kind manner many questions, and as he was leaving, gave her a silver dollar. Unobserved by the President I told the woman who her visitor was and how highly she had been honored. She broke out into exclamations of wonder and praise, clapping her hands in delight and then informed the President, assisted by the jubilant cries, that she would give the baby his name."[1]

This kind of close working relationship would have been an unthinkable, traitorous act for Curry only a decade before.

Hayes, Like Curry, in Transition

With time, Rutherford Hayes underwent a major philosophical transformation. Unlike Curry, who became more like a Radical Republican, Hayes began to doubt the extreme egalitarian principles that he advocated during Reconstruction. The editor of his correspondence said: "Reading Hayes' diary, one notes with growing amazement that this former Civil War general and Republican politician came to doubt gravely the values and standards of the Gilded Age in which he lived." The editor then added: "Sitting in his study, reading such authors as Tolstoy, Emerson, Meredith, Poe, Howells, John Quincy Adams, Lowell, meditating upon his life and times in his own quietly honest way, Hayes would record diary entries like the following: "I do not find a ready word for the doctrines of true equality of rights. Its foes call it nihilism, Communism, Socialism, and the like.' " He began to have an insight into the consequences of Radical Republican ideology.[2]

---

1. Ibid.
2. Louis D. Rubin, Jr., editor, *Teach The Freemen, The Correspondence of Rutherford B. Hayes and the Slater Fund for Negro Education, 1881-1887* (Louisiana State University Press, 1959), p. xxxii.

Simultaneously, Jabez Curry underwent another period of disillusionment, but his malaise did not make him more moderate. He became more radical. It began with the results of schooling for Negroes. "Much of the aid lavished upon the Negro has been misapplied charity, and like much other almsgiving, hurtful to the recipient. Northern philanthropy, disastrously kind, has often responded with liberality to appeals worse than worthless.... The work is too great to be attempted by any other agency, unless by the National Government; the field is too extensive, the offices too numerous, the cost too burdensome."[1]

Jabez Curry had come full circle. The committed believer in state sovereignty, local control of schools, was now pleading for a Federal take-over of Southern children's minds.

---

1. J.L.M. Curry, *Occasional Paper No. 5*, published by the John F. Slater Fund, 1895, from the introduction.

CHAPTER 13. THE BLAIR BILL: A STEP TOWARD NATIONAL-IZED SCHOOLS

Jabez Curry and his Peabody Fund had set the stage for Northern control of Southern education by tying common schools to the carpetbag governments.

Then, Rutherford B. Hayes, both as president and as a Peabody trustee, began the first tentative steps toward the next stage: a Federal take-over.

Hayes and Albion Tourgee: The Take-over Plan

To develop a plan to accomplish this, Hayes corresponded with a former high-ranking army officer colleague; Albion Tourgee. Tourgee had been seriously wounded during the war but had stayed in North Carolina with his family when the fighting ended. He opened a law office, then drifted into the political arena, progressively becoming more radicalized as the Confederates that he hated for his permanent injuries steadily returned to power in the South.

Tourgee joined the Freedmen's Bureau and its Union League and quickly became the most powerful member of the Republican Party in North Carolina.

His extreme hatred of Southern whites led him to become the essence of the stereotypical carpetbagger. "Tourgee the Infamous" and "Tourgee the Cain-Marked" were derogatory terms that followed him, particularly when he was seated on the North Carolina Supreme Court bench in 1868. His decisions were largely unjustifiably biased on behalf of the Negroes.

In 1879, as the carpetbag governments fell, he left the South and turned to novel writing. In the 1880s, *A Fool's Errand, By One of the Fools* and *Bricks Without*

Straw, both best-sellers, were thinly disguised allegories of Radical Republican ideology and his educational plans for the South.

In *A Fool's Errand* Tourgee wrote: "The nation nourished and protected slavery. The fruitage of slavery has been the ignorant poor white man and the arrogant master. Now let the nation undo the evil it has permitted and encouraged. Let it educate those whom it made ignorant and protect those who it made weak. It is not a matter of favor to the black but safety to the nation. Make the spelling book the scepter of national power. Let the nation educate the colored man and the poor white man because the nation held them in bondage and is responsible for their education. Educate the voter because the nation cannot afford that he should be ignorant."[1]

In *Bricks Without Straw*, education for the South was a major theme. One character, believing that ignorance had contributed to white supremacy, said: "It is not my remedy but the only remedy. Educate the people until they are wise enough to know what they ought to do and brave enough and strong enough to do it."[2]

Another fictional character in the book, drawing on the plan of the Peabody Fund, describes how Federal money, on a matching basis, related to illiteracy, could spur intelligence and by-pass untrustworthy, racist state governments.

Tourgee wrote letters to Congress and to President Grant appealing for a common school system "provided and controlled by the General Government, in the former slave states."

As a result of all this effort, the Republican Party platform in 1880 was the first in United States history to recommend Federal help for schools — "It is the duty of the National Government to aid education."[3]

There was another factor, a political element, that led Tourgee to his obsession with education. It would break up Democratic power in the South. To promote this idea he wrote an article in *North American Review*, entitled *Aaron's Rod in Politics*. It was a pure diatribe, rationalizing Federal intervention in Southern schools. Tourgee said that the South contained three-quarters of the nation's illiterates, and that 45 percent of their voters could not read election ballots. Congress should distribute money on the basis of this lack of schooling. All

---

1. Otto Olson, *Carpetbagger's Crusade: The Life of Albion Winegor Tourgee* (Baltimore: The Johns Hopkins Press, 1965), p. 242.
2. Ibid., 244.
3. Stanley Hirshon, *Farewell to the Bloody Shirt* (Chicago: Quadrangle Books, 1962), p. 87.

schools receiving aid must meet Federal regulations. Washington would supply up to one-half of the funds.

Tourgee claimed that this would increase the intelligence of voters (making them intelligent enough to become Republicans, of course) and provide a basis for re-organizing the Republican Party in the former Confederacy to eliminate state sovereignty sentiments and the "Solid South."

In August 1880, at a Union Army reunion in Columbus, Ohio, Rutherford B. Hayes gave a speech which provided an overview of Tourgee's plan. "To perpetuate the Union, and to abolish slavery was the work of the war. To educate the uneducated is the appropriate work of peace."[1]

In another speech Hayes parroted Tourgee: "The total of men of voting age who could not read and write in the late slave-holding states, was in 1870, 1,176,000. In 1880, the number of illiterate voters had increased to 1,350,000. In each of eight Southern states the illiterate voters exceed in number the majority of votes cast even at the most exciting elections. Most seriously important of all, the illiterate voters of the South have in the last ten years increased almost two-hundred-thousand. This increase of ignorant voters alone exceeds the number of votes cast in any one of twenty of the States at the last Presidential election."[2]

These numbers are deceptive. The population of the United States had increased dramatically in the generation after the war, via immigration. Most of the illiterates were Europeans, not poor whites or blacks.

Henry Blair, His Bill, His Idea

In 1882, Senator Henry Blair of New Hampshire put Tourgee's concepts together into a bill. This is a portion of his speech as he introduced Senate Bill No. 151.

"Universal intelligence never makes war. Only ignorance is convertible into brute force. Ignorance is slavery. But for ignorance among the nominally free there would have been no rebellion. The contest we now wage is with that still unconquered ignorance of both white men and black men in all parts of the country who hurried us by remorseless fate to fields of death for four long years. Besides this we confront the demands of hordes incoming from beyond the great oceans, and of the advancing generations of men. I am glad to admit that whenever the State or the local community is able to sufficiently instruct its

---

1. Charles R. Williams, *Diary and Letters of Rutherford B. Hayes* (Columbus: Ohio State Archeological and Historical Society, 1922-1925), vol. 3, p. 591.
2. Speech at Roseland Park, Woodstock, Connecticut, July 4, 1883.

youth it should do so, and that national aid should be invoked only when made necessary by local neglect or inability. But this burden is primarily one of taxation. Civilization must be paid for. Education is the insurance upon civilization. It must be kept up everywhere, for the risk is everywhere."

In describing his plan of supervision, which he envisioned as a mix of State and Federal authority, he mentioned the Peabody Fund. He showed the deceptions in his plan with the following falsehood: "The Peabody Fund, which has been of so much good in every Southern State, is administered practically by one man [Curry] and he is wholly independent of State control."

This was obviously untrue. Peabody was enmeshed with the Freedmen's Bureau and the carpetbagger governments, by sharing subsidies and having the State Education superintendents play a major role in screening and disbursing the funds.

Blair: "We may postpone the remedy but the evil will increase. The issue cannot be evaded. Common-school education must become universal or the form of our government must be changed. I believe the next ten years will decide the question."

Then Blair described the specific provisions of his bill: "That for ten years next after the passage of this act there shall be annually appropriated from the money in the Treasury the following sums, to wit: the first year the sum of fifteen million dollars, the second year the sum of fourteen million dollars, the third year the sum of thirteen million dollars, and thereafter a sum diminished by one million dollars yearly from the sum last appropriated until ten annual appropriations shall have made.... That such money shall be annually divided among and paid out in the several States and Territories in that proportion which the whole number of persons in each, who, being of the age of ten years and over, cannot read or write, bears to the whole number of such persons in the United States, and until otherwise provided such computations shall be made according to the returns of the Census of 1880."

The following shows that Peabody was the model: a matching fund. "That the design of this act, not being to establish an independent system of schools, but rather to aid for the time being, in the development and maintenance of the school systems established by local power, and which must eventually be wholly maintained by the States and Territories wherein they exist, it is hereby provided that no part of the money appropriated under this act shall be paid in any State or Territory which shall not during the first five years of the operation of this act, annually expend for the maintenance of common schools, free to all, at least one-third of the sum which shall be allotted to it under the provisions thereof, and during the second five years of its operation, a sum at least equal to the whole it shall be entitled to receive under this act."

Finally, Blair showed that his so-called concern that the States should have input and equal power in this subsidy, was fraudulent. "The Secretary of the Interior shall be charged with the practical administration of this law through the Bureau of Education."[1]

The next chapter will be devoted to the Bureau of Education and will demonstrate that this was the agency that finally nationalized common schools and viewed State input as an obstacle to be pushed aside and disregarded.

Fraudulent Census of 1870 and 1880

The Census has always been a powerful political tool. Representation in Congress and Washington's "pork-barreling" to states has always been based on Census data. Before there was an Internal Revenue Service, it was the Census questions related to personal and property wealth that were used to assess taxes.

Thus, it can be realistically stated that, from the beginning, the Census has been manipulated. But in the Reconstruction era, fraud reached new heights. As the military controlled voting, it was the soldiers who either conducted the Census questioning of citizens or who "supervised" the questionnaires to "massage" the numbers so that they conformed to the Army's or Washington's requirements.

One contemporary source said that "data primarily from the 1870 & 1880 Census cannot be considered as accurate, in view of the inadequate Census techniques and unreliable appraisals of property values."[2]

"Inadequate techniques" insured the politically correct numbers. "Unreliable appraisals of property values" related to the arbitrary devaluation of confiscated land so it could be purchased by the military or the carpetbaggers for a fraction of its real worth. Land valuation was critical to education. School funding was based on property taxes.

In 1870, the literacy question on the Census form asked "Read" and "Write." In 1880, this had been changed to "Cannot read" and "Cannot write."

---

1. Henry W. Blair's speech in Senate, Tuesday, June 13, 1882, from *Congressional Globe*.
2. Gordon Canfield Lee, p. 30.

These are very different questions, and they elicited different answers and different statistical results.

Senator Roscoe Conkling of New York explained the consequences of inconsistent questions in this speech: "Anterior to 1850 each decade produced its own Census act, each decade of course adding its wisdom to the wisdom of the past. With each act came changes in the form and substance of inquiries, and thus the nation and science were robbed of one of the chief elements of usefulness and instruction, which statistics can possess; unlearned men can appreciate it — I mean continuous identity of inquiries — sticking to the same questions and the same things. The same kind of statistics time after time admit of certain and easy comparisons, changes of growth or decline and the lessons changes teach, constitute the chief object with the students of statistics. Changes can be defined and measured only by comparisons, and he who destroys uniformity among tables which belong to a series, is an enemy of science and knowledge."[1]

The 1880 Census numbers supposedly showed illiteracy rates for all sections of the United States, based only on the question "Cannot write."

By this definition the North had 7.7 percent illiteracy, the Pacific area 15 percent, and the South 42 percent. But the second question, "Cannot read" was discarded to get this fraudulently large difference. When both were utilized, the illiteracy figures for the different regions were much more similar.

Most significantly, the Census questions about the ability to write were asked of the adult heads of household. These were the so-called illiterates. Yet, most children in that era finished school at fifteen. Thus the question, especially when fused with another question, "illiteracy by voters," was skewed to that adult group that would not benefit by school aid. Yet, it was this adult group that was paraded as a conclusive argument for Federal support.

Radicals Claim South Too Poor to Fund Schools

Henry Blair proposed his bill supposedly in part due to the South's inability to pay for its own common schools. Barnas Sears and Jabez Curry also claimed that the South's impoverishment, due to the widespread destruction of the war, made Federal aid imperative.

But, more rational voices presented the more truthful picture. The *Weekly Floridian* newspaper stated: "The debate on the Blair Education Bill has been,

---

1. *Congressional Globe*, 41st Congress, 1st Session, p. 1079.

with the exception of the tariff matter, the most interesting business of the session…. Statistics do show that some, if not all, Southern states raise more money for educational purposes to their population than some of the most prosperous Northern states, and the newspaper press has not neglected to assert the fact."[1]

Then, where did all the money go? The carpetbaggers illegally took that money for their own covert schemes. Here is an example of what occurred throughout the South: "It was a colored man, W.F. Brown, who, as State Superintendent of Education [in Louisiana] called attention in his report of 1873 to the way in which schools funds were being stolen. New Orleans, as a legacy from Banks [General Nathaniel Banks, the brutal commander of occupied New Orleans] and the Freedmen's Bureau, was one of the few Southern states that had a system of public schools. In 1865, there were 141 schools for the freedmen. A school law had been passed in 1869, providing the system of public education without distinction of race and color. This system was not carried out. W.F. Brown reported: 'Stolen in Carroll Parish in 1871, 30,000 dollars; in East Baton Rouge, 5,032 dollars; in St. Landry, 5,700 dollars; in St. Martin, 3,786 dollars; in Plaquemines, 5,855 dollars; besides large amounts in St. Tammany, Concordia, Morehouse and other parishes.' The entire permanent school fund of many parishes disappeared during this period."[2]

Curry Promotes Blair Bill

One might be led to believe that if "Tourgee the Infamous" was behind Blair and promoting Federal aid to common schools, Jabez Curry would have second thoughts about supporting such ideas. But no, still blinded by his belief that the freedmen needed special help, he enthusiastically pressed forward on the wings of the Peabody Fund.

It had started with Barnas Sears; on February 18, 1880, Sears and the Peabody Board met with Rutherford B. Hayes in the library of the White House. At that meeting Sears distributed a report entitled *Education for the Colored Population of the Southern States*. In it, Sears stated that between the impoverished emancipated blacks and the whites who were made destitute by the war, fully one-half of the Southern population was incapable of bearing more taxation. But as has just been shown, what they actually could not bear was more theft of their

---

1. *Weekly Floridian*, April 1, 1884.
2. Habart, p. 406.

taxes. "The only hope that remains of obtaining [funds for schools] is an appeal to the liberality of Congress."[1]

Then Sears tried to terrorize Congress into action: "Several hundred thousand illiterate voters constitute an important factor in national politics.... They may migrate, at pleasure, to any State.... An exodus from the Southern to the Western States has already commenced, and the day may not be far distant when the colored vote may be the controlling power in these States."[2]

In March 1880, along with this report, Sears and the Peabody Board petitioned Congress for such help — with this comment about the "vital necessity of national aid for the education of the colored population of the Southern States, and especially the great masses of colored children who are growing up to be voters under the Constitution of the United States."[3]

After Sears' death, without a moment's hesitation, Curry picked up the ball of Federal aid and, superficially, seemed to have no second thoughts about his position. Yet, in fact, he still held conflicting views.

In March 1882, Curry advised Robert Winthrop, the President of the Board, that he was "identifying the Fund prominently and beneficially" with the movement for "liberal Congressional action," and wondered if Winthrop and the Board might not approve.[4]

Winthrop backed his efforts. Curry then presented his own petition to Congress for school aid in May 1882. This document followed Blair's logic, giving statistics on illiteracy vs. population in all the states, but demonstrating the South's disproportionate share. These numbers were based on the skewed numbers of the 1880 Census.

Curry's petition naively stated: "The help should be given so that it will stimulate rather than supercede the necessity of State effort." It also read: "The safety of the Republic is the supreme law of the land," a motto often used by the Radical Republicans during the war to violate the Constitution, institute martial law, and end the writ of habeas corpus for civilians when that was clearly unjustified. The war and its instability had long past, but not for the newly radicalized Mr. Curry. The petition went on: "The help should be immediate and not remote.

---

1. Proceedings of the Trustees of the Peabody Education Fund, Report of the 18th meeting, 1880, p. 285.
2. Ibid., p. 300.
3. Proceedings of the Trustees of the Peabody Education Fund, Report of the 21st meeting, 1882, Appendix, p. 100.
4. Rice, p. 117

The fortunes of war, and the necessities of legislative action have made citizens of a large mass of ignorant men, whose votes are to shape, for weal or woe, the character of our laws. Education alone can convert this mass of ignorance and element of danger into one of enlightened strength and safety.... In the name of the millions of Christian citizens who we represent, we earnestly urge Congress to help qualify the ignorant voters who are entrusted largely by Congressional action with the ballot, for the duties with which they are charged, believing the power to do is co-ordinate with the power that enfranchised them."[1]

In the summer of 1882, Curry appeared before the Senate and House committees on Education, urging national funding for Southern schools. He quickly saw that this was not their highest priority. He wrote Winthrop that "a few thousand dollars for cleaning out Coon Creek is considered more influential in carrying a particular district than a vital question affecting the perpetuity of our institutions."[2]

Blair, in his speech to the Senate about his bill, had some very harsh words about the South — mostly that its ignorance was the cause of the war. His bill seemed more like an act of revenge. Yet Curry said this about Blair: "I wish as a Southern man, to express my thanks to Senator Blair, for his patience, energy, ability, liberality and comprehensive patriotism with which he has pressed his great plan of national justice and safety."[3]

When the Blair Bill passed the Senate in April 1884, Curry wrote, "It gives hope to the Republic."[4]

Yet, simultaneously, in a newspaper interview, Curry showed that he still faintly recalled his old state sovereignty ideals — but forgot the reality that had prompted them: Federal power, when given an opening, will always dominate and absorb a state power. "State systems should not be superseded. The General Government should act in cooperation with State authorities, and not adopt any plan or practice or method which will subordinate them."[5]

His old ideals quickly faded, as here he sounds more like a promoter of European monarchism and its connecting of schools with the military: "The Absolute governments of Europe are putting us to shame by the extent, variety

---

1. Ibid., p. 118.
2. Ibid., p. 118.
3. Jabez Curry, fragment of an article in an unknown newspaper, unknown date.
4. Rice, p. 119.
5. *Richmond Dispatch*, December 28, 1883.

and value of their educational institutions. Throughout Prussia, Bohemia, Bavaria, Holland, Denmark and the greater part of Austria and France, all the children of both rich and poor are receiving daily instruction, from long and carefully educated teachers. In Prussia, attendance upon school is secured by direct competition, but the males at a certain age are compelled to join the standing army and serve for a term of years."[1]

More of Curry's Contradictions

During this time period, Jabez Curry's mind betrayed a "state of flux." On one occasion he had praised Rutherford Hayes' annual message to Congress but also commented that his recommendation for a National University was antagonistic to "State Rights notions" and Curry felt that the country had "gone far enough in the direction of centralization."[2]

And in a Peabody annual report referring to the same subject, when Curry was still pressing for Federal aid, he made this contradictory statement (which sounds like it was uttered prior to secession, or that there never had been Reconstruction): "In our system of decentralization, or State autonomy, of Home Rule, or community and individual development, we do not need a central, dominating, national university."[3]

At another time, in a hand-written note to himself, Curry wrote: "Our loyalty to the Union ... does not imply any assent to the destruction of what remains of the Constitution or of the Federal system, or the complete absorption of the States into the central mass.... Centralization does not comport with liberty.... Planets should not be plunged into the sun for safety."[4] Yet, centralizing aid to schools in Washington would have the same effect.

James Garfield and Albion Tourgee

In 1880, James Garfield followed Hayes as President of the United States. One-third of his inaugural address was devoted to the idea of nationalized education, mirroring Albion Tourgee's vision almost word for word. Garfield admitted that another of Tourgee's novels, called *Figs and Whistles*, had helped him win the national election because the public believed it to be his fictionalized

---

1. Jabez Curry, hand-written note to probably be used as a guide for an article on education, from Curry Papers.
2. Rice, p. 79.
3. Proceedings of the Trustees of the Peabody Education Fund, 31st meeting, 1892, p. 349.
4. Jabez Curry, hand-written note for a speech or article, Curry Papers.

biography. Garfield said, sweetly: "The race problem will only be solved when the Negro exhibits the native hungering and thirsting for knowledge that the Creator has planted in every child.... So that the hands of the people shall reach out and grasp in the darkness the hand of the government extended to help, and by that union of effort the two will bring what mere legislation alone cannot immediately bring."[1]

Garfield argued that only education could permanently end the "Southern Problem." Soon afterward, the Blair Bill easily passed through the Senate. It then went to the House. If it passed that chamber, education in both the South and the entire United States would be in the hands of Washington.

Counter-Attacks Against Blair

The defenders of decentralized government fought back to block the passage of the Blair Bill. An editorial in the *Nashville American* directly attacked Jabez Curry: "We have received a copy of a circular letter sent by J.L.M. Curry, of Richmond, Virginia, General Agent of the Peabody Fund, which asks us to publish, but which we respectfully decline to do, for reasons which seem to us good and sufficient. The letter is nothing but a prolonged whine about the poverty and destitution of the South, and a piteous appeal to Southern people to unite in a bold assault upon the Treasury, under the leadership of that unspeakable combination of jackass and brigand, Henry W. Blair, of New Hampshire. Mr. Curry thinks the situation of the South is so deplorable that mendicancy and plunder are excusable. Violating the Constitution and rifling the Treasury are the only means, so thinks J.L.M. Curry, whereby we may be rescued from our wretchedness. He thinks 'our liberties and the perpetuity of representative institutions are inseparably interwoven with free schools,' but it has never occurred to him that these liberties and representative institutions could be endangered by trampling the Constitution under foot in order to give every crank and plunderer in the country a whack at the Treasury. Mr. Curry thinks that the next session of Congress will be an encouraging opportunity for the success of his grab scheme. Perhaps it will. And Mr. Curry may felicitate himself upon the fact that a party is in power which has no conscientious scruples in regard to violating the Constitution or robbing the Treasury."[2]

---

1. *Congressional Globe*, 46th Congress, 2nd Session, December 11th and 15th, 1879, p. 104.
2. *Nashville American*, October 29, 1889.

Edwin Burritt Smith was an eminent lawyer in Chicago. He made this speech against the Blair Bill at the Chicago Congregational Club. In the opening phase he presented statistics to demonstrate that whites and blacks had a higher percentage of school attendance in the South than in many Northern states. They stayed in school longer and all the positive numbers kept improving with time. Yet, Smith added, Blair "proposes a vast appropriation on the basis of their incurable illiteracy, to be expended, not upon the illiterates but upon their children, for whose education the South has already shown its ability and willingness to make ample provision."

Smith then turned to other aspects of Blair's bill: "The proposed measure involves a vast extension of the jurisdiction of national authority. It takes the Federal government into a field hitherto wholly occupied by the States.... The supporters of the Blair Bill say it is merely a gift to the States. But it is not true. The bill is filled with conditions which the State is bound to accept or forfeit, not only its share of the appropriation but the sum paid by it in taxes. The Blair Bill, as passed by the Senate last week, is a proposal to participate not only in the support but the management and control of the common school systems which the States have created. The proposal as presented involves only a temporary national aid, to meet a special emergency, and is never to be used as a precedent. But you know the absolute weakness of this plea. Congress never relinquishes a jurisdiction once acquired. Mr. Blair has already abandoned his original position that national aid is to meet the emergency raised by the illiteracy of the colored race and now advocates it as necessary to prevent the growth of illiteracy and anarchy in the North, especially in Massachusetts, Connecticut and New York.... But the final and fatal objection to any measure of national aid for the benefit of the Negro race lies deeper still, and deeper than any mere consideration of public policy. I refer to the effect on the Negro himself. In the deeply significant language of the Supreme Court, in the opinion declaring the Civil Rights Act unconstitutional; 'When a man has emerged from slavery and by the aid of beneficial legislation, has shaken off the insuperable concomitants of that state, there must be some stage in the process of his elevation where he takes the rank of mere citizen and ceases to be the special favorite of the laws, and when his rights, as a citizen or a man, are to be protected in the ordinary modes by which other men's rights are protected.' That man is not the best friend of the Negro, however excellent his intentions, who now seeks to have him treated as a special ward of the nation."[1]

"A Bill to Promote Mendicancy"

In editorials published in the *New York Evening Post* between January to March 1886, Edward Clark hammered away at the dangers of the Blair Bill. Collected together in pamphlet form, the series was called *A Bill to Promote Mendicancy: Facts and Figures Showing that the South Does Not Need Federal Aid for Her Schools.* Samples of Clark's insights are presented: "The plea in favor of the Bill is plausible but we believe it is fallacious, because it takes a short-sighted view of the future. Illiteracy is bad but it is not the worst thing. The vital element of any success that is worth achieving in this world is self-reliance. There is nothing more demoralizing to a state than the assumption of its own duty by the authorities at Washington.

The truth is that the Southern states are already proving they can grapple with the problem alone. Take, for example, South Carolina, which was in the most desperate condition. In 1874, under carpet-bag rule, there were 110,416 pupils in her public schools. In 1884 the number increased to 185,619. In Mississippi; 1876, 166,204 to 266,996 in 1883. Florida; in ten years, 20,911 to 58,311. 63 percent attend in South Carolina, 69 percent in Maine.

A Southerner said: 'The Blair Bill is simply, in another form, the old hallucination of 40 acres and a mule, which has caused more briars and sassafras to grow in Southern fields than all else.' "

In another editorial, Clark said: "Dr. Mayo of the Peabody Fund pointed out that the Southern states raised more money than Northern states for education.... The Reverend A.D. Mayo is a gentleman of the highest character, a clergyman of the highest standing in the Unitarian Church, and a life-long friend of education. Some years ago he abandoned regular church work to devote himself to the cause of education in the South. But he is the most dangerous of guides; a man with a hobby. His former environment causes him to view Southern schools through glasses which distort the situation. Mr. Mayo lived, while his children were going to school, in Cincinnati, and Springfield, Massachusetts. Both cities have excellent systems of graded schools in session nine to ten months a year. He went down South and found that in the rural districts the common schools were open only three to four months a year. He was naturally shocked and jumped to the conclusion that the nation must go to the aid of the Southern states or their children would never get a decent education. His radical mistake was in sup-

---

1. Edwin Burritt Smith, "Education in the South — National Aid," an address before the Chicago Congregationalist Club, February 20, 1888), pp. 10, 11, 14.

233

posing that the situation in the rural regions of the South was much different than the rural regions of the North, or much worse. If he had gone from Springfield through the hill towns of Western Massachusetts, he would have found schools which are but little more effective than exist in the South and are in session but little longer. Official records show that the average length of the school year between 1860 and '70 was 119 days in Vermont, 99 in Maine, 97 in New Hampshire. In eight of sixteen slave states, schools are open 100 days or more, and in only three, less than 75."[1]

Curry and Blair: The Peabody Board Counter-Attacks

As a result of the strong opposition to the Blair Bill, it failed to pass through the House of Representatives. Jabez Curry desperately tried to revive it, for if Blair failed, his hopes for Federal aid would be dashed; but his efforts had serious negative repercussions for him.

In the fall of 1889, Curry published an article, *To Southern Representatives in Congress and to Friends of Free Schools in the South*. He appealed for support of the Blair Bill. He referred to his official position with Peabody. It was published widely in both the religious and secular press. His article was savagely attacked by Peabody Board members, partially because Curry had used his "General Agent" title to gain credibility for his point of view. Robert Winthrop backed Curry, informing the Board members that he had approved the article beforehand but admitting that he did not realize that "General Agent of the Peabody Education Fund" was included.

Overconfident because of this victory, Jabez Curry published a second appeal directed toward Congress. One of the most prestigious Board members, Hamilton Fish, who had been Secretary of State under Ulysses S. Grant and Hayes, was "greatly shocked" that Curry once again used his Peabody title; Fish was strongly opposed to Blair. Angrily, he asked Winthrop if this second piece had been approved; if so, Fish was prepared to resign from the Board.

Winthrop was so alarmed, he said, that "my hand trembles" as he wrote to Fish saying that he had misconstrued the pamphlet. Winthrop believed Curry was making a personal appeal and not in his official capacity.

When Jabez Curry was informed of Fish's distress, he told Winthrop he would resign rather than cause a problem for Peabody. Diplomatically, Win-

---

1. Edward Clark, *A Bill to Promote Mendicancy* (New York: The Evening Post Publishing Co., 1888), pp. 3, 4, 17.

throp smoothed things over for both men and they continued on. Yet, this incident indicates the powerful sentiments that existed against Blair.[1]

Tourgee's Insight

Like Curry, Albion Tourgee relentlessly promoted Blair. But unlike Jabez, he came to a startling understanding of his actions and he "stepped off the train."

Initially, to further his own obsession with Federal aid to Southern schools, Tourgee turned his literary talents toward publishing a magazine, *Our Continent*, which, of course, devoted its editorial content to furthering that goal. Tourgee wrote, "all other questions affecting national life dwindle to insignificance."

Then, Tourgee began to oppose Blair because, instead of giving the funds directly to the Southern school systems Washington's money would be channeled through the "racist, traitorous" state governments. That was intolerable.

As Tourgee backed away, he had an amazing insight. For years he had proclaimed that "knowledge is not only the sole cure for barbarism but the only remedy for prejudice."[2]

Now, he saw the reverse side of his dream. Prejudice, evil, barbarism, could just as easily be spread through the common schools if the political leaders did not share his social perspective.

Soon, the disillusioned Tourgee disappeared from significance; and James Garfield was assassinated. Without their support, the Blair Bill once again failed to pass through Congress, and it also faded into oblivion.

Sadly, Jabez Curry had no such overview. He slogged on and bitterly wrote: "Unfortunately Congress would not rise to the height of the great argument, nor appreciate the unremoved national peril, and the refusal seems a little short of national folly and wickedness, when our policy toward a few Indians and Alaskans is contrasted with our cruel neglect of millions of Negroes."[3]

The forces for federalizing schools had lost the battle, but not the war. They attacked again, from a different, covert angle and took the protectors of liberty by surprise. And once again, Jabez Curry was there, fighting on the side that he had once loathed.

---

1. This section paraphrased from Rice, pp. 152-153.
2. *Continent* magazine, No. 5 (January 30, 1884), p. 150.
3. J.L.M. Curry, *Sketch of George Peabody*, p. 140.

CHAPTER 14. JOHN EATON'S BUREAU OF EDUCATION: THE NEW PSYCHOLOGY

Before common schools were forced upon the South by the carpetbagger constitutions, and long before there was a Blair Bill, in a low-key, covert way the process of nationalizing Southern schools was already under way — but few people realized it. It seemed to be much more innocuous than the headline grabbing plan by Henry Blair.

As noted previously, in 1867, a small agency in the Interior Department was created. It had only five employees: a supervisor and four clerks. It was called the Bureau of Education. Its mandate seemed harmless: "To collect such statistics and facts as show the condition and progress of education in the various States and Territories."[1] Implied but not spelled out was a research function.

Within a few years it employed or had access to 12,000 Interior Department personnel and administered most Southern schools and many in the North. In fact, in one of his annual reports, the Commissioner, John Eaton, made an amusing and revealing gaffe. He complained bitterly that he only had two clerks and a $6,000 budget to do mountains of work and there was no one to wash the office windows. Then he slipped and said that the Bureau of Education had now expanded to the point where it encompassed seventeen rooms![2]

---

1. Annual Report of the Bureau of Education, for the year 1868, p. 2.
2. Annual Report of the Bureau of Education, for the year 1875, pp. vii and viii.

The Bureau of Education succeeded where Blair had failed. It would nationalize American education. This five-man bureau would absorb the Freedmen's Bureau and eventually become the Department of Health, Education and Welfare, one of Washington's largest bureaucracies.

James Garfield Proposes Bureau of Education

In 1866, when future president James Garfield was in the House of Representatives, he submitted a bill calling for a national department of education. Its critics said it was too expensive, and unconstitutional. It was defeated. Then Garfield pleaded: "It is the voice of the children of the land, asking us to give them all the blessings of our civilization."[1] That pushed the Bureau of Education through the House, because Southern Democrats were still excluded from Congress. The Senate and President Andrew Johnson also approved.

Not everyone was pleased. Representative Andrew Rogers of New Jersey presented the negative side: "This bill is similar to the Freedmen's Bureau bill.... I say that this country will compare favorably in respect to education with any country upon the face of the earth.... I am content, sir, to leave this matter of education where our Fathers left it, where the history of this country left it, to the school systems of the different towns, cities and states.... It proposes to collect such statistics which will give a controlling power over the school system of the states. Mr. Donnelly talks about educating the people of the South as though they were a set of men who had no education, learning or intelligence. Sir, when he defames them by saying this, he defames the country."[2]

John Eaton, Second Commissioner

The Bureau of Education's first commissioner was Henry Barnard, a nationally prominent educator with the same views and philosophies as Horace Mann. Barnard's magazine, *American Journal of Education*, has been called the most influential education publication of the 19th century. Unfortunately, he had poor political skills. He refused to compromise with Congress or the Secretary of the Interior. As punishment, Barnard's "Department" was demoted to a "Bureau" and his salary was slashed. He quit.

---

1. B.A. Hinsdale, *President Garfield and Education* (Boston: James R. Osgood and Company, 1882), p. 163.
2. *Congressional Globe*, 39th Congress, 1st Session, p. 2969.

John Eaton replaced Barnard. Eaton was a politically adroit Radical Republican, a close friend of Ulysses S. Grant, and had been a consultant to Abraham Lincoln related to developing a national policy for the freedmen.

It was Eaton who converted the Bureau of Education into a huge force for Federal domination of State school systems throughout the United States. It was Eaton who set the wheels in motion to convert the Bureau from a statistics gathering agency to one that created policy. And he specifically said that the Bureau had the right to call the states to account for how they used Federal aid.

It was Eaton who demanded wider powers than were prescribed, including the by-passing of the budget to get money. He used the same covert and illegal "off-budget" methods pioneered by the Freedmen's Bureau.

John Eaton: His History

Eaton was born in New Hampshire in 1829 and graduated Dartmouth College in 1854. After being the principal of the Ward School in Cleveland, Ohio, he took on a greater responsibility, at 27, as Superintendent of the Toledo school system. He had great executive ability. But, in 1859 he resigned for a higher calling: to study for the ministry at the Andover (Massachusetts) Theological Seminary. He was ordained in 1860 as a Presbyterian minister. Then the war began. Immediately, he volunteered as a chaplain and was assigned to the 27th Ohio Volunteer Infantry.

Eaton, like the other main characters in our story — Curry, Hayes, Grant, and later, William Torrey Harris — all underwent powerful mental changes as time went by. Initially, even as chaplain to the 27th Ohio, Eaton was not an Abolitionist, and he hated both pro and anti-slavery fanatics. By the end of the war he had become an extreme Radical Republican.

In November 1862, Eaton and the 27th Ohio were part of Ulysses S. Grant's forces at Grand Junction in Mississippi. Swarms of slaves came across the Union lines from the surrounding country, driven on by fighting and the destruction of their farms and plantations.

Starving and freezing, the slaves clogged the roads and impeded the movement of the Union army and overwhelmed the resources of the camp at Grand Junction.

They begged for food, clothing and shelter, but although some of them found work with the army as teamsters, cooks and laborers, most (including women and children) seemed destined to die during the coming winter.

Chaplain Eaton devised a plan to put many of the unemployed to work on military projects. They were paid with food. As a former educator, he developed classes in basic literacy for them.

General Grant was very much aware of the slave problem. He said to one of his staff officers, "I wish I knew an honest man, with good sound sense, who could take charge of this business." The officer replied: "I can tell you just the man, General. He is not a red-hot Abolitionist, though." Grant said, "No matter about that, if he is honest, earnest and competent."

Eaton received an order to see Grant. He feared he was being court-martialed for some unknown offense. But Grant greeted him with, "Oh, so you are the man who has all those darkies on his shoulders."[1]

Grant wanted Eaton to follow the same plan that he had so successfully implemented, but now on a much larger scale. First, Eaton was promoted to a colonel so he could give orders to high-ranking army officers. Then he was given a title which indicated the huge scale of his new assignment: "General Superintendent of all Contrabands [slaves who were within Union lines] in the Department of the Mississippi."

Eaton was so successful and the results so profitable to the army that the "contrabands" were now paid for their work.

Eaton had always been a believer that education would be the answer to most moral, social and economic problems. By 1864, he had established schools for the Negroes in Vicksburg, Natchez, Little Rock and Pine Bluff. Altogether, over 13,000 pupils were enrolled.

Jurisdictional conflicts between district commanders in the army and Federal civil agencies like the Treasury Department over how and where to employ the freedmen made Eaton's job extremely difficult, and he asked to be relieved of his assignment. Eaton put together a 34-page report for Grant to help his replacement resolve these issues.

Grant refused to reassign Eaton and was so impressed with the report that he sent it to Abraham Lincoln. The President read it and requested that Eaton come to the White House to discuss it. Eaton suggested that a new independent organization be created to protect freedmen's labor and wages. This was the original impulse for the Freedmen's Bureau. Eaton's report had far-reaching con-

---

1. *Northeast Ohio Quarterly*, "John Eaton and the Freedmen," Leo Siegel, Summer 1957, Vol. XXIX, No. 3, pp. 129-130.

sequences. It would affect national policy and welfare policy into the 21st century.

Another suggestion by Eaton, revolutionary at that time, was that Negroes should be accepted in the military as combatants, in regiments of their own, to avoid friction with white troops.

So, in March 1864, Grant gave Eaton his first military assignment: to command the 63rd United States Colored Infantry. This led, in March 1865, to Eaton's promotion to Brigadier-General of Volunteers.

When the Freedmen's Bureau idea was accepted by Congress, Eaton became an Assistant Commissioner directly under Oliver Otis Howard. This made him the second highest ranking official in the Bureau.

Eaton formulated Bureau regulations as Superintendent of the District of Columbia. His office was in the same building as O.O. Howard. This close association progressively radicalized him.

John Eaton: "Memphis Post" Editor

As a result of his increasing stance as a Radical, Eaton was offered the opportunity to be the editor of a new Republican newspaper, the *Memphis Post*, which spewed hate, contempt, false stories of atrocities against blacks, and threats of violence against Southern whites.

Eaton accepted this role and resigned from the Freedmen's Bureau in December 1865. He said: "A newspaper of strong Union principles was needed in that district and the *Post* was, for a long time, the only sheet of that character published between St. Louis and the Gulf. It supported the policy of the government as represented by Congress [the Radical Republican Congress] and by General Grant as head of the military power but it was opposed to the methods of Andrew Johnson."[1]

A sampling of headlines from the *Post* gives an idea of its tone and intention. January 19, 1866: *Affairs in the South: Persecution of Freedmen and Northerners*. Here, Eaton's false stories of atrocities generated by the Freedmen's Bureau were presented as truths. They were designed to bring an increased Federal military presence into the South.

---

1. John Eaton, *Grant, Lincoln and the Freedmen* (New York: Longmans, Green and Co., 1907), p. 248.

January 20, 1866: *Education in the South: A Set of Confederate Schools Books.* Eaton quotes from the texts to show the traitorous, racist character of Southern education, mostly twisting and misrepresenting them.

February 4, 1866: This article, *Religious Intelligence: Rapid Reconstruction of the Southern Methodist Churches*, explains how Northern Methodist clergy have replaced local ministers for a "purer" religion. He does not say that this transition was achieved at bayonet point.

February 9, 1866: *Accepting the Situation.* Eaton attacks Southern newspapers for stirring defiance and discontent by calling the United States Army in the South a "military despotism," and the bureaucrats and carpetbaggers, as filled with "insolence of office." Eaton says these statements show that the rebel spirit has not been quenched.

February 25, 1866: *What Will Be The Effect of The Veto on The Freedmen?* When President Andrew Johnson vetoed amendments to the Freedmen's Bureau because they would put a military government over the civil state in the South, Eaton, enraged, implicated Johnson with all "political reptiles." He then attacked Johnson for being drunk at his inauguration.

March 23, 1866: *The Necessities of the South.* The agriculture of the Southern states was supposedly in the hands of a small aristocratic group. The large plantations needed to be divided up into small farms and given to the laborers. Here Eaton is advocating a 19th-century variation of Stalinist land re-distribution.

Eaton's ugly, provocative editorials and stories continued until 1870, when the *Post* discontinued publishing. But he took on a second role during the same time that he was editor-in-chief. In the fall of 1867, he became the State Superintendent of Public Education for Tennessee, developing the public school system mandated by the carpetbag constitutions.

While in this position Eaton was investigated by the Tennessee House of Representatives. One of his functions as Superintendent was to place the state's school fund with a bank. Eaton chose the Tennessee National Bank of Memphis. One of that bank's officers, George Rutter, embezzled the money and Eaton was charged with being in collusion, since Rutter used this fund to finance Radical politicians and the *Memphis Post*. Eventually, Eaton was cleared of the charges, but a cloud of suspicion remained.

John Eaton: Bureau of Education Commissioner

When Henry Barnard quite the Bureau of Education over his conflicts with Congress, it was Ulysses S. Grant who asked Eaton to be the new commissioner.

Now, Eaton the Radical was at the center of American education and had the power to make it over in his image. In his memoirs Eaton confided that "during the entire time that Grant remained in the Presidency, he was a kindly counselor and my general support. Indeed, without him, the Bureau could hardly have become the most influential office of education in the world."[1]

Eaton, Curry, and the Peabody Fund

Jabez Curry wrote that on "March 2, 1867 the Bureau of Education was established.... It has become the most efficient and intelligent agency on the continent.... The Bureau and the Peabody Education Fund have been most helpful allies in making suggestions in relation to legislation in school matters."[2]

The 1881 Peabody annual report showed the connection between Peabody and Eaton. In the "Normal Institute for White Teachers in Greenville, South Carolina, in the buildings of Furman University, lectures on subjects of general interest connected with education were delivered at night by J.L.M. Curry, Dr. W.T. Harris [who would be the future commissioner of the Bureau of Education] and General Eaton."[3] It is obvious from the report that it was Curry who brought Harris and Eaton in as speakers.

Later Curry wrote: "It would be ungrateful and unjust not to mention the aid often given by the Bureau of Education at Washington. General Eaton, beyond a technical discharge of office work, delights also to advance the general cause by his abundant information, wide experience, personal counsel and eloquent voice."[4]

Then. "Virginia: The convention of county Superintendents held at Richmond, under the call and direction of the Superintendent, was a pleasant and profitable meeting. General Eaton attended and gave valuable instruction. The expenses of the lectures was paid by the [Peabody] Fund."[5]

---

1. Eaton, p. 259.
2. J.L.M. Curry, *John F. Slater Fund Occasional Paper No. 5*, p. 26.
3. Proceedings of the Trustees of the Peabody Education fund, 20th meeting, 1881, p. 23.
4. Proceedings of the Trustees of the Peabody Education Fund, 22nd meeting, 1883. p. 124.
5. Ibid., p. 130.

Also: "General Eaton ... to whom I am indebted for valuable and cheerful cooperation in all efforts, furnishes me this encouraging statement of educational work in the Southern States." Curry is referring to a statistical table showing the increase in white and black school enrollment.[1]

It is, once again, amazing that Jabez Curry would write such gushing sentiments about John Eaton. As with Grant and Hayes, he completely overlooked the man's Radicalism and his hatred of all things Southern. Curry would work with Eaton for years in the name of federalized schools.

Eaton reciprocated Curry's kind words in the Bureau's annual reports. "Legislation has just been stimulated by Dr. Curry's eloquent appeals, while the course pursued by [Curry] in concentrating the money upon the training of teachers, has accomplished more than any other single agent in creating throughout the South a just appreciation of the paramount importance of this part of public school work."[2]

Eaton also devoted space in his annual reports to Peabody activities, including how and to whom the fund was distributed, listings of Normal schools and the full texts of Curry's speeches to the various state legislatures.

A revealing element about Curry's changed mindset is found in an Eaton annual report, where Jabez wrote an article related to the Freedmen's Bureau. It must be recalled that during Reconstruction, Curry was filled with rage by that agency's ruthless and corrupt activities, including the confiscation of all his property, which left him nearly destitute. From that perspective his comments are astonishingly tepid. "Large and comprehensive powers and resources were placed in the hands on the [Freedmen's] Bureau and limitations of the authority of the Federal government were disregarded in order to meet the gravest problem of the century. Millions of recently enslaved Negroes, homeless, penniless, ignorant, were to be saved from destitution."[3]

The most startling aspect of the Curry-Eaton relationship is exposed in that small, almost unnoticed entry in Jabez's diary for March 27, 1885. Eaton was in declining health and planning to retire: "To Washington City and back. General Eaton asked if I'd accept a place at the head of the Bureau of Education." This position was the ultimate pinnacle for anyone in the world of education. "I replied in the negative."

---

1. Proceedings of the Trustees of the Peabody Education Fund, 24th meeting, 1885, p. 226.
2. Annual Report of the Bureau of Education, 1882, p. lvii.
3. Annual Report of the Bureau of Education, 1895, p. 1377.

Curry gave no explanation, no insight into why he made this decision. One can only surmise that he was aware that, at such a height, Southerners could fully see his collusion with all the forces that were destroying their culture and he would lose all credibility.

The Agriculture Department: Land Control as Mind Control

Long before the Blair Bill and carpetbag school systems, even long before there was John Eaton and his Bureau of Education, the first mind control experiments for Southerners began at the Federal level.

It was 1862; the height of the War for Southern Independence. The South was the world's largest cotton producer. The Confederacy shut off this vital commodity to the North since it was critical for uniforms, blankets, tents, bandages and other military supplies.

Southern rice and sugar cane, also vitally important to feed the Union army, were denied to it. Without these basics, Washington's war effort was severely hampered.

Congress created a new Federal agency, the Department of Agriculture, to create new strains of cotton and sugar cane that would thrive in the less suitable northern climate. In voting for the agency, Senator Joseph Wright of Indiana stated its purpose clearly: "The cotton crop of the South cannot reach Northern spindles. Agriculture must furnish a substitute by the production of upland cotton in the Ohio Valley. The sugar and molasses of the South have ceased to come forward to the North and agriculture must remedy the difficulty by the rapid production of the Chinese and African cane."[1]

Mr. I. Newton, the first Commissioner of the Agriculture Department, echoed this sentiment as soon as this agency became a reality: "The culture of cotton has lately attracted much attention to the free states, especially in Illinois, owing to the rebellion and the consequent scarcity of the staple. Last summer, as a matter of experiment, 300 to 1,000 pounds of cotton were raised per acre by many farmers in Illinois. This department will take early and active measures to induce farmers in Kentucky, Missouri, southern Illinois, Indiana and Kansas; all of which states will undoubtedly produce cotton."[2]

---

1. *The Congressional Globe*, 37th Congress, 2nd Session, p. 1690.
2. Annual Report of the Commissioner of Agriculture, for the year 1862, p. 22.

By 1864, the commissioner reported "sorghum and imphee [sugar cane substitutes] and the dissemination of the seeds of these plants by the Agriculture Department has been worth millions of dollars to the country."[1]

When the war ended the Agriculture Department was once again called upon to make crop experiments, but this time with a higher, more sophisticated objective: new kinds of crops that would influence the behavior of the defeated Confederates.

The Radical Congress saw in the word "cotton" the living metaphor of why the war began and why the "spirit of rebellion" could not be extinguished. "Cotton" endlessly reminded Southerners of the philosophies that drove them to secede: slave labor, state sovereignty, restrictions on Federal power, and free trade. These views had been repudiated as the post-war United States became a centralized, protectionist world power. In this new world, "cotton" would have to be diffused among new crops and its geographic position transformed to erase Southern "reactionary" perspectives.

This statement by the Commissioner of Agriculture indirectly says that cotton caused the war, and gives the solution: "In the re-organization of the Southern states, it is believed that the great mistake of the past, the concentration of labor mainly upon a single branch of a grand division of productive industry [cotton] will be avoided. This mistake cost that section one-half the wealth it might have attained and may have led to the sacrifices in war of the remainder.... Diversification must be applied to reorganized Southern agriculture.... Cotton will never again overshadow and dwarf other interests essential to permanent success in agriculture."[2]

Toward this objective, hardier strains of wheat, grasses and live stock were developed to thrive in the semi-tropical Gulf states. They were disseminated this way: "The distribution, under the special appropriation of $50,000, to be expended in seeds for the Southern states, was promptly and fully made in accordance with the views and intentions of Congress, through the Southern states, post masters, prominent citizens and agents of the Freedmen's Bureau.... These states can produce every article grown in the higher latitudes."[3]

---

1. Annual Report of the Commissioner of Agriculture, for the year 1864, pages 4 and 11.
2. Annual Report of the Commissioner of Agriculture, for the year 1866, p. 6
3. Annual Report of the Commissioner of Agriculture, for the year 1867, pp. x and xvii.

The Morrill Act

Also in 1862, the year that the Agriculture Department was created to provide the necessities of war, another major bill passed Congress with the word "agriculture" in its description. It was called the "Morrill Act" and it has become, even into the 21st century, one of the most far-reaching legislative enactments in United States history. Its effect is more powerful now than in the 19th century. And like the Agriculture Department, and with the Agriculture Department, it played a major role in land control as mind control.

Representative Justin Morrill of Vermont, in 1857, introduced a bill to give 30,000 acres of Federal land for each Congressman in each state for colleges of "agriculture and mechanic arts and military science." That meant research in those three areas.

It passed through Congress but President Buchanan vetoed the Morrill Act, stating: "Should the time ever arrive when the state governments shall look to the Federal Treasury for the means of supporting themselves and to maintain their systems of educational and internal policy, the character of both governments will be greatly deteriorated.... It is extremely doubtful, to say the least, whether this bill will contribute to the advancement of agriculture and the mechanic arts. This bill will injuriously interfere with existing colleges in the different states."[1]

Justin Morrill did not give up. He re-introduced it, and it was passed by Congress and President Lincoln in 1862, since there were no Southern Democrats in Congress to oppose it. It was considered a war measure since war research would be the highest priority to be conducted at the schools. And some of the crop research was unofficially fed to Morrill schools by the Agriculture Department, since land control as mind control was part of the war effort.

From Morrill's research programs came many of the revolutionary inventions of modern warfare: the bullet (as opposed to the traditional "ball"), the repeating rifle, the "iron-clad" vessel, the longer range grooved artillery barrel, and others.

Over time, the Morrill Act would nationalize much of education throughout the country. Today, it forms the basis of the huge state university system.

---

1. Congressional Globe, 35th Congress, 2nd Session, p. 1412.

Fusing Agriculture and Bureau of Education with Morrill

Eventually, the informal relationship between the Agriculture Department (which defined research projects) and the Morrill schools (that fulfilled these requests) solidified into a legal fusion. This was expressed by the Commissioner of Agriculture: "For many years it has become more and more apparent that the one great need of the agricultural interests of the United States, is a better understanding and a more intimate relation between the several agricultural colleges ... and the Department of Agriculture, to develop systems which should better unify experiments and reports on them. These colleges were severally endowed by the one-and-the-same act of Congress [the Morrill Act]. They are now separately carrying on experiments at an expense of time and means and yet without any central head through which to report and compare results with each other.... No suitable provision has been made by the national government for any extended practical experiments in this direction.... The Department of Agriculture can, if wisely conducted, become a vital center for a more general cooperative effort for the promotion of agricultural science."[1]

Two years later, this was formalized: "National legislation has been proposed to extend the work of experimental agriculture, establishing it in every State ... to make the results available to the country at large.... To prevent useless and wasteful duplications and secure cooperation and concerted action when needed, there must be a central station or office, and the natural place for this is in Washington." This legislation of March 2, 1887, is called the Hatch Act.[2]

Then: "Section 3 of the Act of March 2, 1887 provides: that in order to secure, as far as possible, uniformity of methods and results in the work of said [experiment] stations, it shall be the duty of the United States Commissioner of Agriculture to furnish forms, as far as practical, for the tabulation of results of investigations or experiments, to indicate, from time to time, such lines of inquiry as to him shall seem most important." Thus began the classic process by which one agency absorbs another entity. Then, when an amendment to Morrill increased research funding to the colleges, "the Secretary of the Interior was to administer this law. He delegated it to the Commissioner of Education."[3]

---

1. Annual Report of the Commissioner of Agriculture, for the year 1885, pp. 6-7.
2. Annual Report of the Commissioner of Agriculture, for the year 1886, pp. 11-13.
3. Darrell Hevenor Smith, *The Bureau of Education — Its History, Activities and Organization* (Baltimore: Johns Hopkins University Press, 1923), p. 5.

Since the Morrill schools and the Agriculture Department were now legally connected, this really meant that the Bureau of Education could now direct Agriculture to assign experiments to the land-grant schools.

By 1889, "the several States have re-organized the Department of Agriculture in the land-grant colleges as 'experiment stations.' "[1]

With the mergers, the Bureau that John Eaton created stood astride all three and the stage was set for the next phase: mind control experiments for Southern children.

Agriculture Experiment Stations

The Hatch Act, in uniting Morrill and Agriculture, called for something called "agriculture experiment stations." This seemed to mean research related to the improvement of animal breeding and crops. But, was this entirely true?

The first hint that the experiments related to human beings began with: "Another line in which inquiry is especially demanded is the study of food and nutrition of domestic animals and man ... while analysis of feeding stuff are of the greatest service, especially when combined with results of experiments upon digestibility and other physiological research." What other kind of physiological research could that be?[2]

Then: "It is often necessary, in collecting our information, to make apparently wide excursions from the object to be investigated in order to secure a sufficiently broad and accurate basis for the work to be done. This is not infrequently prepared for us by the investigations of other workers, especially in Germany and France, both in the field of human and animal diseases."[3] Why was it necessary to go to Europe to do the research? Was it to hide some aspect of it?

Then: "The result of this work thus far published has awakened great interest in the subject [supposedly animal to human nutritional studies] especially among physicians, teachers, clergymen and officers of the army and navy, the superintendents of benevolent institutions, and persons studying the sociological conditions of modern times."[4] Why did this information interest all these groups? Why not just farmers?

Then, suddenly the issue of education emerged: "In agriculture it is coming to be clearly seen that teaching the boy to plow or to perform other farm opera-

---

1. Annual Report of the Secretary of Agriculture, for the year 1889, p. 453.
2. Ibid., p. 495.
3. Annual Report of the Secretary of Agriculture, for the year 1891, p. 510.
4. Annual Report of the Secretary of Agriculture, for the year 1895, p. 33.

tions is not the most important service which the school can render.... The farmer must be taught to think in the lines where science has shed light." What should he be thinking? And, what has science shed new light on?[1]

Darwin and Comparative Anatomy: The New Psychology

To hide the true nature of the research at the experiment stations, some of it was conducted in Europe and some in remote rural areas in the United States: "The location of experiment stations is now the subject of much discussion. They were first established in isolated estates, generally remote from great cities."[2] But, why?

It wasn't until the 1890s that the first clue emerged that the Hatch Act's "agricultural experiments" mandate had a human educational principle behind it, and a specific scientific theory of learning beneath that: "The application of the comparative method [animal to human physiology] has led the investigator to the mental manifestations of the lower animals.... We are devoting a great deal of attention to the study of children.... From the first we had a little experimental school.... It had the same relation to the Education Department that an experimental farm would have to the Department of Agriculture."[3]

Then, the methodology was expressed as to how these comparative anatomy experiments were conducted: "The laws which express the development and activity of the nervous mechanism must determine pedagogical principles."

This was the conception behind comparative anatomy experimentation. By using the scientific findings of how a cow or a chicken or a horse's brain or nervous system absorbs or transmits information, inferences could be made demonstrating that the same process took place in a child's brain. This was based on the Darwinian principle of evolution wherein, although man was the highest rung in the animal kingdom, he still shared many of the physiological characteristics of the lower life forms.

By this definition, comparative anatomy findings were used to develop a radical new form of curriculum based solely on physiology.

In the 21st century, the conceptions behind comparative anatomy experimentation are commonplace. In the 19th century they were heretical, radically and profoundly hostile to the universally accepted vision that man was vastly

1. Annual Report of the Secretary of Agriculture, for the year 1886, p. 70.
2. Annual Report of the Secretary of Agriculture, for the year 1868, p. 138.
3. Annual Report of the Commissioner of Education, for the year 1894, p. 360.

superior to beasts, both intellectually and, of course, morally. Comparative anatomy as a basis for a philosophy of education demolished man's superior position in the universe and over time converted him, philosophically and legally, into just another beast, with the same civil rights: hardly any.

Behavioral psychology as we know it today was developed from this physiological education research. In the 1870s, the same William James who wrote the classic *Principles of Psychology* (in 1890) began teaching classes at Harvard called "Comparative Psychology" and "The Relation Between Physiology and Psychology." His comparisons of animal to man, physically, would become the basis of "The New Psychology."

One of James' students was G. Stanley Hall. Later on, Hall would become a major figure in this "New Psychology." By 1881, Hall wrote, "at Johns Hopkins University, the first Chair of Experimental Psychology was developed. A score of psycho-physic laboratories are now in operation....[This shows] how transforming for other philosophic disciplines, how all conditioning for education.... Experiments are made on muscle groups with drugs, heat, light, sound. [This is the same approach used in comparative anatomy testing.] It has little ethical power in it, hence few psychologists have the strength to go on. It is psychology without a soul. Another field is comparative psychology. The more we know of animal life the vaster becomes our conception of instincts. The early development of children, from unfocused to reasoning, is the most important for psychologists."[1]

But what was the consequence of the New Psychology as a framework for a curriculum? How did it differ in it objectives from the traditional psychology/curriculum? It completely circumvented culture, values, religion or spiritual ideals for the student, because these were forces that had given the Confederate soldiers their intense courage. Without these externally imposed ideals, the student was reduced to a passive drone who could be manipulated at will. This will be clarified as we proceed.

But, returning to G. Stanley Hall — in 1887, he began publishing *The American Journal of Psychology*. This was one of the "most influential publications for education. Its editorial perspective was experimental.... Inductive studies in animal instincts, psychogenesis in children.... Nervous anatomy, physiology."[2]

---

1. Annual Report of the Commissioner of Education, for the year 1894, p. 445.
2. Dorothy Ross, *G. Stanley Hall: The Psychologist As Prophet* (Chicago: University of Chicago Press, 1972), p. 166.

Darwin and the New Psychology

A 20th century book on educational research had this to say about Darwinism, comparative anatomy and their contribution to the New Psychology: "Evolutionary theory had a profound influence on educational thought, from textbooks to conceptualization. But not all of this was healthy. Its impact was through psychology and sociology, reversing the idea that humans were different. All life is a continuity. Human functioning then could be grasped by lower animal studies. Behaviorism emerged from evolution and it fit laboratory methods of studying simple phenomenon under highly controlled conditions. Educational materials were developed along these lines.... Even consciousness was a simple physical activity."[1]

John Dewey, one of the most successful promoters of the New Psychology as a basis for a specific theory about education and school curriculum (which he called "Pragmatism") explained the difference between the Old and the New psychologies:

> The combination of the words "origin" and "species" embody an intellectual revolt and introduce an intellectual temper easily overlooked by experts.

> The concept that has reigned for 2,000 years [the Old Psychology] rested on the assumption of the superiority of the fixed and final. They rested upon treating "change" and "origin" as signs of defect and unreality. Absolute permanency was a sacred oak. [Darwin's] *Origin of Species* introduced a mode of thinking that transformed the logic of knowledge [the New Psychology] and hence the treatment of morals, politics and religion....

> Few words in our language foreshorten intellectual history as much as "species." The Greeks were impressed by the "characteristic" traits of plants and animals; so impressed that they made these traits the key to defining nature and to explaining mind and society. ["Characteristic traits" implies fixity.]

> In living beings ... the earlier changes are regulated in view of later results; a true final term, a completed, perfected end. This principle seemed to give insight into the very nature of reality itself....

> Species: Fixed form and final cause was a central principle of knowledge as well as nature. Upon it rested the logic of science. [Modern science follows the inverted principle: seeking to prove change instead of fixity.] Change as change is mere flux and lapse; it insults intelligence. To know is to relate all special forms to their one single end and good: pure contemplative intelligence. Since we experience nature changing; nature does not satisfy the conditions of

---

1. Robert M.W. Travers, *How Research Has Changed American Schools; a History From 1840 to the Present* (Kalamazoo: Mythos Press, 1983), pp. 73-76.

knowledge. Neither does sense-perception. Science transcends nature and perception. [Again, this is the complete reverse of the modern era where science only recognizes the perceivable.]

16th and 17th century physical science was the first to question classical assumptions. Galileo said: "The earth is very noble by reason of so many different alterations and generations which are incessantly made therein."

Descartes said: "The nature of physical things is much more easily conceived when they are beheld coming gradually into existence, than when they are produced at once in a finished and perfect state."

Prior to Darwin, the impact of the new scientific method upon life, mind, politics, had been arrested because between these ideals or moral interests and the inorganic world intervened the kingdom of plants and animals. Darwin's philosophy conquered the phenomena of life for the principle of transition, thereby freed the new logic for application to mind and morals and life.

The classic notion of "species" carried with it the idea of purpose.... Since life's regulatory principle is not visible to the senses, it follows that it must be an "ideal" or rational force. Purposefulness accounted for the intelligence of nature and the possibility of science, while the absolute or cosmic character of this purposefulness gave sanction and worth to the moral and religious endeavors of man.

Darwinian "natural selection" undercut this philosophy. If all organic adaptations were due to competitive elimination of unnecessary variations, there was no need for a prior intelligent causal force. Hostile critics charged Darwin with materialism and making chance the cause of the universe.[1]

Origins of the New Scientific Psychology

The 20th century book *The Philosophical Roots of Scientific Psychology* gives a brief historic overview of the New Psychology:

[Modern] psychology studies man's behavior, including covert activity like feeling, perceiving, thinking, by scientific methods. The objective is to describe this behavior and predict it. This psychology occupies a position between the social and biological sciences.

The philosophical viewpoint [the Old Psychology], with respect to man's nature, is more general and broader than the psychological one.

The history of psychology is 2,400 years old. For most of that period it was part of philosophy, without having a differentiated identity. In the 19th century, psychology ceased to be philosophical and became scientific. The advance of physiology was a factor.... Intellectual reflection on man's activities could only bring a general understanding of man's nature.... Philosophy could not scientifi-

---

1. John Dewey, *The Influence of Darwin on Philosophy* (New York: Henry Holt and Company, 1910), pp. 1-12.

cally answer questions on sensation, perception, learning, emotion, etc. Mental abnormalities were previously moral, not scientific provinces.

Laboratory experimentation was via biology, nervous systems, brain functions and physiological functions. Math was used in quantitative analysis. This psychology made contact with the sciences.

This separation occurred in the 1870s. The most important single event signaling the new science was the establishment of the first psychological laboratories.

The first lab was opened in 1878, the first experimental study completed in 1879. This is considered the birthdate of the 'New Psychology.' This was at the University of Leipzig in Germany, under the direction of Wilhelm Wundt. [The reader will recall the statement by the Commissioner of Agriculture that comparative anatomy studies were conducted in Germany and France.] All other scientific disciplines; astronomy, biology, physics, were once part of philosophy but had separated much earlier.

The emancipation of psychology is largely due to the influence of physiology.... Anthropology, sociology, animals studies, education studies contributed to the New Psychology.[1]

What is not expressed in these overviews by Dewey and Misiak and the modern advocates of scientific psychology, comparative anatomy experimentation, etc., is the all-important question of why scientific psychology developed when it did? They do not grasp that its foundations are based on the fervent ideal of erasing and controlling the minds of a hated, defeated enemy. When that element is added, the modern "new" psychology no longer looks like an advance but, instead, a brilliant, frightening retrogression.

The New Psychology Becomes A Curriculum

The physio-psychological and comparative anatomy data slowly congealed into a concept for a revolutionary curriculum. Educational materials would be presented to children based on their neural or cranial maturity, not their intellectual maturity. Those materials that excited a strong electric flow to the brain or induced a rapid heart beat were desirable. "Interest" was defined as this kind of physiological stimulation, not emotions, enthusiasm, purpose or belief in higher spiritual values to propel one forward. Such intangible, unmeasurable ideas were meaningless within the scientific model. "Interest" within this model was also revolutionary. It put the student's temporary excitements into the center of the school's existence. This was precisely the opposite of the tradi-

---

1. Henryk Misiak, *The Philosophical Roots of Scientific Psychology* (New York: Fordham University Press, 1961), p. 36.

tional classroom. Then, the values, vision, beliefs, dreams and ideals of the community were paramount, to make the child "one of us," part of the clan, the group. The child's own interests were discouraged within an educational environment. The community was all-important.

The South was such a close-knit world. It had to be unraveled. A curriculum based on comparative physiology, that was "child-centered," not community-centered, by-passed, isolated and eliminated purpose, beliefs and the culture that engendered them. Only the child's raw ego mattered. Everything else in the world disappeared.

The Agriculture Department and Curriculum

Gradually, step by step, the Department of Agriculture went public about its role in education. In 1897, its annual report stated: "A movement to introduce what is termed 'nature teaching' into the common schools of New York is attracting wide-spread attention. The work is being carried on under the leadership of the colleges of agriculture of Cornell University, which has been given a special appropriation by the State legislation for this purpose.... The chief object of this movement is to secure the training of the powers of observation of young people through the study of natural objects ... such as plants, insects and buds."[1]

Nature training emphasized the observable, the here and now, not the past of tradition or culture. And hadn't John Dewey said that traditional education opposed sense-perception, since it was misleading?

It is also interesting to speculate why New York was chosen for "nature teaching" when this kind of curriculum was intended for the South. During the War for Southern Independence New York had actively sympathized with and aided the Confederacy. As a result, Abraham Lincoln had militarily invaded New York twice, just as his armies had invaded the South. It was occupied after the war as if it was a rebel territory. This probably explains why nature training came to the Empire State and further illuminates why the New Psychology curriculum eventually spread over all the North as well.

Up to this point the Agriculture Department confined its reports to the research done at the Morrill colleges. Now, in 1898, for the first time this agency revealed its connection to the common schools. In an article entitled *Nature Training in the Common Schools* it was stated that "nature-teaching has been introduced into the common schools, but for the most part in the schools of the larger

---

1. Annual Report of the Secretary of Agriculture, for the year 1897, p. 131.

towns, where the teachers have some training in natural science. As a result of the interest in the subject, teachers' manuals and textbooks for the instruction in this branch are being prepared."[1]

At this point we should pause to explain what may seem a contradiction or an irrelevancy. The War for Southern Independence ended in 1865. Thirty-three years later the Department of Agriculture begins to discuss "nature training." It may seem to be stretching reality to connect these educational innovations with the vendettas created by the war, after that great span of time.

First, even beyond 1900 the war was still a major political issue. Into the 20th century few Southerners could get elected to major national positions. If they had lived through the war years, even as civilians or children, they were still called "traitors" and that curse was almost impossible to overcome. If they had not been born until after the war, they were called "the sons of traitors." In 1900, hate and Federal policy still meant the late Confederacy was a quasi-territory of the North.

In addition, there are two kinds of time: human and governmental. Human time is measured over a few decades. Governmental time, in terms of legislative enactments and their fulfillment, is sometimes measured in centuries. From the moment a law passes until it achieves its stated objective may average 140 years. From 1862 (when the Agriculture Department and the Morrill Act were signed into law) and from 1867 (when the Bureau of Education became a reality) to the turn of the 20th century is just a legal twinkle of an eye.

In 1898, an Agriculture Department annual report stated: "Without doubt the greatest difficulty in this matter [bringing 'nature study' into the common schools] is to overcome the conservatism of local boards managing the country schools and to get competent teachers."[2]

This reveals that the New Psychology and the New Education were resisted by those who understood the implications.

In 1900: "The teaching of young children regarding the natural objects and phenomena about them may be so conducted as to lead them to see that a knowledge of nature may be of practical benefit. Their minds will then be easily trained to recognize the intimate relations between scientific knowledge."[3] Science, which emphasized the observable objects of here and now, paralleled

---

1. Annual Report of the Secretary of Agriculture, for the year 1898, p. xviii.
2. Ibid., xviii.
3. Annual Report of the Secretary of Agriculture, for the year 1900, p. 175.

"nature training" to reduce the impact of culture and religion's focus on tradition and bringing forward unobservable ideas from the past to the present.

Then, in 1901: "The time seems favorable for the Department [of Agriculture] to take a more active part in the introduction of nature study into the curricula of rural schools.... Such encouragement may be given by cooperating with the Department of Education in the publication and distribution of suggested courses of study."[1]

1902: "Progress is also being made in the movement for the consolidation of rural schools which has already resulted in improved conditions in schools in Ohio and Massachusetts, Iowa and other states. Such consolidation makes it possible to introduce nature study."[2] Consolidation or, more accurately, centralization, took power away from the "conservatives" so that they could not control local curriculum methods.

William Torrey Harris: The "St. Louis Hegelian"

In August 1886, ill health forced John Eaton to step down as Commissioner of the Bureau of Education. His successor was Nathaniel Dawson, an Alabamian. He only lasted three years. He was followed by William Torrey Harris, an internationally famous Hegelian philosopher and the Superintendent of the St. Louis common school system.

Appointed by Republican President Benjamin Harrison, Harris had openly sided with the Democrats as they renominated their current President, Grover Cleveland. Because of that, Harris hedged about accepting the position. But President Harrison shrugged it off: "It makes no difference. The educators of the country want you."[3]

More than Rutherford B. Hayes, more than Ulysses S. Grant, and even more than Jabez Curry, William Torrey Harris was a man caught in a powerful intellectual paradox. His conflict was the most overt of them all, since he was the only one who was aware that his office and his own ideals were completely at odds.

As a Hegelian, Harris had definite views about how the human mind worked and the importance of the intangible "soul" in creating a civilized human

---

1. Annual Report of the Secretary of Agriculture, for the year 1901, p. 192.
2. Annual Report of the Secretary of Agriculture, for the year 1902, p. – CI.
3. Kurt F. Leideker, *The Life of William Torrey Harris* (New York: The Philosophic Library, 1946), p. 460.

being. He knew that physio-psychology could never achieve this, and he worked to undo the principles of comparative anatomy.

Harris' reluctance had a major impact in slowing the ascent of "child-study" principles into the classroom. William Torrey Harris' stature was so great that when he died, in 1909, Nicholas Murray Butler, the President of Columbia University, said: "With the death of Dr. Harris, there comes to the earthly end the activity of one of the greatest philosophical minds of modern times."[1]

One of Harris' biographers hit his mental contradiction directly on the head when he noted: "He was an Idealist who directed the most powerful Empirical machine in government: the Bureau of Education."[2]

Idealism is the philosophy which puts special value on ideas and ideals as products of the mind — in comparison with the world as perceived through the senses, which is Empiricism. Plato saw eternal ideas a constituting reality and sense experience was only a shadow.

The St. Louis Hegelian

William Torrey Harris was born in North Killington, Connecticut, in 1835. He entered Yale in 1854 but never finished. This school provided a classical education: Greek, Latin, math, rhetoric, ancient history. Harris rebelled against the preoccupation with the past and its formalism. Yet, on his own time he studied German, Mesmerism and Spiritualism. He became a vegetarian.

Harris' father had gone out West to homestead and sent young William clippings describing the life out there. This awakened a fascination for that part of the country; not for its financial opportunities but for its potential to satisfy his reflective temperament in the deep solitude of the vast plains.

It was 1857. He headed with a friend to St. Louis, where he thought he would find his father; but he did not find him, until later.

St. Louis was viewed as the cross-roads of America; the junction between all points on the compass. St. Louis called itself "the future great city of the world" and competed furiously with Chicago. It was a rough, semi-Wild-West cowboy boom town. Everything was dust and rubbish as homes and whole neighborhoods rose out of the barren fields.

To survive, Harris taught shorthand but he had few students. Starving, he took and passed an examination to teach in St. Louis' common schools.

---

1. Ibid., preface, p. vii.
2. Ibid., preface, p. ix.

Lonely and without intellectual stimulation, Harris joined a local philosophical society which was just being formed. It was probably the first group of that kind in the West.

Robert Moore, Harris' friend, fell into debt and returned East. Harris was despondent and wrote his father about suicide. He read all the great philosophers, searching to find meaning in life. This led to his becoming an official of the St. Louis Literary and Philosophical Society.

The Society's membership represented a wide variety of opinions and convictions which were at odds with his emerging Idealism: liberal Christians, skeptics, infidels, atheists, phrenologists, metaphysicians, slavery advocates and abolitionists. They all more or less shared an interest in the natural sciences, which Harris shared, but he gradually came to regard it as responsible for a negative materialistic outlook on life. In the Society's heated debates, he honed his skills in argumentation on behalf of Idealism.

When the prestigious *North American Review* rejected a Harris article attacking materialism, he countered, in 1867, with his own publication, the *Journal of Speculative Philosophy*.

Soon the *Journal* attracted material from major American philosophers of the 19th century: Charles Pierce, William James, John Dewey, and others. It reprinted translations of Kant, Schelling, Hegel, Fichte, Oriental philosophy. There were articles on literature and the fine arts.

The *Journal's* influence spread German philosophy into American universities. St. Louis had a huge German population; many were Socialist revolutionaries. In an early meeting of the Literary and Philosophical Society, Harris debated with Harry Brokmeyer and Denton Snider about the superiority of Kant vs. Hegel. Harris defended Kant. Brokmeyer won the argument with a compelling explanation of Hegel's *Larger Logic*. From that moment on, Harris determined to make "Hegel speak English."

The *Journal of Speculative Philosophy* was the way to do this. It brought Hegel's ideas and German philosophy in general into the mainstream of American thought.

Hegel's absolute Idealism envisioned a world soul that developed out of, and is known through, dialectical logic. The first concept, the thesis, generates its opposite, the antithesis, and the interaction of these leads to a new concept, the synthesis. The universe and man develop through this self-creating plan.

Harris' Educational Career

In 1858, William Torrey Harris began teaching at the Franklin Grammar School, the largest in St. Louis, having over 1,000 students.

Within one year he was the principal of the Clay School and had five assistants. Then, the war came to Missouri. Because St. Louis was a large commercial center, support for secession and slavery was not high. Schools lost teachers to both the Union and Confederate armies, and many were forced to close down.

In the rural areas many schools were destroyed as supporters of the Confederacy fought a guerrilla campaign with the US regular army and loyalist guerrillas. Overt war did not come to St. Louis but Harris witnessed riots, massacres and the public execution of "traitors." Harris himself was exempted from military service because he had lost an eye in a childhood accident.

St. Louis was filled with troops. There was martial law for all citizens. Harris observed, in a letter to a friend, "Haven't we always had a boyish hope that something would happen in our day? The New Englanders all had long been eager for war. Now that war was here they dread it. Nations have moods. They get tired or sated with peace. Like a flock of wild ducks; one will fly, then another, until the whole fly."[1]

Missouri was a slave state. Almost all the votes for Lincoln came from St. Louis. Fear and disappointment resulted from his election. In the countryside, anti-Lincoln men armed themselves and went underground.

Harris, the New Englander, could not understand the secession mentality of Missourians. But the philosopher in him grasped the ideal of state sovereignty.

There were two governments in Missouri. The Union capital was in St. Louis and the secession government in Jackson. At one point the Confederate general, Price, attacked and almost took St. Louis.

With the return of peace, Ira Divoll, the Superintendent of St. Louis' schools, became ill and appointed Harris as his assistant. By May 1868, with Divoll on a leave of absence, William Torrey took over his role. He was 32, and a superb administrator. This skill was tested as the city continued to expand rapidly and the school system also grew by leaps and bounds. To make this growth easier, Harris de-centralized his own authority and gave more responsibility to each principal. Under his leadership St. Louis schools went from near the bottom of the ratings to the top.

---

1. Ibid., p. 193.

His annual reports were not the usual dry list of statistics. There were interesting and even entertaining articles on the latest pedagogical trends. They served as a model all over the world, reprinted by the Bureau of Education.

In 1874, William Torrey Harris became President of the National Education Association. The next year, together with Eaton, he was appointed Counselor-at-large for that organization.

Harris and the Bureau of Education

1889. President Benjamin Harrison selected Harris to head the Bureau of Education. He was expected to continue the policies that John Eaton had initiated; but Harris "was an Idealist who directed the most powerful Empirical machine in government: the Bureau of Education."

In his *Journal of Speculative Philosophy*, Harris presented the difference between the two opposing positions. "Materialists [Empiricists] hold that all phenomena have material equivalents; matter and force are substantial modes [substances] of existence. Mind is one of its many phases. They ask: 'What is the physical equivalent of thought and feeling? What movement of the brain is concomitant with thought? Therefore they study the structure of the nerves, brain, etc. To an Idealist, all phenomena have mental equivalents. Mind and thinking being are substantial; the material is only one of the processes. Matter is the appearance of spirit."[1]

Harris expressed his hostility toward "nature study" this way: "Rousseau was the prophet of the French Revolution. He proclaimed a return to nature. 'Nature' is a word of ambiguous meaning; human nature vs. physical nature. Human history is the revelation of man's nature realized in institutions and not by man as an isolated individual. Nature in time and space is under the dominion of necessity. Rousseau appealed to nature in everything. What we call civilization, was to him a mere artificial form. His plea was to be natural, come back to the point where nature leaves you. The *Social Contract* was an attack on the authority of the State. *Emile* undermined school and Church. He attacked all social institutions: the family, civil society, Church, State. In *Emile*, everything that comes from nature is good, while everything degenerates in the hands of

---

1. John S. Roberts, *William Torrey Harris: A Critical Study of His Educational and Related Philosophical Views* (Washington: National Education Association of the United States, 1924), p. 10-11.

man. Voltaire wittily exposed Rousseau: 'Never has anyone employed so much genius to make us into beasts.' "[1]

Harris was also hostile to the inclusion of nature study in the curriculum because it did "not have a spiritualizing tendency, but rather the opposite." It tended "to further confirm the theory of environmental determinism, external necessity, and to deny self-activity, in all its forms."

This opposition to nature study was presented from another perspective. Resistance to formal subjects is often crystallized in the expression, "things before words"; studying nature instead of languages. Harris believed that such theories undermined society: "It is a delusion to suppose that the study of nature is more practical than the study of man." Things and words cannot be separated. They must develop side-by-side.[2]

As for psychology based on sense-perception, Harris wrote: "Faculty psychology [based on sensory data] is false. Its emphasis on sense perception is based on a false analogy between mind and body. It leaves out the higher faculties, the soul is part of the body."[3]

Also, via sense perception, "everything is an individual object. This leads to an atomistic view of the universe. Knowledge is transient, unrelated, inaccurate. Sense-training should only be a stepping-stone to organized knowledge."[4]

And, "self-activity forces us to view objects as relations to one another; 'forces and processes.' They are abstract ideas because they cannot be seen by the senses. These forces are more real than things of sense-perception because abstract ideas cause 'things' to originate, change, disappear."[5]

Then Harris turned his attention to another major area of the New Psychology: "Physiological psychology puts the cart before the horse; mind directs matter, not vice versa.... Nature is governed by ideals. The attraction of gravity is an ideal."[6]

Physiology was not psychology, said Harris. "The three activities which psychology proper has to deal with, are volitions, ideas and feelings. These are all

1. William H. Goetzman, editor, *The American Hegelians; An Intellectual Episode in the History of Western America* (New York: Alfred A. Knopf, 1973), p. 305.
2. Roberts, p. 71.
3. Vivian Trow Thayer, *Formative Ideas in American Education, from Colonial Times to the Present* (New York: Dodd Mead, 1965), p. 166.
4. Roberts, p. 28.
5. Thayer, p. 169.
6. Ibid., p. 167.

perceived by introspection, and are not matters of objective observation such as brain, nerve cells, muscles, bones and other objects which anatomy and physiology treat of. No amount of external observation, of course, can perceive either will or intellect or feeling as an object of the senses. It can only infer it from certain changes or modifications going on in the physical organism."[1]

Harris believed in a philosophy of education, not a psychology of education like that of the New Psychologists with their focus on "child-centered" pedagogy instead of one that was society-centered. ("All human activities have a psychological side. Education needs a psychology that will show how all activities, whether individual or social, react on children and men so as to develop them.")[2]

Harris further showed his antipathy toward child-centered education when he said: "Modern education seeks to overcome education-by-authority. This is called individual or scientific education, of insight as opposed to authority. The danger of education by insight, if begun too early, is that the individual becomes too self-conceited with what he considers knowledge gotten by his own personal thought and research and that he drifts toward empty agnosticism. So, it is necessary to begin with the safe foundation of education by authority."[3]

And yet, despite all these warnings against the New Psychology, one author describes Harris' work at the Bureau of Education as "the mid-point between the traditional and the New Psychology." And "he was highly instrumental in putting [Horace] Mann's and [Henry] Barnard's ideas into reality. His job at the Bureau was fundamentally at odds with his classical views."[4]

Another commentator described Harris' intellectual conflict by stating: "Harris linked education with the knowledge that was coming out of the labs of the new generation of psychologists. Harris said nature produces animals and not a civilized human but the new sciences of physiology and experimental psychology would be able to help us understand that transition and ultimately exercise some control over it. Science could show the child's transition from a mechanical to an ethical view of the world. Harris published reports on his belief that the classroom became an important laboratory for the psychologist, with the teacher as the experimentor."[5]

---

1. W.T. Harris article, "Is Education Possible Without Freedom of the Will?" from *Education* magazine, January 1896, p. 17.
2. Roberts, p. 64.
3. Goetzman, P. 302.
4. Thayer, p. 175.
5. Travers, p. 42.

Even Jabez Curry made this comment, indicating William Torrey Harris' ambiguous and contradictory stance: "Dr. W.T. Harris thinks that the investigations which have been stimulated will enable us to enter on 'a new and more scientific epoch of educational theory and practice.' "[1]

---

1. Proceedings of the Trustees of the Peabody Education Fund, Report of the 33rd meeting, 1894, p. 77.

CHAPTER 15. THE NEW PSYCHOLOGY BECOMES A CURRIC-ULUM

The experimental New Psychology which was designed to be implanted into Southern schools and minds, a 19th century form of intellectual ethnic cleansing, slowly worked its way North in the 20th century.

One reason for this perhaps unintended movement into the Union states was expressed by New York's former governor, Horatio Seymour, during Reconstruction: "We cannot have a government whose Northern face shall smile devotion to the popular will, and whose Southern aspect shall frown contempt, defiance and hate to the people of eleven states."[1]

In other words, however the Federal government deals with one part of the country, it must deal with all other sections the same way. And, as was stated before, several Northern states were considered Confederate sympathizers, or worse, and were subjected to the New Psychology curriculum in order to purge the minds of the children of unpatriotic adults.

G. Stanley Hall

There were many educators, politicians, bureaucrats, scientists and philosophers who contributed to making the New Psychology into the New Curriculum in the 20th century.

---

1. Thomas M. Cook and Thomas Knox, editors, p. 290.

To include all would require another book, so we shall focus on three high-visibility men who were major figures in the process: G. Stanley Hall, John Dewey, and Edward Thorndike.

Like many of the characters in our drama, G. (Granville) Stanley Hall was a man filled with conflicts, both intellectual and emotional. Hall pioneered "child-study" education in the 1890s and that gave John Dewey's "Progressivism" an enormous influence as a curriculum philosophy through much of the 20th century.

Hall was one of the earliest of the New Psychologists and, together with William James, established that field as an academic discipline. As founding President of Clark University, he made that institution one devoted to educational-psychological-scientific research.

G. Stanley Hall believed that science[1] aided education and religion; he was an ordained Presbyterian minister whose first major conflict was over the supremacy of faith or science.

His central focus for the science-based New Psychology was understanding childhood, sex and psychopathology. One of the many weaknesses which hurt his career was his extreme ambivalence of thought, brought about by his early religious and later scientific training. As a result, his writings, his rhetoric, his ideas, were permeated by incompatible faith[2] and scientific ideals. Hall saw himself simultaneously as a village preacher and a cosmopolitan experimenter. He sensed his own vacillation that lurked behind every belief, often professing both positions at once.

As a young man, Hall's pious parents pushed him toward a career in the ministry even though he was a skilled musician and dreamed of being a concert pianist. He loved poetry and edited a literary quarterly. Reading Emerson and the German Romantics opened him to ideas that were powerfully unorthodox compared to his Christian teachers.

---

1. Paraphrasing the 2000 *Columbia Encyclopedia*, p. 2540, science is defined by the scientific method and the scientific attitude. Gathering data by the observation of phenomena (meaning only the "here and now") by deductive reasoning, (meaning from a particular to a generalization, which is the reverse of the traditional generalization to a particular) the scientific "attitude" rests on a rational impartiality (meaning that no moral hesitations can interfere with the findings and the observer's own mind becomes the standard for defining the data. This eliminates the external world; like child-centered psychology).
2. Christianity works in the inverted way in terms of science: from a general universal truth to a particular.

At Williams College he was taught (and influenced by) philosophy, Darwin and physio-psychology. It is surprising that Williams College, a liberal Protestant school, had courses in these topics, since they were so hostile to religion.

John Stuart Mill's empiricism[1] captured Hall's imagination, leading him to combine that form of materialism with the Romantic's tendency to see man's impulses, appetites and feelings as the core of human nature. "Man's nature is only his emotional nature." This was later transferred into Hall's evolutionary biology, but that would mean escaping his religious background. Instead, he employed a method which he used all his life: maintaining a traditional veneer to disguise his radicalism.

In 1863, at 23 years old, he graduated from Williams College. Hall wanted to continue his education in science-minded Germany, but he could not afford to do so. At that time, the only road open to a man interested in philosophy was through theology. He enrolled in New York's Union Theological Seminary, spending two years there, and was again trained in Liberal Protestantism — which still meant the empirical approach to theology. This "New Method" or "New Direction," which paralleled science's methods, contradicted Christianity's "eternal truths." This background made his next step much easier. His dream now was to be a professor of philosophy. Again, that meant Germany.

G. Stanley Hall received a grant to study at the University of Berlin for a year. In its scientific, materialistic atmosphere, religion was despised. He was told that faith "was neither knowledge or doing but a modification of feeling or immediate self-consciousness." This shifted Christianity away from a supernatural God toward a subjective, natural phenomenon God.

Wilhelm Wundt, in Germany, had opened a psychological laboratory in 1878, possibly funded by the Agriculture Department. Wundt studied consciousness via sensations and reflex actions in animals.

Unfortunately for Hall, the Franco-Prussian War of 1870 ended his hope for earning a PhD there. He came back to the United States and finished his last year at Union Theological Seminary. In its more conservative atmosphere, he felt like a radical.

---

1. Empiricism is the philosophical doctrine that claims all knowledge is derived from experience and sense perception. (All knowledge is "here and now.") Thus, once again, all awareness of the physical world is a generalization from a particular instance and that implies that truth can never be more than a probability.'

The harsh, mechanical universe of science which had no rational meaning or moral purpose drove Hall to conceptualize a philosophy similar to that which Tennyson had achieved in poetry: finding divinity within cold, heartless nature.

He taught English at Antioch College in Ohio after receiving his divinity degree; his philosophical positions were much too extreme for that provincial institution, or most other colleges in America.

Hall corresponded with William Torrey Harris, then visited him in St. Louis, and his empirical experiment articles were published in the Bureau of Education's annual reports. But, Hall became disillusioned with Harris, probably because he could not enter the tight-knit clique that surrounded the "St. Louis Hegelian."

In 1876, Hall left Antioch for Harvard, still only a lowly English instructor. There, William James was lecturing on the "New Psychology." This was the only school in the United States where this subject was taught.

Hall worshipped James. He enrolled in the Philosophy Department as a PhD candidate in order to be James' student. Under James, "philosophy" meant physio-psychology, using experimental equipment to measure nervous reactions in animals and humans. For his devotion, Hall was brought into James' select inner circle, the "Philosophy Club."

Both men shared a similar goal: creating a philosophy/psychology that would encompass the claims of religion and naturalism via empiricism. Of course, through physio-psychology, human consciousness, the basis of religious morality, retreated from the individual mind into a neural motor function. Thus, their hope was an absurdity.

Hall's doctoral dissertation was a study of muscular "perception" of space. Through this he was attempting to prove that mind and matter were connected by muscular properties. Motion sensations were connected to consciousness through nerves within muscles.

"Motion" would eventually become "activity"; the Mind was an active agent. But William James disapproved. Linking thought to neural motor activities robbed the Mind of free-will.

Hall went back to Germany, which was more supportive of such theories and where muscle systems were regularly studied. He joined Wundt's laboratory; he was the first American to be accepted.

Between 1880 and 1890 G. Stanley Hall became one of the leading figures in American scientific and intellectual life. Other than William James, he was America's first psychologist, climbing to fame on the tide of "natural science," defined as the opposite of Idealism and sometimes equated with Empiricism and materialism.

Yet, at 35, he still had trouble finding a job. Fearing that "neither psychology nor philosophy would ever make bread," he joined Johns Hopkins University, which was dedicated to original scientific research and especially the application of psychology to education.

While in Germany, Hall observed the wide-spread belief that the educational system —established after the expulsion of Napoleon — had been the chief instrument for national regeneration. Hall saw the same possibility for America; pedagogy would be the chief field for the practical application of psychology and the key to moral progress — at least, his definition of moral progress.

He lectured on the fusion of Christianity and science, believing that Christianity had to give up "the old and baseless claim of absoluteness and universal validity."[1]

The Child-Centered Movement

By the 1880s, the child-centered viewpoint had already shown its radical potential to subvert the traditional educational framework. Francis Parker of Quincy, Massachusetts was the first American educator to promote these revolutionary ideas. Parker followed Darwin; allowing the child to be himself, permitted him to ascend through natural steps to maturity, ala evolution. Later Parker, took this conception to the Cook County Normal School in Chicago.

G. Stanley Hall also elevated child-centered doctrines from a covert governmental ideology to a dominant pedagogical "reform" movement through his lectures. For him, the child's physiological nature dictated the curriculum and its order of presentation, based on his development. This was also a form of Darwinism.

Hall's lectures prompted his election to the elite National Council of Education, where he was on the same committee with William Torrey Harris.

At Johns Hopkins, G. Stanley had the first New Psychology Chair in the United States but this powerful position showed up his personality flaws: deceit and paranoid views emerged. John Dewey was one of his students. Hall pushed him out of the university, fearing him as a threat.

---

1. Ross, p. 109.

Hall included consciousness under instinct (along with impulses, desires and appetites), making it easier to bring it under empirical study, but, as William James had warned, this too denied free-will. Hall's "unconscious," predating Freud, was a part of human automatic nature, which one again implied that free-will did not exist. In that context, Hall said that animal instincts — which we cannot escape — rather than reason, "make the human soul great and good."[1]

In 1887, G. Stanley Hall published his *American Journal of Psychology*. Its editorial perspective was "psychological work of a scientific, as distinct from a speculative character [parallel to Idealism, where ideas and ideals are products of the mind, independent of the senses] ... experimental ... inductive [a particular to a general] studies in animal instincts, psychogenesis in children, morbid and anthropological psychology, [the study of primitive peoples, based on Darwinism] nervous anatomy, physiology and morphology" [a branch of biology that deals with the form and structure of animals and plants without regard to function].

Hall then added, "Controversy, so far as possible, will be excluded," but by the definition of the *Journal's* purpose, it was a highly controversial and viciously attacked by traditionalists.[2]

William James warned G. Stanley about making the American Journal too empirical, but he would not listen. The *Journal* was his bid for the New Psychology's leadership.

In 1888 Hall left Johns Hopkins to become President of Clark University, which emphasized graduate work in science and physio-psychology. Clark was considered the most "progressive" school in the United States. To insure that reputation, Hall hired German professors for his staff.

By 1897, the US granted more doctorate degrees in psychology than in any other science except biology. Students flocked to it because it gave them, as it had given Hall, originally, a scientific format for earlier religious beliefs.

Near the dawn of the 20th century, Clark University and the University of Chicago were the major centers for child-study. John Dewey directed the Laboratory School at Chicago. Dewey was a philosopher-psychologist whose concern with the development and adaptability of reason led him into educational theory.

---

1. *New Psychology*, Part I, 1885, pp. 122-123.
2. *American Journal of Psychology*, October 1887, pp. 3-4.

At this stage child-study was gaining popular acceptance through women's clubs and PTAs. But, predictably, the emphasis on the physical produced illiteracy. This reality did not deflect Hall. He countered with his statistics that proved the muscles and nerves involved in reading and writing did not develop until the age of eight or nine years. So, teaching these skills before that age was dangerous. Dewey's "Progressive" schools postponed reading and writing until the same age range, delaying and weakening hard drills in the critical primary years.

The emphasis on physiology included an emphasis on "health." But now, health took on a new meaning. It became the New Morality of nature, not unlike the morality of healthy stud animals or the "kill or be killed" struggle for survival, where the healthier devour the weaker in the wild.

This worship of nature set the child against civilization, democracy and intellect. And G. Stanley Hall's Romanticism constantly carried him into the sentimental idolizing of "ignorance." He said: "We must overcome the fetishism of the alphabet, of the multiplication table, of scales and bibliolatry and must reflect that but a few generations ago the ancestors of all of us were illiterate.... That scholars have argued that Cornelia, Beatrice and even the blessed, beloved mother of our Lord knew nothing of letters."[1]

In his vision of child-study, Hall fused psychology with adolescence and its sexuality, and anthropology, which led him to the psychoanalytic theories of Freud. Hall's "self-expression" for children paralleled Freud's "overcoming of repressions." Freud's "childhood sexuality" was another form of child-study.

It is not surprising, then, that for the 20th anniversary of Clark University, G. Stanley Hall brought Sigmund Freud to the campus to speak. This was Freud's first trip to the United States. At Clark, Freud gave five lectures, along with several Nobel Prize winners. Freud admitted that his sexual theories were despised in Europe, and his first positive recognition came at Clark.

In 1904, Hall's book, *Adolescence*, "blamed society, like Rousseau had, before him, for the negative acts of children."

Freudianism spread into the United States through Clark's Psychology Department largely because Hall believed it profoundly deepened the understanding of child-nature. Freud said that Hall enjoyed being a "king-maker" and then deposing those he had elevated, and needed to promote heretical thinkers.

---

1. Ross, p. 312.

Hall was also seen as representing a "Fifth Column." Emma Goldman, the famed anarchist, told how she had heard Hall speak to parents on the need for Christian churches to teach modern sex education based on "health," "to safeguard chastity, morals and religion." Then, in 1917, he published *Jesus the Christ in the light of Psychology*, offering a rational view of Jesus at odds with the biblical version.

During the First World War, Hall promoted applied psychology to motivate American troops.

In 1920, he resigned from Clark University, retired, and died in 1924 at age 80.

John Dewey

G. Stanley Hall's influence in education was felt most powerfully until the 1920s but John Dewey lived much longer and he was active into mid-century. His mark on educational theory, for better or worse, was apparent even toward the end of the 20th century.

Firstly, more so than G. Stanley Hall, John Dewey hated the America that he grew up into — with its private enterprise competitive economy and its Christian piety, where inherited values and world-view were critically important. He was called a Socialist or a Communist, based on his own statements which often mirrored Karl Marx. Dewey saw education as a way to create the revolutionary common man for the new millennium's Utopian social order. And just by coincidence (or was it coincidence?), these same educational principles fulfilled the national policy of emptying out the contents of Southern children's minds.

History of the Laboratory School

Sidney Hook, the Socialist intellectual, said this about John Dewey: "The Dewey Laboratory School was the most important experimental venture in the whole history of American education. Long before 'Progressive Education' [Dewey's term for his school curriculum philosophies] became a movement or even an identifying phrase, its basic principles were experimentally developed in a short period of seven years, by people whose original concern had been the education of their children; but on scientific as well as social grounds, soon became interested in the education of every child. An imposing galaxy of scientists and philosophers from the University of Chicago cooperated in elaborating the curriculum, adapting it to various age levels and also in teaching."[1]

1. Sidney Hook, *John Dewey: An Intellectual Portrait* (New York: The John Day Co., 1939), p. 15.

The *Encyclopedia of Modern Education* defines the Progressive movement this way: "Progressivism began in the latter part of the 19th century but spread only slowly until the end of the 1920s. Then it spread rapidly, both in the elementary school and in the theory and practice at teacher's colleges. Its acceptance has been slower but increasingly present in the colleges."[1]

John Dewey came to the University of Chicago in the summer of 1894 as head of the Philosophy, Psychology and Pedagogy Department. The next year the University established an educational Laboratory. There were twelve pupils, six to nine years old, and two teachers. One of them was in charge of manual training.

Dewey placed great emphasis on manual, "practical" training, in opposition to intellectual training. Because of his association with the University, his ideas spread world-wide, based on the rebellion against the formal, verbal methods of the past which emphasized quiet absorption of book learning. Books reflect the bringing forward of culture from the past to the present. Books are not "empirical," not the "now" of sense perception.

Dewey believed there should be no break between the home and the school. Manual training first, the 3R's thereafter, which would be integrated into the child's "practical activities." The child would learn in and for the present, rather than as a preparation for adult life, for the future. This would, of course, destroy all ambition, all sense of a bigger picture of life, of the importance of one's community. In other words, the system was perfect for the defeated South.

Supposedly, at least through Dewey's eyes, the child would find his own solutions to problems, using his own inventiveness and creativity. There would be no rote learning, because that would indicate a transmission of ideas from the past to the present. "Creativity" was child-centered and negated connections with the past. Dewey believed his system developed self-discipline so no rewards were given for excellence. This reduced or denied excellence.

Great emphasis was placed, for all groups, on manual, practical training, sweeping away all pretense of intellectual development. Pupils were not divided into grades but instead grouped together on the basis of "community interests," a metaphor for the new collectivist Utopian social order. There were no exams, no marks.

1. Harry Rivlin, editor, *Encyclopedia of Modern Education* (New York: The Philosophical Library of new York City, 1943), p. 615.

"More eyes are now fixed upon the University Elementary School at Chicago [the newer name for the Laboratory School] than upon any other elementary school in the country and probably in the world."[1]

Then came conflict, fragmentation and changes in direction toward more nihilism. Around 1900, Francis Parker's school in Quincy, Massachusetts, became part of the University of Chicago. Parker became the director of the elementary school. The Deweyites feared their school would be swallowed up. To prevent that, the two schools split into two divisions. One became a teacher-training school, with the Lab School under Dewey. But, by 1904, Dewey finally resigned because of constant factionalism between the two sections. He would move to Columbia University.

In 1909, Charles Judd Hubbard directed the Chicago elementary school and transformed the child-centered Deweyian model into the G. Stanley Hall empirical physio-psychology approach. Now, the principle became "concerted analysis of the learning process under laboratory conditions." The pupils referred to themselves as "guinea pigs."

Dewey's Own Views on Progressivism

Dewey's statements more than fulfill the objectives of John Eaton, Oliver Otis Howard and Thaddeus Stevens for the complete mental elimination of Southern culture and ideals, but now it had become the national standard.

"The child is the starting point, the center and the end. His development, his growth, is the ideal. Not knowledge or information but self-realization is the goal. To possess all the world of knowledge and lose one's self is an awful fate in education as in religion. Moreover, subject-matter can never be got into the child from without. Learning is active. It involves reaching out of the mind. It involves organic assimilation, starting from within."[2]

William Heard Kilpatrick was a disciple of Dewey who was hugely successful in promoting Progressivism to the general public. He demonstrated how perfectly Dewey had fulfilled John Eaton's policy. "Less and less do the young yield themselves to the mere word of their elder's command. Less and less do they accept existing customs and convention as binding.... With external authority gone, the school must help young people to find the only

---

1. Ida B. dePencer, *The History of the Laboratory Schools: The University of Chicago, 1896-1965* (Chicago: Quadrangle Books, 1967), p. 38.
2. Thayer, p. 252.

real authority that can command respect, the internal authority of 'how it works when tried.'"[1]

Here, Dewey sounds like a Stalinist: "Political democracy cannot stand in isolation. It can be effectively maintained only where democracy is social, where it is moral.... The national counterpart to free and universal public education is a system of universal industry [meaning the nationalizing of private companies] in which there are no idlers or shirkers or parasites and where the ruling motive is interest in good workmanship for public ends, no exploitation of others for private ends. That is why industrial democracy and industrial education [state control of business and schools] should fit each other like hand-in-glove."[2]

Dewey and the New History

John Dewey's Progressivism influenced the telling of history, by the creation of the "New History," which also fit perfectly into Washington's requirements for the next generation of Southern children. "To what avail if we learn to read and write, and learn geography and history, if in the process the individual loses his own soul and loses his appreciation of things worthwhile."[3]

Although Dewey never exclusively treated history extensively in any single work, he consistently used history to "reconstruct" philosophy. He gave the "New History" of his fellow Columbia associates, Harvey Robinson and Charles Beard, a philosophical foundation. Thus Robinson came to believe that history should delete useless political and military facts. History was justified only to solve current social problems. Robinson followed Dewey's dictum that "the present has been the willing victim of the past. She should turn on the past and exploit it in the interest of advance," and proposed the revolutionary idea that history must "alter its ideals and aims with the general progress of society and of the social sciences."[4]

In 1907, Robinson and Beard wrote *The Development of Modern Europe*. The next year Dewey wrote *Ethics*. Both works were similar, combining history and current social problems. For Robinson, Beard and Dewey, history should not be objective because it was always colored by a contemporary frame of reference.

---

1. William Heard Kilpatrick, *Education for a Changing Civilization* (New York: The Macmillan Co., 1926), pp. 80, 82.
2. Rena L. Vassar, p. 190.
3. John Dewey, *Experience and Education* (New York: A Touchstone Book, published by Simon and Schuster, 1938), p. 49.
4. James H. Robinson, *The New History* (New York: Macmillan and Co., 1912), pp. 17 and 24.

History should always be an "imaginative creation." They called this Instrumentalist History. The knower makes the truth, rather than finds it. The past is subordinated to current problems. The changing present needs a changing past. Dewey: "History can liberate us from the past."[1] He added: "The past is the past. There are too many urgent demands in the present, too many calls over the threshold of the future, to permit the child to become deeply immersed in what is forever gone by."[2]

Dewey also wrote on the methodology of the New History: "The historical method, like the experimental method in physics, enables us to isolate any particular fact and study it in terms of antecedents and consequences, and this gives us intellectual control over it." Then Dewey described what he considered to be the central problem of history: "The present is the true past."[3]

Charles Beard then echoed Dewey: "Every man must be his own historian."[4]

Progressivism As Totalitarian Model

"We are told," wrote Dewey, "that the complexity of human relations makes it impossible to have large-scale social planning and direction by intelligence."[5]

Large-scale social planning is the hallmark of the totalitarian models, where the human factor is eliminated and "intelligence" resides with the power-manipulating leaders.

Dewey continued on in this vein, stating that "students should be introduced to scientific subject-matter and be initiated into its facts and laws through acquaintance with everyday social applications.... The application of science in production and distribution."[6] Science, in deleting human motivation and values, leads to the so-called "efficiency" of a centralized command totalitarian economy and ends the "waste and inefficiency" of private enterprise.

---

1. John Dewey, "The Evolutionary Method as Applied to Morality," in *The Philosophical Review II*, 1902, p. 113.
2. John Dewey, "History for the Educator," *The Progressive Journal of Education*, March 1909, No. 5,
3. John Dewey, "Reconstruction," an address before The Students Christian Association, at Michigan University, in *The Monthly Bulletin*, No. 15, June 1894, p. 155.
4. John Blewitt, editor, *John Dewey, His Thought and Influence* (New York: Fordham University Press, 1960), p. 153.
5. John Dewey, *Experience and Education*, p. 81.
6. Ibid., p. 80.

Progressivism Leads to Madness, No Past or Future

Dewey: "When experiences are disorderly, not in continuity, it causes a divided personality. At a certain point, that person becomes insane."[1]

"Traditionally, the subject-matter of education consisted of bodies of information and skills that have been worked out in the past. The chief business was to transmit them to the new generation, along with rules of conduct, moral conduct.... The attitude of pupils must be docility, receptivity, obedience. Progressive education is discontented with this philosophy."[2]

"When preparation [for the future] is made the controlling end, then the potentialities of the present are sacrificed to a suppositious future. Thus the actual preparation for the future is missed or distorted."[3]

Progressivism's Stamp on Education

"From the closing decades of the 19th century, Progressivism permeated every aspect of American life. It dominated the educational scene until the 1950s." Then it seemed to fade, but in actuality that indicated it was being absorbed into the national system. By 1929 over 200 cities in 41 states had adopted Progressivism. One wing of it was Communist, the American Historical Association, which condemned individualism and capitalism: "The Progressive school is a place where children go, not primarily to learn, but to carry on a way of life.... It perpetually criticizes the competitive character of the present social order."[4]

"The State" Imposes Values on Experience

The terms "child-centered" and "experience" seemed to mean that the student was king, and the world of outside values did not impinge on the pristine classroom. But it also implied that the State was controlling the environment, the school, the classroom, and the curriculum, so that only its worldview reached the child.

Beginning in the 1930s and expanding after World War II, State-funded public schools became more aggressive and overtly imposed values, not only on the environment, but directly on the pupil. There was great pressure to create a "planet-wide democratic order," and "Experimentalism" was superimposed on

---

1. John Dewey, *Experience and Education*, p. 44.
2. Ibid., p. 17.
3. Ibid., p. 49.
4. Vassar, pp. 232, 261.

277

"Progressivism," proclaiming that this new ideal "expresses the mood, the values and the practice of a culture in transition between two greatly different eras in modern history." This meant that the new dream would be a rationally-planned totalitarian world. Experimentalism merged once again, now called, appropriately, "Reconstructionalism" education, which takes sides. "It encourages students and all members of the community, not merely to study knowledge and problems crucial to our period of culture but to make up their minds about the promising solutions and then to act accordingly."[1]

In the 1940s, Walter Lippmann, the famed writer and newspaperman, said: "During the past fifty years educators have progressively removed western culture studies which have created democracy, so the youth do not understand the principles of the free society in which they live. This education will destroy Western civilization."[2]

And how was this accomplished? Let John Dewey give us a clue: "When external control is rejected, all authority is not rejected, there is a need to search for a more effective source of authority."[3] Yes, the Bureau of Education!

Dewey's Disillusionment

By the 1920s, John Dewey showed a transition, a disillusionment with the results of his own ideals. He began to claim that the sciences of man had become materialistic and mechanistic and psychology had now become a dangerous reductionism of man to a mere algebraic summation. Dewey's schoolroom emphasis on "activity" (like manual training) rather than on reason did not have the liberating effect which he had predicted. Rather than being progress, the extreme environmentalism, wherein the child and the classroom form a complete insulated world, appeared to Dewey to be just as cruel and unloving, just as selfish and anti-social, as traditional schooling had once seemed.

Edward Thorndike

"I just can't understand Dewey!" said Edward Thorndike. His own educational vision was far more statistically oriented.

Thorndike primarily was an experimental scientist. Yet, his influence was felt in psychology, education, social science, and statistics, for better or worse.

---

1. Thayer, pp. 319, 321.
2. Ibid., p. 343.
3. John Dewey, *Experience and Education*, p. 21.

It must be understood that the "experimental scientific method" generates statistics and it was Horace Mann who said that statistics were the only presentation that politicians understood in order to enact legislation.

Thorndike's dream was to establish an experimental science of man, a science of human nature, describable in terms of matter and energy. This would be an applied science to guide policy-makers in law, government and education.

Thorndike said: "Science is the only sure foundation for social progress."[1] This is absurd. By the encyclopedia definition of science, its inductive reasoning of working from a "particular" undermines the "general" principle through which law develops. The "objectivity" of science undermines morality which binds communities and stabilizes governments. Thorndike's dream results in an anarchic dictatorship.

Thorndike: Science as Religion

Edward Thorndike's father was a Methodist minister who put his three sons on display as models of virtue. This negatively influenced them and they rebelled against his strict code. Thereafter, religion would mean very little to them. But young Edward could not escape his father's messianic fervor; science itself took on the character of a crusade.

Edward went to Wesleyan, a Methodist university, where he rejected religion for science. This meant adopting an exclusively naturalistic view of man. He saw scientists as heroes and religious men as perpetuators of superstition and repression. He distrusted all traditional modes of thought, including philosophy.

Wesleyan emphasized science because "Methodism is experimental Christianity. Its spirit is scientific." This meant that Wesleyan had New Psychology courses, emulating the physical sciences and breaking psychology away from philosophy by forming a separate department for it. This was revolutionary in the 1880s.

Indirectly, one Thorndike biographer gave evidence of the covert power of the Bureau of Education's hand at Wesleyan, in subsidizing physio-psychology research: "Colleges and universities tumble over one another in their zeal to establish psychological laboratories and graduate programs, both evident before 1900."[2]

---

1. Geraldine Joncich, *The Sane Positivist; a Biography of Edward L. Thorndike* (Middletown: Wesleyan University Press, 1968), preface, p. 4.
2. Ibid., p. 69.

Edward Thorndike planned for a graduate degree. His intention was to teach. He selected Harvard, where he took advanced New Psychology courses with William James.

In 1897, he conducted his first tests on children — studying facial expressions or movements made unconsciously during mind-reading experiments — despite Harvard's ban on testing children. Thereafter, Thorndike substituted chickens and kept them in William James' basement.

Initially James' psychology was metaphysical and moralistic. This was not revolutionary enough for the New Psychologists and his work had little impact on them. Eventually he fell in line with "Radical Empiricism," which overturned the classic religious dualism of Mind vs. Matter; now, the Empiricists proclaimed that man is part of nature and psychic and physical laws function under the same laws. This translates into Dewey's Progressivism and Thorndike's brand of empirical educational theories.

In yet another demonstration of how Federal funding of schools for Agricultural Experiment Stations was revolutionizing the entire mental framework of the United States; even the more conservative periodicals of the time increasingly reported the moral superiority of science. In 1898, the *Atlantic Monthly* editorialized: "America has become a nation of science. There is no industry, from agriculture to architecture, that is not shaped by research and its results. There is no law on our statutes, no motive in our conduct, that has not been made more just by the straight forward and unselfish habit of thought fostered by scientific methods."[1]

As the 19th century came to an end, the term "pure science" came to stand for not only an activity and a motive, but an ethic as well. Science was now understood, for the first time, to offer an ethical and moral superiority over Christianity.

But — there was a huge flaw in the empirical, observable, here and now methodology as the New Religion. The most basic example of this flaw lies in "Power," that potentially deadly force that government can hold over people. The effects of power cannot be seen or observed until after it has entrapped its victims. The empirical method, the scientific experimental method, cannot perceive it until it is too late.

---

1. Ibid., p. 111.

Columbia

Thorndike planned for a PhD in philosophy, to teach psychology. He chose Columbia University. James Catell was a professor of psychology there. He was a great popularizer, promoting the New Psychology in publications like *Popular Science Monthly* and *School and Society*.

Catell edited the *Men of Science* biographies, applying to all human affairs, especially education, scientific principles. Catell turned Columbia into a leading New Psychology center.

Nicholas Murray Butler, President of Columbia, said: "The great activity and human interest called education might be subjected to scientific examination and analysis."[1]

It is Butler who taught Thorndike and sparked his interest in the areas of zoology, comparative neurology, the study of brain and nervous systems of animals.

1898: Thorndike produced a doctoral thesis called *Animal Intelligence, An Experimental Study of the Associative Process in Animals*. Learning and adaptive changes in behavior were explained by the forming of associations between situations in which the animal finds itself and its impulse to action.

For Thorndike, since animal studies revealed human parallels, then child-study would be an avenue to understanding adult behavior. But, by the definitions of 19th century science, the truth could never be found; science had become "continual change." Truth and knowledge were endlessly relative.

Thorndike's experiments for *Animal Intelligence* were done with mazes. His methodology conformed to the New Psychology's mechanistic procedures, which denied the possibility of free will and minimized consciousness to sense impressions..

Animal Intelligence was immediately ranked as a classic and is considered to be the real starting point of general acceptance of the use of comparative anatomy psychology.

Until World War I, educational psychology remained the only kind of psychology.

1899: New York State's Department of Education supported child-study. This gave child-study national acceptance.

---

1. Ibid., p. 120.

Thorndike Teaches at Columbia

Edward Thorndike's first job was teaching pedagogy at Western Reserve University. In 1899, he moved back to Columbia, which had come to epitomize the "New American University" along with Clark University and the University of Chicago.

Within six months he was the Chair of Columbia's Psychology Department. In five years, this was one of the highest visibility posts in the academic world.

At the Teachers College division of Columbia, educational research had become a major function. It would also train teachers for leadership roles in government. Its alumni would become local and state administrators within the Bureau of Education.

1903: Thorndike is teaching "Educational Psychology." This is still an unfamiliar term. Then, "Application of Psychological and Statistical Methods to Education."

Within fifteen years there is a "Division of Educational Psychology." This becomes the most important center of psychological training in the United States.

One title of Thorndike's several books is *Notes on Child Study*. It is geared toward parents since the child-centered movement was as much a lay movement as a professional one. Another book, *Educational Psychology*, presented how science and statistics could be applied to school problems. This required another book, *Elements of Psychology*, to promote empirical psychology.

In these writings, Thorndike made the word "experimental" synonymous with "scientific." He was engaging in methodological reductionism, fusing the procedures of one science to those of another. When psychologists spoke of "mental atoms" or "conservation of psychic energy," they were following physics.

Each science was responding to the other's "revolution." Even as specialization erected fences, others had come down. Chemistry had assaulted the barrier between the organic and inorganic, as a result of Darwinism. This synthesis had discredited the concept of a "life principle," since evolution proceeded seamlessly from the inorganic to living organisms.

Thorndike believed that Darwinism had the potential to unify all fields of knowledge: humanistic and scientific. "Human psychology shared with physiology, anthropology and sociology the study of all human nature and activities. Psychology in general shares with zoology the study of all animal nature and activity." (Once again, this reduced consciousness to "activity.") "Nowhere more truly than in his mental capacities is man more a part of nature."[1] This inverted the traditional position which saw man's intelligence as elevating him to understand the concept of volition, or choice, which separated him from the "necessity" of nature.

In Darwinian biology, nature is essentially statistical; thus, Thorndike's experiments with fish and monkeys confirmed to him the validity of the statistical and non-rational concept of intelligence and learning. "Intelligence is behavior appropriate to the situation; simply a collection of associations. There can be no over-riding conception." As a result, learning was reduced from trial and error to trial and accident, since "error" indicated "choice."[2]

Transfer of Faculties

Transfer of faculties was a basic foundation of classical, formal, education. "Formal" refers to the bringing forward the past to the present.

Traditionally, students were required to take Latin and higher math to develop their general problem-solving skills, but the New Psychology challenged these assumptions. Thorndike created biased experiments to disprove the validity of transfer of faculties training. From these he showed that there was nothing general about the operations of the mind. This brought the entire assumption of formal pedagogy under fire. Thorndike said: "The mind is a machine for making particular reactions to particular situations."[3]

Nicholas Murray Butler countered, that: "As a result of a few hopelessly superficial and irrelevant experiments it was announced that there was no such thing as general discipline.... This new notion spread among the homes and schools of the United States to the undoing of the effectiveness of our American education."[4]

Teachers College was closely connected to the Bureau of Education. One of its commissioners, Elmer Ellsworth Brown, taught at Teachers while he was in office. Brown called Thorndike to Washington to do a statistical survey, *The Elimination of Pupils from Schools*, to find out why students dropped out. The survey found that ninety-one percent left school by the time they were eighteen. On the

---

1. Edward Thorndike, "Darwin's Contribution to Psychology," *University of California Chronicles*, 12 (1909), p. 65 and Joncich, p. 260.
2. Jonich, p. 266.
3. Ibid., p. 273.
4. Nicholas Murray Butler, *Laws and Lawlessness*, from *Tracts for Today*, No. 11, 1923, pp. 6- 7.

basis of this evidence, the radical policy of "social promotion" was instituted, where failing students were not left back.

In the 1920s, the *Thorndike Arithmetics* and the *Thorndike Dictionary* were published. These books had the strongest direct influence upon education. He said: "Nothing is included for mental gymnastics. Only content of intrinsic value.... Preparation for the problems of actual life.... The unrealizable pretensions of deductive reasoning [general principles, transfer of faculties] are omitted."[1]

The *Arithmetics* sold millions of copies. Thorndike, in the 1920s, is listed among the three hundred most famous men in American history. Only fourteen of them are educators.

Among the scientists in Catell's *American Men of Science*, ninety percent are advisors to the Federal government in World War I. Afterward they appear with ever-greater frequency. Universities are now dependent on Washington, which eventually supports half the scientists and engineers. Thorndike believes in Federal support, since science, when applied to psychology or sociology for human engineering, can reconstruct society. In the Marxist tradition, Thorndike hardly questions the supposition that progress in science is synonymous with social advance.

In the 1930s, under Franklin D. Roosevelt, Secretary of the Agriculture Department Henry Wallace was overlord of the largest science program in the Federal government. Wallace develops a radical concept of progress through research: to make the social sciences on a par with the exact sciences.

1939: Thorndike retires.

1946: One year after the surrender of Japan in World War II, General Douglas MacArthur requests that Thorndike and thirty other major educators "assist Japan in gearing its educational system to democratic principles." Thorndike cannot go; he is too old and ill.

It must be recalled that the United States viewed the Japanese as fanatical warriors, much the same way as the Confederate soldier was, eighty years before. The Japanese would get the same form of cultural re-education as the South. And it was successful there, too. Their samurai culture largely disappeared and was replaced by Western relativism, where no values remained to inspire a man to fight to the death.

1949: Thorndike dies.

---

1. Joncich, p. 398.

Chapter 16. Ambassador to Spain on the Edge of War

We return to Jabez Curry in the final phase of his life, as an ambassador, and then, his disillusion with "all he hath wrought" in education.

In September 1885, Jabez Curry was preaching in the small East Tennessee town of Rogersville. While he was there, Mary Curry forwarded him a letter from President Grover Cleveland's Secretary of State, Thomas Bayard. "I wish to enlist you in the public service, and believe that an opportunity for high usefulness is open to you in which it may be in your power to render important service to your country. The mission to Spain is now vacant and I consider that point in our foreign relations as second in importance to none."[1]

In conflict, Jabez Curry wrote to Robert Winthrop. "President Cleveland tenders me the mission to Spain.... In my confusion I turn to you as my most valued and trusted friend. What shall I do?[2]

Winthrop's reply expresses that he desperately wished for Curry to remain with Peabody but he also fully grasped the significance of this prestigious appointment. "You are the very pivot of George Peabody's great Southern benefaction. All its success turns upon you.... However you may decide the question, my own regard and affection for you and Mrs. Curry cannot be changed."[3]

---

1. Thomas Bayard letter to Jabez Curry, September 7, 1885, in Curry Papers.
2. Jabez Curry letter to Robert Winthrop, September 14, 1885, in Curry Papers.
3. Robert Winthrop letter to Jabez Curry, September 16, 1885, in Curry Papers.

Curry decided in favor of the ambassadorship, although he admitted, "I love the Peabody work."

He had several reasons to be conflicted. This would be his first opportunity to be more directly involved in the world of politics after an absence of twenty-one years. Curry had turned down two major political offices: Commissioner of the Bureau of Education, and membership in Rutherford Hayes' Cabinet. Yet, this was different. Grover Cleveland, as the first Democratic President since James Buchanan in the 1850s, had a real chance to restore the South to an equal status in the Union.

Curry, as a Southerner, understood how important that was. Years later, in a speech to the students of Tulane University, he explained his decision: "The trouble with the South, to use a common term, is 'we are not in it.' I am sorry to hear you laugh. I am serious. I am desperately serious. We are not in it. I am speaking of general results. In appropriations, appointments, recognition, in every part and parcel of government, we are not in it. We were in it once, and you, the university men, must put the South back in it. When I accepted the appointment of Minister to Spain, I told Mr. Cleveland, the greatest statesman and public man in the United States, that I did so because I wanted to show that a Southern Democrat will protect American interests and uphold American honor as well as an Ohio or a Massachusetts Republican."[1]

The announcement of Curry's appointment was greeted with mixed comments by the press because he was a Baptist reverend, an avowed opponent of the Church of Rome, and Spain was very much a Catholic country. Curry had often expressed his anti-Catholic sentiments in writing and in sermons. And yet, he was easily confirmed by the Senate.

Of course, Senator Henry Blair was distressed by Curry's departure; his Federal aid to education bill was still hanging by a thread in the Senate. Blair said that the fate of his bill depended on Curry and without his help it could not pass. Blair was correct in that assumption.

To prepare for his unfamiliar consular role, Jabez Curry went to Washington to study the diplomatic questions pending with Spain. Secretary of State Bayard invited him to dinner with both the Spanish Minister to the United States and John Foster, the former Minister to Spain.

---

1. J.L.M. Curry, article in an unknown newspaper, unknown date, but after 1890, from Curry Papers.

Both of Curry's biographers, Jessie Pearl Rice (1949) and Edwin Anderson Alderman (1911), as well as Robert Winthrop, were in agreement that this Spanish post was an unimportant sinecure. They all saw Spain as a backwater European power with little political significance. History proved them to be completely wrong. Before and during Curry's tenure, Spain and the United States were inching toward war and he would be a participant in the process.

Spain was also convulsing through a period of radical political change, shifting from an absolutist monarchy toward something faintly resembling a modern republic. Curry witnessed this turmoil and was asked to take sides, as ambassador, in a coup.

Jabez Curry would write a book about these events, *Constitutional Government in Spain*, which, like his previous works, was partially an allegory of the constitutional travesties that the South was compelled to accept during Reconstruction.

For more than a century Spain was a declining power. In the generation before Curry became Minister, there was virtually continual instability. In 1868, the notorious Queen Isabella II was deposed, causing great turmoil. Amedeo of Savoy then ascended to the throne but it swayed so precariously that he abdicated in 1870. Then, "The Republic" was established, but without popular support, it quickly gave way to a dictatorship that pretended to be the heir to "The Republic." It so mismanaged the country that it fell in a year.

Then Alfonso XII, the seventeen-year-old son of Isabella II, came to the throne in 1875. He restored order through a limited constitutional monarchy. At Spain's height of empire, her colonies had stretched from the Caribbean to the tip of South America. By the rein of Alfonso XII, Spain's only remaining colonial possessions in the Western hemisphere were Cuba and Puerto Rico. These two possessions, especially Cuba, would be grounds for war with the United States.

Jabez and Mary Curry left for Spain in November 1885, on the steamship *Germanic*. They dallied in London and Paris until they learned that Alfonso XII was seriously ill. They rushed to Madrid to be formally presented to him, but Alfonso died just as they arrived. This created a protocol problem. Curry would need new credentials for the Queen Regent, his successor. This was solved when Curry was designated the "Special Envoy of the United States" for the King's funeral.

Curry described the funeral with some humor and sarcasm; there occurred at "the Church of St. Sebastian, with great pomp and display, the funeral of the deceased King. The house was packed. Seats were assigned to, and reserved for, the diplomatic corps and the dignitaries. All the governments of Europe had authorized Special Ambassadors, who, with the Cabinet and some others, had seats of honor in the choir. Being a Special Envoy, equivalent to an ambassador, I was honored with a seat behind the 'elect few'; and being just behind the Papal Nuncio, Cardinal Rampolla, I watched him, and was thus able to go through the various 'risings and sittings,' which were frequent, and without such experienced guidance, would have been embarrassing. The diplomatic corps sat below the choir, as did various other officials and especially invited guests. All were in their gorgeous uniforms and decorations, except the representatives of the United States; and we, restrained by the absurd instructions of our Government, wore the dress-suits of a head-waiter in a hotel."[1]

Given Spain's instability, Jabez Curry feared that Alfonso's death would cause more uprisings and attempted coups. He put Mary on a train for Paris until he was certain that order and calm would prevail.

It was almost a month after his arrival before the Queen Regent received Curry officially as Minister. Then he made the required calls of courtesy on members of the Cabinet and diplomatic corps.

Diplomacy, Free Trade vs. Protectionism

One of the factors that had moved the Old South to secede was the issue of "protectionism." Abraham Lincoln and his Republicans instituted high tariff barriers to keep foreign products from competing with American manufactured goods. This was important for the industrialized Northeast but disastrous for the agricultural South which depended on, and required, a national free trade policy since it exported most of its cotton and tobacco overseas.

Similar issues plagued relations between Spain and the United States over Cuba and Puerto Rico; and, because they were never resolved, tensions continued to build, moving both nations ever closer to war.

In the specific language of this situation, the United States objected to the tonnage fees which Spain had levied on the cargoes of vessels leaving the US for Spanish ports. Another irritant for the United States had to do with differential "flag duties." Foreign goods carried in Spanish ships from American ports paid twenty-five percent less duty in Cuba and Puerto Rico than when transshipped in American vessels. The third and potentially most explosive issue was the

---

1. Alderman and Gordon, p. 298.

payment of claims growing out of the Cuban revolutionary wars against Spanish rule.

Curry, with his usual enthusiasm, began immediately to try to resolve all these difficulties but he believed what he considered the Spanish characteristic of *mañana* prevented a settlement and nearly drove him mad. He wrote Robert Winthrop of "the national habit of procrastination" of officials whose "ideas of time and space" seemed "altogether subjective and ideal."[1]

Curry added, "My predecessors had written letters. In the course of time, dilatory responses came. Dialectical diplomacy found exercise.... My policy has been to divide and conquer. To present each matter separately and on its own merits.... Rejecting the common notion of diplomacy as being synonymous with evasion and duplicity, I have emphasized frankness and directness but with some little loss of self-respect. I have been as persistent as a needy creditor in making demands on a reluctant debtor."[2]

The "procrastination" and the endless delays that Curry found so galling were probably not due to the supposed inherent laziness of Spaniards or their diplomatic corps; it is far more likely they were deliberately obstructing an agreement because they hated America and Americans. *Mañana* was a form of snub, a punishment for the war-like posture that the United States had taken over Cuba since the 1860s.

As evidence that the Spanish government was toying with Curry, Jabez believed he was having success in most areas of dispute; flag differentials were to be removed, consular tariffs to be reduced on tonnage taxes in foreign ports. But again, delay followed delay and in the end most of these promises were nullified by the Cortes, the Spanish Congress.

The continued threat of war with the United States intensified Spain's internal instability. Another military coup took place while Curry was in Madrid. A cavalry squadron and an infantry company revolted and proclaimed a republic on September 19, 1886. Most of the army remained loyal and the insurrection was crushed in a day, but this incident had a lasting effect. When a new ministry was formed on October 10, the United States immediately reimposed tariffs that had been removed, possibly in protest.

Another after-effect of this abortive coup directly involved Curry. Salmeron, a deputy in the Cortes and a leader of the republican faction, called on

---

1. Jabez Curry letters to Robert Winthrop, June 2 and September 1, 1886, in Curry Papers.
2. Jabez Curry letter to Robert Winthrop, June 12, 1886, in Curry Papers.

Curry and told him that arrangements had been made for the rescue of the prisoners taken in the revolt. Salmeron asked that in case of "hot pursuit" by the police they be given protection in the American legation. Curry emphatically declined, believing that leaving the embassy door unlocked was tantamount to an invitation and that would make him an accomplice.

Although Jabez Curry had always advocated republicanism over monarchy, he was not overly sympathetic to the Spanish republicans. He felt that Spain was not ready for such an advanced form of government. Its ignorance, superstition, and fusion of Church and State were all serious impediments.

The Other Life of a Diplomat

It was here in Spain that Mary Curry came to the foreground for the first time. The Spanish newspapers reported that Mary was both beautiful and distinguished, and she sustained in Madrid the standard of hospitality of the rich and powerful American republic through her afternoon receptions and evening banquets. Jabez wrote home that her weekly teas were becoming popular; they were elegant, she had beautified everything and shed so much light and warmth that the "etiquette-bound Spaniards" enjoyed the relaxation from the rigidity to which they were accustomed. And to Robert Winthrop he described Mary's social conquests with her dinners and said that her receptions were crowded with the best and most notable people of Madrid, which greatly enhanced his "ability and opportunities for usefulness." Members of royalty and nobility, the leaders in the ministry and Cortes, his colleagues of the diplomatic corps, all attended Mary's parties.[1]

Castelar and Canovas

Curry made the following comments about two major political figures: "Mary accompanied me to Congress [the Cortes] and we heard Castelar, the distinguished Republican, of whom I wrote some time ago. Enthusiasts write of him as the Orator of Humanity, as the peculiar, unparalleled product of Spanish environment. I was disappointed. He is full of poetry, imagination, fervor. He has read widely, and his language is full, chaste, appropriate. He is the most impassioned speaker I ever heard; rants excessively, gesticulates vehemently and ludicrously. The pantomime — and it was not much more to me in my unfamiliarity with the language, and my bad position for hearing — was not effective. His

---

1. Jabez Curry letters to Mrs. Thomas, Mary's mother, November 15, 1886 and to Robert Winthrop, December 28, 1886, in Curry Papers.

voice was not distinct nor musical, probably the result of hoarseness, and the use of too much fluid. Do not misunderstand me: he is very temperate; does not smoke nor even drink wine, and that in Spain is something unique. I was not moved. I have heard men in a foreign tongue, who, by voice or acting, stirred me. Castelar did not. He is not to be compared to Yancey. Who is?"[1] [William Yancey was the famed Southern politician who wrote Alabama's ordinance of secession and was a member of the United States and Confederate Congress.]

On another occasion Curry wrote this humorous note to Robert Winthrop about Castelar and another major political figure, Canovas: "in a former letter, I think I mentioned our formal or State dinners, which bring us into pleasant social intercourse with leading men and women. I do not share in his political opinions, but no statesman here has impressed me as much as Canovas. He has firmness, courage, intelligence, political experience, breadth of view and much wit. He talks at a dinner-table exceedingly well, but both he and Castelar monopolize the 'talk.' Canovas, speaking of Castelar's well-known and inoffensive vanity, and peacockish display, said of him, that he never saw a marriage without wishing to be the bride, nor a funeral without wishing to be the corpse."[2]

Curry also had these flattering comments to make about Sigismund Moret, who "was the Minister of State, with whom I had all my official intercourse. Physically and intellectually he is a superb man. With enlightened views, varied experience, unusual ability, unquestioned patriotism, unfailing suavity and courtesy of manner, it was a pleasure to deal with him; and our relations were most cordial. In politics, he is a Liberal.... During the Spanish-American War he was Secretary for the Colonies, and would have favored large concessions to Cuba. In May 1888, he [had] said Cuba should be Americanized. If in the course of years it desired independence, such was the course of life. To give up Cuba then would be the overthrow of the monarchy; and in these utterances his chief, Sagasta, agreed. I am sure that to have allowed Cuba to hold the relation to Spain, that Canada does to England, would not have been objectionable. The insular American possessions, being the last of Spain's continental dominion, were regarded with special pride, and the sensitiveness of the people could not brook such a loss."[3]

---

1. Alderman and Gordon, p. 311.
2. Jabez Curry letter to Robert Winthrop, December 28, 1886, in Curry Papers.
3. Alderman and Gordon, p. 308.

The Birth and Baptism of the New King

During Curry's first year as ambassador in Madrid, a new Spanish king was born, Alfonso XII's son born posthumously. Curry wrote: "On Monday, the 17th of May [1885], about sunrise, a messenger from the Palace came post haste to summon my immediate attendance.... I went to the Palace and found some of the diplomatic corps and government officials, in full uniform, with cocked hats, swords, gold bands, and all the decorations to which they were entitled....

"We waited half or three-quarters of an hour, when the Cabinet was called. Soon the President, Senor Sagasta, returned, and standing at the door, proclaimed in Spanish, 'Long live the King!' This announced the birth and sex of him, who, so far as I know, was the first human being ever born a King.

"Passing at once through a suite of rooms, we were halted next to the chamber of the Queen. Arranging ourselves in a semi-circle, and waiting for what might occur, a lady, one of the Queen's waiting-women, came out, holding in her hands a beautiful silver basket, or waiter. In this, enveloped in soft cotton, was the new-born babe, His Royal Highness, Prince of Asturias, King of Spain. The babe was passed around, naked, for our inspection; but I did not see the divinity which hedges in a King. He soon proved his common humanity by crying, and was withdrawn to be clothed. This ceremony, once so common, to prevent imposition of false heirs, is peculiar to Spain; and I am one of the few now living who 'assisted' at such a function. The birth was soon made known by firing of cannon, ringing of bells, and noisy, tumultuous demonstrations on the streets....

"On the 22nd the baptism of the babe was performed in the royal chapel in the Palace, and was a splendid ceremonial.... The whole distance was lined with people, four or five rows in depth; but the Civil Guard kept an open avenue, wide enough for the gorgeously dressed favored few, who had access to the chapel.

"While marching through the avenue, the Introducer of Ambassadors met us, and offering his arm to Mrs. Curry, conducted her to the tribune which had been erected in the chapel for the diplomatic corps. It was with much personal and national pride that an American saw the female representative of his country encountering with such calmness the battery of a thousand eyes; for, as her train swept gracefully behind, she was the cynosure of universal admiration, and elicited a thousand compliments. She wore a white satin dress, a point-lace over-dress looped with feathers, a white satin train lined with green velvet, and trimmed with sable, a point-lace mantilla, white feathers, a diamond aigrette, emeralds in hair and a diamond brooch in front.

"The royal babe, gorgeously dressed, preceded by civil and ecclesiastical dignitaries, was brought in by Infanta Isabel, aided or attended by the Papal Nuncio, Cardinal Rampolla, and the first lady of the Court. The little fellow screamed lustily, showing his protest against such fuss and folly. The 'baptism,' I suppose, was after the usual ceremony of the Church of Rome, emphasized and prolonged for the occasion, and the exceptional 'subject.' The Pope, through the Nuncio, stood sponsor, or godfather; and the whole function consumed an hour and-a-half.... The King was christened Alfonso Leon Fernando Santiago Maria Isidro Pascual y Anton."[1]

Cuba, the Thorn That Leads to War

At its height, Spain ruled a world-wide empire and a substantial portion of it was centered in the "New World." By Curry's time in Madrid, most of it had been stripped away. Only Cuba and Puerto Rico remained.

Cuba began to show a strong desire for independence in 1810, when its representation in the Spanish Cortes was withdrawn. There were several insurrections but they were quickly and ruthlessly extinguished.

Spain could not part with Cuba as she had with her other possessions. Jabez Curry explained why: "I found the people of Spain absolutely a unit on one question. Royalty, aristocracy, government, the Church, the masses, conservatives, liberals, republicans, all were united in opposition to the separation of their country from the control of Cuba. Nothing would excite the people more than the suggestion of even a remote possibility of the transference of Cuba to another power. I think that this feeling is due very much to national pride and sentimentalism. Cuba is the last vestige of their immense possessions in the Western continent; and they clung to it with a tenacity that is thoroughly Spanish."[2]

In 1868, Cuban discontent again escalated into violence, over excessive taxation, trade restrictions and the virtual total exclusion of native Cubans from governmental posts.

Carlos de Cespedes began the revolt. It became known as "The Ten Years War." He proclaimed the existence of the "Revolutionary Republic of Cuba," with its capital at Bayamo. The fighting was mostly guerrilla fighting, except in

---

1. Ibid., p. 303.
2. J.L.M. Curry article, March 15, 1896, in a fragment of an unknown newspaper, Curry Papers.

the eastern provinces where it raged with great fury. The Spanish general Weyler retaliated with atrocities against thousands of the "rebels."

United States sympathy for the insurgents and antagonism against Spain intensified with the destruction of American property by Spanish troops.

Curry became involved in resolving the claims against Spain for that destruction: "Another matter I inherited," he wrote, "gave annoyance and trouble. For years the Legation was burdened with Cuban claims; and the claimants, personally, through attorneys, and through instructions from the State Department, were urgent and insistent in demanding payment for enormous alleged injuries and losses. Instead of making a drag-net of claims of varied worth and proof, my accomplished secretary, E.H. Strobel, and myself, after thorough consideration, decided to select one, apparently the best sustained, and make a test of it, with the hope that an agreement to pay one would settle the principle and establish a precedent for paying others. After scores of interviews, annoying delays, wearing patience threadbare, I succeeded in getting an agreement to pay the claim of Mora for $1,500,000. This agreement bound the government, committed the members of the Cabinet, but aroused active opposition in the Cortes, threatened the existence of the government.... The claim was delayed in payment for some years; and Spain, in her impecunious condition, finally yielded to heavy pressure brought to bear on her by the United States government."[1]

After a decade of brutal warfare, Spain's General de Campos concluded the treaty of Zanjon, nominally granting reform and governmental representation to the Cubans, which never was fulfilled. This bitter, bloody conflict seemed futile to the Cubans but it actually foreshadowed the next phase: the war of independence in 1895.

In October 1873, in the midst of the Ten Years War, an event took place which brought the United States to the brink of war with Spain. This was twelve years before Jabez Curry became ambassador but the repercussions were still felt in both countries while he was in Madrid.

The *Virginius* was a marauding privateer, fraudulently flying the American flag and carrying arms to the Cubans. It was captured by the Spanish, off the coast of Cuba. The captain and 52 of the crew and passengers, including Americans, were executed. More would have been killed except for the intervention of the British ship, *Niobe*.

---

1. Alderman and Gordon, p. 306.

America and Spain went head to head. Unfortunately, General D. E. Sickles, who had been one of the ruthless Radical commanders in the occupied South, was the United States minister. He was not a diplomat and his intemperate attitude and actions seemed to be designed to provoke overt hostilities. It is significant that Sickles was minister in such a sensitive time, given that he had a long combat record.

Hamilton Fish, the Secretary of State, the same Mr. Fish who had been in President Ulysses S. Grant's Cabinet and had strong reservations about Grant's military provocations in the South, stepped in, pushed Sickles aside and settled the crisis, at least temporarily, with Spain agreeing to pay a large indemnity.

Later, Jabez Curry would comment on this continuing crisis: "The situation is certainly very perplexing, and I don't know exactly what is the duty of this country [the United States], all things considered, more than to stand together as one man, whenever a positive policy is announced and entered upon. Cuba seems lost to Spain; I do not see how her authority can be regained, whatever course we may take in the matter. But I have no confidence in the insurgents; I do not believe they are capable of managing a government that we would want to have alongside of us, and if we should today acknowledge the independence of the island, it would simply mean that we have taken the side and espoused the cause of one part of its population. We should have to make treaties with the rebels, and in a measure be under obligation to defer to them in formulating our Spanish policy. In these circumstances, I certainly hope Congress will not make the mistake of recognizing independence now. To the annexation of the island I should be positively opposed, although, in the event of shaking off of Spanish rule, which must come sooner or later, I can hardly see any other way out. In framing this republic, our Fathers made no provision for the government of colonies or alien dependencies; our theory in the annexation of territory has been to take such as might eventually be incorporated into states on an equal footing with the original Union. We cannot go much further in the way of territorial expansion without an altogether new system of colonial control, which, I believe, is incompatible with a republican government, and practically speaking, an altogether unsafe experiment. Hence, this is the situation; Cuba must be either subject to Spain, independent, or annexed to the United States; the first is not much longer a possibility; the second, as I have said before, would be mightily inconvenient; and the third I regard as wholly unwise.... The only chance I see for bringing Spain to reason is through the Pope. There is no country on the face of the earth and no monarchy so intensely loyal to

Rome as Spain; her Catholicism is genuine, and differs radically from that of France or even Italy. What the Pope says is tremendously potent. Now I can see how a decision of [Pope] Leo XIII, to the effect that Spanish control of Cuba must cease, might be accepted, although with extreme reluctance, by throne and people. I overheard a man say today that he thought the Pope would 'mediate' in the affair. That is the proper verb. If the Pope, through mediation, realizes all that war with the United States may mean, he may possibly give Spain the advice that will make peace possible."[1]

Later, Curry would add this about United States policy on Cuba: "As I told the Spanish Minister of Foreign Affairs at the time I presented my credentials, the United States will never consent, under any circumstances or at any sacrifice, that Cuba should pass out of the hands of Spain into the possession of any other European power. The United States would never allow a strong naval power to hold it, because all the commerce of the Gulf of Mexico passes at its very door."[2]

As ambassador, Curry tried to create new trade agreements that would modify the national policies of both the United States and Spain, to reduce tensions and divert their hostile intentions away from Cuba. One way was through reciprocal treaties involving Cuban exports to the US. This would require both countries to lower their protectionist barriers for certain Cuban products. President Grover Cleveland refused to accept this.

Finally, in 1895, the last act of this long drama was played out. Another revolt broke out, with the brilliant poet, José Martí, as its chief spokesman. His fiery words created a stronger sentiment in the United States for the Cuban insurgents. A major factor which moved America toward overt military action was the anticipated construction of the Panama Canal, since Cuba was now seen as strategically critical to Central America, where the canal would be located.

By this phase, Jabez Curry was no longer ambassador but was an activist to prevent war. He favored international arbitration as a solution. In April 1896, when the National Arbitration Conference met in Washington, Curry was on the committee which drafted the resolutions and memorial to the President. He called at the White House and presented the papers to Grover Cleveland personally.

---

1. J.L.M. Curry article in the *Evening Post* newspaper, February 9, 1894, from Curry Papers.
2. J.L.M. Curry article in fragment of unknown newspaper, March 15, 1896, from Curry Papers.

When war did come, in 1898, in the form of the sinking of the USS Maine in Havana harbor, Curry clearly understood how uneven the fight was. He wrote, in effect, that it was like the heavyweight champions, Bob Fitzsimmons or Jim Corbett, fighting a ten-year-old.

Hostilities ended quickly and the peace treaty established Cuba as an independent republic under United States protection. Military occupation continued until 1902.

"Constitutional Government in Spain"

In August 1888, Jabez Curry resigned as Minister to Spain. In accepting his departure, Secretary of State Bayard wrote: "The impairment of your health by the unfavorable climate of Madrid, to which alone I must attribute your resignation, I trust will be speedily restored in your native land."[1]

The winters in Madrid were damp and cold and Jabez was often sick. The summers were intolerably hot, and Curry said that the climate was treacherous.

But the New York *Tribune* editorialized that Curry left Spain due to disagreements with the administration. Possibly his frustration was a factor, as he had worked with great effort to reduce trade barriers and resolve Cuban claims but had little to show for it — especially when his attempts proved to be at odds with Cleveland's policies.

Whatever the true reason, Jabez was welcomed back to the Peabody Fund with open arms. He immediately resumed his former role as General Agent. Then he wrote another book, called *Constitutional Government in Spain*. It reflected his views of all the reasons that democracy and republican government had never been able to take hold in monarchist Spain.

And, as in his previous publications, there is the inescapable element of allegory throughout it. Once again, there is the parallel story of the travesties and tragedies accompanying the legal and constitutional reconstruction of the South.

No attempt will be made here to follow the through-line of *Constitutional Government in Spain*, since it covers the political spirals of that country during the entire 19th century. A few paragraphs will be extracted to indicate the tone and bitter sense of the same horrors being committed in the two nations, one great and the other formerly great.

In the first chapter the opening headline states that "Evolution of constitutional government is slow: the sketch is helpful in appreciating and guarding our

---

1. Alderman and Gordon, p. 318.

republic." Curry explained: "People fail to realize how reluctantly privilege relaxes its grip, or traditional wrongs and usurpations yield to the demand of liberty, equality and fraternity. The excesses of the French Revolution, so commonly used to point censures of popular rule, had their occasion in the violence of popular passion, but their cause was in the tyrannies and corruption of government and aristocracy and church. The most harmful and indefensible of all usurpations, a State religion, contests every inch in the struggle for freedom and conscience, and rallies and conquers even when victory seemed to have been won by the opposition."[1]

Wasn't this precisely the case in the Reconstruction South when the conquering carpetbag governments, the military and the Northern religious sects fused?

Curry went on: "In Spain the battle for constitutional government has been waged for eighty years in the face of the most formidable odds and most persistent and virulent antagonism. In this period there has been a litter of constitutions. [1812, 1836, 1837, 1845, 1869, 1873, 1876]. New constitutions have superseded the older, to in turn be disregarded or overthrown by the favorite of the hour.... The history of these tentative and ephemeral constitutions, superficially considered, is apt to provoke ridicule, but a closer examination will discover an undercurrent moving onward, with many eddies and obstructions, toward a freer government and a better definition and a more stable guarantee of popular rights."[2]

The same can be said for the South, which took a century to legally transform itself from an occupied territory to having a relatively equal status with the rest of the United States, through progressive amendments to the carpetbag constitutions.

The following may seem far-fetched in finding a parallel with the South, but it certainly is there, beneath the surface. It closely resembles the continual armed intervention by President Ulysses S. Grant every time Southern home rule and democratic process emerged: "The Peninsula Wars, growing out of the restless ambition of Napoleon and the weakness of Charles IV, threw Spain into anarchy. [The 1812 constitution] was the first in a series in a long struggle to overcome kingly misrule.... [It] provided for only one legislative assembly. It

---

1. J.L.M. Curry, *Constitutional Government in Spain, A Sketch* (New York: Harper and Brothers, 1889), p. 2.
2. Ibid., p. 4.

formed a democratic monarchy. This constitution was overthrown by Ferdinand VII at his restoration..... Backed by military force.... Provision was made for trial by jury. Ferdinand, although he committed himself to the constitution, by every variety of gratuities and supererogatory perjury, eagerly violated his oaths, and used all his power and influence to crush the spirit of the people. [In the 1820s] the Holy Alliance [England, France, Spain] asserted its right to interfere in every case where new institutions were established not consistent with 'the monarchist principle.'... France invaded Spain, and by armed intervention put down the constitution of 1812."[1]

Here, Jabez Curry gives an example of his most consistent theme: the dangers and instability associated with centralized power. In the United States, as power concentrated in Washington following the War for Southern Independence, it came to reside in Congress, which was dominated by Radical Republicans: "As a result of the Franco-Prussian War, the Napoleonic dynasty collapsed. The Papal temporal jurisdiction, no longer supported by French bayonets, disappeared. Italy was unified. The German States were consolidated into an empire.... In Spain, there were eight ministers in two years. In 1873, Philip resigned as Regent because of instability. The Cortes assumed supreme sovereignty and power over the nation "[2]

Curry: "When Prim [Juan Prim, Spanish general and statesman] was asked why he did not establish a republic in 1868, he replied, 'It would have been a republic without republicans.' ... In 1873 there seemed to exist a strong republican feeling but the government policy of Spain has never been favorable to the growth of republican practices, to the training of the people for democratic institutions, to familiarizing them with home rule, individual judgment, personal independence.... During the Republic three wars were in progress: the Cuban war, the Federalist in the South, and the Carlist."[3]

This comment by Curry about 19th century Spanish history applies word-for-word to America's 19th century Reconstruction era, even the word "monarchy." Hadn't Ulysses S. Grant, as President, said to Reverend Smith that he intended to be emperor, and that Governor Holden of North Carolina should also have a royal title?

---

1. Ibid., pp. 6-14.
2. Ibid., p. 39, 43, 46.
3. Ibid., pp. 66-67, 69.

Curry: "Absolute monarchy, constitutional monarchy, military dicta-torship, have come and gone with celerity. Militarism, flagrant violations of con-stitutions and laws, oscillations between despotism and anarchy, have marked the unhappy history of this century and the people have often quietly acquiesced in these rapidly occurring mutations as things to be expected in the course of human events. Power has been sought, not by legal methods or through consti-tutional forms, but by revolts, insurrections, conspiracies. The bayonet has superseded the ballot-box or the vote of the Cortes. The army has been a political engine. [Exactly like the Freedmen's Bureau.] Military officers have been intriguers. Estelair once said that in the crisis of every party question the inquiry is, 'Which side controls the cannons?' "[1]

Curry concluded with: "The evil of political ambition in the army and of the association of political consequences with military insurrections is not easily cured. The French army has always honorably abstained from being an instrument pf political revolution.... A vast horde of poorly paid and unemployed officers are an inviting field for political intrigue, and constitute a band of ready conspirators."[2]

Curry speaks as if this was unique to Spain, but within his own experience and as presented before, both Ulysses Grant and General Phil Sheridan attempted coups to overthrow Andrew Johnson; some occupied Southern states had three competing Republican governors, each using mercenary troops and United States forces to crush the others. The Treasury Department hired merce-naries to terrorize other Federal agencies and made war on them, to block their efforts to take the cotton, tobacco and other booty which were worth millions of dollars to the personal accounts of major Treasury officials. And the United States army controlled the voting and terrified or killed those who did not vote Republican, which guaranteed that the military's party of choice remained in power.

---

1. Ibid., p. 101
2. Ibid., p. 184.

CHAPTER 17. PEABODY AGAIN, SPAIN AGAIN, DISILLUSION

Within three weeks after returning to the United States from Spain, Jabez Curry resumed his Peabody work and it seemed to be the same as it ever was; speaking before legislatures, speaking to educators and school boards, at education conventions, all in the name of tax-supported, state and Federally controlled schools. And, until its final defeat in March 1890, the Blair Bill continued to absorb much of Curry's attention. Curry continued to travel thousands of miles per year for these efforts and his diary still showed how proud he was of the distances.

As soon as he walked off the ship from Madrid, Curry was wooed by the Democratic Party to enter the main political stage again. But his age [he was now in his mid-60s] and a long-term bladder disorder which had been aggravated by the "treacherous" Madrid weather made him turn away from the political arena.

Disillusionment

But at Peabody, all was not the same. He had been away for two years. Spain was profoundly different and antagonistic to the American cultural model. This allowed Jabez to see familiar things from an inverted perspective, whether he wanted to or not.

Upon his return he experienced a low-key disenchantment with all he had been trying to achieve. This change was not as dramatic as Albion Tourgee's, who, after years of zealous promoting of the Blair Bill, had a life-altering insight and disillusionment, and completely backed away. Tourgee had the shattering revelation that nationalizing Southern children's minds could not only be a

301

means to achieving the good (his idea of the good) but could just as easily be harmful, depending on who was in power. It was, in itself, no panacea for bringing peace or unity.

Curry came to see, piecemeal, that the goals he and Peabody had been fighting for were seriously flawed. First, he recognized the real consequence of a tax-supported school system where politicians, not educators, selected the officials: "The evils of rotation [where school superintendents are installed by the political party assuming power] are aggravated when changes are the consequence of the varying fortunes of political parties.... and the tendency to convert the school organization into a political machine for retaining power ascendancy. Instead of the schools and their administrations being sacredly kept as the appointed means for educating children, they are subordinated to the irrelevancy of party success and personal aggrandizement. Instead of being for the general weal, the school system may be wickedly perverted to secure the supposed interests of a fraction of the people."[1]

Jabez Curry and Peabody had been a major force in politicizing Southern schools. By the 1890s, he could boast: "The South is now in a rapid transition from private education to an education prescribed and supported by public authority."[2]

His comment meant (and Curry was fully aware of it) that John Eaton's "empirical" and "laboratory" curriculum had entered State schools. As a revolutionary abstraction, Curry was highly enthusiastic. As a reality, Jabez was disturbed by the results: "The spirit of the age has set in strongly toward the mechanical, the empirical, the practical. This spirit has become rampant in Normal schools. Teachers are no longer to be educated, but 'trained,' and this 'training' is to be done in laboratories, where students are encouraged to operate on children. The inevitable but deplorable consequence of this is that Normal schools have lost the respect of educated men, and it is very commonly taken for granted that a teacher 'trained' in these schools is a man or a woman of slender scholarship who expects to succeed by 'devices' and 'methods.' ... Just now the 'hobby' of the Normal school is the so-called 'laboratory.' The term, deliberately chosen, marks the height or the depth of the experimental method as applied to education. The name is pathetically suggestive. Children are 'material,' and on

---

1. Proceedings of the Trustees of the Peabody Education Fund, Report of the 23rd meeting, 1883, p. 126.
2. Proceedings of the Trustees of the Peabody Education Fund, Report of the 37th meeting, 1898, p. 342.

this material young men and women are to operate for the double purpose of making discoveries in infant psychology, and of learning the art of teaching by the experimental method, as vivisection, so much in vogue in biology, redis-covers from year to year, at the cost of numberless [animal] lives, what is well-known in physiology; so the 'pedagogical laboratory' rediscovers truths in the mental life that in one form or another have been well known for centuries. It is barely conceivable that after countless experiments and disasters, some essential new truth may be added to what is already known; but it is infinitely more probable that in each bushel of new chaff there will be found only one grain that in kind is as old as the Pharaohs and their mummies. It is easy to assume that there are no ancient landmarks which our forefathers have set! So modern and so scientific for each callow scholar to mark off the highways of knowledge with milestones of their own devising."[1]

Being an aristocrat, and proud of it, Jabez Curry detested and was disillu-sioned by the leveling process that was emerging and expanding. He also seems to have faintly understood that State-controlled schools played their part in homogenizing Americans, since "universal suffrage" had created "universal edu-cation." An "evil of a different character has grown out of universal suffrage and the means adopted to control votes. Modern democracy is usurping and leveling. It is not simply clamorous for political equality, but would break down the walls of partition and remove the real and ineffaceable distinctions, between 'refinement and coarseness, education and ignorance.' Good breeding and vul-garity, the ease and grace of high culture and the stiffness and dullness of imperfect civilization. Nay, it is despotic and claims the right to universal espi-onage. No public man's house is his castle. The voter and the party supporter claims the right of entrance, at any time, regards social intercourse, as a party obligation, demands hospitality and entré into all circles of society. Its can-didate, a public officer, is not supposed to have the right to protect the privacy of himself and family, from their intrusion. Democracy in America requires the rep-resentatives, the servants, the deputies, to walk and ride and drive and associate familiarly, at home, with persons of little education."[2]

Since Jabez Curry's life was on a long, swift trajectory, its speed and con-stant motion did not leave much time for contemplation. And contemplation would have revealed to him that he had "advocated all that he hated."

---

1. Ibid., pp. 343 and 350.
2. Fragment of undated letter by Jabez Curry to unknown person, Curry Papers.

Albion Tourgee took that moment, and he walked away. Jabez never allowed himself the time to reflect, so he continued on to the end, embittered, disillusioned, but never truly grasping that it was his own life-work that had created this brave new world.

Yet, as we have seen, he did have insights. In 1898, at the time of the Spanish-American War, he once more "caught the brass ring," as he had before the War for Southern Independence, and he once again wrote about the higher truth of home rule. And as always, by implication, he was speaking of the destructiveness of nationalized schools, of centralized control of children's minds, which produced students who would glorify their master, the State, instead of their own lives: "Centripetalism, drawing into the hands of the government a large part of the direct powers of control and administration, aggregation of authority in the central head, may have stimulated national pride and vanity and coarse militarism, but has not increased national happiness or promoted the general welfare. It has originated or intensified problems, difficult and apparently insoluble, arrayed capital against the masses, stimulated 'vast plutocratic combinations of incorporated wealth,' excited foreign ill-will, and created perils which menace personal freedom, individual liberty and State autonomy.... It has been announced 'ex-cathedra' to be 'the divine purpose that America should depart from her isolated position and take her place among the foremost nations of the earth [as a result of the Spanish-American War]. Others, not assuming to speak as 'the oracles of God,' say, 'we are going on to the Sandwich Islands [Hawaiian Islands] and as much further as duty and destiny call.' ... We may have the Roman and English aptitude for colonization, but certainly colonial aggrandizement upsets, reverses all the principles and traditions of the Fathers."[1]

Spain Again

In January 1902, Mary Curry received this letter from the Spanish princess, Eulalia, who had become a close friend during the ambassadorship period: "I am so happy to hear that Mr. Curry is appointed Special Envoy to Madrid upon the coming of age of our King next May." This was for the same Alfonso XIII whose magnificent birth ceremony Jabez had attended in 1886.

Between the 1880s and 1902, much had occurred between Spain and the United States. There had been the short but bloody war in which, in addition to

---

1. J.L.M. Curry, *Principles, Acts and Utterances of John C. Calhoun, etc.*, p. 26.

Cuba and Puerto Rico, the United States acquired the Philippine Islands. The Filipinos, like the Cubans, had been fighting a prolonged insurrectionary war to attaint their independence. Initially, they saw the Americans as liberators but it wasn't long before they realized they had traded one harsh master for another. Again, insurrection and guerrilla war resumed, drawing the United States army into at least four years of malarial jungle warfare in some of the most rugged and inhospitable places on earth. Atrocities were inflicted on both sides. This "Philippine Insurrection," as it has been officially called, has been considered by many historians as America's first Vietnam.[1]

Jessie Pearl Rice and Edwin Anderson Alderman do not mention any of this in their biographies, but Jabez Curry did, in a veiled way, in his address at Alfonso's coming of age ceremony.

In his second crossing to Spain, Jabez had a new title — "Ambassador Extraordinary on Special Mission." He and Mary left the United States in April 1902 by steamship. In ten days they were in Paris, where they were met by the same Princess Eulalia and Queen Isabel.

On arriving in Madrid, the Currys were treated like royalty. A beautiful villa was put at their disposal, with servants, guards, and a royal carriage with a driver in full livery.

When Curry presented his credentials, as he had years ago, he made a speech to the Queen Regent and the young King. Peace, war, and Spain's military past were behind his words, diplomatically phrased in the most positive light. "I am charged as Special Ambassador Extraordinary to bear you the greetings of the President and of the government of the United States, as you stand with joyous expectation on the threshold of hope and progress, and to felicitate you on a long life, blessed by the example and spirit and teachings of a noble and world-honored mother, and to assure you of the most cordial sympathy and cooperation in all efforts for development of resources for adhering to the basal principle of law and order, and for the settlement of all differences. On the basis of the equality of nations and stability of just governments.... The object of this mission is to confirm anew the former utterances of my country's honored representative, and to reassure, in a most emphatic manner, the earnest desire of the President and of the people, to cement in indissoluble bonds the friendship of

---

1. John Chodes, *A Howling Wilderness*, a play, in the New York Public Library's Lincoln Center Theater Collection, 2001. This play deals with the true court-martial of a Marine Corps Major, Littleton Waller, who was accused of committing atrocities against Filipino civilians during the Philippine Insurrection.

the new nations [Cuba, Puerto Rico, the Philippines]. There can be no political antagonism, no well-founded or enduring antipathy, between two peoples alike anxious of, and equally proposing, the closest relations of amity. This mission is the strongest assurance, may it be the guarantee, of peace and friendship, of social and commercial intercourse, in the pursuit of a common end, a nobler civilization, choosing the good, rejecting the evil.... America can never forget, must always honor, Spain's early and commanding history, her unquestioned superiority in the arts of policy and of war, her pre-eminence in art and literature, her chivalrous courage, tenacity of conviction, irrepressible vitality.... Peace is not a period of preparation for war, a whetting of swords for another conflict. It has a deeper, a diviner meaning, the emulation of brotherhood, which by infrangible bonds of a common interest and by international arbitration will make wars impossible."[1]

On the following day Curry was invited to a royal banquet and was seated near the King. Then, he was given the Royal Order of Charles III decoration. The Currys left Madrid on May 22, taking a much-needed two-month vacation in France and Switzerland before returning home.

The Last Act

For the last six months of the War for Southern Independence, Jabez Curry and the Fifth Alabama Cavalry had fought in the mosquito-filled swamps and freezing hill country of northern Alabama. Malaria, and the prolonged hunger and exhaustion of the final stages of the war, caused permanent injury to his bladder. Immediately afterward, he began having gall stone attacks. They continued, with increasing intensity, frequency and pain over the years, but Jabez Curry courageously maintained his demanding Peabody schedule.

By 1902, his kidneys were also failing and he declined rapidly. In October of that year, shortly after a Peabody Board meeting in New York, he had an agonizing kidney problem. A specialist came in from Philadelphia and performed an emergency operation on October 17. Jabez seemed to recover and he prepared to fulfill his usual grueling speaking and travel commitments.

On November 30, he spoke to the students at the Nashville Normal College but he was in so much pain and so weak that he could not stand to give his address.

---

1. Alderman and Gordon, p. 370.

On December 9, he underwent an unsuccessful bladder operation. Mary was also very ill. Jabez Curry died on February 12, 1903, in the Asheville, North Carolina home of his brother-in-law, "of Bright's Disease, complicated by uremia." He was 77. Mary would die three months later.[1]

---

1. Rice, p. 181.

Addendum

Even in his last months, despite continual debilitating pain, Jabez Curry was involved in the creation of one grand new educational project that would be a major force in the 20th century.

His diary of February 27, 1902 states: "Left for New York.... We went to Mr. and Mrs. John D. Rockefeller, Jr.'s, to dinner.... We signed our names to a paper defining the purpose of an Education Association, for which an incorporation was effected, and Mr. Rockefeller, for his father, agreed to place one million dollars in the hands of the Association, to be used at the rate of one hundred thousand dollars a year for education in the South."[1]

This was the beginning of the General Education Board, which in time became one of the most powerful educational philanthropies in the world.

In 1905, two years after Curry's death, Mr. Rockefeller established the Curry Memorial School of Education at the University of Virginia.

When Jabez Curry died he was still the General Agent for the Peabody Fund. Despite his disillusionment, he continued to press forward to nationalize Southern schools. Amazingly, 38 years after the War for Southern Independence, the former Confederate states continued to resist. Jabez Lafayette Monroe Curry, the former champion of home-rule, fought to the end of his life to make the South a ward of Washington, and near the end, only faintly realized the consequence of his labors.

---

1. Rice, p. 181.

Anderson Alderman's Memorial Address

Three months after his death, Edwin Anderson Alderman delivered a eulogy for Curry, in Richmond, under the auspices of the Conference for Education in the South. This section is particularly touching: "The intense, rich life of our leader and friend covered an equally intense and rich period of his country's history. His thoughtful boyhood looked out upon a crude, healthy, boastful nation, drunk with a kind of demonic passion, and getting used, in a rough way, to the shrewd air of popular government, and yet clinging to the concept of orderly nationality. His young manhood was passed in the isolated lower South, amid the storm of great argument, as to the nature of this Union, made necessary by the silence and indecision of the Constitution. To our minds, cleared of the hot temper of the time, that age seems an unhappy, contentious, groping age; but I believe that it was a good age in which to be born, for men were in earnest about deep, vital things. It was indeed the age of passion, but of passion based on principles, and enthusiasms, and deep loyalties. The cynic, the political idler, the self-seeker, fled before these fiery-eyed men who were probing into metaphysical, governmental theories and constitutional interpretations, and who counted their ideas as of more value than their lives. The time had its obvious faults, and was doomed to fall before the avatar of progress; but there lived in it beauty and force and a greater central note of exaltation of personality above social progress. To this was due the romantic beauty of many of the personalities of this period and section, and also the industrial inefficiency of the total mass. Around the fireside, in that frontier world of his, the talk did not fall so much upon the kind of man who forms the syndicate or corners the stock market or who wages the warfare of trade around the world, but rather upon simple, old questions which might have been asked in the Homeric age; is he free from sordidness or stain? Has he borne himself bravely in battle? Has he suffered somewhere with courage and dignity? Has he kept faith with ideals?"[1]

---

1. Edwin Anderson Alderman, *J.L.M. Curry, A Memorial Address* (Brooklyn: Eagle Press, 1903), p. 5.

BIBLIOGRAPHY

War for Southern Independence

Ainsworth, Brigadier-General Fred C. and Kirby, Joseph W., *The War of the Rebellion: A Compilation of the Official Records of the Union and Confederate Armies*, Washington: Government Printing Office, 1900.

Armstrong, O.K. and Armstrong, Marjorie M., *The Indomitable Baptists*, Garden City: Doubleday and Co., 1967.

Confederate States of America, *Journal of the Congress of the, 1861-1865*, Document No. 234, 58th United States Congress, 2nd Session, February 1904, Washington, D.C., Government Printing Office.

Croly, David, *Seymour and Blair, Their Lives and Services*, New York: Richardson and Co., 1868.

Curry, Jabez and others, *An Address to the People of the Confederate States*, pamphlet in Curry Papers, Library of Congress, Washington, D.C.

Curry, Jabez, *A Soldier's Life*, hand-written autobiographical notes, from Curry Papers, Library of Congress, Washington, D.C.

Curry, Jabez, *Joseph Eggleston Johnston*, in Washington Post newspaper, March 24, 1891.

Davis, Jefferson, *The Rise and Fall of the Confederate Government*, New York: D. Appleton and Company, 1881.

Dean, Henry, *Crimes of the Civil War*, Baltimore: J. Wesley Smith and Brother, 1869.

Dowdy, Clifford, *Experiment in Rebellion*, Garden City: Doubleday and Company, 1946.

DuBose, John W., *General Joseph Wheeler and the Army of Tennessee*, New York: The Neale Publishing Company, 1912.

Dyer, John P., *Fighting Joe Wheeler*, University, Louisiana: Louisiana University Press, 1941.

Eckenrode, Hamilton James, *Life of Nathan B. Forrest*, Atlanta: B.F. Johnson Publishing Company, 1918.

Fogel, Robert W. and Engerman, Stanley L., *Time On the Cross*, New York: W.W. Norton & Company, 1974.

Hall, C.R., *Andrew Johnson, Military Governor of Tennessee*, Princeton: Princeton University Press, 1916.

Hay, Thomas Robson, *James Longstreet*, Baton Rouge: Louisiana University Press, 1952.

Johnson, Bradley T., editor, *A Memoir of the Life and Public Service of Joseph E. Johnston*, Baltimore: R.H. Woodward and Company, 1891.

Kennedy, James Ronald and Kennedy, Walter Donald, *The South Was Right*, Gretna: Pelican Publishing Company.

Keys, Thomas, B., *The Uncivil War*, Biloxi: The Beauvoir Press, 1991.

Lytle, Andrew Nelson, *Bedford Forrest and his Critter Company*, New York: Minton, Balch and Company, 1931.

Maxwell, William Quenten, *Lincoln's Fifth Wheel: The Political History of the United States Sanitary Commission*, New York: Longmans, Green and Company, 1956.

McReynolds, Edwin, *Missouri, A History of the Cross-Roads State*, Norman: University of Oklahoma Press, 1962.

Meredith, Roy, editor, *Mr. Lincoln's General*, New York: E.P. Dutton and Company, 1959.

Neely, Mark E., *The Fate of Liberty: Abraham Lincoln and Civil Liberties*, New York: Oxford University Press, 1991.

Olmstead, Frederick, *Journeys and Explorations in the Cotton Kingdom of America*, New York: Mason Brothers, 1862.

Owsley, Frank Lawrence, *State Rights in the Confederacy*, Chicago: University of Chicago Press, 1931.

Siegel, Leo, *John Eaton and the Freedmen*, Northwest Ohio Quarterly, Summer 1957, volume xxix, no. 3.

War, Secretary of, annual reports, Washington: Government Printing Office.

Sifakis, Stewart, *Who's Who in the Confederacy*, New York: Facts on File, 1988.

Wilkins, J. Steven, *America: The First 350 Years*, Monroe, Louisiana: Covenant Publications, 1988.

Yearns, Wilfred Buck, *The Confederate Congress*, Athens: University of Georgia Press, 1961.

Reconstruction

American Missionary Association, *History of the American Missionary Association: Forty Years of Missionary Labor, 1847–1886*, New York: American Missionary Association, 1886.

Badeau, Adam, *Grant in Peace*, Hartford: S.S. Scranton and Company, 1887.

Barnes, William Wright, *The Southern Baptist Convention, 1845–1953*, Nashville: Broadman Press, 1954.

Bellows, Henry Whitney, *Historical Sketch of the Union League Club of New York: Its Origins and Work, 1863–1879*, New York: Union League Club, 1879.

Bentley, George, *History of the Freedmen's Bureau*, Philadelphia: University of Pennsylvania Press, 1955.

Bowers, Claude, *The Tragic Era*, Cambridge: The Riverside Press, 1929.

Chodes, John, *The Union League: Washington's Klan*, Tuscaloosa: League of the South Institute for the Study of Southern Culture and History, 1999.

Congressional Globe, Washington, D.C.: United States Historical Documents Institute, reprint edition, 1970.

Thomas M. Cook and Thomas Knox, editors, *Public Record of Horatio Seymour*, New York: I.W. England, at the offices of the New York *Sun*, 1868.

Deforest, John William, *A Union Officer in the Reconstruction*, New Haven: Yale University Press, 1948.

Dubois, W.E.B., *Black Reconstruction in America*, New York: S.A. Russell Company, 1935.

Dunning, William Archibald, *Reconstruction: Political and Economic, 1865–1877*, New York: Harper and Brothers, 1907.

Eaton, John, *Grant, Lincoln and the Freedmen*, New York: Longmans, Green and Company, 1907.

Eaton, John, editor, Memphis *Post* newspaper.

Fitzgerald, Michael, *The Union League Movement in the Deep South*, Baton Rouge: Louisiana State University Press, 1969.

Fleming, Walter, *Civil War and Reconstruction in Alabama*, New York: Columbia University Press, 1905.

Foner, Eric, *A Short History of Reconstruction*, New York: Harper and Row, 1990.

Hasseltime, William, *Ulysses S. Grant, Politician*, New York: Frederick Ungar Company, 1957.

Herberg, Will, *The Heritage of the Civil War*, New York: Workers Age Publishing Association, 1932.

Herbert, Hilery, editor, *Why The Solid South*, New York: Negro University Press, 1969, reprinted from the original publication date of 1890.

Hill, Michael, "The Fourteenth Amendment," in *Southern Events*, November–December 1999.

Hirshson, Stanley, *Farewell to the Bloody Shirt*, Chicago: Quadrangle Books, 1962.

Horn, Stanley, *The Invisible Empire: The Story of the Ku Klux Klan, 1866–1867*, Cos Cob, Ct.: John E. Edwards, 1969.

Howard, Oliver Otis, *Autobiography of Oliver Otis Howard, Major-General, United States Army*, New York: Baker & Taylor Company, 1907.

Johnson, Thomas C., *The Life and Times of Robert Lewis Dabney*, Richmond: The Presbyterian Committee of Publication, 1903.

LaFevre, General Benjamin, *Campaign of '84*, Chicago: Baird and Dillon, 1884.

Leigh, Frances Butler, *Two Years on a Georgia Plantation Since the War*, London: Richard Bentley and Son, 1883.

McFeeley, *Yankee Stepfather: O.O. Howard and the Freedmen*, New Haven: Yale Publications in American Studies 15, Yale University Press, 1968.

Morris, Robert, *Reading, 'Riting and Reconstruction*, Chicago: University of Chicago Press, 1976.

Morrow, Ralph, *Northern Methodism and Reconstruction*, East Lansing: Michigan State University Press, 1956.

Nevins, Allan, *Hamilton Fish, The Inner History of the Grant Administration*, New York: Dodd, Mead & Company, 1936.

Pearson, Charles Chilton, *The Readjuster Movement in Virginia*, New Haven: Yale University Press, 1917.

Pike, James, *The Prostrate State*, New York: Loring & Mussey, 1935.

Robinson, Lloyd, *The Stolen Election; Hayes vs. Tilden, 1876*, Garden City: Doubleday and Company, 1968.

Sefton, James E., *The United States Army and Reconstruction, 1865-1877*, Baton Rouge: Louisiana State University Press, 1967.

Singletory, Otis, *Negro Militia and Reconstruction*, Austin: University of Texas Press, 1957.

Spain, Rufus B., *At Ease In Zion: A Social History of Southern Baptists, 1865-1900*, Nashville University Press, 1967.

Thompson, Clara Mildred, *Reconstruction in Georgia: Economic, Social, Political, 1865-1872*, New York: The Columbia University Press, 1915.

Welles, Gideon, *Diary of Gideon Welles*, Boston: Houghton Mifflin Company, 1911.

Wickersham, J.P., *Education as an Element in the Reconstruction of the Union*, Boston: L.C. Rand and Avery, 1865.

Williams, T. Harry, editor, *Diary of a President*, New York: David McKay Company, 1964.

Education

Agriculture Department, annual reports of the Secretary, Washington, D.C.: Government Printing Office.

Alderman, Edwin Anderson, *J.L.M. Curry: An Address*, Brooklyn: Eagle Press, 1903.

Allen, Gay Wilson, *William James*, New York: The Viking Press, 1967.

Alvord, John W., *Letters from the South*, Washington: Howard University Press, 1870.

Balch, William Ralston, *The Life of James Abram Garfield, Late President of the United States*, Philadelphia: J.C. McCordy & Company, 1881.

Blewitt, John, editor, *John Dewey, His Thought and Influence*, New York: Fordham University Press, 1960.

Bloom, Allen, *The Closing of the American Mind*, New York: Simon and Schuster, 1987.

Clark, Edward, *A Bill to Promote Mendicancy*, New York: The Evening Post Publishing Company, 1888.

Curry, J.L.M., *A Brief Sketch of George Peabody and a History of the Peabody Education Fund Through Thirty Years*, Cambridge: University Press, John Wilson and Son, 1898.

Curry, J.L.M., *Difficulties, Complications and Limitations Connected with the Education of the Negro*, John F. Slater Fund Occasional Paper No. 5, Baltimore: Published by the Trustees of the John F. Slater Fund, 1895.

Curry, J.L.M., *Education of the Negro Since 1860*, John F. Slater Fund Occasional Paper No. 3, Baltimore: Published by the Trustees of the John F. Slater Fund, 1894.

Curry, J.L.M., *The Alliance of Church and State*, London: Society for the Liberation of Religion from State Patronage and Control, 1873.

dePencer, Ida B., *The History of the Laboratory Schools: The University of Chicago, 1896–1965*, Chicago: Quadrangle Books, 1967.

Dewey, John, *Experience and Education*, New York: A Touchstone book, published by Simon and Schuster, 1938.

Dewey, John, *How We Think*, Boston: D. C. Heath and Company, 1933 revision of 1909 edition.

Dewey, John, *The Influence of Darwin on Philosophy*, New York: Henry Holt and Company, 1910.

Dillingham, George, *The Foundation of the Peabody Tradition*, Lanham: University Press of America, 1989.

Education Bureau, annual reports of the Commissioner, Washington: Government Printing Office.

Glasser, William, *The Quality School*, New York: Perennial Library, 1990.

Goetzman, William H., *The American Hegelians, An Intellectual Episode in the History of Western America*, New York: Alfred A. Knopf, 1973.

Grosser, Paul, *The Nihilism of John Dewey*, New York: Philosophical Library, 1955.

Hall, G. Stanley, *American Journal of Psychology*.

Hedges, Charles, editor, *Speeches of Benjamin Harrison, 23rd President of the United States*, Port Washington: Kennikat Press, 1971, reprinted from 1892 edition.

Himmelfarb, Gertrude, *Darwin and the Darwinian Revolution*, Glouster: Peter Smith, Inc., 1967.

Hinesdale, B.A., *President Garfield and Education*, Boston: James R. Osgood and Company, 1882.

Hollis, Allen, *The Federal Government and Education*, New York: McGraw-Hill, 1950.

Hook, Sidney, *John Dewey: An Intellectual Portrait*, New York: The John Day Company, 1939.

Illich, Ivan, *De-Schooling Society*, New York: Harper and Row, Publishers, 1970.

Joncich, Geraldine, *The Sane Positivist; A Biography of Edward L. Thorndike*, Middletown: Wesleyan University Press, 1968.

Journal of the 4th Biennial Session of the House of Representatives of the State of Alabama, Session of 1853–1854, Montgomery: Britton & Blue, State Printers, 1854.

Kilpatrick, William Heard, *Education For a Changing Civilization*, New York: The Macmillan Company, 1926.

Lancaster, Joseph, *The Lancaster System of Education with Improvements*, Baltimore: William Ogden Niles, 1821.

Lee, Gordon Canfield, *The Struggle for Federal Aid*, New York: Teachers College, Columbia University, 1949.

Leideker, Kurt F., *The Life of William Torrey Harris*, New York: The Philosophic Library, 1946.

Marrin, Albert, *Nicholas Murray Butler*, Boston: Twayne Publishers, 1976.

Meyer, Adolphe E., *Grandmasters of Educational Thought*, New York: McGraw Hill Book Company, 1975.

Misiak, Henryk, *The Philosophical Roots of Scientific Psychology*, New York: Fordham University Press, 1961.

Neuhaus, John Richard, *Democracy and the Renewal of Public Education*, Grand Rapids: William B. Eerdmans Publishing Company, 1987.

Olson, Otto, *Carpetbagger's Crusade: The Life of Albion Winegor Tourgee*, Baltimore: The Johns Hopkins Press, 1965.

Peabody Education Fund, Proceedings of the Trustees.

Reimer, Everett, *School Is Dead*, Garden City, Doubleday and Company, 1971.

Rivlin, Harry, editor, *Encyclopedia of Modern Education*, New York: The Philosophical Library of New York City, 1943.

Roberts, John S., *William Torrey Harris, A Critical Study Of His Educational and Related Philosophical Views*, Washington: National Education Association of the United States, 1924.

Robinson, James H., *The New History*, New York: Macmillan and Company, 1912.

Ross, Dorothy, *G. Stanley Hall: The Psychologist As Prophet*, Chicago: University of Chicago Press, 1972.

Rubin Jr., Louis D., editor, *Teach The Freedmen, The Correspondence of Rutherford B. Hayes and the Slater Fund for Negro Education, 1881–1887*, Baton Rouge: Louisiana State University Press, 1959.

Salmon, David, *Joseph Lancaster*, London: Longmans, Green and Company, 1904.

Second Capon Springs Conference for Education in the South, Proceedings, 1899, Raleigh: Edwards and Broughton, 1899.

Slater, John F. Fox Fund for the Education of the Freedmen, Proceedings of the Trustees, Baltimore: 1901.

Smith, Darrell Hevenor, *The Bureau of Education, Its History, Activities and Organization*, Baltimore: Johns Hopkins University Press, 1923.

Smith, Edwin Burritt, *Education in the South—National Aid*, address before Chicago Congregationalist Club, February 20, 1888.

Thayer, Vivian Trow, *Formative Ideas in American Education, From Colonial Times to the Present*, New York: Dodd, Mead, 1965.

Tilley, John S., *Facts the Historians Leave Out*, Montgomery: The Paragon Press, 1951.

Travers, Robert M.W., *How Research Has Changed American Schools; A History from 1840 to the Present*, Kalamazoo: Mythos Press, 1983.

Vassar, Rena, *Social History of American Education*, Chicago: Rand McNally, 1965.

Williams, Charles R., *Diary and Letters of Rutherford B. Hayes*, Columbus: Ohio State Archeological and Historical Society, 1922–1925.

Additional books by or about Jabez Curry

Alderman, Edwin Anderson and Gordon, Armistead Churchill, *J.L.M. Curry, A Biography*, New York: The Macmillan Company, 1911.

Curry, J.L.M., *Civil History of the Government of the Confederate States, With Some Personal Reminiscences*, Richmond: B.F. Johnson Publishing Company, 1911.

Curry, J.L.M., *Constitutional Government In Spain, A Sketch*, New York: Harper and Brothers, 1889.

Curry, J.L.M., *Establishment and Disestablishment; Progress of Soul Liberty in the United States*, Philadelphia: American Baptist Publication Society, 1889.

Curry, J.L.M., *Protestantism: How Far A Failure?*, Philadelphia: American Baptist Publication Society, 1880.

Curry, J.L.M., *Struggle and Triumph of Virginia Baptists*, Philadelphia: American Baptist Publication Society, 1873.

Curry, J.L.M., *William Ewart Gladstone*, Richmond: B.F. Johnson and Company, 1891

Rice, Jessie Pearl, *J.L.M. Curry: Southerner, Statesman, Educator*, New York: King's Crown Press, Columbia University, 1949.

ABOUT THE AUTHOR

John Chodes is a New Yorker and a writer, in equal parts.

The War for Southern Independence and the problems of Reconstruction have been the subject of more than 20 articles and three monographs published by the author. *The Paradox of Jabez L.M. Curry: State Sovereignty to Federalized Schools* led to the writing of the current work. In *The Constitution and State Sovereignty*, Mr. Chodes condensed the classic book by Jefferson Davis, *The Rise and Fall of the Confederate Government*, which documents the fact that the United States Constitution was only ratified on the condition that secession would be an accepted alternative in case the Federal Government overstepped its mandated powers. Chodes's third monograph, *The Union League: Washington's Klan*, demonstrates that the federal government's agency, the Union League, equaled or surpassed the Ku Klux Klan in brutality toward Southern freedmen.

Articles by Mr. Chodes, mostly relating to the history of the federalizing of Southern education, culture and property, have appeared in *Chronicles*, *The Freeman*, *Social Justice Review*, *The New York Tribune*, *Southern Partisan*, *Southern Events*.

His nonfiction books include *Bruce Jenner* (a biography of the 1976 Olympic decathlon gold medalist), and the award-winning *Corbitt* (a biography of the first African-American runner to compete in an Olympic marathon, and Chodes's mentor); *Corbitt* led Chodes to a position as technical advisor to Dustin Hoffman in the Paramount Pictures film, *Marathon Man*.

Seven plays by John Chodes have been performed Off-Broadway in New York City:

> *A Howling Wilderness* (2001)
> *Molineaux*, a musical (1995)

The Longboat (1987)
Frederick Two (1985)
Slaves (1982)
Molineaux (1979)
Avenue A Anthology (1969 and 1970)

Mr. Chodes has also written extensively for the Libertarian Party of New York, with over 100 articles, editorial replies and chapters published, promoting the "free market" in *The New York Times, Chronicles, Reason, The Freeman,* and on CBS-TV, NBC-TV, ABC-TV, and FOX-TV.

His photographs have appeared in *Newsweek, Track and Field News, Athletics Weekly* (England), *Long Distance Log, Town and Country,* the *Brooklyn Daily Eagle, Brooklyn Heights Press, The Phoenix,* and the *Brooklyn Record.*

Chodes's next book, *Horatio Seymour: Governor of New York, Ally of the Confederacy,* is scheduled for release shortly.

INDEX

W

Waddell School, 53
Waddell, Dr. Moses, 53
Wade, Ben, 97, 144, 201
Walker families, 48
Walker, LeRoy Pope, 30
Walker, Richard, 163, 167
Walker, Robert, 16, 28
Wallace, Henry, 284
War Department, 129, 143
War for Southern Independence, 7, 15, 17, 20, 25, 64, 68, 100, 141, 210, 245, 255–256, 299, 304, 306, 309
Ward School in Cleveland, Ohio, 239
Warrington, Alabama, 119
war-time Unionists, 93
Washington City, 52, 127, 244
Washington, George, 49, 64
Watson, Judge, 216
Watterson, Henry, 209
Weekly Floridian newspaper, 226
Welles, Gideon, 159, 201
Wesleyan University, 279
West Indies, 30
West Point, 31, 64, 69
West Virginia, 18, 176, 180, 210, 214
West, John, 131
Western relativism, 284
Westminster Abbey, 104
Westminster Palace, 104
Wetumpka, Alabama, 119

Wheeler, Joseph, General, 70–75, 77, 79–80
White House, 206, 213, 227, 240, 297
White Sulphur Springs, West Virginia, 180
White, Josiah, 78
Why the Solid South, 176
Wickersham, J.P., 145, 150, 154–156
Wigfall, Mr., 40
Williams College, 267
Wilmot, David, 15
Wilmot, David, 15, 163
Wilson, General James, 82
Wilson, Senator, 111
Winn, General, 48
Winn, Susan, 49
Winthrop, Robert, 182, 190, 194, 228, 234, 285, 287, 289–291
Withers, General, 70
World War I, 272
World War II, 1, 277, 284
worship of nature, 271
Wright, Joseph, 245
Writ of Habeas Corpus, 46
Wundt, Wilhelm, 254, 267–268
Wyandotte Convention, 17

Y

Yancey, William, 38, 161, 291
Yankee ingenuity, 165
Yazoo frauds, 55
Young Men's Christian Association, 112

Printed in the United States
47532LVS00005B/32

9 780875 864013